# Financial Analysis:
## Tools and Concepts

Also by Jerry A. Viscione

*Analyzing Ratios: A Perceptive Approach*
*Cases in Financial Management*
*Financial Analysis: Principles and Procedures*
*Flow of Funds and Other Financial Concepts*
*How to Construct Pro Forma Statements*

# Financial Analysis:

## Tools
## and
## Concepts

### Jerry A. Viscione
Professor of Finance
Boston College

Publications Division
National Association of Credit Management
475 Park Avenue South, New York, N.Y. 10016

This publication is designed to provide accurate and
authoritative information in regard to the subject matter
covered. It is sold with the understanding that the
publisher is not engaged in rendering legal, accounting, or
other professional service. If legal advice or other expert
assistance is required, the services of a competent
professional person should be sought.

Library of Congress Cataloging in Publication Data

Viscione, Jerry A.
  Financial analysis.

  Bibliography: p.
  Includes index.
  1. Corporations—Finance.  2. Business enterprises—
Finance.  I. Title.
HG4026.V577  1984      658.1'51       84-16530
ISBN 0-934914-56-7

Manufactured in the United States of America

First Printing

*To Albert, Keith, Kelly and Joe*

# Table of Contents

## PART I: FINANCIAL STATEMENTS

# Tables

# Figures

# Preface

*Financial Analysis: Tools and Concepts* was written for credit managers, other business professionals and students who want to develop skills in organizing and interpreting financial information. Its primary objective is to explain how financial analysis can be used productively in the decision-making process.

The book can be used in formal courses either as a primary or supplementary text, in management development seminars, and for self-study. It can also serve as a handy reference for financial managers, financial analysts and bankers. Although illustrations and examples pertain to business firms, most of the tools and principles covered in this book are relevant for not-for-profit organizations.

We have tried to explain finance terms and concepts as clearly and concisely as possible. Theoretical issues are covered in terms of practical applications. We explain briefly what the theory says and then discuss how it can help the decision maker. References for further discussion are available for the interested reader.

To enable readers, particularly those studying on their own, to solidify their grasp of topics covered in the chapters, the book contains an ample supply of problems and their solutions. There are numerous unsolved problems that can be employed for home study assignments in courses. A solutions' manual with answers to unsolved problems will be sent to instructors who adopt the book.

The book begins with a brief introductory chapter giving an overview and hints for studying financial analysis. This is followed by three major sections. The first deals with financial statements and covers basic accounting principles and procedures, ratio analysis, and flow of funds analysis. The second explains tools and concepts needed for planning and control. The third discusses the time value of money and valuation and explains the basic tools and concepts that assist managers in making investment and financing decisions. Topics covered include capital budgeting techniques, valuing bonds and common stock, selecting hurdle rates for capital budgeting techniques, the cost of capital, analyzing a debt versus equity choice, and evaluating the cost of a financial or capital lease.

To achieve the goal of providing a handy reference, we have tried to make the chapters as self-contained as possible. However, some familiarity with accounting is essential background for all the chapters, so the chapter on this topic should be read first by those who have had no formal training in accounting or who believe they need a review. Further, an understanding of the time value of money is required for most topics covered in the final section of the book.

Because of this self-contained feature, instructors have considerable flexibility with respect to the order in which chapters are assigned. For example, some instructors may want to cover the chapters on the time value of money and valuation and required rates of return first so that valuation can serve as a unifying framework for the course.

# Acknowledgements

I owe a substantial debt to many capable people who helped me complete this project. Many of the ideas of Professors George Aragon, Gail Chu, Louis Corsini, Gordon Roberts, and Hassan Tehranian are included in this book. These distinguished academicians reviewed chapters for content and writing style and provided suggestions that helped in a significant way to improve quality. To show the practical relevance of theory, I needed assistance from practitioners who are able managers and bankers and who also are up to date on recent developments in the accounting and finance disciplines. Fortunately, the following people who possessed these desired qualities were quite generous with their time—John Balboni, Elaine Kiuber, Bill Nyhan and Frank Wey. Henry Ahn, Darlene Bator, Michelle Cheung, Ellen Goss, Steve Kwiathowski and John Sheridan, assistants in the Boston College Finance Department, performed many essential tasks, including researching various topics, selecting references, developing problems, checking solutions, and constructing tables and figures. Ms. Mary Sullivan performed editorial work and also did much of the required typing. James J. Andover, Director of Publications for NACM, carefully reviewed each chapter. Many of his excellent suggestions were incorporated. I am sincerely grateful to all these kind people. Finally, I am solely responsible for any errors that may remain.

Jerry A. Viscione
Boston, Massachusetts

# Introduction

In this introduction we will discuss how financial analysis relates to decision making, explain what it does and does not do for the manager, and give some hints for studying the tools and concepts covered in subsequent chapters. The primary purpose is to establish a common framework for all topics in the book and to present ideas related to the approach you must take to become a good analyst.

A variety of definitions exist for the phrase "financial analysis." For our purposes, we will rely on the following:

> *Definition of Financial Analysis*
> Financial analysis is a set of principles, procedures, and tools that help you organize and interpret financial, economic, and other business data.

We perform financial analyses because they help us make better decisions. These analyses do not make decisions for us; rather, they give us *information* that can improve the quality of our decisions.

## STANDARD FOR FINANCIAL DECISIONS

Many of a financial manager's tasks pertain to a firm's investment and financing decisions. How much should we invest? Which investments should we select? How should we finance our investments? Frequently, when we hear the word investments in the context of a firm, we think of issues like expanding a plant or introducing a new product. In fact, these two decision areas are much more general. For example, when a firm alters its policy with respect to how much inventory to carry, it is making an investment decision. When a firm extends credit to a customer, it is making an investment in an asset called accounts receivable. Further, we think about these decisions in the context of an industrial corporation, but investment and financing decisions are made by all kinds of organizations, such as banks and other financial institutions, including not-for-profit establishments.

We cannot make a decision unless we have a goal or standard to guide us. An important financial objective for a business is to increase the value of the firm for its owners. Managers do this by increasing returns accruing to the business and/or by reducing risks. Hence, a useful way of viewing financial decisions is in the context of risk versus return. When we make a financial decision, a basic issue is: Is the return worth the risk we are taking? (Putting it another way: Will this increase or decrease the value of the firm?) Related issues are: How can we improve the return on an investment? How can we lower an investment's risk? How can we minimize financing costs?

Much of financial analysis is concerned with providing information about risk and return. Considerable "number crunching" is involved because we attempt to quantify risk and return. Numerous concepts are essential because we must have a firm grasp of the many principles that pertain to risk and return. Let's look at a simple example. Suppose you are going to buy a car for your business for $14,000. Your banker will lend you $14,000 for three years at an interest rate of 13%. The car dealer offers to lease the car to you for three years, charging you $5,500 per year and giving you the option to buy the car for $1,000 in three years. A financial analysis technique, that is based on the notion of the time value of money and other finance concepts, will enable you to estimate which is the cheaper alternative.

Later in the book we will explain the required computations and the underlying concepts. For now, we just want to point out that financial analysis can't provide an exact answer to the alternative you should choose. One reason is that several of the numbers used in the analysis are estimates. For instance, to perform an analysis of the above example, we need to estimate what your firm's income tax rate will be in three years and what the car will be worth at that time. Another reason why an exact answer is not possible is that we cannot quantify precisely qualitative factors such as how important it might be for you to own the car instead of leasing it. Despite the inherent limitations, we will see that financial analysis can give considerable insight toward solving complicated problems.

To summarize, financial analysis can provide us with useful information for making decisions, particularly when the outcome is not certain. But it is crucial to keep in mind that financial analyses provide *information, not decisions*. This latter point cannot be emphasized enough because too many people expect too much from financial analysis. For example, we have heard such statements as: "The numbers prove that this is a good investment decision." Rarely, if ever, can quantitative analysis alone prove that an investment should be undertaken. Another sign of expecting too much is this statement: "The rate of return on this investment is 12.86%." For most investments, it simply is not possible to be that exact, and to state rates of return to two decimal places is misleading because it implies a precision that does not exist.

## HOW TO STUDY FINANCIAL ANALYSIS

Before closing, we have some advice regarding how you should study and apply the tools and concepts of financial analysis.

We will see that financial analysis includes a large number of procedures and formulas. It's tempting to focus on learning rules because it enables you to see some results immediately. But, you will never, in our opinion, be a good analyst if you view financial analysis as a bunch of rules and formulas. To be a good financial analyst, you must acquire and continuously develop analytical skills which involve a way of thinking that is not mechanical.

It's hard to give specific guidance because so much depends on the individual, but here are some ideas to consider:

1. *Why and then how.* When we cover a specific procedure, make sure you understand why we do it before learning how to do it.

2. *Logic.* Focus on the underlying rationale of a tool. This is especially important because some tools are derived from well-developed theory, while others are based primarily on experiences of users (ratios being a good example).

3. *Pencil pushing.* People too often start to make calculations before properly understanding the task. The first step in an analysis is to define and to think about the problem.

4. *Beware of models.* Advances in technology have certainly eased the burden of financial analysts by eliminating much of the "grunt work" and also by enabling us to expand the scope of many financial analyses. However, many people use computers and calculators to make computations without properly understanding the tool and/or underlying concept. Make sure you have a firm grasp of a topic before relying on calculators and computers.

5. *Try something new.* The text and problems will demonstrate numerous applications of tools and concepts. We suggest that you apply what you learn here to actual business situations. For example, when studying ratio analysis, you perhaps should try to apply the tool to financial statements of an actual business. It will not be easy, and at first you likely will not obtain productive results. But eventually you will develop

the skill of being able to apply financial analysis in unique and creative ways, and this is a quality that every analyst hopes to possess.

6. *Patience.* It takes time and patience to become a good analyst. It often is very frustrating for beginners, especially students, to have an experienced analyst point out insights in their work that they "never would have dreamed of." It takes practice and patience to learn the finer points.

# Part
# I

# Financial Statements

# 1
# Financial Accounting

This chapter provides an overview of financial accounting. It is designed primarily for those who have had little or no formal training in accounting (or need a review) but who have some skill and experience reading and interpreting financial statements. We first describe assumptions, principles and procedures underlying the preparation of the income statement and balance sheet. After that we discuss individual items—called accounts—that appear on these statements. Emphasis throughout is on the needs of various users, rather than preparers of financial statements; therefore, it will not be necessary to discuss debits and credits, T-accounts, trial balances and similar subject areas. Finally, an appendix covers additional financial accounting topics.

The accounting discipline is frequently subdivided into two areas: managerial accounting and financial accounting. Mangerial accounting refers to reports and other information prepared for the exclusive use of managers and others within the organization. These reports are prepared according to internally established policies and procedures. Financial accounting refers to reports and data prepared primarily for external users such as stockholders, creditors, customers, employees, government bodies, and other interested parties. Managers and other internal users employ financial accounting information in their work, but it is the needs of external users that are given priority when financial accounting principles and procedures are formulated.

Portions of this chapter are taken from Chapters 1 and 2 of *Flow of Funds and Other Financial Concepts* by Jerry Viscione, National Association of Credit Management, 1981.

## CRITERIA FOR FINANCIAL ACCOUNTING PRINCIPLES AND PROCEDURES

The purpose of accounting is to provide information which is useful for decision-making purposes. Accountants strive to supply appropriate information on a timely basis and in an understandable manner. Therefore, the fundamental criterion is: Do the principles and procedures lead to the generation of useful information?

Who decides which principles and procedures to use in preparing financial statements? For accounting reports prepared for people within the organization, the managers of that organization decide. For accounting reports prepared primarily for external users, the answer is not that simple because the managers of the organization are not the only ones setting the rules. It is beyond our scope to discuss all the parties involved; we will briefly describe three: the Internal Revenue Service, the Securities and Exchange Commission and the Financial Accounting Standards Board.

The Internal Revenue Service (IRS) was created to administer the federal tax laws. Its many duties include establishing reporting requirements for businesses. The tax rules are such that often the information required for the IRS is not suitable for other parties. For example, the income statement a firm submits to the IRS often differs from the one issued to its shareholders in numbers and format. Thus, the amount of net income that a firm reports to the IRS often will differ from the amount reported to its stockholders. We will discuss this difference again later but the relevant point here is that the IRS generally does not get involved in setting the rules governing the preparation and presentation of financial statements issued to investors.

The Securities and Exchange Commission (SEC) is a government agency established by the 1933 and 1934 Securities Acts. Its many duties include specifying reporting requirements for firms which sell securities (e.g., stocks and bonds) to the public. With respect to this activity, its mission is to ensure that investors receive reliable information on a timely basis. The SEC has generally, but not always, relied on the accounting profession to formulate accounting principles and procedures.

The Financial Accounting Standards Board (FASB) is the rule-making body of the accounting profession. It is an independent body whose purpose is to formulate accounting principles and procedures. The FASB issues statements which become "generally accepted accounting principles" (GAAP), also referred to as generally accepted accounting standards. With minor exceptions, most firms, including all publicly traded companies, must adhere to these principles in preparing reports for external users, and there are specialized rules for specific industries such as insurance companies and not-for-profit organizations.

# *Financial Accounting Principles and Procedures*

To explain principles and procedures, we will rely on the income statement and balance sheet of the Eagle Hill Company, shown in Table 1-1. Table 1-2 is a checklist of topics addressed in this section and should prove useful for reference purposes.

An income statement presents an entity's profit performance for a stated period such as one year. The overriding consideration in the selection of accounting procedures is to choose those which best show the results of operations, that is, the measure of net income for a specific period of time. A balance sheet is a report which displays an entity's assets, liabilities and owners' equity at a specific point in time.

Each statement begins with the name of the organization. This illustrates the *entity concept,* financial data measured for a certain entity, separate and apart from its owners. It can be a business, a hospital, a church or any other unit for which it makes sense to gather economic data. In other words, most entities engaged in financial transactions maintain accounts and report the results of operations and financial position.

The line beneath the name of the statement shows the *time principle,* also known as periodicity. An income statement, also called profit and loss statement (or simply P&L) always relates to a certain period of time such as a month, a quarter or a year. In contrast, a balance sheet always relates to a specific point in time. The balance sheet, known also as a statement of financial position (or condition), lists an entity's assets, liabilities and owners' equity at a specific date. Assets are economic resources owned by the firm. Liabilities are obligations of the firm. Owners' equity represents what the owners have invested plus the profits retained in the business. An alternative definition of owners' equity is that it equals the excess of assets over liabilities. Therefore, by definition we have the following *accounting identity:*

$$\text{Assets} = \text{Liabilities} + \text{Owners' Equity}$$

Bookkeeping systems are designed so that this equality is maintained at all times.

Before proceeding to explain the remaining topics in Table 1-2, several

**TABLE 1-1**
**EAGLE HILL CORPORATION**
Income Statement
for Year Ending December 31, 19XX

| | |
|---|---:|
| Net sales | $175,000 |
| Less cost of goods sold expense | 90,000 |
| Gross profit | $ 85,000 |
| Less operating and financial expenses; | |
| selling, general and administrative expenses | 10,000 |
| Less interest expense | 15,000 |
| Profit before income taxes | $ 60,000 |
| Less income taxes | 20,000 |
| Net income | $ 40,000 |

**EAGLE HILL CORPORATION**
Balance Sheet
at December 31, 19XX

| | | | | |
|---|---:|---|---:|---:|
| Cash | $10,000 | Accounts payable | | $ 6,000 |
| Accounts receivable | 15,000 | Notes payable (bank) | | 5,000 |
| Inventory | 9,000 | Accrued liabilities | | 3,000 |
| Other | 3,000 | Total current | | $14,000 |
| Total current | $37,000 | | | |
| | | Long-term debt | | 14,000 |
| | | Total liabilities | | $28,000 |
| Fixed assets (net) | 54,000 | | | |
| Total assets | $91,000 | Paid-in capital: | | |
| | | Common stock | 2,000 | |
| | | Additional paid-in | | |
| | | capital | 26,000 | 28,000 |
| | | Retained earnings | | 35,000 |
| | | Total liabilities | | |
| | | and owners' equity | | $91,000 |

observations pertaining to the use by analysts of these statements are in order.

1. Analysts and managers (and finance professors) are not always as precise as they should be when describing financial statements. For example, we sometimes hear remarks like: "I am going to analyze X Company's balance sheet for 19X6." This is not precise because it implies that the balance sheet is for all of 19X6, when in fact the balance sheet must be as of some specific date in 19X6. This precision is important because

**Table 1-2**  *Checklist of Principles and Concepts*

| | |
|---|---|
| Entity Concept | Footnotes |
| Time Principle | Materiality Principle |
| Accounting Identity | Consistency Principle |
| Unit of Measure | Auditor's Opinion |
| Historical Cost Principle | Accrual versus Cash Accounting |
| Lower of Cost or Market Rule | Realization Principle |
| Conservatism | Matching Principle |
| Disclosure Principle | |

it clarifies the fundamental difference between an income statement and a balance sheet.

2. If assets are resources owned by the firm and liabilities are the entity's obligations, does the difference, owners' equity, represent what the firm is worth? The answer is "no." The worth or value of a going concern depends on its ability to earn income.

3. For purposes of financial analysis, it is often helpful to think of assets as the resources the firm uses to generate sales. For example, machinery, an asset, is needed to produce products. Liabilities and owners' equity represent the sources relied upon to finance the acquisition of these resources. Putting it another way, assets represent a firm's uses of resources, and liabilities and owners' equity are the sources. A later chapter explores sources and uses of funds in more detail. We will learn that sources and uses are more complex than presented here. Still, it is often helpful for the financial analyst to think about the balance sheet in the following terms:

Assets = Liabilities + Owners' Equity
Uses of Resources = Sources of Resources

Returning to the topics listed in Table 1-2, each item is stated in terms of dollars, illustrating the *unit of measure* notion, that is, the dollar is the unit of measure. This measurement approach allows us to raise two issues. The first is: How do we account for the fact that the value of the dollar changes? For example, if the firm has the same amount of cash today as it had two years ago, this cash has less purchasing power because of inflation. The second issue is a related one: How do we account for the fact that the prices of individual assets may change? For example, if the firm owns inventory, inflation and/or other factors can cause the market value of the inventory to vary.

The answers to these questions are that we do not account for changes in the purchasing power of the dollar or for changes in the market values of individual assets. Existing practice is to rely on the *historical cost principle* which means that transactions are recorded at cost and maintained at this amount on the company's books. In other words, income statement and balance sheet amounts are not adjusted for variations in the general price level or for changes in the market value of individual assets.

A major reason for relying on the historical cost principle is the notion that accounting reports, to the extent possible or feasible, should be based on factual data rather than estimates. This is known as the *objectivity principle*. Recording transactions at cost is easy to verify, for it avoids any bias the preparer might possess. However, as we shall see later, the goal of objectivity is not always achieved because in some instances estimates and/or subjective judgments are necessary or desirable.

We have said that we do not account for changes in market value of specific assets. That is not an exact statement because decreases in market value sometimes are recorded. For example, suppose a firm purchases a marketable security for $10,000 and the market price subsequently drops to $5,000. It is likely that it would be shown on the statement as $5,000 instead of $10,000. This is known as an application of the *lower of cost or market rule*. This rule which generally applies only to inventory and investments states that if the market value or replacement value of an asset is lower than the original cost of the asset, the lower amount should apply.

The rationale for showing value reduction is supported by the notion of *conservatism*. This standard provides the following guidance for the accountant: When reasonable evidence exists for alternative measurements of net assets and income, select the one which tends to understate net assets and net income.

Many accountants and users of financial statements argue that there should be further departures from the historical cost principle. It is beyond our scope to debate this here, but we should mention a couple of points. First, opponents of historical cost thus far have been successful in requiring certain firms to present supplementary data showing the effects of general price level changes and changes in replacement values of specific assets.[1] Second, those advocating the incorporation of the effects of price level changes have shown that because of historical cost it is possible for a firm

---

[1] Statement No. 33 of the Financial Accounting Standards Board outlines the basic requirements. The jury is still out on how useful this information is. Our view is that it is very valuable and so we recommend that the analyst pay particular attention to these data when they are available. Some firms have argued that the data are not realistic for their business and actually present a distorted view of economic reality. This is probably true in some instances. Nevertheless, generally the data are helpful and normally there will be enough information for the analyst to make a judgment on its usefulness.

to report increasing net income numbers when its true profitability is declining.

This issue raises the *disclosure principle,* which states that information required for a fair presentation of the firm's financial position must be provided. If the information cannot be included on the statement, it must be contained in the supplementary materials. When analyzing a firm's financial performance and condition you frequently obtain the most perceptive insights by examining the information accompanying the financial statements. *Footnotes* which typically accompany financial statements are quite useful in this regard. For example, the balance sheet of the Eagle Hill Company shown in Table 1-1 includes long-term debt. When must the debt be repaid? What are important provisions of the loan? The footnotes accompanying the financial statements may help answer these questions.

In general, footnotes to financial statements contain two types of information. The first is a brief explanation of the accounting principles and procedures used in constructing the statements. The second is an elaboration of information which cannot be included in the statements themselves. Many inexperienced analysts do not pay sufficient attention to footnotes because they find them too tedious. This is a serious mistake because, as noted, you may often obtain the most perceptive insights by carefully studying footnotes. In fact, they are so important that many experienced analysts begin an analysis of financial statements by reading the auditor's opinion (discussed shortly) and then studying the accompanying footnotes.

A problem that accountants frequently encounter is what information to disclose. They cannot disclose everything; if they did, reports would be too costly and perhaps useless because of the information overload. In making this judgment they rely on the principle of *materiality* which means that you do not have to deal with unimportant matters. Thus, certain facts can be omitted and in some cases accounting principles can be violated if this treatment does not have a significant effect on the firm's financial condition. For instance, there would be no need for the Eagle Hill Corporation (Table 1-1) to mention a lawsuit for $500, but it should mention one for $100,000.

We are now in a position to raise a problem that is discussed in depth later, and that is that there are certain types of events for which more than one accounting method is acceptable. In theory at least, the preparer should select the principle which most clearly reports periodic net income. In practice, whether selection is based on the fairest or the highest level of net income is an interesting issue. At any rate, the variety of acceptable methods makes financial statement analysis more difficult. A key element in analyzing a firm's financial status is: (1) to make comparisons of the firm's progress over time and (2) to make comparisons to similar companies. Because different accounting approaches are acceptable, comparisons among firms can be quite difficult, if not impossible. Two firms can experience identical economic events and still show very different revenue and expense numbers. With respect to comparisons over time, the same company can face identical economic events in two different years and report very different revenue and expense numbers each year. Fortunately, in this latter case, we are helped by the *consistency principle* which states that once a particular method is adopted it should be maintained. If a firm wishes to change an accounting method, it may do so but it must disclose the effect of the change on reported results.

Before proceeding with principles, we should discuss the *auditor's opinion*. Firms whose securities are publicly traded on the stock exchanges are required to have their financial statements audited by independent accountants. Even firms whose shares are not traded might be required by creditors to have an audit or they may decide on their own to do so. A major purpose of an audit is to judge whether the firm's financial statements were prepared in accordance with generally accepted accounting principles (GAAP). The auditor will issue an opinion which is included in the firm's report. If GAAP was not followed, it will be mentioned in the opinion. Also, if there was a change from one acceptable accounting method to another, this will also be noted in the opinion along with the dollar effect the change had on reported results.

When mention is made in the opinion of a departure from GAAP or some other matter, this is called an exception or a qualification (versus the auditor issuing a clean or unqualified opinion). If there is a qualification, it is considered a "red flag" and analysts are extra careful in conducting the analysis.

We now come to three important principles: accrual accounting versus cash accounting, the realization principle and the matching principle. To understand financial accounting it is essential that you have a firm grasp of each of these three principles.

## ACCRUAL ACCOUNTING VERSUS CASH ACCOUNTING

According to the cash basis of accounting, revenues are recorded when the cash is received, and expenses are recorded when payment for them is made. Under the accrual basis of accounting, revenues are recognized and recorded when they are earned, provided that receipt is reasonably assured. Expenses are recognized and recorded when they are incurred, that is, when the economic resources needed to generate sales are used up. (The meaning of earning revenue and incurring expenses will become more clear when we discuss the realization and matching principles.) Accrual accounting provides the foundation of generally accepted accounting principles (GAAP). It is the preferred method because it provides a better measurement of a firm's profit performance and its financial condition.

Because of the use of accrual accounting, there is a difference between net income and cash flow. The amount of net income a firm earns during a period will be different from the amount of cash that it generates. And very often the difference will be substantial. Since net income is not cash, we must recognize that it can't be used to pay bills, purchase assets, etc. More will be said about the distinction between income and cash flow later in this chapter and in other chapters as well. This emphasis is warranted because it is crucially important for analysts to appreciate the difference between the two.

## REALIZATION PRINCIPLE

The realization principle states that revenues should be recognized and recorded when the earning process is virtually completed, that is, when the product is sold or the service is rendered. Cash might be received at the time of sale, prior to the sale, or in a subsequent period. The amount of revenue to record is the amount of cash that has been received or that will be received in the future. With respect to future payments, revenue should be recorded only if there is a reasonable expectation that the customer will pay. Let's look at some examples.

1. *The Reservoir Company is a wholesaler of men's clothing.* It sold suits for $50,000 to a department store in December on terms of net 30 days which means the customer is supposed to pay in January. According to the realization principle, the $50,000 is recorded as revenue during December, not in January. (If the cash basis of accounting was employed, the $50,000 would be recorded as revenue in January when the cash is received.) The rationale is that the earning process is completed in December. Stated another way, the customer has received the product and the Reservoir Company has the right to collect cash. This right to collect cash is an asset called accounts receivable.

2. *A publisher sells a three-year subscription to its monthly magazine for $180 on January 1 and on that day it sends the first issue to the customer.* In this instance, revenue of $60 would be recorded each year for three years (or $5 per month). The logic is that the revenue is not earned until the magazine is sent to the subscriber. During the first year only

12 of the 36 issues are sent, so only one-third of the $180 is earned the first year. If for some reason the firm cannot supply the magazine in the future, the customer is due a refund.

3. *In late March, Joe Holt made an appointment to receive a $10 dancing lesson on April 2.* He received the lesson April 2 and paid for it the same day. The firm would record the revenue of $10 on April 2 when the lesson is given. The logic of waiting until April 2 instead of recording it at the end of March is that the earning process is not completed until the lesson is given. (The number of appointments a studio has might be relevant to readers and might be disclosed as supplementary information on a financial report. We frequently see this type of information listed as orders received or as backlog for certain types of manufacturers.)

The above examples reveal the three basic situations: cash received subsequent to, prior to, and at the time of sale. For uncomplicated transactions like these, applying the realization principle is straightforward. For situations that are more complex, application is more difficult. We will explain two of these: installment sales and construction projects.

Installment sales normally represent high priced items, like a refrigerator, for which payment is made over several years. In some instances, accountants recognize the revenue when cash is received rather than at the time of sale. Is this practice consistent with the realization principle? The answer is, it depends. The realization principle says that revenue is recognized when the earning process is completed. Obviously, the process is completed when the product is sold. However, the realization principle also states that one should record the amount that is expected to be received. Thus, if there is considerable doubt as to full payment being made, then the installment method is appropriate and consistent with the realization principle. The problem is that it is normally a judgment call and accountants might differ in the way they record the transaction.

Actually, the installment method is not common in preparing financial statements. However, it does point out the importance of judgment in financial accounting. Moreover, as we shall see, it is a common method for tax purposes and thus has important implications for analyzing a firm's financial statements.

Another complex situation is a construction project that takes more than one accounting period to complete. For example, suppose a firm receives a contract to build a structure for $6 million. It is estimated that it will take three years to complete the project. When is the earning process completed? Some would argue when the project is completed, while others would contend that it is inappropriate to recognize all the revenue in one year since only a portion of the work will have been performed during that year. Two methods are acceptable for financial reporting. One is the completed contract method, which records all the revenue when the project is finished. The second is the percentage completion method, which records a portion of the total revenue each year that work is performed.

Long-term construction projects illustrate a problem mentioned earlier: There is more than one acceptable method for the same transaction. Thus, financial statement analysis is made more difficult and some standard techniques can be misleading. For example, creditors typically calculate financial ratios and then look at the industry averages. If various accounting procedures are common within the industry, such comparisons may be misleading.

To summarize, the realization principle's basic contention is that revenue is recognized when the product is sold or the service is rendered, that is, when the earning process is completed. For some types of situations the application of the principle is straightforward, while for others, it is more complex. For our purposes two points are worth emphasizing. First, since various accounting treatments for the same transaction are possible, comparisons are often difficult. Second, the amount of revenue that is reported is not necessarily a good indication of how much cash has flowed into the firm.

## MATCHING PRINCIPLE

The matching principle is concerned with the recording of expenses. It states that expenses incurred to generate revenue should be recorded in the same period the revenue is recorded. To improve our understanding of this principle, we will first discuss cost of goods sold and then consider other expenses.

Cost of goods sold expense is the cost of the products or services sold during the period. The composition of the account will vary depending on the type of firm. For a manufacturing firm, cost of goods sold includes the cost of the labor, materials and overhead used to produce the products sold during the period. For firms that purchase and resell a product, which we will call merchandising firms, cost of goods sold expense consists of the cost of the purchased products sold during the period. To show the difference and the application of the matching principle, we will rely on the first three examples used to explain the realization principle.

*The first example was the Reservoir Company which sold men's suits* for $50,000 in December on terms of net 30 days. Suppose the suits were purchased by the Reservoir Company from the manufacturer for $35,000. The $35,000 would be recorded as an expense in December, the same month the revenue was recorded. What if the suits were purchased by Reservoir in November? The $35,000 would be recorded as an asset, called inventory, and then eliminated and recorded as an expense when the suits were sold. Note the asset would be recorded as an expense in December regardless of when payment for the suits was made. Payment might occur prior to December, in December, or in a subsequent month.

The rationale is that to measure the profitability of the $50,000 sale, we must record the costs incurred in generating the sale in the same period the revenue is recorded. For example, suppose Reservoir purchased the suits for $35,000 cash in November, sold them in December and collected the cash in January. There were no other costs or transactions of any nature. If we employed the cash basis of accounting, the monthly income statements would be as follows:

|  | November | December | January |
|---|---|---|---|
| Revenues | $      0 | $      0 | $50,000 |
| Expenses | 35,000 | 0 | 0 |
| Profit (Loss) | ($35,000) | $      0 | $50,000 |

These statements show that November was a bad month, December was uneventful, and January was good. Actually, the firm sold suits for $50,000 in December, making $15,000 on the transaction. Only by adhering to the realization principle would we know the revenue was earned in December and only by following the matching principle would we know that the profit on the transaction was $15,000 as shown below:

|  | November | December | January |
|---|---|---|---|
| Revenues | $      0 | $50,000 | $      0 |
| Expenses | 0 | 35,000 | 0 |
| Profit | $      0 | $15,000 | $      0 |

*The second example involved a publisher who sold a three-year sub-scription* for $180 on January 1. For the month of January revenue of $5 would be recorded. Suppose the magazine was produced during December and the firm incurred the production costs in that month. These production costs would have been recorded as an asset, called inventory, and then the asset would have been eliminated and recorded as an expense during January when the revenue was recorded. This is the appropriate treatment because the goal is to measure the profitablity of the $5 sale.

*The final example concerned Joe Holt who purchased a dancing lesson for $10* on April 2—a cash sale. Suppose the person who gave the lesson was paid $5, but payment to this person was not made until May. The $5 would be recorded as an expense in April, the same month that the sale was recorded. But what about the fact that the firm didn't pay the dance instructor until May? In terms of measuring the profitability of the sale, it does not matter. Moreover, in April the firm incurred a legal obligation to make the payment and this obligation would be recognized by recording a liability of $5.

See if you can apply the matching principle to the following example: The Hassa Company incurs material, labor and overhead costs of $450 to produce a refrigerator which it sells to Joe Shaki for $600, payable in three equal annual installments of $200. Because of Shaki's poor credit rating, the firm decides to use the installment method, recognizing revenues of $200 per year. How would the costs of $450 incurred in manufacturing the refrigerator be treated? One third of the total cost, $150, would be recorded as an expense each year.

With respect to other expenses, some are matched with sales in the same manner as cost of goods sold expense. For example, commissions based on sales should be recorded as expenses in the same period that sales are recorded. There are some expenses, however, that are incurred to generate sales but are not matched to sales because it is not feasible or possible to do so. Examples are the president's salary, office supplies used in the accounting department and interest on debt. These types of expenses are called *period* expenses because they are incurred with the passage of time. Thus, they are matched with the period rather than with sales.

Recognizing that matching with the period rather than sales is due largely to practicality will help to avoid confusion when we see different treatments for the same type of costs. For example, suppose we start a manufacturing firm and hire two people, one to be the firm's credit manager and one to produce the products we manufacture. Both employees are paid a fixed salary. The credit manager's salary would be a period cost. The production worker's salary would be part of the product's cost, which first becomes an asset and then an expense when the product is sold. The reason for the dual treatment is that it is feasible to match the production worker's salary directly to sales, but most likely this is not the case for the credit manager's salary.

Certain categories of expenses will be matched with the period in one firm and with sales in another, depending on whether the firm is involved in manufacturing activities. For example, heat, light and power would always be treated as a period cost in a merchandising firm, but a portion of these costs would be treated as product costs in a manufacturing firm.

To summarize, the matching principle states that costs incurred to generate sales should be recorded as expenses in the same period that the revenues are recorded. This is done to measure the profitability of the sales during the period, a primary goal of financial accounting. It is not feasible, however, to match all costs directly with sales and thus some are matched with the period.

## YOU CAN ONLY SPEND CASH

Because of accrual accounting, net income and cash flow are not the same thing. It is crucial for an analyst to keep this point in mind. Look back at the Reservoir Company. Suppose the firm had to pay a bill for $10,000 in December. Net income for that month was $15,000. Could the firm pay? The answer is "no," unless the firm could find some source other than operating the business. That's because the firm did not generate one cent of cash during December.

The importance of cash flow does not imply, however, that net income is unimportant. If revenues are not greater than expenses by a sufficient margin, the firm is simply uneconomic and cannot survive—eventually its cash inflows will not be sufficient to cover its cash outflows. You will realize this critical insight about the economics of the business by measuring net income using the realization and matching principles.

# Income Statement and Balance Sheet Accounts

We will now turn our attention to discussing individual items, called accounts, that appear on income statements and balance sheets. We will rely on the statements of the Hypothetical Company, shown in Tables 1-3 and 1-4, as the basis for explaining accounts.

## INCOME STATEMENT

The first account is *gross sales* which represent the total amount of goods or services sold during the period. There may be more than one gross sales figure. For example, if a manufacturer of equipment sells and leases its

**TABLE 1-3**
**HYPOTHETICAL COMPANY, INC.**
Income Statement
for Year Ended December 31, 19XX

| | | |
|---|---:|---:|
| Gross sales | $320,800 | |
| Less sales returns and allowances | 32,800 | |
| Net sales | | $288,000 |
| Cost of goods sold | | 126,500 |
| Gross profit | | $161,500 |
| Selling, general and administrative expenses | | 84,000 |
| Depreciation expense | | 8,500 |
| Income from operations | | $ 69,000 |
| Interest expense (net of interest income) | | 5,100 |
| Income before taxes and extraordinary items | | $ 63,900 |
| Income taxes on operations | | 18,700 |
| Income before extraordinary item | | $ 45,200 |
| Loss from fire, net of tax of $4,000 | | 6,000 |
| Net income | | $ 39,200 |
| Earnings per share | | $ 1.90 |
| Dividends per share | | .95 |

product, these two sources of revenue may be listed separately. One or two items are deducted from gross sales to compute the net sales figure—*sales returns and allowances* and *sales discounts*.

If a customer is not satisfied with a product he or she may return the product and obtain either a cash refund or a credit against future sales. Alternatively, the customer may be granted a price concession, paying an amount lower than the original transaction price. These transactions are called sales returns and allowances, and the total for the period is deducted from the gross sales figure.

The second item, sales discounts, is a price concession granted for payment within a specified period of time. These discounts, frequently referred to as *cash discounts,* are normally recorded. Prompt payment discounts are not to be confused with quantity discounts which are price concessions granted for purchasing a specified amount. These and other types of *trade discounts* normally do not enter accounting records.

The *net sales* figure represents the economic resources, usually cash, the firm has received or expects to receive in the future. Sometimes firms present only the net sales figure and do not show the other two items described above. When we see only a net sales figure we know something

**TABLE 1-4**
**HYPOTHETICAL COMPANY, INC.**
Balance Sheet
at December 31, 19XX

### Current Assets

| | |
|---|---:|
| Cash | $10,400 |
| Marketable securities, at cost (approximates market value) | 16,300 |
| Accounts receivable, net of allowance of $400 | 24,500 |
| Inventory | 32,100 |
| Prepaid expenses | 4,400 |
| Other | 4,300 |
| Total current | $92,000 |
| Property, plant and equipment (net) | 40,100 |
| Long-term investments | 8,700 |
| Notes receivable | 6,900 |
| Goodwill | 6,300 |
| Other | 3,000 |
| Total assets | $157,000 |

### Current Liabilities

| | | |
|---|---:|---:|
| Accounts payable | | $ 20,700 |
| Accrued expenses | | 10,100 |
| Short-term debt | | 8,000 |
| Current portion of long-term debt | | 18,600 |
| Deferred taxes | | 2,200 |
| Total current | | $ 59,600 |
| Long-term debt | | 38,500 |
| Deferred taxes | | 14,800 |
| Deferred revenue | | 8,800 |
| Total liabilities | | $121,700 |
| Shareholders' equity | | |
| Paid-in Capital | | |
| Common stock | $ 2,000 | |
| Additional paid-in capital | 18,500 | 20,500 |
| Retained earnings | | 14,800 |
| Total shareholder's equity | | $ 35,300 |
| Total liabilities and shareholders' equity | | $157,000 |

has been deducted, but we can't tell whether it is one or two items or what the amount of each is. For example, the fact that sales returns and allowances are reported by the Hypothetical Company indicates that most likely there are no cash discounts. However, if this information was not provided, we would not be able to deduce this fact. Are firms justified in presenting only the net amount? The materiality principle discussed earlier is the guide. If the amounts are significant, they should be shown on the statement.

Suppose Joe Jones' Co. has a large number of sales returns, say, equal to 25% of total sales. As analysts we want to know this fact because it signifies that a large number of customers were so unhappy they may no longer be customers of Joe Jones. This, of course, would affect the firm's future sales and profits. Suppose Joe decides 25% is not material and does not report it. When independent accountants, usually certified public accountants, perform the annual audit or review,[2] they will insist he show the returns separately. And if he does not, they will issue a qualified opinion noting this fact. Of course, if Joe's statements are not reviewed or audited, we would never know.

There are two things to be learned from the above example. First, as analysts we want an audit. If we are lenders, we should insist on this unless there is some overriding consideration. Second, we should be concerned about a large number of sales returns and allowances not only because of the impact on that year but also because of what it implies for future years. When we analyze financial statements, we are primarily concerned about the future. After all, firms repay debts in the future, not in the past. The price of the stock is influenced by the future progress of the firm, etc.

## COST OF GOODS SOLD EXPENSE

Cost of goods sold expense represents the cost of the product or services sold during the period. For a manufacturing firm, it is calculated as follows:

> Beginning inventory of finished goods
> + Cost of goods manufactured
> − Ending inventory of finished goods
> = Cost of goods sold expense

Table 1-5 presents an illustration of a statement of cost of goods manufactured which might be included as part of the income statement. It might

---

[2] A review consists of an evaluation of the firm's accounting procedures based primarily on inquiries of its personnel. The scope is much less than a full audit and the fee also is much less. Sometimes an independent accountant is retained merely to prepare statements. This is called a compilation and it may be even less rigorous than a review.

also be shown as a supplementary statement, or might not be presented at all. At any rate, the last item on that statement, the $360,000 figure in Table 1-5, is part of the cost of *goods sold* calculation for a manufacturing firm.

As we can see from Table 1-5 cost of goods manufactured includes the cost of the raw materials, direct labor and overhead used to produce the products during the period. A manufacturing firm will have three categories of inventories: raw materials, which are goods purchased for production but not yet in the production process; work in process inventory, which includes the cost of the materials, labor and overhead incurred to produce products that are not completed as of the end of the period; finished goods, which represent the cost of the raw materials, labor and overhead incurred to produce products completed at the end of the period but not yet sold.

For a firm which does not manufacture the products it sells, the calculation is as follows:

> Beginning inventory
> + Purchases
> − Ending inventory
> = Cost of goods sold expense

This kind of firm has only one category of inventory. (The Hypothetical Company is this type.)

A major complication is that goods are purchased at different prices. This issue is especially critical when the rate of inflation is high and/or it changes in a dramatic fashion, or when replacement costs change due to technological change and/or demand-supply factors. To illustrate, let's discuss a firm which sells a single product purchased ready for sale. During the first year purchases are as follows:

| Month | Amount | Total Cost |
|---|---|---|
| January | 100 units @ $5.00 | $   500 |
| March | 200 units @ $5.50 | 1,100 |
| June | 200 units @ $6.00 | 1,200 |
| September | 200 units @ $6.50 | 1,300 |
| December | 300 units @ $7.00 | 2,100 |
| | 1,000 | $6,200 |

At year end there are 400 units on hand, indicating that 600 units were sold during the year. To calculate cost of goods sold expenses we must use the formula: beginning inventory + purchases − ending inventory = cost of goods sold expense. Beginning inventory was zero and purchases were

**TABLE 1-5**
**MANUFACTURING COMPANY**
Statement of Cost of Goods Manufactured
for Year Ending June 30, 19X1

| | | |
|---|---:|---:|
| Work in process inventory beginning of period | | $100,000 |
| Raw Materials | | |
| Beginning inventory of raw materials | $40,000 | |
| Purchases of raw materials | 80,000 | |
| Less ending inventory of raw materials | 50,000 | |
| Raw materials used | | 70,000 |
| Direct labor | | 90,000 |
| Overhead | | 150,000 |
| Total | | $410,000 |
| Less work in process inventory, end of period | | 50,000 |
| Cost of goods manufactured | | $360,000 |

$6,200. What value do we place on the ending inventory of 400 units? Various costing methods are permitted. We will discuss the following three: weighted average cost; first-in, first-out (FIFO); last-in, first-out (LIFO).

The weighted average cost approach uses an average cost per unit to value the ending inventory as shown below:

$$\frac{\text{Total Dollar Cost of Inventory}}{\text{Total Units}} = \frac{\$6,200}{1,000} = \$6.20$$

| | |
|---|---:|
| Beginning inventory | $    0 |
| + Purchases | 6,200 |
| − Ending inventory (400 × $6.2) | 2,480 |
| = Cost of goods sold expense | $3,720 |

The second method, FIFO, assumes for costing purposes that the first items purchased are the first sold. In our example the ending inventory would consist of the 300 purchased in December and 100 of the 200 purchased in September, giving an ending inventory of $2,750 and hence a cost of goods sold of $3,450.

The third method, LIFO, assumes for costing purposes hat the last items purchased are the first sold. Thus, the ending inventory figure would include the cost of January's, March's, and one-half of June's purchases, for a total of $2,200. This amount produces a cost of goods sold figure of $4,000.

The three approaches give substantially different numbers as the following summary indicates:

|  | Cost of Goods Sold Expense | Ending Inventory |
|---|---|---|
| Weighted average cost | $3,720 | $2,480 |
| FIFO | 3,450 | 2,750 |
| LIFO | 4,000 | 2,200 |

We can generalize from our example that when prices are rising, LIFO will give the highest cost of goods sold figure, FIFO the lowest, and the weighted average cost method an amount in between the two other approaches. As noted above, all three methods are acceptable; thus we see another instance of how varying accounting procedures can make inter-firm comparisons difficult. With respect to comparisons over time, if a firm decides to change methods it has to disclose this fact along with the dollar impact of the change on the firm's income statement and balance sheet.

Earlier we noted that generally it is permissible to use one accounting procedure for tax purposes and another for financial accounting purposes. LIFO is an exception. If LIFO is used on the tax reports, it must be employed for financial accounting purposes, though there are some exceptions. Since in a period of rising prices LIFO would produce the lowest tax liability (because expense would be highest under this method), why would a firm ever use FIFO? Minimizing taxes is certainly in the best interest of a firm's owners and we would certainly expect managers to minimize taxes. However, although we should be extra careful in our analysis when we see FIFO, we must not jump to conclusions because a firm might be minimizing taxes by using FIFO. For example, in the late 1970s many computer firms experienced decreasing product costs while the economy as a whole was experiencing rapid inflation.

We should note that the view expressed in the preceding paragraph represents the theoretical position that differences in accounting methods do not affect stock prices (because analysts are smart enough to discern the impact). Some would argue that firms use FIFO because it maximizes reported net income which in turn has a positive effect on the common stock price.

You might have noticed that if the purchase prices of a firm's inventories are rising, the use of LIFO will produce inventory values on the balance sheet that are below their market or replacement values. This is an example of a problem created by relying on the historical cost principle described earlier. Hopefully, supplementary data and/or accompanying footnotes would enable the analyst to make reasonable judgments concerning the true value of a firm's inventory.

A major problem with LIFO is that it provides an opportunity for manipulating the net income figure. (Although manipulation is also possible with other methods, it is less likely to occur when FIFO is employed.) Managers are often expected to achieve certain profit targets. Moreover, they like to show steadily increasing earnings per share figures over time. LIFO might provide these managers with an opportunity to achieve these goals.[3] To illustrate let us assume that the firm used in the example to explain the three costing methods adopts LIFO. As noted above the firm sold 600 units the first year but purchased 1,000 units as shown below:

| Month | Amount | Total Cost |
|---|---|---|
| January | 100 units @ $5.00 | $  500 |
| March | 200 units @ $5.50 | 1,100 |
| June | 200 units @ $6.00 | 1,200 |
| September | 200 units @ $6.50 | 1,300 |
| December | 300 units @ $7.00 | 2,100 |
| | 1,000 | $6,200 |

Let us assume that the firm's profit performance for the year is above target. It could in December purchase 400 units instead of 300. The result would be a cost of goods sold expense figure of $4,100 instead of $4,000. Now suppose the firm's profit performance is worse than expected either because it anticipated selling more than 600 units or certain expenses were higher than projected. It could postpone December's purchases until January. The result would be a cost of goods sold expense figure of $3,600 rather than $4,000.

Cost of goods sold expense is often the largest expense for a firm that sells products. We have just seen that the selection of an inventory costing method can have a substantial impact on the measurement of cost of goods sold expense. Thus, we see another instance of how inter-firm comparisons can be difficult because alternative accounting treatments are acceptable. (We should add, however, that if procedures are clearly stated, often adjustments to financial statements can be made for comparison purposes.)

Turning to the other items, the difference between net sales and cost of goods sold expense is known as *gross profit* or *gross margin*. The next line on the income statement: selling, general and administrative expenses, summarizes a number of accounts. Selling expenses are costs incurred by the firm in its sales activities. Examples are advertising, promotion, salespersons' salaries and commissions. General and administrative expenses would include the costs of various staff departments.

---

[3] As noted earlier, generally accepted accounting principles allow alternative accounting treatments for certain types of transactions. Relying on this choice to influence reported results is often referred to as income smoothing, although many analysts call it "creative accounting." In any event, you should recognize that the use of LIFO to manipulate figures is only one example of income smoothing.

*Depreciation expense,* which is not always reported separately, represents the allocation of the cost of a tangible asset that has a life of more than one year and that will help to generate revenue for more than one year. For example, suppose a firm purchases a machine for $5,000 which has an estimated useful life of five years and an estimated salvage value of $1,000, that is, it could be sold for $1,000 at the end of five years. It would be a violation of the matching principle to charge the entire $5,000 as an expense in the year the machine is purchased because it will help to generate revenues for five years. Therefore, a portion of the cost is allocated to each of the five years and is called depreciation expense.

We will illustrate by relying on the *straight-line method* which is one of several acceptable cost allocation procedures. It is computed as follows:

$$\frac{C - SV}{n} = \text{Depreciation Expense per Period}$$

Where:

    C = Cost of asset
  SV = Estimated salvage value
    n = Number of periods

For our example, depreciation expense will be $800 per year as shown below:

$$\frac{\$5,000 - \$1,000}{5 \text{ years}} = \$800$$

Each year depreciation expense of $800 will be recorded. The asset will not be reduced by $800 each year; rather a contra-asset account, called accumulated depreciation, will be established and will be increased by $800 each year. The process for five years is:

| Year | Depreciation Expense | Machine | Accumulated Depreciation | Book Value |
|------|---------------------|---------|--------------------------|------------|
| 1 | $800 | $5,000 | $ 800 | $4,200 |
| 2 | 800 | 5,000 | 1,600 | 3,400 |
| 3 | 800 | 5,000 | 2,400 | 2,600 |
| 4 | 800 | 5,000 | 3,200 | 1,800 |
| 5 | 800 | 5,000 | 4,000 | 1,000 |

The machine account is part of a category commonly called *fixed assets* or *property, plant and equipment.* The difference between the machine account and its related accumulated depreciation account is known as the asset's book value. The sum of the book values of fixed assets is shown on the balance sheet as *net fixed assets* or *property, plant and equipment (net)*.

As was the case with cost of goods sold expense, alternative procedures for computing depreciation expense are acceptable. These are known as accelerated methods because they give higher depreciation expense figures in the earlier years of the asset's life. An accelerated procedure should be used for financial accounting purposes when it would provide a better matching of revenues and expenses. For example, if the machine described above would help to generate more revenues in the earlier years of its life, an accelerated method should be employed.

None of the accelerated methods will be illustrated because a productive discussion would require that we raise a number of tax regulations that are beyond the scope of this chapter. We should point out, however, that it is permissible to use an accelerated method such as the Accelerated Cost Recovery System (ACRS) for tax purposes and the straight-line method for financial accounting purposes, and many firms do this.

On the balance sheet in Table 1-4 we have an asset section called "property, plant and equipment (net)." These are the fixed asset accounts. What the firm did was to sum all of its gross fixed asset accounts and then all of the corresponding accumulated depreciation accounts. It then subtracted the second total from the first and presented only the difference or the net amount. An alternative presentation would be the following:

Fixed assets
Less accumulated depreciation
Net fixed assets

In the context of financial statements, depreciation refers simply and only to a procedure for allocating cost over time. We must stress what it does not mean.

1. It does not necessarily reflect the physical deterioration or obsolescence of the asset.

2. It does not necessarily indicate a decline in the asset's market value.

3. It does not imply that the firm has established a fund or intends to establish a fund to replace an asset.

Selling, general and administrative expenses, and depreciation expense are subtracted from the gross margin figure to compute *income from operations*. This figure measures the profit performance of the firm from normal continuing operations before considering financing activities, income taxes and unusual items. The next item, *interest expense,* is the cost of borrowed funds. Firms typically invest temporary surpluses of cash and sometimes make permanent financial investments (e.g., stocks and bonds). Income from these sources would be reported in this section of the profit and loss (P&L) as interest income and/or dividend revenue. In our example in Table 1-4, this revenue was subtracted from interest expense and only the difference was reported. (You might see just the word "net" next to interest expense to signify this.) We should note that this revenue should be reported separately if the amount is material.

## INCOME TAX EXPENSE

The next expense category, *income tax expense,* represents the income taxes that would be due based on the income reported on the income statement. The taxable income on the firm's tax return, and hence the amount actually due for the period, often will be different from the amount reported on the income statement; and the difference can be substantial. There are three basic causes: (1) permanent difference, (2) differences due to the carryback and carryforward provisions of the tax laws and (3) timing differences.

A permanent difference arises because certain revenues are non-taxable and certain expenses are not tax deductible. An example of the former is interest on municipal securities; an example of the latter is the insurance premium paid on a life insurance policy on a firm's officer with the firm as beneficiary. The accounting impact of a permanent difference is on the reported income tax expense figure. More specifically, nontaxable revenues and expenses that are not tax deductible are excluded from the reported profit before income taxes figure in deriving the income tax expense figure. To illustrate, suppose a firm whose income tax rate is 50% regardless of its level of taxable income, reported profit before income taxes of $100,000 on its income statement. This amount includes nontaxable interest on municipal bonds of $10,000. All other revenues are taxable and all expenses are tax deductible. The income tax expense figure reported on its income statement would be $45,000, 50% times $90,000. The income statement would show the following:

| | |
|---|---:|
| Profit before income taxes | $100,000 |
| Income tax expense | 45,000 |
| Net income | $ 55,000 |

If there were no carrybacks or carryforwards or timing differences (discussed next), the firm's actual income tax liability would be $45,000 for the period, or 45% of its profits before income taxes. In other words, permanent differences have the effect of altering a firm's average income tax rate.

If a firm incurs a loss, it may carry it back for three years and forward for 15 years.[4] Carryback of a loss means a firm can obtain a refund for income taxes paid during the previous three years. To illustrate, assume the following information for a firm.

|  | Three Years Ago | Two Years Ago | One Year Ago |
|---|---|---|---|
| Taxable income | $300,000 | $150,000 | $50,000 |
| Income taxes paid | 150,000 | 75,000 | 25,000 |

In the current year the firm incurred a taxable loss of $100,000. The firm would apply this loss against the figures for three years ago as shown below:

|  | Original | Revised | Change |
|---|---|---|---|
| Taxable income | $300,000 | $200,000 | − 100,000 |
| Income taxes paid | 150,000 | 100,000 | − 50,000 |

The firm would receive a tax refund of $50,000 because of the loss and this amount should be reported on the current year's income statement. One way of reporting this information is as follows:

| | |
|---|---|
| Operating loss | ($100,000) |
| Income tax benefit of carryback | 50,000 |
| Net loss | ($50,000) |

If taxable income during the previous three years was not large enough to offset the loss, then the balance of the loss would be used to offset future income for up to 15 years. Suppose the firm in our example was formed in the current year and incurred a loss of $100,000 in the first year. Since the firm has never paid taxes, it obviously cannot obtain a refund. Thus, the loss would be used to offset future income, that is, this amount can be deducted from taxable income in future years and hence will lower future tax liabilities. For instance, if the firm earned income of $100,000 in its

[4] The investment tax credit, which is a reduction in taxes created by investment in certain kinds of fixed assets, also can be carried back and forward if the firm cannot utilize the full amount in the year the fixed asset is acquired.

second year, its tax liability would be zero because the firm could deduct the previous year's loss.

The benefit of a carryforward should not be reported on a firm's income statement in the year of the loss unless receipt is virtually assured. For instance, if the loss was $100,000 in the first year, normally the presentation on the income statement would be the following:

| | |
|---|---|
| Operating loss | ($100,000) |
| Income taxes | 0 |
| Net income | ($100,000) |

Given the principle of conservatism discussed earlier, the rationale for this treatment is clear. Realization of the benefit depends on earning income in the future, and since this is uncertain we generally do not recognize the benefit until the income is earned. In rare situations, it is permissible to recognize the future benefit in the year of the loss. For instance, suppose the firm in our example had contracts with the United States Government that guaranteed profits of much more than $100,000 during the next several years. In this situation, the tax benefit of the carryforward could be recognized because realization is virtually assured. We must emphasize that this treatment is rare. Putting it another way, when analyzing financial statements if you see the recognition of the benefit of a carryforward in the year of a loss, worry! This is a red flag indicating you must be extra careful in analyzing the statements because the firm might have very "creative accountants."

Before proceeding to discuss a timing difference, a word is in order regarding why we are paying so much attention to income taxes. Income taxes can consume 50% or more of a firm's pretax income. However, there are legal ways of reducing this tax burden and so business decisions must carefully consider the impact of income taxes. Further, to analyze financial statements properly, we must know how to evaluate the impact of taxes. For instance, the next two chapters cover ratio analysis and flow of funds analysis, respectively. To conduct these analyses effectively, we must understand how the impact of income taxes is reflected on financial statements.

A timing difference means that the period during which a firm reports revenues and/or expenses on its income statement differs from the period when these revenues and/or expenses are reported on its income tax return. Theoretically, a timing difference is the result of actions to minimize income tax payments while at the same time adhering to the realization and matching principles. (We say "theoretically" because it is not clear whether some managers are concerned about accounting principles or reporting the highest possible profits.) Let's look at several examples.

1. *A firm uses the installment method of recognizing revenue for tax purposes but reports the full sales price on its income statement.* As we saw earlier, a firm should recognize the full sales price on its income statement unless there is considerable doubt with respect to payment. The tax laws permit the use of the installment method. Since this method would normally postpone the payment of taxes, one would expect firms to rely on it for tax purposes.

2. *Accelerated methods of depreciation are allowed for tax purposes.* Since they have the effect of postponing taxes, many firms rely on these methods in preparing their tax returns. Straight-line depreciation, however, might be more appropriate for the firm's income statement in the sense that it provides a better matching of revenues and expenses than an accelerated procedure. (Many firms employ straight-line depreciation for income statement purposes, but one must wonder if it is due to accounting theory or the fact that this procedure often produces a higher earnings per share.)

3. *A firm rents space in its building and receives rent for two years when the contract is signed.* The entire amount is taxable in the year of receipt. However, for income statement purposes, the rental revenue must be spread over two years in accordance with the realization principle. Thus, in this case, tax expense on the income statement would be less than the amount actually paid. This difference is also reported on the balance sheet as an asset called deferred charges, prepaid taxes or some similar title.

You will more frequently encounter the type of situation described in the first two examples. To illustrate the accounting treatment, we will assume the following:

### Income Statement

|  | Year 1 | Year 2 | Year 3 | Total |
|---|---|---|---|---|
| Income before taxes | $450,000 | $450,000 | $450,000 | $1,350,000 |
| Income tax expense | 225,000 | 225,000 | 225,000 | 675,000 |
| Net income | $225,000 | $225,000 | $225,000 | $ 675,000 |

### Tax Return

|  | Year 1 | Year 2 | Year 3 | Total |
|---|---|---|---|---|
| Taxable income | $300,000 | $350,000 | $700,000 | $1,350,000 |
| Income taxes | 150,000 | 175,000 | 350,000 | 675,000 |
| Net income | $150,000 | $175,000 | $350,000 | $ 675,000 |

Note that the totals are the same for the three years but the firm has chosen to defer taxable income as long as possible—the third year. By doing so, in the first year it saved $75,000 ($225,000 − $150,000) and in the second year it saved $50,000 ($225,000 − $175,000). Thus, the firm had an additional $125,000 ($75,000 + $50,000) to work with. Of course, in the third year the $125,000 must be paid along with the $225,000 for that year.[5]

How do we account for the difference? A liability account is established, normally called *deferred taxes,* and the difference is reported there. Say the deferred tax account had a zero balance at the beginning of Year 1. At the end of Year 1 it would show $75,000. It would be increased by $50,000 to $125,000 at the end of Year 2 and then decreased by $125,000 at the end of Year 3.

This accounting treatment is called a timing difference because in theory as the above example shows, there will be a reversal, that is, initially taxes paid will be less than tax expense but in a future period (Year 3 in our example) taxes paid will be larger. Often, in practical situations the reverse will not occur for a long time—if ever. To see this important point, let's look at a simple example. The facts are:

1. The Installment Company is organized to sell a product for $200 each. It sells one unit in Year 1, two units in Year 2, three units in Year 3 and three units each year thereafter.

2. Customers pay over two years, $100 per year. Since payment is virtually assured, the firm will record revenues of $200 in the year of sale.

3. For simplicity only, it will be assumed that there are no expenses other than taxes; thus, pretax income from each sale is $200. Finally, we will assume a tax rate of 50%.

Given the above facts we can derive the information shown in Table 1-6.

We are most concerned with deferred taxes, which are shown as a liability on the firm's balance sheet. In the first year deferred taxes amount to $50— the difference between tax expense and taxes paid. In each of the next two years deferred taxes again increase by $50. After that they do not change, for taxes paid equals tax expense. Thus, in this example, deferred taxes represent a liability which will never be paid!

To be more precise, it should be noted that taxes in each individual account will be paid, but these taxes will be offset by new accounts. In other words, taxes are paid each year on part of the previous year's income,

---

[5] I am grateful to Professor Louis Corsini of Boston College for suggesting the approach presented in this paragraph.

**Table 1-6**    *Installment Company: Selected Financial Data*

| Year | Pretax Income Per Income Statement | Tax Expense | Taxable Income[1] | Taxes Paid | Deferred Taxes Per Balance Sheet |
|------|------|------|------|------|------|
| 1 | $200 | $100 | $100 | $ 50 | $ 50 |
| 2 | 400 | 200 | 300 | 150 | 100 |
| 3 | 600 | 300 | 500 | 250 | 150 |
| 4 | 600 | 300 | 600 | 300 | 150 |
| 5 | 600 | 300 | 600 | 300 | 150 |
| • | | | | | |
| • | | | | | |
| • | | | | | |
| • | | | | | |
| Infinity | 600 | 300 | 600 | 300 | 150 |

[1] Taxable income equals cash collections from sales. In Year 1, $100 is collected; in Year 2 one-half of sales for Years 1 and 2 are collected; in Year 3 one-half of the sales for Years 2 and 3 are collected. In each subsequent year collections will equal $600.

but a segment of the taxes on the current year's income are postponed, automatically recreating a liability.

The above example depicted a firm that stopped growing because many people rely on the following rule of thumb: Growing firms should treat deferred taxes as a liability that will never be paid. Actually, a firm that is growing will show a continuously increasing liability. The only time that the deferred taxes account might be reduced is when there is a decrease in sales. Note that we said *might be reduced*. When sales decline, the firm might incur a loss. This, of course, would mean no income taxes would have to be paid.

In situations where it appears that the liability account might not be paid for a considerable time, if ever, many analysts adjust the firm's financial statements. They would argue that in these cases it is really a permanent difference rather than a timing difference. This, they say, would lead to a reduction in the firm's effective tax rate. The effect of this would be to increase net income, increase earnings per share, reduce the firm's deferred taxes account and increase the firm's owners' equity. Some analysts who agree with this point of view merely treat the deferred taxes account as part of owners' equity rather than debt.

Now that we have given you the "party line," we must conclude by noting that we personally are hesitant to treat deferred taxes as an equity account. A firm can experience a decline in sales and still be profitable. In such a case deferred taxes can become a very damaging liability, especially in times when funds are desperately needed for other purposes.

The next category on the income statement is the *extraordinary items* section. These are events, both gains and losses, which are unusual in nature and do not occur frequently. Both conditions must be met to treat an item as extraordinary. An example would be a volcanic explosion. The extraordinary event is reported net of the tax effect. This is done because of the matching principle.

The final item on the body of the statement is *net income,* the difference between net sales and all expenses. It represents the increase in the firm's owners' equity, that is, total assets less liabilities, produced by day-to-day operations (i.e., generating revenues and incurring expenses).

Suppose you owned a share of stock in one of two firms. The first has a net income of $100 and the second $1,000. Both firms will earn the existing level of net income for many years into the future. Which would you choose? Your initial reaction might be to select the second. But suppose you were told that there was a total of two shares outstanding for the first firm and 1,000 for the second, that is, there are two equal owners for the first and 1,000 equal owners for the second. If you choose the first you would own $50, one-half the net income; the second would give you ownership of $1, one-thousandth of $1,000.

The above example demonstrated the importance of *earnings per share* (EPS). It is calculated as follows:

$$EPS = \frac{\text{Net Income} - \text{Preferred Dividends}}{\text{Weighted Number of Common Shares Outstanding for Period}}$$

*Preferred stock* normally offers a fixed return that must be paid before the claims of common stockholders. *Common shares outstanding* refers to the number of shares owned by investors. To compute EPS we rely on a weighted average of the number of shares outstanding at various times in the period. Firms frequently purchase their own shares. These shares, known as *treasury stock,* may not be voted. They are not entitled to dividends, nor are they eligible for any other benefits of ownership. Since they are no longer in the hands of investors, they are not included in the number of common shares outstanding.

There are a number of instruments and arrangements that may be used to obtain shares. Examples are convertible debt, options and warrants. Should these potential shares be included? It is beyond our scope to delve into this issue. We will merely note that for hybrid securities, it is sometimes necessary to compute an additional earnings per share figure showing the maximum potential dilution should all instruments be converted to common stock. This second ratio is called *fully diluted earnings per share*. Specific rules are provided by the accounting profession for guidance in its computation.

Earnings per share does not necessarily represent the entire amount that common shareholders can receive. Because of accrual accounting, earnings per share does not represent the amount of cash flow per share generated. Moreover, even if it did represent cash flow, it is not necessarily available because the firm might need the cash to pay debt or satisfy other needs. The last item on the statement, *dividends per share* (DPS), indicates the amount declared for each share. It is through dividends that stockholders receive cash from the firm.

Before proceeding to balance sheet items, we should observe that we have already referred to many of the items on the balance sheet. This illustrates the fundamental relationship between the two statements. For our purposes this means that one cannot understand and evaluate the income statement without referring to the balance sheet and vice versa.

## BALANCE SHEET

As noted previously, a balance sheet, also known as a statement of financial position, is a listing of a firm's assets, liabilities and owners' equity at a specific point in time. Assets are divided into two categories: current and noncurrent. A current asset is one which is either cash, or will turn into cash or be consumed within a relatively short period, normally one year. Noncurrent assets do not satisfy this criterion.

*Cash* represents currency on hand and deposits in banks. *Marketable securities* are temporary investments of cash. They normally consist of money market instruments, which are short-term debt instruments with a maturity of one year or less. In Table 1-4 the original cost of the securities was $16,300. This figure was about equal to the current market value.

*Accounts receivable* are amounts expected to be received from credit sales to customers. Receivables from other sources should be classified separately or lumped in with other current assets. One such example is a loan to an employee. The word net signifies that a contra-asset account, called *allowance for doubtful accounts*, has been subtracted from total accounts receivable. In our illustration the allowance is $400. The difference between the two accounts is called the net realizable amount. It is this quantity that is included in the calculation of total assets.

*Inventory* was discussed in conjunction with cost of goods sold expense.

In a manufacturing firm three separate inventory accounts might be presented on the balance sheet: raw materials, work in process and finished goods. *Prepaid expenses* represent items which have been paid for but are not yet expenses because of the matching principle. Examples are prepaying rent and premiums on fire insurance policies. *"Other"* current assets are assets that meet the test of being classified as current but because of their size are not listed separately.

Turning to long-term assets, the property, plant and equipment account has already been considered in connection with our discussion of depreciation expense. We will only add here that for an asset to be included in this category it must satisfy two criteria. First, it must be tangible; second, the purpose of acquiring the asset is for normal business use and not resale. For example, suppose a firm is a retailer of furniture. A desk used in this firm's accounting department would be a fixed asset, but desks on hand for sale to customers would be included in inventory. Finally, earlier we discussed the issue of supplying readers of financial statements with information on replacement costs. For many firms the most difficult part of this process is dealing with fixed assets because market value data are not always readily available for them.

The next asset is the *long-term investments* account which represents a financial commitment made by the firm with some long term or permanent objective in mind. For example, if a firm purchases shares of stock in another firm, with the intention of strengthening business ties or ultimately acquiring control of the firm, this purchase would be classified as an investment. Another example is information on subsidiaries that are not included in the consolidated statement. (We discuss the issue of consolidated statements in the Appendix to Chapter 1.)

The *notes receivable* account represents amounts due to the firm. The word "note" signifies that there has been a written agreement. The inclusion in the noncurrent section indicates that receipt is not expected within one year from the balance sheet date. If it were due within one year, it would be listed as a current asset.

The next category is intangibles. An intangible asset is any noncurrent asset such as *goodwill*. (Financial investments such as stocks and bonds are not included in this category.) The term "goodwill" has many connotations but if it appears on a balance sheet, it means the firm has paid for it. Specifically, goodwill arises when a firm acquires another firm at a price that is greater than the fair market value of the identifiable assets acquired. Goodwill, like most intangible assets, must be written off over the periods during which it helps to generate revenues—the expense is called *amortization*. It is usually difficult to estimate the useful life of goodwill. The Financial Accounting Standards Board has set 40 years as the maximum period over which goodwill must be amortized and for some transactions a shorter amortization period is required.

Firms try to avoid the presence of goodwill on their balance sheet. The reason being that it is "a drag" on net income and earnings per share since it must be written off, and it's *not* a tax deductible expense. (There are two methods of accounting for mergers: purchase and pooling of interests. The latter eliminates the possibility of creating in the asset column additional goodwill through the merger. The terms of the merger dictate the accounting method to be employed. The decision is not left to the firm. However, there have been cases where the terms of a merger were allegedly altered so that the desired accounting method could be employed.)

The final asset is *other* which represents accounts that meet the test of being classified as noncurrent but are not separately listed because of their size. An example is a piece of equipment being held for resale. After this item, the amount of total assets is listed.

Turning to the liabilities we see that they are also divided into the categories of current and noncurrent. Current liabilities normally include those that must be eliminated within one year from the balance sheet date. Noncurrent include all obligations that do not qualify as current.

The first item is *accounts payable.* It can represent any short-term liability, but it usually refers to credit buying of products for resale, raw materials used in production, and supplies. *Accrued liabilities,* also known as accrued expenses, are expenses that have been incurred but not paid for as of the balance sheet date. Examples are labor expenses, payroll taxes, income taxes due, and utilities. *Short-term debt* normally includes borrowings for temporary and/or seasonal financing requirements. *Current portion of long-term debt* is the principal portion of long-term debt due in one year. The remainder is reported as long-term debt in the noncurrent section.

Deferred taxes was discussed in the section on timing differences. Here we will only point out the difference between deferred taxes and accrued taxes. The latter is a current liability either classified separately or lumped in with other accrued expenses. You will recall that deferred taxes can be a questionable liability which might never be paid. Conversely, accrued taxes represent a very real liability, one that will be paid within one year from the balance sheet date.

When we considered deferred taxes, we did not cover its balance sheet classification. If taxes are postponed for one year or less, they are listed as a current liability. If postponement is for more than one year, they are a noncurrent liability. If a portion is deferred for one year or less and another part is for more than a year, both accounts will appear on the balance sheet. This is the case with Hypothetical Company in Table 1-4. The important point, however, is that the nature of the liability is the same irrespective of its balance sheet classification. Do not infer that since it appears as a current liability there is a high probability the account will be reduced. For example, in the illustration we used for the deferred taxes account that would never be reduced (the Installment Company in Table 1-6), that account would be listed as a current liability.

The *deferred revenue* account, also known as unearned revenue, is for cash received but not yet earned. An example is a magazine publisher who receives payment prior to sending the magazine to the subscriber. As was explained earlier, revenue received in advance is a liability because it must be returned if the firm does not deliver the good or provide the service. There is a subtle point, however, which should be explicitly stated. This is an example of a liability which is not quite the same as other liabilities. Note that the amount listed beside the account in Table 1-4 is $8,800. This figure represents the amount that has been received in advance. It does not represent the dollar amount that the firm must pay (as is the case with most liabilities). Obviously, the firm will have to expend resources to provide the goods or services, but if the sale is a profitable one, the amount will be less than $8,800.

The last segment of the statement is the stockholders' equity section, which is what the owners' equity section is frequently called when the entity is a corporation. This section reports the amounts of capital paid in by stockholders and the earnings retained in the business. When a corporation sells *common stock,* it increases the common stock account by the par or stated value of the stock. If it sells the stock at a price above the par or stated value, which is virtually always the case, it will increase the *additional paid-in capital* account for the remainder. (This latter account is also known as paid-in capital or capital surplus.) For example, suppose a firm issues one share of stock with a par value of $1 for $20. It would increase the common stock account by one dollar and increase the additional paid-in capital account by $19.

Par value for all practical purposes has no meaning today—common stock is virtually always issued without a par value or at a price above its par value. Par value bears no relationship to market value nor is it useful for any analytical purpose. Indeed, its only significance is to meet certain legal state statutes.

The final item is the *retained earnings* account which represents the portion of net income retained by the business since its inception. Putting it another way, it equals the total amount of net income earned less dividends paid out since the start of the business. Many firms have been profitable for a long time. Most of these firms will have a large retained earnings balance. However, the funds have already been spent and the account does not represent cash. As shown in Table 1-4, the retained earning balance is $14,800. This does not mean that the firm has a pool of cash of $14,800 sitting somewhere. The $14,800 figure means simply and only that the company has retained and reinvested $14,800 of its net income since its inception. Where is the $14,800? We can't tell. It was either used to acquire assets directly or to pay off liabilities created when the assets were acquired. All we know for sure is that it is not a pool of money laying around. How much money does the firm have? To answer this question we look to the cash account which shows a balance of $10,400.

We emphasized that the retained earnings account does not represent cash because the phrase can and does confuse many people. We should add that other items appearing on the right hand side of the balance sheet can also be confusing in this regard. Therefore, it is important to keep in mind that all the economic resources owned by the firm will always be reported as assets and will never appear in the liability or owners' equity sections of the balance sheet.

An understanding of the topics covered in this chapter and some experience will enable you to analyze financial reports. Of course, you will encounter items we have not addressed in the chapter or in the following Appendix, but searching through accounting references should no longer be an ominous undertaking. (A list of references for this and remaining chapters is provided at the end of the book.)

# Appendix to Chapter 1
# Additional Financial Accounting Topics

Chapter 1 explained financial accounting principles and terms appearing on income statements and balance sheets. We avoided many details and complexities to keep the presentation as simple as possible. In this appendix we will address several of these.

## OTHER FINANCIAL STATEMENTS

Public companies are required to issue an annual report and a 10-K report each year. These contain financial data and other information. We will discuss briefly some of the financial data included in these reports.

Included are an income statement for the most recent fiscal year ended and one for the prior year. There are also two balance sheets—one as of the end of the most recent fiscal year and one as of the end of the prior fiscal year. Two consecutive annual statements are provided to help the reader make comparisons. There are also summary annual financial data for the last five or ten years. Finally, selected quarterly data for the previous eight quarters are included.

In addition to the above, the annual and 10-K reports normally include the following statements:

1. Statement of Changes in Financial Position.

2. Statement of Retained Earnings.

3. Statement of Paid-In Capital.

The latter two may be combined into a single Statement of Shareholders' Equity. Following is a brief description of each of these statements:

The Statement of Changes in Financial Position provides information on the firm's investment and financing activities. In the chapter on flow of funds analysis, we consider this statement in more depth.

The Statement of Retained Earnings explains the change in the balance in the retained earnings account between two periods. The two basic items affecting this account are net income and dividends. Generally, it is the difference between net income and dividends that accounts for the change in retained earnings as shown below:

> Retained earnings, beginning of period
> + Net income for the period
> − Dividends declared
> + Retained earnings, end of period

Sometimes there will be other items affecting the retained earnings balance. These are called prior period adjustments and are relatively rare.

The Statement of Paid-In Capital will explain changes that have occurred in the common stock and paid-in capital accounts. Items in this statement include the following: new issues of stock, exercise of stock options, stock splits, exercise of warrants, conversion of debt and purchase of Treasury shares. This statement often appears ominous to the inexperienced reader but once understood the terms are not so difficult. We will give a brief description of each of them, except for new issues and treasury stock which were described in the chapter.

Many firms give their employees the option to purchase common stock in the firm as an inducement to act in the best interest of the common shareholders, who are the owners of the firm. The option gives the employee the right to purchase stock at a certain price for a stipulated period of time. Exercising the stock option refers to the actual purchase of shares and this transaction affects the common stock and additional paid-in capital accounts.

Warrants are similar to stock options. Generally, they are given to someone outside the firm as an inducement or for services provided. For example, sometimes warrants are attached to a debt instrument. In this case, the warrant gives the lender the option to purchase shares for a certain price for a stipulated period of time. Exercising the warrants refers to the actual purchase of shares by the owner of the warrants, and this transaction affects the common stock and additional paid-in capital accounts.

Sometimes firms issue convertible debt which can be exchanged for common stock. When the debt is exchanged for stock, debt on the balance sheet is reduced and the common stock and additional paid-in capital accounts are increased.

## DISTRIBUTIONS OF STOCK

For a variety of reasons firms issue stock dividends and/or stock splits, which are additional shares, or a fraction of a share, to existing stockholders.

In all cases, new shares are distributed in proportion to existing shares. For example, if a firm with 100 common shares outstanding issues ten additional shares, each existing share is entitled to one-tenth of a new share. For financial accounting purposes, we must distinguish among stock splits, small stock dividends and large stock dividends. We will explain by relying on a simple example:

The shareholders' equity section of Firm A is as follows:

| | |
|---|---|
| Common stock, par value of $1 | $10,000 |
| Additional paid-in capital | 40,000 |
| Retained earnings | 30,000 |
| Total | $80,000 |

There are 10,000 common shares outstanding. Firm A is contemplating giving existing shareholders new shares, and three options are being considered:

1. Two-for-one stock split.

2. 10% stock dividend.

3. 50% stock dividend.

The market price of the firm's shares is ten dollars per share.

A two-for-one stock split means that for each share owned, a stockholder will receive one additional share. The only effect of this event on the shareholders' equity section shown above is to change the par value from $1 to 50¢. The balances shown in the accounts do not change.

A stock dividend is basically the same as a stock split. However, the accounting treatment differs and there are different treatments for small and large stock dividends. Let's first explain how many new shares are issued. A 10% stock dividend means Firm A would issue 1,000 new shares, and each existing share would be entitled to one-tenth of a new share. A 50% stock dividend means Firm A would issue 5,000 new shares, and each existing share would be entitled to one-half of a new share.

For accounting purposes, 20% to 25% is the key to the appropriate treatment. Stock dividends less than 20%–25% are considered small and receive the following treatment: The par value is not changed. The retained earnings account is reduced by the market value of the new shares issued. The common stock account is increased by the par value of the new shares issued and the additional paid-in capital is increased by the remainder. In our example of a 10% stock dividend, 1,000 new shares would be issued. Given the market value per share of $10, the retained earnings balance would be reduced by $10,000, and the common stock and additional paid-in capital accounts would be increased by $1,000 and $9,000, respectively, as shown below:

| | |
|---|---|
| Common stock, par value $1 | $11,000 |
| Additional paid-in capital | 49,000 |
| Retained earnings | 20,000 |
| Total | $80,000 |

Notice that total stockholders' equity has not changed.

A large stock dividend is treated more like a stock split. In this case the retained earnings account is reduced by the par value of the new shares issued and the common stock account would be increased by the same amount. In our example of a 50% stock dividend, there would be 5,000 new shares. Recalling that par value per share is $1, we can recompute the stockholders' equity section as shown below:

| | |
|---|---|
| Common stock, par value $1 | $15,000 |
| Additional paid-in capital | 40,000 |
| Retained earnings | 25,000 |
| Total | $80,000 |

Notice that total stockholders' equity does not change.

We explained the three different accounting treatments for stock distributions to help the reader analyze the stockholders' equity accounts for firms that distribute stock. It is beyond our scope to explore the rationale for distributing stock and for the different accounting treatment they receive. We should point out, however, that there is considerable controversy on both issues.

## CONSOLIDATED STATEMENTS

Many firms consist of several legal entities, a parent and subsidiaries. This raises two issues: the extent to which these entities should be combined for financial reporting purposes and how to accomplish this. For these complex matters we can merely highlight important points. Let's begin by listing a summary of the accounting rules:

1. When one firm (parent) has a controlling interest in another firm (subsidiary), consolidated financial statements normally should be prepared.

Controlling interest means owning more than 50% of the outstanding stock of the subsidiary.

2. The equity method normally should be used if one firm owns between 20%–50% of the outstanding common stock of another firm.

3. The cost method usually is employed if stock ownership is less than 20% or for some reason the other two methods are inappropriate.

We will now briefly describe each method.

### *Consolidation and Minority Interest*

Consolidation means that the separate legal entities are treated as a single economic entity for financial reporting purposes. The financial statements of the separate entities are combined. Suppose Firm C, a manufacturer of widgets, purchases 100% of the common stock of Firm D which also manufactures widgets. For various legal, tax or other considerations, Firm C decides to leave Firm D as a separate corporation. Given this, Firm C would be the parent and Firm D would be the subsidiary. Most likely, consolidated statements would appear in the annual report. This means the financial statements (i.e., income statements, balance sheets, etc.) of Firm C and Firm D would be added together.

What if Firm C only purchases 90% of the common stock of Firm D? Since more than 50% is owned, Firm C controls Firm D; therefore, consolidated statements would be prepared as described above. However, the statements must recognize the fact that there are other owners besides Firm C. This is done by reporting *minority interest*. In our example, minority interest equal to 10% of the net income of Firm D would be reported on the consolidated income statement. The dollar amount is deducted in computing consolidated net income. The 10% ownership of the equity of Firm D would also be recognized on the consolidated balance sheet. It would be called minority interest and would be reported as either part of shareholders' equity or listed as a separate category between the liabilities and shareholders' equity sections.

Sometimes it is not useful to prepare consolidated statements, even if one firm owns 100% of a subsidiary. This is appropriate when combining the statements would make the data less useful. For example, many manufacturing and retailing firms that have finance subsidiaries do not include this subsidiary in their consolidated statements. Instead they use the equity method and also report financial data for the subsidiary in the footnotes or as part of the supplementary data.

### Equity Method

Suppose Firm C purchased 30% of the shares of Firm D and decided to use the equity method. The purchase price would be reported on Firm C's books as an asset called investment in subsidiary, or something similar. Each year Firm C would report its share, 30%, of the net income in Firm C as other income on its income statement (or 30% of the net loss as other expenses). This amount would also be added to the asset account. Dividends are not reported as income. However, the asset account is reduced by the amount of the dividend.

### Cost Method

Suppose Firm C purchases only 15% of Firm D and decides to use the cost method. The purchase price would be reported on Firm C's books as an asset called investment in subsidiary, or something similar as was constructed for the equity method. Unlike the equity method, however, this amount is not changed unless the firm purchases more shares or sells some of the shares bought. Moreover, Firm C does not report any of the earnings of Firm D on its books. All that is reported are dividends received from Firm D, and these are shown as other income on Firm C's income statement.

## LEASES

This section briefly describes the accounting treatment of capital leases and other kinds of leases. After defining a lease, we will provide an example to give the reader an intuitive sense for the distinction between the two types. Then we will generalize and note some problems for financial analysts.

When one party, the lessee, pays another party, the lessor, to use his or her asset for a stipulated period of time, this transaction is a lease arrangement. Note that the lessee does not own the asset.

A firm that recently purchased a small computer was offered a lease arrangement by the vendor. The essential elements for our purposes were the following:

1. The lease term was five years and the lessee could not cancel. This meant lease payments had to be made for five years even if the firm decided it no longer wanted the computer.

2. The estimated useful life of the computer was five years.

Let's assume the firm accepted the transaction. How would it have reported the arrangement on its books? The accounting rules for this kind of transaction changed in 1976. Let's first review what the accounting rules were prior to 1976. The firm would have recorded the lease payment as an expense when it was incurred. Moreover, it would have included details of the arrangements in the footnotes to its financial statements.

Now let's look at what this treatment does for financial analysts. Here we have a firm with a legal commitment to make payments for five years, yet there is no liability on the books. Moreover, the firm has the use of an asset for its entire useful life. Analysts would figure out what an equivalent asset amount and equivalent liability amount would be and they would adjust the balance sheet. Analysts also complained to the accounting profession. Fortunately, the accounting profession listened and in 1976 the Financial Accounting Standards Board issued Statement No. 13. This said that a lease like the one described above should be classified as a capital lease. More generally, a capital lease is one that meets *any one* of the following criteria:

1. The lessor transfers title to the lessee before or at the end of the lease period.

2. The lease agreement contains a clause allowing the lessee to purchase the asset at a bargain price.

3. The lease period is greater than or equal to 75% of the economic life of the asset.

4. At the outset of the lease, the present value of the minimum lease payments equal 90% of the market value of the asset (less any tax credits).

Capital lease accounting is complex, but basically the lessee must account for the transaction as if he or she purchased the asset and financed it with debt. Lease arrangements that do not meet one of the above four conditions would be accounted for as an operating lease. In this case, no asset or liability would appear on the balance sheet. Lease expense would be recorded when incurred, and details would be provided in the footnotes.

Lease accounting shows how the accounting profession tries to respond to the needs of financial statement users. Experience with the new rules has also shown that no set of standards is foolproof. We have seen lease arrangements that are basically capital leases, but managers have figured a way to have them qualify as operating leases.

## INTERNATIONAL OPERATIONS

Many firms have subsidiaries outside the United States. This raises the issue of dealing with different currencies when preparing consolidated financial statements. Past pronouncements have created considerable controversy because some managers have argued that the accounting rules require them to report amounts that are not realistic.

To see at least part of the difficulty let's rely on a simple example. Suppose our Canadian subsidiary purchases a piece of land for one million Canadian dollars when the Canadian dollar is worth one United States dollar, that is, you can exchange one Canadian dollar for one United States dollar. Assume that two years later the Canadian dollar is worth 80 cents, which means we can exchange a Canadian dollar for .8 of a United States dollar. Let's also assume that the market value of the land is still one million Canadian dollars. When we prepare our consolidated statements which are stated in United States currency how do we value the land? It is only worth $800,000 in United States currency. Thus, you can argue that there has been a loss of $200,000 because if we sell the land for one million Canadian dollars we would end up with only 800,000 United States dollars. On the other hand, you can also argue that we have no intention of selling the land and so we should not recognize the loss.

There are many issues such as the one described above that have created controversy. Disagreement on all of these issues is focused on whether or not to report gains and losses caused by fluctuations in exchange rates and how to report them. Here is a simplified summary of what is done when a foreign subsidiary is being consolidated:

1. Assets and liabilities of the subsidiary are translated, say from French francs to United States dollars, at the exchange rate in effect at the balance sheet date. Revenues and expenses for the period are translated at an average of exchange rates for the period.

2. Translation gains and losses are classified into two categories depending on the nature of the item.

3. Net gain or loss for one category is reported on the consolidated income statement and net gain or loss for the other category is reported as a separate item in the stockholders' equity section of the consolidated balance sheet. (The land example in the preceding paragraph would fall into the category reported on the balance sheet.)

This short appendix covered a number of additional financial accounting topics that you are likely to encounter in conducting financial statement analyses. It was beyond our scope to discuss these topics in more depth. The references at the end of the book will enable you to explore all topics covered in the chapter and this appendix in more detail and to deal with other financial accounting terms and issues as well.

# Problems and Discussion Questions

## A. Solved Problems

### Problem 1-1A

Accounts from the income statement for the year ended December 31, 19X1 and the balance sheet at December 31, 19X1 for Henderson, Inc. are listed in Table 1-7. Your task is to prepare an income statement and balance sheet in proper form.

TABLE 1-7
HENDERSON, INC.
Income Statement and Balance Sheet Accounts

| | | | |
|---|---:|---|---:|
| Paid-in capital | $ 47,800 | Total current liabilities | $ 64,975 |
| Sales discounts | 10,500 | Earnings per share | 4.43 |
| Selling and administra- | | Allowance for bad debts | 1,050 |
| tive expenses | 104,450 | Accrued expenses | 9,475 |
| Goodwill | 5,075 | Cash | 4,700 |
| Accounts receivable (net) | 51,850 | Interest expense (net) | 5,100 |
| Gross sales | 500,000 | Accounts payable | 47,500 |
| Loss from fire, net of tax | | Long-term debt | 41,400 |
| of 300 | 800 | Sales returns and allowances | 5,000 |
| Inventory | 74,600 | Total current assets | 151,325 |
| Net income | 53,830 | Gross fixed asets | 462,500 |
| Marketable securities | 18,100 | Net sales | 484,500 |
| Accumulated depreciation | 147,800 | Deferred income taxes | |
| Current portion of long- | | (non current) | 9,100 |
| term debt | 8,000 | Common stock, par | |
| Research and develop- | | value $1 | 12,154 |
| ment expenses | 47,400 | Fixed assets (net) | 314,700 |
| Income taxes on operations | 36,420 | Total assets | 471,100 |
| Gross profit | 248,000 | Cost of goods sold | 236,500 |
| Total liabilities and | | Retained earnings | 295,671 |
| shareholders' equity | 471,100 | Income before taxes and | |
| Income from operations | 96,150 | extraordinary items | 91,050 |
| Total liabilities | 115,475 | Prepaid expenses | 2,075 |
| Income before extraor- | | | |
| dinary items | 54,630 | | |
| Total shareholders' equity | 355,625 | | |

*Solution 1-1A*

Label each item as belonging to the income statement and balance sheet. Then prepare an outline of an income statement and a balance sheet. The final step is to prepare the statements. Table 1-8 has the income statement and Table 1-9 has the balance sheet.

TABLE 1-8
HENDERSON, INC.
Income Statement
for the Year Ended December 31, 19X1

| | | |
|---|---:|---:|
| Gross sales | $500,000 | |
| Less sales returns and allowances | 5,000 | |
| Less sales discount | 10,500 | |
| Net sales | | $484,500 |
| Cost of goods sold expense | | 236,500 |
| Gross profit | | $248,000 |
| Selling and administrative | | 104,450 |
| Research and development | | 47,400 |
| Income from operations | | $ 96,150 |
| Interest expense (net) | | 5,100 |
| Income before taxes and extraordinary items | | $ 91,050 |
| Income taxes on operations | | 36,420 |
| Income before extraordinary items | | $ 54,630 |
| Loss from fire, net of tax of 300 | | 800 |
| Net income | | $ 53,830 |
| Earnings per share | | 4.43 |

**TABLE 1-9**
**HENDERSON, INC.**
Balance Sheet
at December 31, 19X1

| Current Assets | | |
|---|---|---|
| Cash | | $ 4,700 |
| Marketable securities | | 18,100 |
| Accounts receivable, net of bad debt of $1,050 | | 51,850 |
| Inventory | | 74,600 |
| Prepaid expenses | | 2,075 |
| Total current | | $151,325 |
| Gross fixed assets | $462,500 | |
| Less accumulated depreciation | 147,800 | |
| Fixed assets (net) | | 314,700 |
| Goodwill | | 5,075 |
| Total assets | | $471,100 |
| | | |
| Current liabilities | | |
| Accounts payable | | $ 47,500 |
| Accrued expenses | | 9,475 |
| Current portion of long-term debt | | 8,000 |
| Total current | | $ 64,975 |
| Long-term debt | | 41,400 |
| Deferred taxes | | 9,100 |
| Total liabilities | | $115,475 |
| Shareholders' equity | | |
| Common stock, par value $1 | | 12,154 |
| Paid-in capital | | 47,800 |
| Retained earnings | | 295,671 |
| Total shareholders' equity | | $355,625 |
| Total liabilities and shareholders' equity | | $471,100 |

*Problem 1-2A*

You are given the following information for a new firm, Downs, Inc.

• Annual net sales for each of the first four years is $50,000. All sales are for cash.

• There are only two expense categories—labor and depreciation.

• Labor expense is $20,000 per year for each of the first four years. This is a cash expense.

- The firm employs the straight-line method of depreciation for financial accounting purposes and an accelerated method for tax purposes. The annual amounts are:

| Year | Depreciation For Financial Accounting | Depreciation For Income Tax Return |
|------|---------------------------------------|------------------------------------|
| 1    | $20,000                               | $30,000                            |
| 2    | 20,000                                | 25,000                             |
| 3    | 20,000                                | 20,000                             |
| 4    | 20,000                                | 5,000                              |

- The firm's income tax rate is 40%.

1. Prepare annual income statements for Downs, Inc. for the four years.

2. Compute the firm's income tax liability for each of the four years.

3. Are the differences between annual income tax expense and annual income tax liability reported on the firm's financial statements? If so, how?

### Solution 1-2A

1. The income statements are shown below:

|                    | For Year 1 | For Year 2 | For Year 3 | For Year 4 |
|--------------------|-----------|-----------|-----------|-----------|
| Net sales          | $50,000   | $50,000   | $50,000   | $50,000   |
| Labor              | 20,000    | 20,000    | 20,000    | 20,000    |
| Depreciation       | 20,000    | 20,000    | 20,000    | 20,000    |
| Income before taxes| $10,000   | $10,000   | $10,000   | $10,000   |
| Income tax expense | 4,000     | 4,000     | 4,000     | 4,000     |
| Net income         | $ 6,000   | $ 6,000   | $ 6,000   | $ 6,000   |

2. The income statements shown on the firm's income tax returns are:

|                 | For Year 1 | For Year 2 | For Year 3 | For Year 4 |
|-----------------|-----------|-----------|-----------|-----------|
| Net sales       | $50,000   | $50,000   | $50,000   | $50,000   |
| Labor           | 20,000    | 20,000    | 20,000    | 20,000    |
| Depreciation    | 30,000    | 25,000    | 20,000    | 5,000     |
| Taxable income  | $    0    | $ 5,000   | $10,000   | $25,000   |
| Income taxes due| 0         | 2,000     | 4,000     | 10,000    |

3. The differences between income tax expense and the actual tax liability for the period is reflected on the firm's balance sheet

in a liability account called deferred taxes. The balance in this liability account at the end of each year is shown next:

| Year | Income Tax Expense | Income Tax Due | Deferred Taxes |
|------|--------------------|----------------|----------------|
| 1 | $4,000 | $    0 | $4,000 |
| 2 | 4,000 | 2,000 | 6,000 |
| 3 | 4,000 | 4,000 | 6,000 |
| 4 | 4,000 | 10,000 | 0 |

# B. Discussion Questions

### 1–1B
What is the difference between depreciation expense and accumulated depreciation?

### 1–2B
Explain the difference between the cost method and the equity method of accounting for a subsidiary. (Appendix)

### 1–3B
Explain the difference between cost of goods sold expense and cost of goods manufactured.

### 1–4B
Evaluate the following statement: Earnings per share (EPS) is computed by dividing net income after taxes by the number of common shares outstanding plus treasury stock.

### 1–5B
Describe the difference between the cash basis and accrual basis of accounting.

### 1–6B
Your study group is analyzing a business policy case. The firm wants to introduce a new product which will cost $15 million. The firm's balance sheet shows cash plus marketable securities of $5 million, retained earnings of over $50 million and current maturities of long-term debt of $10 million. The footnotes accompanying the financial statements indicate that the $10 million liability is due three months from the balance sheet date. A member of your study group makes the following observation: "Resources will be no problem. Retained earnings are sufficient to pay off the $10-million debt and the cost of introducing the new product." How would you respond to this remark?

## C. Study Problems

### Problem 1–1C

Accounts from the income statement for the year ended June 30, 19X2 and the balance sheet at June 30, 19X2 for Trevento, Inc. are shown in Table 1-10. The amounts for some accounts are omitted. You are to prepare an income statement and balance sheet in proper form with the missing amounts filled in.

### Problem 1–2C

The Mangen Company was formed on January 1, 19X5 to sell widgets. All widgets are purchased ready for sale. During 19X5 purchases were as follows:

**TABLE 1-10**
**TREVENTO, INC.**
Income Statement and Balance Sheet Accounts

| | | | |
|---|---:|---|---:|
| Depreciation and amortization expense | $ 25,765 | Net income | $ 69,110 |
| | | Accumulated depreciation | 120,500 |
| Paid-in capital | 150,000 | Accrued expenses | 15,765 |
| Goodwill | 43,750 | Cost of goods sold expense | ? |
| Total shareholders' equity | 457,450 | Sales discounts | 4,600 |
| Interest expense (net) | 25,100 | Total assets | 693,515 |
| Notes payable-bank (short term) | 84,500 | Gross fixed assets | ? |
| | | Total current liabilities | 130,415 |
| Net fixed assets | 454,600 | Sales' returns and allowances | 9,475 |
| Gross sales | ? | Common stock | 20,000 |
| Other operating expense | 18,430 | Marketable securities | 2,075 |
| Retained earnings | ? | Net sales | 891,775 |
| Inventory | 101,510 | Cash | 5,355 |
| Gain from sale of subsidiary—net of tax of 4,000 | 11,500 | Advertising and selling expenses | 87,870 |
| Long-term debt | ? | Accounts receivable (net) | ? |
| Income taxes on operations | 47,185 | Deferred taxes (noncurrent) | 30,150 |
| Other current assets | 2,150 | Accounts payable | ? |
| Total liabilities | 236,065 | Gross profit | 356,710 |
| Income before extraordinary items | ? | Income from operations | 129,895 |
| | | Total current assets | 195,165 |
| General and administrative expenses | ? | Income before taxes and extraordinary | ? |
| Total liabilities and shareholders' equity | ? | | |

| Month | Amount | Total Cost |
|-------|--------|-----------|
| January | 5,000 units @ $7.00 | $ 35,000 |
| April | 1,000 units @ 7.10 | 7,100 |
| July | 7,000 units @ 7.15 | 50,050 |
| October | 5,000 units @ 7.29 | 36,450 |
| December | 2,000 units @ 8.00 | 16,000 |
| | 20,000 | $144,600 |

During 19X5, 17,000 units were sold and 3,000 units were in inventory at December 31, 19X5.

1. Compute cost of goods sold expense for the year and ending inventory at December 31, 19X5 for each of the following inventory costing methods: (a) Weighted Average Cost, (b) LIFO, (c) FIFO.

2. Redo the calculations assuming no widgets were purchased during December 19X5.

## Problem 1–3C

You are given the following information for the Ho Manufacturing Company.

• The raw materials and work-in-process inventories at 1/1/19X6 were $20,500 and $40,750, respectively. At 12/31/19X6 the balance in raw materials inventory was $10,210 and the work-in-process inventory was $50,100.

• Total purchases of raw materials during 19X6 were $155,000.

• Direct labor and overhead for 19X6 was $175,500 and $52,900, respectively.

• Finished goods inventory was $10,000 on 1/1/19X6 and the balance in this inventory account was $60,000 at 12/31/19X6.

1. Compute cost of goods manufactured for the Ho Manufacturing Company for the year ended 12/31/19X6.

2. Compute cost of goods sold expense for the Ho Manufacturing Company for the year ended 12/31/19X6.

## Problem 1–4C

You are given the following income statements for the Anderson Corporation which was formed on January 1, 19X2.

|  | For Years Ended | | |
|  | 12/31/19X2 | 12/31/19X3 | 12/31/19X4 |
|---|---|---|---|
| Net sales | $550,000 | $640,000 | $750,000 |
| Cost of goods sold | 275,000 | 320,000 | 375,000 |
| Gross profit | $275,000 | $320,000 | $375,000 |
| Selling, general and administrative | 200,000 | 220,000 | 240,000 |
| Depreciation expenses | 30,000 | 30,000 | 30,000 |
| Income before taxes | $ 45,000 | $ 70,000 | $105,000 |
| Taxes @ 50% | 22,500 | 35,000 | 52,500 |
| Net income | $ 22,500 | $ 35,000 | $ 52,500 |

Except for depreciation expense, all amounts for revenues and expenses reported on the above statements were also reported on the firm's income tax returns. For income tax purposes, the firm used an accelerated method of depreciation and the following amounts were reported.

| Year | Depreciation Expense for Tax Purposes |
|---|---|
| 1 | $40,000 |
| 2 | 35,000 |
| 3 | 30,000 |

1. Compute the firm's income tax liability for each year. (Use a tax rate of 50%.)

2. Compute the balance of the deferred taxes account at the end of each year.

# Case Study

## Nelson School of Music and Dance, Inc.

Early in June 19X4, Christopher Nelson, founder and president of the Nelson School of Music and Dance, Inc., was working on his new firm's monthly financial statements for April and May. These statements were being prepared for a meeting with an officer of the local bank. The purpose of the meeting was to discuss a loan of $10,000 to purchase fixtures and musical instruments.

### Background

Christopher Nelson was a gifted dancer and musician. Throughout high school and college he worked part time for a private school of music and dance where he gave dancing and piano lessons. After graduating from college as an accounting major in 19X1, he joined a "Big 8" public accounting firm. He liked his new profession but he also missed teaching so he began to give lessons one evening a week. Mr. Nelson soon realized that he wanted to devote full time to teaching and he began to save money to open his own school.

In late 19X3 he approached Lynn Gosster, the owner of the school where he had worked part time, for advice. He told her about his goal and noted that with his own savings and a loan from his parents, he would have $25,000 by the end of 19X3. Ms. Gosster believed that this amount was enough to begin on a small scale, provided his commitment was genuine. For the first several years he would have to work long hours and take as little salary as possible. Instructors typically received 60% of the fee charged the customer. Thus, by teaching many lessons himself, he would minimize labor costs and in her opinion this is what he would have to do to build a successful school. Mr. Nelson assured her that he was indeed ready and able to make the necessary commitment.

They then discussed a location. Ms. Gosster advised him to buy an established business in a growing community in which there was no dominant school. Many schools were operated on a part-time basis by an individual who had a full-time position or by someone nearing retirement. In her view buying from someone nearing retirement was ideal because often the purchase price was very reasonable. Also, the new owner had a small customer base upon which to build. At the conclusion of the conversation, Ms. Gosster said she would contact some people for him and also offered to help with other matters.

Mr. Nelson then met with John Lawrence, an attorney, who was his closest personal friend. Mr. Lawrence was happy to hear that Ms. Gosster was so cooperative. He observed that it is typical for owners of successful small business to help someone who wants to enter the same business. He urged Mr. Nelson not to make a move without checking with her.

In January 19X4, Ms. Gosster called Mr. Nelson about an opportunity. The owner of a small dancing studio planned to sell his business. He was 62 years old and for the last several years, he had operated the business on a part-time basis. The existing owner was willing to accept $9,000 which was the book value of the furniture and fixtures. His studio was in a centrally located office building and the monthly rent was $500.

Ms. Gosster and Mr. Nelson visited the owner of the business, met with the landlord, and studied the community. They concluded that it was an excellent opportunity. The purchase price of $9,000 was a bargain in the sense that if Mr. Nelson purchased secondhand furniture and fixtures of similar quality, he likely would pay more than $9,000. The landlord was a reasonable man. The existing lease expired in December 19X4. The landlord would allow Mr. Nelson to sublet at the same rent and also give him the option to renew the lease in January 19X5 on terms that Ms. Gosster and Mr. Nelson believed were quite attractive.

The investigation also revealed that the existing owner had a loyal customer base, that there was no dominant school in the area, and the community was growing. The only concern was that the existing owner and the other schools extended credit to many customers. However, credit customers usually paid within 30 days and bad debts were rare.

Mr. Nelson was also concerned about the fact that it was only a dancing school. He wanted to offer piano lessons and instructions in other instruments as well. Ms. Gosster believed that there was plenty of opportunity. She discussed how effective advertising prior to opening would bring in immediate business and he could build from there.

Mr. Nelson decided to buy the studio.

### A Studio Is Born

Late in March 19X4 the Nelson School of Music and Dance came into existence. This new corporation had 1,000 common shares with a par value of $1 each. Mr. Nelson purchased all the shares for $25 per share for a total investment of $25,000. On April 1, 19X4, he paid $9,000 for the furniture and fixtures of the existing dancing school and $1,000 to the landlord—$500 for April's rent and $500 for December 19X4, the last month of the lease. On that day he also paid $9,000 for a piano and $600 for a one-year insurance policy on all fixed assets. The final expenditure on April 1 was $500 for a series of advertisements in the local newspaper which began in the second week of March and ran through the end of April.

Mr. Nelson learned that legal fees to form the corporation normally would be $600 including a $50 expenditure incurred by John Lawrence to file forms. Mr. Lawrence did not want to accept a penny, not even for his out-of-pocket costs. Mr. Nelson insisted and after much discussion, Mr. Lawrence agreed to accept a $600 fee, which included the filing fees, provided that the entire amount was not paid by the firm until May 19X5.

Revenues for the month of April were $6,400, including $5,200 on credit, which were still outstanding at the end of April. Payments for instructors and his own salary were $1,200 and $1,000, respectively, for the month.[1] Other operating expenses (utilities, supplies, etc.) were $2,100 for the month, and all but $200 of this total was due and paid by April 30.

Revenues increased during May. Total revenues for the month were $12,575. Collections for the month were $7,550—$2,350 from May's sales plus the $5,200 outstanding from April. Payments for instructors and his own salary were $3,200 and $1,000, respectively. Mr. Nelson spent $200 on advertisements for May. Other operating expenses were $2,450 for the month and all but $450 of this amount was due and paid by the end of the month. The $200 of April's operating expenses that were due in May were paid on schedule.

Mr. Nelson was pleased with the first two months. Appointments scheduled indicated that revenues would exceed $15,000 in June. However, he believed he could have done even more business in April and May if he had more musical instruments. In addition, he wanted to purchase some new fixtures. He considered borrowing $20,000 for capital investments but after talking to Ms. Gosster he decided to aim for $10,000.

Mr. Nelson was able to interest a bank officer in his business. The officer suggested that Mr. Nelson bring financial statements to an interview.

Mr. Nelson decided he would prepare monthly income statements for April and May and balance sheets as of the end of each of these months. He planned to rely on the straight-line method of depreciation. For the $9,000 of furniture and fixtures he would assume a five-year life and a zero salvage value. A ten-year life and zero salvage value would be assumed for the $9,000 piano. The initial expenditure of $500 for advertising would be charged as an expense for April. He considered allocating the $600 legal

---

[1] The reader may ignore payroll taxes in preparing this case.

fee over several months but decided to expense the total amount in April. Finally he estimated that his effective income tax rate would be 25%[2] and decided to round all figures to the nearest dollar.

As Mr. Nelson began to organize the financial data, he wondered what kind of questions the loan officer would ask. He planned to develop a list of possible questions and prepare appropriate responses.

---

[2] The reader may ignore the investment tax credit in preparing this case and assume that income tax expense for the month will be paid during the month. Finally, assume that all earnings will be retained.

# 2
# Ratio Analysis

This chapter explains how to apply ratio analysis. After defining ratio analysis and providing a classification scheme, we discuss selected ratios. The final part of the chapter discusses the limitations of ratio analysis and how to use this analysis effectively by taking what we call a perceptive approach. The basic message of the chapter is this: Ratio analysis can be a very valuable tool provided it is applied properly.

The focus of the chapter will be on how ratios help us interpret and evaluate the information contained in financial statements. We analyze financial statements to make decisions; more specifically, financial statement analysis includes the following goals:

- Evaluate management's performance in earning a rate of return.

- Appraise the firm's financial soundness.

- Help make predictions about the firm's future financial performance and position.

## WHAT IS RATIO ANALYSIS AND WHY DO ANALYSTS USE IT?

Ratio analysis is the process of calculating and interpreting financial ratios. A ratio is an index which relates numbers and is derived by dividing one quantity by another. Very often the two numbers are taken from the firm's financial statements. For example, suppose a firm on a certain date has current assets of $50,000 and current liabilities of $25,000. A commonly employed measure is the current ratio which is computed by dividing current assets by current liabilities.

$$\text{Current Ratio} = \frac{\text{Current Assets}}{\text{Current Liabilities}} = \frac{50{,}000}{25{,}000} = 2{:}1$$

The 2:1 means that at that date the firm had $2 of current assets for each $1 of current liabilities.

Ratios are used in analyzing financial statements because they reduce the data to workable form, thus making the information more meaningful. To see why, let's assume a firm had net income of $83 for the year and shareholders' equity was $7,342. We can readily see that this is not a good return, but by computing the rate of return on equity ratio, the information is more meaningful.

$$\frac{\text{Rate of Return}}{\text{on Equity}} = \frac{\text{Net Income}}{\text{Shareholders' Equity}} = \frac{83}{7{,}340} = 1.1\%$$

## *Ratio Classification*

For discussion purposes we will classify ratios into four categories.

1. *Liquidity.* Ratios in this category are designed to assist one in judging if a firm can pay its current liabilities when due.

2. *Financial Leverage.* These ratios provide insight into the extent to which a firm is relying on debt financing. They can also aid one in judging a firm's ability to raise additional debt and its capacity to pay its liabilities on time.

3. *Efficiency.* These ratios can help one evaluate how well a firm is managing and controlling its assets. Moreover, they can assist one in estimating the amount of capital necessary to generate sales.

4. *Profitability.* Ratios in this category can assist one in appraising management's ability to control expenses and to earn a return on the resources committed to the business.

We will discuss selected ratios in each of the four categories relying on the financial statements in Tables 2-1 and 2-2 for the Rockwell Company, a hypothetical firm. Table 2-3 summarizes all the ratios we will discuss and also includes industry averages for Year 2. We will rely on a single company throughout to illustrate the importance of an integrated analysis—a ratio analysis which includes ratios from all four categories.

Before proceeding, we should emphasize that a ratio in isolation means very little. Its utility comes from comparing it to something else. The something else could be the same ratio for prior time periods, an industry average, and/or some other benchmark. *The Annual Statement Studies* of the Robert Morris Associates and the data collected by Dun and Bradstreet are two examples of sources of industry averages.[1] We will make computations for two years to illustrate the importance of comparisons over time. Realize, however, that while we can make the essential points about comparisons by relying on a two-year period, frequently comparisons should be made for longer time spans (five years or even longer). Note also that it is often helpful to rely on monthly or quarterly data when available.

## TABLE 2-1
### ROCKWELL COMPANY
Income Statement
Years Ended December 31
(000 omitted)

|  | Year 1 | Year 2 |
|---|---|---|
| Net sales | $37,634 | $40,228 |
| Cost of goods sold | 22,580 | 25,746 |
| Gross profit | $15,054 | $14,482 |
| Research and development | 3,768 | 3,218 |
| Selling, general and administrative | 6,731 | 7,804 |
| Profit before taxes | $ 4,555 | $ 3,460 |
| Income taxes | 2,097 | 1,522 |
| Net income | $ 2,458 | $ 1,938 |

Notes:
1. Selling, general and administrative expenses include interest expense of $432,000 in Year 1 and $756,000 in Year 2.
2. Depreciation included in the above expenses was $335,000 in Year 1 and $417,000 in Year 2.
3. Purchases were $21.4 million in Year 1 and $29.111 million in Year 2.

[1] The industry averages in Table 2-3 are hypothetical and do not come from the cited sources. We mention this because these sources do not gather data on all the ratios we will discuss and/or use alternative definitions for certain ratios. Further, they present data on ratios we will not explain. The issues of selection of ratios and alternative definitions are discussed further later in the chapter.

**TABLE 2-2**
**ROCKWELL COMPANY**
Balance Sheet, at December 31
(000 omitted)

|  | Year 1 | Year 2 |
|---|---|---|
| Cash | $    394 | $      19 |
| Marketable securities | 252 | — |
| Accounts receivable (net) | 3,147 | 5,749 |
| Inventory | 2,823 | 6,189 |
| Prepaid expenses | 892 | 743 |
| Total current | $ 7,508 | $12,700 |
| Fixed assets (net) | 6,017 | 6,368 |
| Other | 327 | 536 |
| Total assets | $13,852 | $19,604 |
| Notes payable (bank) | $    436 | $    872 |
| Accounts payable (end) | 2,019 | 3,029 |
| Accrued expenses | 867 | 1,018 |
| Current maturities of long-term debt | 300 | 650 |
| Total current | $ 3,622 | $ 5,569 |
| Debentures | 1,200 | 4,200 |
| Deferred taxes | 469 | 513 |
| Total debt | $ 5,291 | $10,282 |
| Common stock | $ 1,473 | $ 1,473 |
| Paid-in capital | 2,842 | 2,842 |
| Retained earnings | 4,246 | 5,007 |
| Total equity | $ 8,561 | $ 9,322 |
| Total liabilities and stockholders' equity | $13,852 | $19,604 |

We should also mention before continuing that numerous ratios are used in practice and it is not feasible to discuss all of them. However, the approach taken will enable you to deal with other ratios you will encounter in practice. We should add that while numerous ratios are employed, most analysts use a comparatively small number because generally it is not necessary to use a large number to gain the desired insight. Incidentally, do not infer that the ratios discussed in this chapter are the ideal combination. In our view, there is no such thing as an "ideal combination" of ratios because so much depends on the issues of interest, the company involved, and the particular

**TABLE 2-3**
**ROCKWELL COMPANY**
Selected Ratios for Year 1 and Year 2
and Industry Average for Year 2

|  | Year 1 | Year 2 | Industry Average Year 2 |
|---|---|---|---|
| Current Ratio | 2.07:1 | 2.28:1 | 2.3:1 |
| Acid Test | 1.05:1 | 1.04:1 | 1.1:1 |
| Debt to Asset Ratio | 38.2% | 52.5% | 30% |
| Capitalization Ratio | 16.3% | 33.6% | 20% |
| Debt to Equity Ratio | 61.8% | 110.3% | 75% |
| Interest Coverage | 11.5 times | 5.6 times | 10.0 times |
| Burden Coverage | 5.1 times | 2.2 times | 5.0 times |
| Total Asset Turnover | 2.72 times | 2.05 times | 3.0 times |
| Fixed Asset Turnover | 6.25 times | 6.32 times | 6.0 times |
| Days Sales Outstanding Ratio | 30.1 days | 51.5 days | 40.0 days |
| Days Payables Outstanding Ratio | 34.0 days | 37.5 days | 35.0 days |
| Inventory Turnover | 8.0 times | 4.16 times | 6.0 times |
| 100% Income Statement |  |  |  |
| Net sales | 100.0% | 100.0% | 100.0% |
| Cost of goods sold | 60.0% | 64.0% | 62.0% |
| Gross profit | 40.0% | 36.0% | 38.0% |
| Research and development | 10.0% | 8.0% | 10.0% |
| Selling, general and administrative | 17.9% | 19.4% | 16.0% |
| Profit before taxes | 12.1% | 8.6% | 12.0% |
| Income taxes | (.46) | (.44) | (.45) |
| Net income | 6.5% | 4.8% | 6.6% |
| Return on assets | 17.7% | 9.9% | 19.8% |
| Return on owner's equity | 28.7% | 20.8% | 29.7% |

circumstances. In some cases, we might need six or seven ratios, while in others we may need 15 or even more. In any event, keep in mind that in all cases, we should include one or more ratios from each of the four categories described above.

Finally, keep in mind that ratios provide clues and hints, not conclusive answers. They lead you to ask the right questions and help to pinpoint areas requiring further study. An experienced analyst can gain considerable insight into what may be wrong, but definite answers are simply not possible. Hence, we must be careful not to jump to conclusions. This caution is very important because as we will see, ratios can give misleading signals.

The first step is to think about the issue or problem at hand and to carefully read the financial statements. With respect to the issue, let's assume we are trying to evaluate Rockwell's financial performance and position in Year 2 versus Year 1 to gain insight into its future financial performance and position. Experience will help you learn what to look for in the financial statements, but when we read the statements we usually try to gain an appreciation for the size of the firm, the nature of assets (e.g., a large proportion of fixed assets versus a large proportion of current assets), the nature of expenses (e.g., a large proportion of revenues consumed by operating expenses versus a large proportion of revenues consumed by cost of goods sold), liquidity and debt levels, etc. Further it is wise to compute annual sales growth. Rockwell's net sales grew by 6.9% in Year 2. Growth in sales tells us something about performance. However, the rate of growth must be viewed in the context of the inflation rate and the industry growth rate. Say the inflation rate in Year 2 was 2%. This implies that Rockwell had real sales growth (i.e., sold more goods or services). On the other hand, had inflation been 10% for Year 2, then a decline in real activity would have been signalled.[2] Moreover, it would be one thing if real growth in this industry was two to three percent per year and quite another if it was 20%. Assuming for a moment that inflation was zero percent, a sales growth of 6.9% for Rockwell would indicate increased market share if the industry grew by two to three percent, but a substantial decline would be indicated if industry growth was 20%.

The rate of growth of sales also alerts us to possible ratio measurement problems. As we will see when a firm's sales are growing rapidly, ratios, particularly efficiency ratios, can give misleading signals.

## LIQUIDITY RATIOS

Liquidity ratios help the analyst judge if a firm can pay its current liabilities when due. We will discuss two liquidity ratios: the current ratio and the acid test ratio (quick ratio).

[2] A published inflation rate like the Consumer Price Index does not necessarily indicate the impact of price level changes on a firm's revenues and costs. For example, in the early 1980s prices of computers decreased while broad measures of inflation were high.

### Current Ratio

The current ratio is derived by dividing current assets by current liabilities.

|  |  | Year 1 | Year 2 | Industry Average<br>Year 2 |
|---|---|---|---|---|

$$\frac{\text{Current}}{\text{Ratio}} = \frac{\text{Current Assets}}{\text{Current Liabilities}} = \frac{7,508}{3,622} = 2.07{:}1 \quad \frac{12,700}{5,569} = 2.28{:}1 \qquad 2.3{:}1$$

There was an increase in the second year and the level is consistent with the industry average. Thus, no problem is indicated. A widely used rule of thumb is that a firm with a current ratio of 2:1 or more is in good shape in terms of being able to pay maturing current liabilities. Most experienced analysts realize this rule may be misleading.

### Acid Test Ratio

The acid test ratio, also known, as the quick ratio, is designed to provide a more rigorous test than the current ratio of a firm's ability to pay its current liabilities on time. It does this by excluding relatively illiquid current assets from the numerator as shown below:

$$\frac{\text{Acid Test Ratio}}{} = \frac{\text{Cash + Marketable Securities + Accounts Receivable}}{\text{Current Liabilities}}$$

| Year 1 | Year 2 | Industry Average<br>Year 2 |
|---|---|---|

$$\frac{394+252+3,147}{3,622} = 1.05{:}1 \qquad \frac{19+0+5,749}{5,569} = 1.04{:}1 \qquad 1.1{:}1$$

Although there was a decline it was quite small and the level is in line with the industry average. Therefore, no problem is indicated.

Some analysts use a different version of the acid test ratio than the one shown above. The most common alternative is to use current assets minus inventory as the numerator.

A widely used rule of thumb is that an acid test ratio of 1:1 or more indicates current liabilities will be able to be paid as they mature. However, most experienced analysts realize that this rule may be misleading.

### Evaluation of Liquidity Ratios

A current asset is one that is cash or will turn into cash within one year. A current liability is one that is due within one year. Comparing these two quantities gives insight into a firm's ability to pay. If a firm has more of the former than the latter, ability to pay is indicated. Certainly, a firm is in good shape if current assets are twice as large.

Although the above logic seems sensible, there is a basic flaw in the reasoning. Comparing current assets (or liquid current assets) with current liabilities gives no information on the level and timing of cash flow, which is the essential determinant of ability to pay when due. Critical questions are: When during the year must current liabilities be paid? At what rate and when will new current liabilities be created? How much cash will the firm generate? Will it be available to pay current liabilities? The current and acid test ratios give little information on these issues. Hence, they are at best rough measures of a firm's ability to pay on time.

These ratios are widely used. If they are less than perfect, why do so many analysts employ them? Experienced analysts realize that current and acid test ratios provide only a rough indication. Nevertheless, when used in conjunction with ratios in other categories they can give a hint of ability to pay on time.

## FINANCIAL LEVERAGE RATIOS

Financial leverage ratios, also known as solvency or debt ratios, are designed to:

- Provide insight into how much debt a firm is employing relative to equity.

- Help evaluate a firm's ability to raise debt.

- Assist an analyst in judging a firm's ability to pay its debt when due.

The ratios we will discuss are: (1) total debt to total assets, (2) capitalization ratio, (3) debt to equity ratio, (4) interest coverage and (5) burden coverage.

### Debt to Assets Ratio
This ratio is derived in the following manner:

|  | Year 1 | Year 2 | Industrial Average Year 2 |
|---|---|---|---|
| Total Debt to Total Assets $= \dfrac{\text{Total Liabilities}}{\text{Total Assets}} =$ | $\dfrac{5{,}291}{13{,}582} = 38.2\%$ | $\dfrac{10{,}282}{19{,}604} = 52.5\%$ | $30\%$ |

The substantial increase is troublesome especially since the level is well above the industry average. This is certainly an area we would want to investigate further because it hints that the firm will have difficulty paying its debt when due.

### Capitalization Ratio

The capitalization ratio focuses on long-term debt usage. It is calculated as follows:

$$\frac{\text{Capitalization}}{\text{Ratio}} = \frac{\text{Long-Term Debt}}{\text{Long-Term Debt and Owners' Equity}}$$

|  |  | Industry Average |
|---|---|---|
| Year 1 | Year 2 | Year 2 |
| $\frac{1,669}{1,669+8,561} = 16.3\%$ | $\frac{4,713}{4,713+9,322} = 33.6\%$ | 20% |

This ratio also increased substantially and is well above the industry average of 20%, providing the same signal as the total debt to total assets ratio.

Many analysts calculate both ratios because together they can help isolate the source of change in debt usage. For example, if a firm financed the purchase of a building with short-term debt, the debt to assets ratio would be affected but not the capitalization ratio. It is dangerous to finance permanent needs like a building with temporary source of funds like a short-term bank loan. Analysts look for signals of improper financing and these two ratios may give the signal. (Liquidity ratios may help confirm the signal.)

### Debt to Equity Ratio

The debt to equity ratio is derived as follows:

$$\text{Debt to Equity Ratio} = \frac{\text{Total Debt}}{\text{Total Equity}}$$

|  |  | Industry Average |
|---|---|---|
| Year 1 | Year 2 | Year 2 |
| $\frac{5,291}{8,561} = 61.8\%$ | $\frac{10,282}{9,322} = 110.3\%$ | 75% |

This ratio can be derived from the debt to assets ratio and provides essentially the same information.

### Interest Coverage Ratio

The interest coverage ratio, also known as times interest earned, is designed to help you evaluate a firm's capacity to meet interest payments.

It is calculated by dividing earnings before deducting interest and taxes (EBIT) by interest expense. Footnote 1 in Table 2-1 states that interest expense was $432,000 for Year 1 and $756,000 for Year 2. We add these amounts to the profit before taxes figures to compute EBIT. For Rockwell we have the following:

|  |  | Year 1 |  | Year 2 | Industry Average Year 2 |
|---|---|---|---|---|---|
| Interest Coverage | $= \dfrac{\text{EBIT}}{\text{Interest}} =$ | $\dfrac{4{,}987}{432} = 11.5$ times | | $\dfrac{4{,}216}{756} = 5.6$ times | 10.0 times |

In Year 1, $11.50 was earned for each dollar of interest, and coverage fell to 5.6 times in Year 2, substantially below the industry average. The decrease confirms the signal of the previous two ratios.

### Burden Coverage Ratio
The burden coverage ratio provides insight into a firm's ability to meet interest and principal payments.

$$\frac{\text{Burden}}{\text{Coverage}} = \frac{\text{EBIT}}{\text{Interest} + \dfrac{\text{Principal Payments}}{1 - \text{Tax Rate}}}$$

Principal payments represent the portion of debt due in one year. This information is shown in Table 2-2 by the account called current maturities of long-term debt. These amounts ($300,000 for Year 1 and $650,000 for Year 2) are divided by one minus the tax rate to convert them to pretax equivalents (Principal payments are not tax deductible.) The tax rates can be derived by dividing income tax expense by profit before tax. They are 46% and 44% for Years 1 and 2, respectively.

|  |  | Year 1 |  | Year 2 | Industry Average Year 2 |
|---|---|---|---|---|---|
| Burden Coverage | $=$ | $\dfrac{4{,}987}{432 + \dfrac{300}{1-.46}} = 5.1$ times | | $\dfrac{4{,}216}{756 + \dfrac{650}{1-.44}} = 2.2$ times | 5.0 times |

The substantial decline and large deviation from the industry average confirms our concern that Rockwell may have difficulty meeting required debt payments.

Many analysts include other items such as rent in the denominator of the coverage ratios. The intent is to test the ability of the firm to meet all required payments.

### Evaluation of Financial Leverage Ratios

Financial leverage ratios are quite helpful in measuring debt usage but they are at best a rough guide with respect to appraising ability to pay. Firms pay liabilities in the future with cash available at that time. The first three ratios discussed above provide no direct information on size or timing of required debt payments, or on how much cash the firm will have. The coverage ratios incorporate required debt payments. However, they look at past earnings. Also, it's important to note that earnings and cash flow are not the same thing. There can be a substantial difference between earnings and cash flow for extended periods of time. To deal with this defect, many analysts use cash flow from operations in the numerator of coverage ratios. This quantity can be derived from the statement of changes in financial position discussed in the next chapter.

## EFFICIENCY RATIOS

Efficiency ratios, also known as turnover or activity ratios, can help you judge management's performance in managing and controlling assets. They also provide insight into how much capital is required to support sales. Later in the chapter we will explain how changing sales levels from year to year and within the year create measurement problems leading to distorted signals. This is a serious problem and is most damaging for efficiency ratios. To reduce the severity of the problem, but not eliminate it, analysts use various kinds of averages (and rely on quarterly data). For example, most efficiency ratios have an asset in the numerator or denominator. Rather than use the year-end level, it is often helpful to employ an average at various points during the year. However, for illustrative purposes we will use year-end asset levels.

The ratios we will discuss are: (1) total asset turnover, (2) fixed asset turnover, (3) days sales outstanding, (4) days purchases outstanding and (5) inventory turnover.

### Total Asset Turnover

The total asset turnover helps the analyst appraise the overall efficiency of asset employment and the level of capital intensity. It's computed as follows:

$$\begin{array}{c}
\textit{Year 1}\\[4pt]
\begin{array}{c}
\text{Total}\\
\text{Asset}\\
\text{Turnover}
\end{array}
= \frac{\text{Net Sales}}{\text{Total Assets}} = \frac{37{,}634}{13{,}852} = 2.72 \text{ times}
\end{array}$$

| | *Industry Average* |
|:---:|:---:|
| *Year 2* | *Year 2* |
| $\dfrac{40{,}228}{19{,}604} = 2.05 \text{ times}$ | 3.0 times |

The decrease is disturbing especially in light of the industry average. It is a signal that the firm is too capital intensive and/or is not managing and controlling assets efficiently. The remaining ratios in this category help us isolate which assets are causing the decrease.

### Fixed Asset Turnover

Fixed asset turnover helps us appraise capacity utilization and the quality of fixed assets. A declining fixed asset turnover might be a signal that a firm has excess capacity, while an abnormally high turnover may indicate the firm is relying on old fixed assets. It is computed as follows:

$$\begin{array}{c}
\textit{Year 1}\\[4pt]
\begin{array}{c}
\text{Fixed}\\
\text{Asset}\\
\text{Turnover}
\end{array}
= \frac{\text{Net Sales}}{\text{Net Fixed Assets}} = \frac{37{,}634}{6{,}017} = 6.25 \text{ times}
\end{array}$$

| | *Industry Average* |
|:---:|:---:|
| *Year 2* | *Year 2* |
| $\dfrac{40{,}228}{6{,}368} = 6.32 \text{ times}$ | 6.0 times |

We see that there is only a slight change. Hence, fixed assets are not causing the decrease in the total asset turnover.

### Days' Sales Outstanding Ratio

The days' sales outstanding ratio (DSO) helps one judge if a change in receivables is due to a change in sales or to something else such as a lengthening of the time it takes customers to pay. It is computed by dividing receivables from customers by a daily average of credit sales. If credit sales are not available, total sales are employed.

$$\begin{array}{c}
\text{Days'}\\
\text{Sales}\\
\text{Outstanding}
\end{array}
= \frac{\text{Receivables from Customers}}{\dfrac{\text{Net Sales for Year}}{360 \text{ days}}}$$

|  | | Industry<br>Average |
| Year 1 | Year 2 | Year 2 |
| $\dfrac{3,147}{\dfrac{37,634}{360}} = 30.1$ days | $\dfrac{5,749}{\dfrac{40,228}{360}} = 51.5$ days | 40.0 days |

The increase is disturbing. It indicates that receivables have increased at a greater rate than sales, implying either that customers are taking longer to pay or Rockwell is granting longer terms.

As noted above, changing sales can cause a distortion. To reduce this problem, but not eliminate it, some analysts compute a daily average of sales based on the previous 30, 60 or 90 days and/or employ an average of accounts receivable at various points during the year for the numerator of the ratio. Even if these refinements could eliminate the problem (which they cannot), another difficulty could cause the ratio to give a misleading signal. The other difficulty would arise when the intra-year pattern of sales varies from year to year. For example, suppose a firm that normally sells 15% of its total annual sales during December produces 30% of its sales in December one year. This different pattern could cause the days sales outstanding ratio to increase even if there was no lengthening of the collection period. Note that such a distortion could occur even if annual sales do not change.

The days sales outstanding ratio frequently is called the average collection period. This is an unfortunate label because the ratio often does not indicate the length of a firm's collection period.

### Days Payables Outstanding Ratio

The days payables outstanding (DPO) ratio gives information on whether a firm pays its trade payables on time. (This ratio is not concerned with asset efficiency, but we treat it here because it is similar in scope to efficiency ratios.) It's derived as follows: (Purchases are shown in footnote 3 in Table 2-1.)

$$\text{Days Purchases Outstanding} = \frac{\text{Trade Accounts Payable}}{\dfrac{\text{Purchases}}{360 \text{ days}}}$$

|  | | Industry Average |
| Year 1 | Year 2 | Year 2 |
| $\dfrac{2,019}{\dfrac{21,400}{360}} = 34.0$ days | $\dfrac{3,029}{\dfrac{29,111}{360}} = 37.5$ days | 35.0 days |

There is an increase and the level is above the industry average. The deviations are not that great, however, so no problem is indicated. Viewing this information in the context of financial leverage ratios, we can infer that the increased debt usage is not due to stretching payables. (Stretching means not paying suppliers on time.)

We should note that variability of sales affects this ratio in the same way the DSO is affected. Also, the same refinements (i.e., shorter averaging period, etc.) are made. Finally, although credit purchases should be used in the denominator, total purchases are used if this information is not available.

### Inventory Turnover

The inventory turnover ratio helps judge how well inventory is controlled and managed. It assists you in evaluating whether a change in inventory is due to a change in sales or to some other factor such as a slowdown in the time it takes for the firm to produce and/or sell its inventory. It's derived as follows:

$$\frac{\text{Inventory}}{\text{Turnover}} = \frac{\text{Cost of Goods Sold}}{\text{Ending Inventory}} = \overset{\textit{Year 1}}{\frac{22,580}{2,823}} = 8.0 \text{ times}$$

$$\overset{\textit{Year 2}}{\frac{25,746}{6,189}} = 4.16 \text{ times} \qquad \overset{\substack{\textit{Industry Average} \\ \textit{Year 2}}}{6.0 \text{ times}}$$

The substantial decline is disturbing and we would want to investigate further. It could be a signal of purchasing problems or even worse, obsolete inventory.

We must add that changing sales levels can cause distortions. Moreover, some analysts rely on net sales in the numerator and this creates the possible problem of a false signal due to a change in gross profit rate (i.e., gross profit ÷ net sales).

### Evaluation of Efficiency Ratios

Efficient utilization of assets is a key factor in determining overall profitability and a firm's ability to generate cash. Ratios in this category help us evaluate efficiency. Since there are measurement problems, we must often make adjustments. Also, we must be alert to factors that can cause these ratios to give false signals.

## PROFITABILITY RATIOS

Profitability ratios help one judge how well the firm has done in controlling expenses and earning a return on the resources committed to the business. The ratios we will discuss are: (1) 100% income statements, (2) rate of return on assets and (3) rate of return on owners' equity.

### 100% Income Statement

The 100% income statement is actually several ratios in one. We set net sales equal to 100% and each expense, except for income taxes, is listed as a percentage of net sales. This is done by dividing each expense by the net sales figure. The income tax expense figure is stated as a percentage of profit before taxes, and it is calculated by dividing income tax expense by the profit before taxes figure. (Some analysts prefer to treat income taxes like all the other expenses and state it as a percentage of net sales.) Table 2-3 presents all the percentages and we will illustrate by showing how the cost of goods sold and income tax figures were computed for Year 2.

$$\textit{Year 2}$$

$$\frac{\text{Cost of Goods Sold}}{\text{Net Sales}} = \frac{25,746}{40,228} = 64\%$$

$$\frac{\text{Income Tax Expense}}{\text{Profit Before Taxes}} = \frac{1,522}{3,460} = 44\%$$

It's useful to begin with the net income percent, which is called the net profit margin. In 19X3 Rockwell earned 6.5¢ on each dollar of sales and in 19X4 the net profit rate fell to 4.8%. This is disturbing especially in light of the industry average of 6.6%.

The expense categories identify the sources of the decreases. In this instance, there is a strong signal of a problem. Cost of goods sold expense increased from 60% to 64% while the industry average stood at 62%. This raises such questions as the following: Has the firm become inefficient in purchasing? Is it paying too high a price for the products it purchases? (If the firm was a manufacturer, we would investigate production costs to see if they were out of control.) Is the firm caught in a cost price squeeze, making it difficult to pass on cost increases? Has there been a change in product mix? Is the firm now selling a greater proportion of products that have relatively low gross profit margins? Is the firm's pricing policy ineffective?

The next category, Research and Development (R & D), shows a decrease from 10% to 8% and the latter figure is below the industry average of 10%. It is difficult to interpret a decrease in R & D because it is an example of a *managed cost.* (Other examples are advertising and repairs and maintenance.) These costs can more easily be changed than others and management can cut them even if it's not in the best interest of the firm. Reductions in such expenses tend to improve profits in the short run but may be detrimental to long-term profitability. Selling, general and administrative expenses increased from 17.9% to 19.4% and we want to find out which specific items caused the change.

The financial leverage and efficiency ratios indicated possible problems. The 100% income statement not only reinforces these signals but also causes more concern. Often if a firm has solid profits, it will be given time to work out problems in other areas. Rockwell was profitable in Year 2, earning almost $2 million. However, the trend is downward and if it were not for the cut in R & D, the situation would have been much worse. (Trends are difficult to identify and this is why normally we would examine annual data for more than two years. Moreover, we would also study quarterly data to see if a decrease was caused by one or two bad quarters.)

## Rate of Return Measures

The final two ratios we will consider are concerned with the amount earned on the resources committed to the business. Each is frequently referred to as the Du Pont formula because it was perhaps the first firm to use them as part of its control system.

## Rate of Return on Assets

Rate of return on assets is derived as follows:

$$\frac{\text{Rate of Return}}{\text{on Assets}} = \frac{\text{Net Income after Taxes}}{\text{Total Assets}}$$

| | | Industry Average |
|---|---|---|
| *Year 1* | *Year 2* | *Year 2* |
| $\frac{2{,}458}{13{,}852} = 17.7\%$ | $\frac{1{,}938}{19{,}604} = 9.9\%$ | 19.8% |

Before discussing the implications for Rockwell, we should mention that many versions of this ratio are employed in practice. We used year-end assets but often an average or the beginning of the year amount is employed. Also, frequently net income after taxes plus interest expense or earnings before interest and taxes (EBIT) is the numerator. There are other variations as well. We must be extra careful when reference is made to rate of return on assets because it could refer to a variety of relationships.

Rockwell's ratio has declined sharply and is well below the industry average of 19.8%. We have already discussed the reasons. To see why, let's examine a more illuminating definition:

$$\text{Rate of Return on Assets} = \frac{\text{Net Income after Taxes}}{\text{Total Assets}} = \frac{\text{Net Income after Taxes}}{\text{Net Sales}} \times \frac{\text{Net Sales}}{\text{Total Assets}}$$

$$9.84\% \qquad = \qquad 4.8\% \qquad \times \quad 2.05 \text{ times}$$

(The difference between the 9.84% and the 9.9% derived earlier is due to rounding.) The essential point is that return on assets is a function of profit earned on sales and asset efficiency. Many firms work very hard at keeping expenses under control but are not as diligent in controlling asset levels. We see that overall profitability depends on careful attention to both areas.

### Rate of Return on Equity
Rate of return on equity is computed as follows:

$$\frac{\text{Rate of Return}}{\text{on Owner's Equity}} = \frac{\text{Net Income after Taxes}}{\text{Owners' Equity}}$$

|  |  |  | *Industry Average* |
| --- | --- | --- | --- |
| *Year 1* | | *Year 2* | *Year 2* |
| $\frac{2,458}{8,561} = 28.7\%$ | | $\frac{1,938}{9,322} = 20.8\%$ | 29.7% |

Before discussing the figures, we should note that alternative versions of this ratio are employed. For example, often the beginning of year owners' equity or an average is used in the denominator. Also, if a firm has preferred stock outstanding, preferred dividends may be subtracted from the numerator and the book value of preferred may be subtracted from the denominator to focus on the return to common stockholders.

Although the return on owners' equity has declined, it has not decreased by the same proportion as the rate of return on assets. Why? The answer is that the firm is now financing a greater proportion of its assets with debt. This can be seen by restating the return on equity ratio as follows:

$$\frac{\text{Rate of Return on Owners' Equity}}{} = \frac{\text{Net Income after Taxes}}{\text{Net Sales}} \times \frac{\text{Net Sales}}{\text{Total Assets}} \times \frac{\text{Total Assets}}{\text{Owners' Equity}}$$

(Total assets divided by owners' equity is a financial leverage ratio which provides the same insight as the total debt to total assets ratio.) The net profit margin and total asset turnover ratios decreased for Rockwell but these were partially offset by the increased use of debt.

### Rockwell Company Summary

Our analysis implies that Rockwell's performance and financial position deteriorated in Year 2. Expenses increased more than sales as indicated by the 100% income statement. The turnover ratios signal a problem with receivables and inventory. The debt ratios indicate that the firm may have trouble servicing debt. We cannot jump to conclusions because of the possibility of false signals. Nevertheless, ratios have pointed out the areas requiring further study. Moreover, they are providing a strong signal that something is wrong.

## ADDITIONAL RATIOS

We will now discuss several ratios that are quite common but do not fit neatly into our four category scheme.

### Common-Size Balance Sheets

A common-size balance sheet is computed as follows: total assets are set equal to 100% and each asset is stated as a percentage of the total; the total of liabilities plus owners' equity is set equal to 100% and each liability and equity account is stated as a percentage of the total. Analysts find it useful to compare common-size balance sheets for a firm over a number of years. Such comparisons can help you spot trends over time with respect to the proportion of total resources committed to various asset categories and will enable you to detect shifts in the proportion of resources obtained from various sources. These statements are also useful when comparing firms of varying sizes.

### Price Earnings Ratio

The price earnings ratio for a firm may be computed as follows:

$$\frac{\text{Market Price per Share of Common Stock}}{\text{Earnings per Share}}$$

This ratio is used by analysts for several purposes. One is to judge how investors view the firm in terms of risk and growth prospects. Increases in risk exert downward pressure on a firm's price earnings ratio, while increases in expected earnings growth will raise it. Like other ratios, comparisons are made over time and to some benchmark like an average for the industry, similar companies, or the market as a whole. (The last refers to an index such as an average of the price earnings ratios of all firms listed on the New York Stock Exchange.)

Security analysts work with price earnings ratios in trying to estimate the true worth or intrinsic value of a firm's common stock. Here's what they do: They estimate what the firm's earnings per share will be in the future, say the next year. They also estimate what price earnings ratio investors will pay for the firm's earnings. They then multiply the price earnings ratio by the earnings per share figure. The result is the estimate of intrinsic value. Finally, they compare this value to the existing market price to see if the purchase (or sale) of the firm's stock would be a good investment (disinvestment).

### Market Value to Book Value Ratio

This ratio is computed as follows:

$$\frac{\text{Market Price per Share of Common Stock}}{\text{Book Value per Share of Common Stock}}$$

Book value per share is calculated as follows:

$$\frac{\text{Owners' Equity—Preferred Stock}}{\text{Number of Common Shares Outstanding}}$$

In the past, security analysts relied on this ratio to help judge the risk involved in investing in a firm's common stock. A ratio substantially greater than one implies a high degree of risk. This ratio is now used more to help identify potential acquisition candidates. Supposedly, a ratio of less than 1 to 1 implies that the firm may be the target for a takeover.

## EFFECTIVE RATIO ANALYSIS

To apply ratio analysis effectively takes experience (so be patient) and a perceptive approach. We talked about the possibility of false signals. A list of rules for adjustments, ratio limitations and measurement problems would require several books. The basic approach is the key. We call this a perceptive approach. Below are some guidelines and cautions.

### Preliminary Steps

When using ratios to analyze financial statements, inexperienced analysts too quickly turn to the computation of ratios. The first step is to think about the issue or problem at hand and to read carefully the financial statements, including the footnotes that accompany them. Then you select the combination of ratios you want to compute.

Many experienced analysts compute certain basic ratios and then decide if they need more. The set of basic ratios that is used varies from analyst to analyst and depends on the individual's experience and the nature of his or her job. For instance, a credit analyst in a credit department of a retail firm would probably have a different set than a security analyst working for a mutual fund. However, generally the sets of basic ratios include at least one or two ratios from each of the four categores described above. We believe this is a reasonable approach. However, we also think it is best in most instances to start from the rate of return on equity ratio and to develop the analysis from that starting point. This approach is described below.

### Integrated Analysis

A ratio analysis should include one or more ratios from each of the four categories listed earlier. We have seen that a ratio in one cateory is much more enlightening when viewed in the context of ratios in other categories. For example, the financial leverage ratios indicated that Rockwell may have a problem paying liabilities but the liquidity ratios signalled that there would be no difficulty meeting maturing current liabilities. What is causing the difference? The answer is the decrease in the inventory turnover and the increase in the DSO caused the liquidity ratios to appear stable.

In conducting a ratio analysis, it's a good idea to start with the rate of return on equity ratio. More specifically, you will find it useful to set up a schedule like the one shown in Table 2-4 to compute the elements for the last five or ten years, and also to have a column for the industry average or some other standard. This will give you an overview and help you pinpoint the causes of the change in return on equity over time. You can delve into the ratios in each category. (If you follow this approach, include liquidity ratios in the financial leverage category.)[3]

### Relationships

When learning ratios, you should focus on underlying relationships rather than definitions. For example, the current ratio was defined as current assets

---

[3] We should point out that many experienced analysts would say that this recommendation is too general. They think this approach is suitable for investment analysts but not other analysts such as short-term creditors. In our opinion, it is suitable for short-term creditors because it insures an integrated analysis.

**Table 2-4** *Schedule: Rate of Return on Equity*

Rate of Return on Equity $= A \times B \times C \times D$
A $= 1 -$ Tax Rate
B $=$ Profit before Taxes / Net Sales
C $=$ Net Sales / Total Assets
D $=$ Total Assets / Owners' Equity

| Year | Rate of Return | A | B | C | D |
|------|----------------|---|---|---|---|
| 1 |  |  |  |  |  |
| 2 |  |  |  |  |  |
| 3 |  |  |  |  |  |
| 4 |  |  |  |  |  |
| 5 |  |  |  |  |  |
| 6 |  |  |  |  |  |
| 7 |  |  |  |  |  |
| 8 |  |  |  |  |  |
| 9 |  |  |  |  |  |
| 10 |  |  |  |  |  |

Net Profit Margin $= A \times B$

$$\frac{\text{Net Income after Taxes}}{\text{Net Sales}} = \left(1 - \frac{\text{Income Tax Expense}}{\text{Profit before Taxes}}\right) \times \frac{\text{Profit before Taxes}}{\text{Net Sales}}$$

This expansion enables the analyst to judge the extent to which variations in rate of return are due to taxes.

divided by current liabilities. When you hear the phrase current ratio, you should visualize a ratio with current assets in the numerator and current liabilities in the denominator. Moreover you should be skeptical and ask: Does the relationship tell me what the experts say it does?

There are many reasons for the above advice and we will mention two that are especially relevant. First, most ratios were developed by analysts who found that they could pick up useful information by studying certain relationships. While analysts have contributed a great deal to the development of ratios and other financial analysis tools, some ratios lack economic content. Moreover, rules of thumb prevail which are notable for their numerous exceptions. On the other hand, we believe that analysts will continue to develop new ratios with more insight. The only way we can learn to deal with new measures is by "thinking about the logic," and not merely memorizing a definition.

The second reason is that individual ratios are known by a variety of names and more importantly, different definitions are employed for specific ratios—that is, two analysts might refer to the same ratio and then proceed to include different quantities from the firm's financial statements in performing the calculations. For example, there are numerous definitions of rate of return in practice and unfortunately we hear people talk about ROI and simply assume that others will know what they are talking about. We have seen people compute a ratio and then make a comparison to an industry average that is computed another way! The point is, when consulting a source for industry averages, make sure you understand the source's definition.

### *Inference Not Fact*
Ratio analysis is best suited to help us ask the right kinds of questions and to pinpoint areas that need further study. They enable us to infer things about the firm but they do not enable us to reach firm conclusions. Putting it another way, ratios provide clues and hints about certain issues but not definite answers. However, as we have seen, often the clues and hints are very strong.

### *Limitations of Industry Averages*
A major message of this chapter is that a ratio in isolation means very little. Its utility comes from use in combination with other ratios and in comparison with prior periods, an industry average and/or some other predetermined standard. The most common benchmark for comparison is an industry average. We advocate comparisons to industry averages, but it is crucial to recognize the inherent limitations. Below we discuss some of these and suggest ways of dealing with them.

For many business transactions, more than one accounting treatment is possible. For instance, cost of goods sold can be computed using FIFO or LIFO, depreciation expense can be calculated using a straight line or an accelerated method, and sometimes options are available regarding the timing of revenue recognition. (See Chapter 1 for a discussion.) The choice of an accounting method can have a substantial impact on reported results. Thus, it is possible for two firms to experience identical economic events and to report financial statement numbers that are very different. The upshot is that if firms within an industry choose different accounting procedures, an industry average may be a meaningless benchmark for comparison. We should point out that analysts sometimes adjust the financial statements of firms within the industry to make them more comparable.

Even in the absence of accounting problems, we have to face the reality that classifying firms by industry is not an easy task and frequently the result is far from perfect. Thus, quite often there will be substantial differences among firms listed in the same industry category. Because of this, we believe it is often best to focus on comparisons to selected firms rather than an overall average for the industry. (Incidentally, relying on a group of firms makes it more feasible to do a thorough job in adjusting for differences in accounting procedures to eliminate the problems discussed above.)

Finally, it is important to keep in mind that an industry average is not a standard of achievement or an objective. Suppose you could not be present for an examination. Before taking a "make up" the next week, the professor tells you the class grade average was F. This might be useful information but (hopefully) it would not lead you to choose a grade of F as a goal.

Here's the punch line: We use industry averages all the time. When doing an in-depth analysis we focus on selected firms but also look at the industry averages. For "quick and dirty" analyses, there is generally not enough time to gather and adjust selected data so we only look at the industry average. However, we are well aware of the inherent limitations and do not make unwarranted inferences. Industry averages are helpful when there are large deviations (in either direction) because we are alerted to the possibility that something may be wrong and further investigation is needed. (Large deviations from previous years' levels are also cause for concern.)

### Trends Tell the Story

A financial crisis like bankruptcy is usually the result of problems that have developed over a period of time. Generally, effective financial statement analysis will enable us to identify these problems and to take appropriate action. But to identify a deteriorating trend often requires a ratio analysis encompassing the past five years or even longer. As noted earlier, we explained ratios by relying on two consecutive years of data. We used this time frame because it was sufficient to make the essential points of the chapter. Please bear in mind that two-year comparisons are usually not sufficient.

### Ratio Manipulation and Income Smoothing

Ratios can be manipulated and we will illustrate using the current ratio. Assume the following for a firm:

#### Balance Sheet Data

| | | | |
|---|---|---|---|
| Cash | $15,000 | Short-term debt | $12,000 |
| Receivables | 5,000 | Accounts payable | 4,000 |
| Inventory | 5,000 | | |
| Total current | $25,000 | Total current | $16,000 |

The firm's current ratio is:

$$\frac{25,000}{16,000} = 1.56{:}1$$

This is below 2:1 which is a widely used rule of thumb. Suppose that just prior to year-end the firm uses $10,000 of cash to pay down its short-term debt. At the start of the new year, it will borrow the $10,000 again. This action would reduce current assets to $15,000 and current liabilities to $6,000 and the current ratio computed on year-end figures, those that analysts have, would be 2:5 to 1.

Perhaps a more serious problem is income smoothing (which was discussed in the previous chapter). As noted above, different accounting treatments are permitted for certain transactions. Relying on this choice to influence reported results is known as income smoothing. The effect of income smoothing on financial statements and hence the ratios derived from them can be substantial.

### Distortions Created by Variability in Sales

Changes in sales can produce distortions and cause false signals. For example, suppose you invest $1,000 in a piece of land on January 1, 19X1 and earn $20 per month or $240 for the year. Assuming this is your only asset, you would report a return on assets of 24% for the year. Now assume that on December 1, 19X2, you purchase an identical piece of land for $1,000 which also provides $20 per month. At December 31, 19X2, your total assets would be $2,000 and since your second piece of land produced profits starting in December, net income for the second year would be $260. Thus, your reported rate of return would be 13%. This is a substantial decrease from 24% yet there has been no real deterioration. It's a measurement problem. Earlier we noted that using an average can reduce the severity of the problem but not eliminate it. An average of beginning and end-of-year asset levels in this example is $1,500. If we use this figure in the denominator, the rate of return is 17.3% ($260 ÷ $1,500), still a substantial distortion.

More generally, changing sales causes distortions and we can separate three sources of variability.

1. Annual sales changes. Typically, a firm's sales will change each year and this can cause distortions. You will see in practice that the greater the change in annual sales, the greater the chances of false signals.

2. Seasonality. Often we want to monitor the performance of a firm during the course of the year. If sales are seasonal, ratios may be misleading.

3. Intra-Year Pattern of Sales. Pattern of sales refers to the proportion of annual sales realized during some segment of the year, say a month. For example, 10% of the firm's annual sales are sold in January, 8% in February, 12% in March and so on. If the pattern changes from year to year ratios can be misleading.

Because of changes in the pattern of sales and/or seasonality, it can be hazardous to compare ratios at different points during the year. For example, comparing a firm's current ratio at December 31 and June 30 could be misleading.

As noted earlier, analysts frequently rely on various kinds of averages to compute efficiency ratios to reduce the severity of the impact of varying sales. For instance, the National Association of Credit Management recommends that the DSO be computed by taking an average of the month-end receivable balances for the last three months and an average of credit sales for the previous 90 days. This and other averaging procedures can be quite useful, but keep in mind that they cannot eliminate the problem.

Finally, note that the use of averages requires the use of quarterly and monthly data. In the beginning of the chapter we discussed how it is often wise to rely on these data. We should point out, however, that monthly data often are not available to the external analyst and many smaller firms do not issue quarterly financial reports. In other words, sometimes analysts work only with annual data because they are the only data available.

The message of this chapter is that ratio analysis, if applied properly, can be a very valuable tool. However, to learn to apply ratio analysis effectively, you must take a perceptive approach and be aware of the limitations of ratios. Also, experience is required, so it's important to be patient. If you practice the art of ratio analysis, you will be amazed at how quickly you will improve.

Finally, to assist you in making computations, Table 2–5 has a list of the ratio computations discussed in the chapter.

**Table 2-5**  *Summary of Ratios Discussed in the Chapter*

1. Current Ratio $= \dfrac{\text{Current Assets}}{\text{Current Liabilities}}$

2. Acid Test Ratio $= \dfrac{\text{Cash} + \text{Marketable Securities} + \text{Accounts Receivable}}{\text{Current Liabilities}}$

   *quick*

3. Debt to Assets Ratio $= \dfrac{\text{Total Liabilities}}{\text{Total Assets}}$

4. Capitalization Ratio $= \dfrac{\text{Long-Term Debt}}{\text{Long-Term Debt} + \text{Owners' Equity}}$

5. Debt to Equity Ratio $= \dfrac{\text{Total Debt}}{\text{Total Equity}}$

6. Interest Coverage Ratio $= \dfrac{\text{EBIT}}{\text{Interest}}$

7. Burden Coverage Ratio $= \dfrac{\text{EBIT}}{\text{Interest} + \dfrac{\text{Principal Payments}}{1 - \text{Tax Rate}}}$

8. Total Asset Turnover $= \dfrac{\text{Net Sales}}{\text{Total Assets}}$

9. Fixed Asset Turnover $= \dfrac{\text{Net Sales}}{\text{Net Fixed Assets}}$

10. Days Sales Outstanding Ratio $= \dfrac{\text{Receivables from Customers}}{\dfrac{\text{Net Sales}}{360 \text{ Days}}}$

11. Days Purchases Outstanding Ratio $= \dfrac{\text{Trade Accounts Payable}}{\dfrac{\text{Purchases}}{360 \text{ Days}}}$

12. Inventory Turnover $= \dfrac{\text{Cost of Goods Sold}}{\text{Ending Inventory}}$

13. Income Statement $=$ Set net sales equal to 100%. Each expense, except for income taxes, is listed as a percentage of net sales by dividing each expense by net sales. Income tax expense is set as a percentage of income before income taxes by dividing income tax expense by pretax income.

14. **Return on Assets Ratio** $= \dfrac{\text{Net Income after Taxes}}{\text{Total Assest}} = \dfrac{\text{Net Income after Taxes}}{\text{Net Sales}}$

$$\times \dfrac{\text{Net sales}}{\text{Total Assets}}$$

15. **Return on Equity Ratio** $= \dfrac{\text{Net Income after Taxes}}{\text{Owners' Equity}} = \dfrac{\text{Net Income after Taxes}}{\text{Net Sales}}$

$$\times \dfrac{\text{Net Sales}}{\text{Total Assets}} \times \dfrac{\text{Total Assets}}{\text{Owners' Equity}}$$

# Problems and Discussion Questions

## A. Solved Problems

### Problem 2-1A

Mr. Howard Zinn, president of Fala, Inc., was pleased with his firm's performance during 19X5 and was prepared to report to the firm's stockholders that measures of profitability and efficiency had improved. Moreover, he planned to comment that the company was in a stronger financial position at the end of 19X5 versus 19X4 because of the improvement in liquidity and the reduction in financial leverage. Using the data in Tables 2-6 and 2-7, study the financial statements, compute the ratios presented below, and after analyzing them, assess Mr. Zinn's remarks.

Current Ratio
Acid Test
Total Debt to Total Assets Ratio
Capitalization Ratio
Total Asset Turnover
DSO
Inventory Turnover
100% Income Statement
Return on Assets
Return on Owners' Equity

### Solution 2-1A

Frequently, individuals turn too quickly to computations. The first step is to ponder the issue at hand and to read carefully the financial statements, including the footnotes. The purpose of this analysis is to assess the remarks of Mr. Zinn regarding the firm's financial performance and position.

With respect to reading the financial statements, experience will help you learn what to look for but normally we try to gain an appreciation for the size of the firm, the nature of assets (e.g., fixed assets comprising a large proportion of total), the nature of expenses (e.g., heavy operating expenses versus a large proportion going to cost of goods sold), liquidity and debt levels, etc. Further it is wise to compute annual sales growth. In this case, net sales grew by 31.3%. This is a healthy growth rate but keep in mind that rate

### TABLE 2-6
### FALA, INC.
#### Balance Sheet at December 31
#### (In $ thousands)

| Assets | 19X4 | 19X5 |
|---|---|---|
| Cash | $ 83 | $120 |
| Marketable securities | 8 | 9 |
| Accounts receivable | 93 | 146 |
| Inventory | 89 | 130 |
| Total current | $273 | $405 |
| Fixed assets | 215 | 284 |
| Less accumulated depreciation | 101 | 120 |
| Net fixed assets | $114 | $164 |
| Other assets | 3 | 4 |
| Total assets | $390 | $573 |
| Liabilities and Owners' Equity | | |
| Accounts payable | $ 43 | $ 63 |
| Other current liabilities | 88 | 114 |
| Total current | $131 | $177 |
| Long-term debt | — | 94 |
| Other long-term liabilities | 13 | 12 |
| Total liabilities | $144 | $283 |
| Common stock | 10 | 10 |
| Additional paid-in capital | 26 | 27 |
| Retained earnings | 210 | 253 |
| Total owners' equity | $246 | $290 |
| Total liabilities and owners' equity | $390 | $573 |

of growth in sales must be assessed in the context of the inflation rate. Say a firm had sales growth of 10%. Is this good or bad? Well, if inflation were three to four percent, it would indicate real growth, but if inflation were 12%–13% it would imply a decline in real sales activity. We must also view growth in the context of the industry. Real growth of five or six percent might be very good in markets that are growing at a rate of two to three percent per year, but it would be a cause for concern in a market that is growing at a rate of 20% per year.

The rapid growth of Rockwell should alert us to two potential problems. First, many firms that grow rapidly lose "control of operations," which means that expense and asset levels get out of

**TABLE 2-7**
**FALA, INC.**
Income Statements
for Years Ending December 31
(In $ thousands)

|  | 19X4 | 19X5 |
|---|---|---|
| Net sales | $665 | $873 |
| Cost of goods sold | 471 | 616 |
| Gross profit | $194 | $257 |
| Selling expense | 61 | 95 |
| General and administrative | 64 | 60 |
| Profit before income taxes | $69 | $102 |
| Income tax expense | 32 | 39 |
| Net income | $ 37 | $ 63 |

hand. Second, rapid sales growth can cause ratios, particularly efficiency ratios, to give misleading signals. Specifically, rapid growth can cause turnover ratios to decrease when in fact there was either no deterioration or improvement.

Now we can turn to the ratios which are shown in Table 2-8. As noted, we advocate working from the return on equity ratio. We can see that it increased substantially, from 15.0% in 19X4 to 21.7% in 19X5. This change can be explained by other ratios—leverage, 100% income statement and efficiency ratios.

The net profit margin increased from 5.6% to 7.2% and this is a positive sign. A closer examination reveals that part of the increase was due to a decrease in the firm's average tax rate. When there is a decrease, we try to figure out if it's temporary or permanent. In other words, will Fala's tax rate for 19X6 stay at 38% or will it return to 46%? Turning to operating expenses, the cost of goods sold percentage increased and this is always troublesome. Selling expenses inceased as a percentage of sales, and this should be looked into further. While general and administrative expenses showed improvement, it could be due to reductions in managed costs like maintenance. In any event, while we cannot reach a firm conclusion without checking the above items, the improvement in net profit margin is a positive sign and Mr. Zinn's statement on this point is correct.

Mr. Zinn said that efficiency measures improved, but this is incorrect as we can see from Table 2-8. However, we must keep

**Table 2-8**   *Ratio Computations for Solved Problem 2-1A*

|  | 19X4 |  | 19X5 |  |
|---|---|---|---|---|
| Current Ratio | 2.1:1 |  | 2.3:1 |  |
| Acid Test | 1.4:1 |  | 1.6:1 |  |
| Total Debt to Total Assets | 36.9% |  | 49.4% |  |
| Capitalization Ratio | 5.0% |  | 26.8% |  |
| Total Asset Turnover | 1.7X |  | 1.5X |  |
| DSO | 50 days |  | 60 days |  |
| Inventory Turnover | 5.3X |  | 4.7X |  |
| Net Sales | 100.0% |  | 100.0% |  |
| Cost of goods sold | 70.8% |  | 70.6% |  |
| Gross profit | 29.2% |  | 29.4% |  |
| Selling expense | 9.2% |  | 10.9% |  |
| General and administrative expenses | 9.6% |  | 6.9% |  |
| Profit before taxes | 10.4% |  | 11.7%* |  |
| Income taxes | (46.4%) | — | (38.2%) | — |
| Net income | 5.6% |  | 7.2% |  |
| Return on assets | 9.5% |  | 11.0% |  |
| Return on equity | 15.0% |  | 21.7% |  |

* Does not equal gross profit minus operating expenses because of rounding.

in mind that there could be a distortion caused by rapid sales growth. For instance, there may not have been a decrease in the rate at which the firm is selling its inventory, even though the turnover decreased.

The decrease in the asset turnover did offset somewhat the improvement in net profit margin—that is, had this measure not decreased, return on equity would have increased further. We know it is only a partial offset because the return on asset ratio increased. (Recall that the return on assets ratio is a function of the net profit margin and the total asset turnover.)

We can see that the return on assets ratio increased at a much lower rate than return on equity. The only way this could happen is if there was an increase in the ratio of owners' equity to total assets, which means more financial leverage. Thus, there was not a reduction in financial leverage as Mr. Zinn claimed. We should note, however, that the increase was in long-term debt which is the right kind of financing. Incidentally, the liquidity ratios also signal that the right kind of debt was employed, although these were distorted to a certain extent by the decrease in inventory turnover and increase in DSO.

## Problem 2-2A

You are given the following information for the Jackson Company.

| | Credit Sales | |
|---|---|---|
| Month | Year 1 | Year 2 |
| January–September | $120,000 | $120,000 |
| October | 5,000 | 25,000 |
| November | 5,000 | 10,000 |
| December | 30,000 | 5,000 |

Credit terms are net 30 days, customers pay on time, there are no bad debts and for simplicity, assume 30-day months.

1. Compute the DSO ratio, for Years 1 and 2, using the end-of-year accounts receivable balance in the numerator and an average daily sales figure in the denominator, for the last 360 days.

2. Would you recommend a different averaging period? If so, what should we employ for the numerator and denominator of the ratio?

## Solution 2-2A

1. The accounts receivable balance is $30,000 at the end of Year 1 and $5,000 at the end of Year 2, given that all sales are collected in 30 days. The DSO ratios are:

| Year 1 | Year 2 |
|---|---|
| $\dfrac{30,000}{\dfrac{160,000}{360 \text{ days}}} = 67.5 \text{ days};$ | $\dfrac{5,000}{\dfrac{160,000}{360 \text{ days}}} = 11.25 \text{ days}$ |

Notice that neither measure gives an accurate indication of how long it takes the firm to collect its receivables. More importantly, the DSO indicates a very substantial improvement when in fact there is no change. This shows how a change in the intra-year pattern of sales can produce misleading signals.

2. Averaging procedures can help but keep in mind that quarterly and monthly data are not always available to the external analyst (especially monthly data). All sorts of averages can be used and we will illustrate two. The first is year-end receivables and a daily average of sales for the last 60 days.

$$\begin{array}{cc} \textit{Year 1} & \textit{Year 2} \\[4pt] \dfrac{30,000}{\dfrac{35,000}{60 \text{ days}}} = 51.4 \text{ days}; & \dfrac{5,000}{\dfrac{15,000}{60 \text{ days}}} = 20 \text{ days} \end{array}$$

We still are obtaining a false signal but it is not as bad as the use of an annual average of daily sales. This will usually be the case, but sometimes there will be a greater distortion.

The second illustration is what NACM recommends, which is to use an average of month-end receivables for the last three months for the numerator and an average of daily sales for the last 90 days for the denominator.

$$\begin{array}{cc} \textit{Year 1} & \textit{Year 2} \\[4pt] \dfrac{\dfrac{5,000+5,000+30,000}{3}}{\dfrac{40,000}{90 \text{ days}}} = 30 \text{ days} & \dfrac{\dfrac{25,000+10,000+5,000}{3}}{\dfrac{40,000}{90 \text{ days}}} = 30 \text{ days} \end{array}$$

We see the distortion has been eliminated. Generally, this procedure will work best. However, this will not always be the case, so you should not infer that we can eliminate measurement problems altogether with the right kind of averaging procedure.

## B. Discussion Questions

### 2-1B

Evaluate the following: "Short term creditors should focus on analyzing liquidity ratios."

### 2-2B

Explain why varying sales levels can cause misleading signals. Be prepared to give one or two examples.

### 2-3B

What is income smoothing?

### 2-4B

Is it wise to compute annual sales growth figures as part of a ratio analysis? Why?

### 2-5B

What are managed costs?

### 2-6B

Why must we be cautious in comparing a firm's ratios to industry averages?

## C. Study Problems

### Problem 2-1C

Tables 2–9 and 2–10 contain income statements and balance sheets for two years for the Blanco Company.

1. Relying on ratio analysis, comment on the firm's financial performance in 19X5 relative to 19X4 and its financial position.

2. Based on your analysis decide whether you would extend this company a loan of $50 million.

### TABLE 2–9
### BLANCO COMPANY
Income Statements
for Years Ending December 31
(In $ millions)

|  | 19X4 | 19X5 |
|---|---|---|
| Net sales | $504 | $630 |
| Cost of goods sold | 252 | 347 |
| Gross profit | $252 | $283 |
| Selling, general and administrative expense | 105 | 151 |
| Research and development | 50 | 35 |
| Profit before taxes | $ 97 | 97 |
| Income taxes | 48 | 48 |
| Net income | $ 49 | $ 49 |

Notes:
1 Purchases were $240 million in 19X4 and $396 million in 19X5.

## Problem 2-2C

You are given the following information for the Sertel Company.

| | Credit sales | |
|---|---|---|
| | *Year 1* | *Year 2* |
| January–August | $215,000 | $15,000 |
| September | 5,000 | 30,000 |
| October | 5,000 | 5,000 |
| November | 5,000 | 5,000 |
| December | 30,000 | 5,000 |

The firm was forced to close down for the first half of Year 2. That is why sales were only $15,000 from January to August. Credit terms are net 45 days, customers pay on time, sales are spread evenly during the month, and for simplicity, assume 30-day months. Given this information, the accounts receivable balances at the end of the last three months were:

| | *Year 1* | *Year 2* |
|---|---|---|
| October | $ 7,500 | $20,000 |
| November | 7,500 | 7,500 |
| December | 32,500 | 7,500 |

1. Compute the DSO for Year 1 and 2 using the end of December receivables balance in the numerator and average daily sales for the last 360 days in the denominator.

2. Compute the DSO for Years 1 and 2 using the NACM procedure. (Review this chapter and Problem 2-2A for explanation.)

3. Comment on the impact of the use of averages on ratios.

## Problem 2-3C

Relying on the following information complete the balance sheet shown in Table 2-11:

| | |
|---|---|
| Net profit margin | 8% |
| DSO (based on year end receivables and an average of sales' for the year) | 15 days |
| Total Debt to Total Assets | 50% |
| Total Asset Turnover | 3X |
| Acid Test | .65 |

**TABLE 2–10**
**BLANCO COMPANY**
Balance Sheet at 12/31
(In $ millions)

|  | 19X4 | 19X5 |
|---|---|---|
| Cash plus marketable securities | $ 30 | $ 10 |
| Accounts receivable | 42 | 47 |
| Inventory | 70 | 119 |
| Total current | $142 | $176 |
| Fixed assets (net) | 270 | 310 |
| Intangibles | 10 | 18 |
| Total assets | $422 | $504 |
| Accounts payable | $ 20 | $ 66 |
| Short-term bank debt | 30 | 130 |
| Total current | $ 50 | $196 |
| Long-term debt | 210 | 191 |
| Total | $260 | $387 |
| Common stock | $ 10 | $ 5 |
| Additional paid-in capital | 80 | 40 |
| Retained earnings | 72 | 72 |
| Total owners' equity | $162 | $117 |
| Total liabilities and owners' equity | $422 | $504 |

**TABLE 2–11**
Balance Sheet
at 12/31

| | |
|---|---|
| Cash plus marketable securities | $ 34,750 |
| Accounts receivable | ? |
| Inventory | ? |
| Net fixed assets | 100,000 |
| Total assets | 500,000 |
| | |
| Accounts payable | $ 50,000 |
| Short-term debt | ? |
| Total current | ? |
| Long-term debt | ? |
| Common stock and additional paid-in capital | 150,000 |
| Retained earnings | ? |
| Total liabilities and owners' equity | ? |

## Problem 2-4C

You are given the following information for the Georgan Company.

| End of Year | Cost of Goods Sold | Year-End Inventory |
|---|---|---|
| 1 | $ 960 | 160 |
| 2 | 1,920 | 320 |
| 3 | 3,840 | 640 |
| 4 | 7,680 | 1,280 |

The inventory balance at the beginning of Year 1 was $80. The firm sells its products ready for sale, gross profit is 20% for all sales, sales are spread evenly during the year. A one month's supply of inventory is needed to support sales, and inventory required for the month are purchased on the last day of the preceding month. Thus, it takes the firm 30 days to sell its inventory. (For simplicity, we are assuming 30-day months.)

1. Compute inventory turnover for each year using year-end inventory in the denominator. Redo the calculation using an average of beginning and end-of-year inventory levels in the denominator.

2. Are the inventory turnovers giving an accurate signal with respect to how long it takes the firm to sell its inventory? What impact does the use of average inventory levels have?

## Problem 2-5C

You are given the following information for the Hartek Company.

| Year Ending 12/31 | Net Sales | Net Profit | Total Assets at 12/31 | Total Debt at 12/31 |
|---|---|---|---|---|
| 1 | $ 100 | $ 10 | $ 20 | $ 0 |
| 2 | 200 | 20 | 50 | 10 |
| 3 | 500 | 50 | 150 | 60 |
| 4 | 1,200 | 120 | 420 | 210 |
| 5 | 3,000 | 300 | 1,050 | 540 |

1. Compute the net profit margin, total asset turnover and ratio of owners' equity to total assets for each year. Using a schedule like the one in Table 2-4 compute rate of return on equity. (You may assume the firm's income tax rate was 50% each year.)

2. Based on the above analysis comment on the firm's performance.

### Problem 2-6C

Table 2-12 has the income statements for the years ended 12/31/19X1 and 12/31/19X2 and Table 2-13 has the balance sheets at 12/31 for these years for the Canton Manufacturing Company.

Relying on ratio analysis, compare Canton's financial performance for the two years and comment on the change, if any, in financial position.

### TABLE 2-12
### CANTON MANUFACTURING COMPANY
Income Statements
for Years Ended 12/31
(000 omitted)

|  | 19X1 | 19X2 |
|---|---|---|
| Net sales | $1,032 | $1,352 |
| Cost of goods sold | 717 | 949 |
| Gross profit | $ 315 | $ 403 |
| Selling expenses | 106 | 112 |
| General and administrative expenses | 99 | 136 |
| Operating profit | $ 110 | $ 155 |
| Interest expense | 12 | 50 |
| Interest income | (11) | (15) |
| Profit before taxes | $ 109 | $ 120 |
| Income taxes | 54 | 54 |
| Net income | $ 55 | $ 66 |

**TABLE 2–13**
**CANTON MANUFACTURING COMPANY**
Balance Sheets at 12/31
(000 omitted)

|  | 19X1 | 19X2 |
|---|---|---|
| Cash | $128 | $186 |
| Marketable securities | 12 | 14 |
| Accounts receivable | 144 | 226 |
| Inventory | 138 | 202 |
| Total current | $422 | $628 |
| Property, plant and equipment (net) | 178 | 238 |
| Other assets | 5 | 7 |
| Total assets | $605 | $873 |
| Accounts payable | $67 | $98 |
| Notes payable (banks) | 130 | 130 |
| Other current liabilities | 6 | 47 |
| Total current | $203 | $275 |
| Long-term secured bonds | — | 147 |
| Other long-term liabilities | 21 | 18 |
| Total liabilities | $224 | $440 |
| Common stock | 16 | 16 |
| Additional paid-in capital | 40 | 42 |
| Retained earnings | 325 | 375 |
| Total liabilities and owners' equity | $605 | $873 |

# 3

# Flow of Funds Analysis

This chapter explains flow of funds analysis, which is the process of constructing and interpreting a statement of changes in financial position. Specific goals of the chapter include the following:

- Show how to construct a statement of changes in financial position.
- Provide a solid understanding of the concepts of net working capital from operations and cash flow from operations.
- Show the relationship between the statement of changes in financial position and the income statement and balance sheet.
- Explain the suitability principle.
- Teach how to evaluate a firm's financing strategies and policies.
- Clear up the confusion surrounding the phrase "funds flow" and the practice of adding depreciation expense to net income and calling the total something it is not.
- Discuss the nature of assets and liabilities that vary automatically with sales.

After some preliminary remarks, we will explain how to prepare a statement of changes in financial position and this will serve as our vehicle for discussing the other topics listed above.

Flow of funds analysis makes it possible for analysts to address issues such as the following:

1. What happened to the net income earned during the period? Why was net income for the period not accompanied by a similar increase in cash? As we will see, it is possible, and not uncommon, for net income to be high and for cash flow from operations to be low or even negative.

2. Did the current assets of the firm increase during the period? If so, by how much, why, and was the increase properly financed?

3. How did the firm finance its expenditures for fixed assets?

4. Of the resources committed during the period, what portion was provided by the day-to-day operations of the business? What other sources were relied upon to finance the resources committed? Did the firm select appropriate sources?

5. Was it wise for the firm to pay dividends? Where did the money come from?

6. Did operating the business during the period, provide or use cash? If it generated cash, how was it employed? If it used cash, where did the money come from and were the sources appropriate?

7. How has the firm financed growth? Assets are needed to generate sales. To produce more sales, a firm generally needs more assets. Higher sales, even if they are quite profitable, can create severe financial problems if they are not properly financed.

We can see from the above that flow of funds analysis is a valuable tool for analyzing financial statements. But we also see it is much more. If we are to understand the financial operations of a business, we first need to understand flow of funds analysis.

We will begin with the preparation of the statement, which is known by a variety of names including the following: (1) statement of changes in financial position (most common in annual and other published reports), (2) sources and uses of funds statement and (3) flow of funds statement. We will use flow of funds statement because it is shorter and still common in practice.

# Preparation of a Flow of Funds Statement

A flow of funds statement is prepared from the information on income statements and balance sheets. Thus, we are not eliciting new information; instead we are organizing existing data in a more useful manner for analysis. The statement is prepared for a specific period. Therefore, we first select the time horizon of interest and collect the necessary income statements and balance sheets. For example, for an annual flow of funds statement, we need an income statement for that year, a balance sheet at the beginning of that year, and another balance sheet at the end of that year.

To illustrate the preparation of a flow of funds statement, we will construct one for the Andrel Corporation for Year 2. Table 3-1 has annual income statements and balance sheets.

The first step is to calculate the change in each balance sheet item and label it a source or a use according to the following guidelines.

*Source*
1. Increase in a liability account.
2. Increase in an owners' equity account.
3. Decrease in an asset account.

*Use*
1. Increase in an asset account.
2. Decrease in a liability account.
3. Decrease in an owners' equity account.

Let's for a moment discuss the logic of the guidelines. A source means that the specific item provided the means of financing one or more of the uses. For example, if a firm issues long-term debt to finance the purchase of a building, a liability account would increase (source), as would an asset account (use). If the firm collected some of its accounts receivables and used the money to pay off a bank loan, there would be a decrease in an asset account (source), and also a decrease in a liability account (use).

Seems simple enough, so let's begin.

|  | At End of Year 1 | At End of Year 2 | Change |
|---|---|---|---|
| Cash | $40,000 | $55,000 | +$15,000 |

There is an increase of $15,000. Cash is an asset so it is a use of $15,000. If the firm now has $15,000 more, how can we call it a use? The firm is

**TABLE 3-1**
**ANDREL CORPORATION**
Income Statements

|  | *For Year 1* | *For Year 2* |
|---|---|---|
| Net sales | $4,500,000 | $6,750,000 |
| Cost of goods sold | 3,605,000 | 5,400,000 |
| Gross profit | $ 895,000 | $1,350,000 |
| Depreciation expense | 155,000 | 233,000 |
| Selling expense | 260,000 | 390,000 |
| General and administrative | 320,000 | 487,000 |
| Profit before taxes | $ 160,000 | $ 240,000 |
| Income taxes | 80,000 | 120,000 |
| Net income | $ 80,000 | $ 120,000 |

**ANDREL CORPORATION**
Balance Sheets

| Assets | 12/31/Year 1 | 12/31/Year 2 |
|---|---|---|
| Cash | $ 40,000 | $ 65,000 |
| Accounts receivable | 750,000 | 1,125,000 |
| Inventory | 300,000 | 450,000 |
| Total current | $1,090,000 | $1,630,000 |
| Fixed assets (net) | 1,450,000 | 1,850,000 |
| Total assets | $2,540,000 | $3,480,000 |
| Liabilities and owners' equity |  |  |
| Accounts payable (trade) | $ 150,000 | $ 225,000 |
| Notes payable (bank) | 10,000 | 607,000 |
| Accrued income taxes | 25,000 | 38,000 |
| Other accrued expenses | 10,000 | 15,000 |
| Total current | $ 195,000 | $ 885,000 |
| Deferred income taxes | 100,000 | 120,000 |
| Common stock | 300,000 | 355,000 |
| Paid-in capital | 1,195,000 | 1,310,000 |
| Retained earnings | 750,000 | 810,000 |
| Total liabilities and owners' equity | $2,540,000 | $3,480,000 |

committing $15,000 more to its cash account and this amount had to come from some source. That's what a use means. Why did the firm increase its cash account? Was it a good idea? We are performing an analysis to gain insight into such issues.

Note that all sources and uses of financing are included, not only those involving cash. Later we will discuss how the word "funds" in the context of a flow of funds statement generally means cash or net working capital. (Net working capital equals current assets minus current liabilities.) However, usually a flow of funds statement is prepared according to an "all resources" notion. This means we include sources and uses of all economic resources and not just those that directly involve cash or net working capital. For example, suppose Firm A purchases a building from Mrs. B. for $1 million and the means of payment is a stock issue from Firm A worth $1 million. The increase in fixed assets is a use and the offsetting source is the $1 million stock issue. Cash or net working capital were not directly involved but according to the all-resources concept, we would still include this transaction. How do we reconcile this treatment with our earlier statement that the word "funds" generally refers to cash or net working capital on a flow of funds statement? Since the above transaction is important for analyzing flows of resources, the all-resources concept basically tells us to assume that the firm had an inflow of funds by issuing stock and these funds were used to buy the building.

Now we can proceed with the first step, which is to compute each change on the balance sheet (as we did for cash) and label it as a source or use following our guidelines.

## Step 1. Compute Balance Sheet Changes

| Sources | | Uses | |
|---|---:|---|---:|
| +Accounts payable | | +Cash | $15,000 |
| (trade) | $ 75,000 | +Accounts receivable | 375,000 |
| +Notes payable (bank) | 597,000 | +Inventory | 150,000 |
| +Accrued income taxes | 13,000 | +Fixed assets (net) | 400,000 |
| +Other accrued expenses | 5,000 | | |
| +Deferred income taxes | 20,000 | | |
| +Common stock | 55,000 | | |
| +Paid-in capital | 115,000 | | |
| +Retained earnings | 60,000 | | |
| | $940,000 | | $940,000 |

After labeling each change as a source or a use we total the sources and uses. The two totals must equal because every use requires a source. If they do not, then a change was not classified correctly or a numerical error was made.

Let's pursue further the exact meaning of a source and a use. Asset accounts represent uses of resources, and liability and owners' equity accounts depict sources of resources. The items listed above are sources and uses for Year 2. For example, at the end of Year 1, $300,000 was tied up in inventory; that is, the firm was employing $300,000 to support inventory. At the end of Year 2, $450,000 was tied up in inventory; that is, the firm was using $450,000 to support inventory at that time. The increase of $150,000 represents a use for Year 2 in the sense that this was the amount of added financing that was needed for inventory for Year 2.

We should also note that these items represent net sources and net uses for Year 2 and do not indicate how much was needed or how much was supplied for various periods within Year 2. To understand this point, let us assume the following inventory balances at various times during Year 2.

| | | |
|---|---|---|
| 12/31/Year 1 | $300,000 | |
| 3/31/Year 2 | $160,000 | |
| 6/30/Year 2 | $700,000 | $\triangle$ $150,000 |
| 9/30/Year 2 | $700,000 | |
| 12/31/Year 2 | $450,000 | |

As explained above, the use for Year 2 was $150,000. This figure is the net amount required for Year 2. However, we can see that for the first quarter, inventory declined from $300,000 to $160,000, making it a source for this period. From the end of the first quarter to the end of the second quarter, it was a use of $540,000. It was neither a source nor a use for the third quarter. For the fourth quarter it was a source of $250,000. We could continue and show monthly, weekly, or even daily changes. The message we'd like to get across is this: When looking at annual changes in individual items, do not infer that the amount specifies the total or the maximum inflow or outflow related to that item for the year.

## Step 2. Adjustments

Normally, the following three adjustments are made to the above statement to make it more informative.

1. Remove the change in retained earnings from the above statement and substitute net income as a source and dividends as a use. (A net loss would be a use.)

2. Show the amount of net working capital provided by operations. This

is done by adding (or subtracting) certain items to net income. (As we will see later, net working capital provided from operations is frequently referred to as funds flow or funds provided by operations.)

3. Remove the change in net fixed assets from the above statement and substitute the net amount spent on fixed assets.

We will now explain each adjustment and we will see that we need income statement data for Year 2 to make them.

### Retained Earnings Adjustment

Let's first state the procedure and then explain how to apply it.

> *Procedure*
> Remove the change in retained earnings from the statement prepared in Step 1 and substitute net income as a source and dividends as a use.

The income statement for Year 2 indicates that net income was $120,000. Information regarding dividends is normally given on the income statement or on the statement of retained earnings. In this case we do not have a retained earnings statement, and dividends are not shown on the income statement, so we must estimate the amount.

You may recall that the two major items affecting the retained earnings account are net income and dividends. Specifically, the end of period retained earnings balance may be calculated as follows:

> Retained earnings balance, beginning of period
> + Net income for period
> − Dividends for the period
> = Retained earnings balance, end of period.

For our example, we can use this formula to derive the amount.

| | |
|---|---:|
| Retained earnings balance, end of Year 1 | $750,000 |
| + Net income for Year 2 | $120,000 |
| − Dividends for Year 2 | ? |
| = Retained earnings balance, end of Year 2 | $810,000 |

Since we know three of the four items in the equation, we can figure out that dividends were $60,000.

Now we can apply the rule. We remove the $60,000 change in retained earnings from the statement and substitute income of $120,000 as a source, and dividends of $60,000 as a use. (Later we show how to incorporate the adjustment.)

Why do we make this adjustment? The answer is to make the statement contain more useful information. The change in the retained earnings account of $60,000 could be the result of literally an infinite number of combinations of net income and dividends. For example, net income of $5.06 million and dividends of $5 million would produce a change of $60,000. Whether net income and dividends were these amounts, or $120,000 and $60,000 as they were for Andrel Corporation, is obviously important information which cannot be gleaned by looking only at the change in retained earnings.

Before turning to the next adjustment, we should point out that although net income and dividends are usually the major items affecting the retained earnings figure, sometimes there are others. If this is the case, the information will be on a statement of retained earnings. (When the other items are relatively small, many analysts ignore them and do not make further adjustments.)

One final point. The retained earnings account represents the proportion of the profits reinvested in the business since its inception. These funds have already been used. Thus, retained earnings does not represent a pool of money held somewhere in the firm. The amount of cash a firm has is listed as cash on the balance sheet. We give the following advice to students who cannot keep this crucial point in mind. When you see the phrase, retained earnings, cross it out and in its place insert: not money!

## NET WORKING CAPITAL ADJUSTMENT

We will state the procedure and then explain how to apply it. Before we do, note the following two points: First, the procedure gives an estimate, not an exact figure. Second, we will be referring to a firm's current assets as working capital and the difference between current assets and current liabilities as net working capital. This is the definition typically employed by finance people. Accountants generally call the difference between current assets and current liabilities, working capital.

Here's the procedure:

> *Procedure*
> Remove the change in the long-term deferred taxes liability
> from the statement constructed in Step 1. To the net income fig-

ure add an increase (or subtract a decrease) in the long-term deferred taxes account. Also, add expenses on the income
statement that do not decrease net working capital.[1]

Before illustrating how to apply the rule, we should briefly explore its logic.
Generally, the only source of net working capital from operating the business is revenues. Some expenses decrease net working capital, but not all
expenses decrease it. In preparing a flow of funds statement we could
present revenues that increase net working capital as a source and expenses
that decrease it as a use. While this perhaps should be done, it is not normal
practice. Instead, analysts usually adjust the net income number. Specifically, they make the following calculation:

Net income (or net loss) for period
+ Expenses that do not decrease net working capital
= Increase (or decrease) in net working capital from operations
    for period.

It is beyond our scope to describe all the expenses that do not decrease net
working capital. However, we should mention three expenses: depreciation,
amortization and a portion of income taxes. Amortization expense and depreciation expense are simply added to the net income figure. The portion
of income tax expense that does not decrease net working capital is derived
by adding the increase (or subtracting the decrease) in the long-term deferred income taxes account. The liability, deferred income taxes, could be
current or non-current and some firms have both on their balance sheets.
It is only the change in the long-term liability that is involved in this
calculation.

Let's now apply the procedure to Andrel. We start with net income for
Year 2 or $120,000. To this figure, we add depreciation expense for the
period of $233,000 and the increase of $20,000 in long-term deferred
income taxes as shown below:

| | |
|---|---:|
| Net income for Year 2 | $120,000 |
| Add depreciation expense for Year 2 | 233,000 |
| Increase in long-term deferred income taxes | 20,000 |
| Net working capital provided by operation for Year 2 | $373,000 |

[1] To obtain a more accurate estimate, one should also subtract from net income revenues that do not increase net
working capital. Moreover, it is possible to have a long-term deferred taxes asset account. If so, an increase in it
would be subtracted and a decrease would be added. In most cases, these items will not exist or will be relatively
small. These refinements will not be included in the discussion.

The significance of this quantity will be discussed after we complete the preparation of the statement.

We said above that we could show revenues that increase net working capital as sources, and expenses that decrease net working capital as uses. Let's do it for Andrel for Year 2.

| *Sources* | | *Uses* | |
|---|---|---|---|
| Net sales | $6,750,000 | Cost of goods sold expense | $5,400,000 |
| | | Selling expense | 390,000 |
| | | General and administrative | 487,000 |
| | | Income taxes | 100,000 |
| Total | $6,750,000 | Total | $6,377,000 |

Our tax figure is different from the income tax expense shown on the income statement. We will explain the reason in a moment but first notice that the difference between the two totals is $373,000, the same answer we got from using the adjustment procedure. This equivalence is no surprise because the procedure is merely a mathematical derivation of the difference between the revenues and expenses listed above. Now we will explain taxes.

The increase in the deferred taxes liability of $20,000 tells us that income tax expense shown on the income statement is $20,000 more than the amount actually due for the period. The nature of deferred taxes was explained in the Income Tax Expense Section of Chapter 1. If you do not have a thorough understanding of deferred taxes or other aspects of accounting for income taxes, you should study that section because a knowledge of this is important for various financial analyses. For instance, in that chapter we explain the difference between accrued income taxes and deferred income taxes. Accrued income taxes is a liability representing an expense that has been incurred but not yet paid. Generally, it will be paid early in the next period. The deferred income taxes account arises from treating transactions one way for income tax purposes and another way for financial accounting purposes. In effect, the firm defers paying income taxes, and as explained in Chapter 1, this deferral produces a liability on the balance sheet that may not be paid for a very long time or may never be paid.

One final point before we proceed to the next adjustment. How do we know that the revenues and expenses listed above affect net working capital? The answer is we don't know for sure because that would require us to analyze the firm's internal records. Therefore, we must keep in mind that the procedure used to derive net working capital from operations gives an estimate and not an exact figure. However, generally the estimate will be a good one.

### Fixed asset adjustment

Firms acquire and sell fixed assets. The purpose of this adjustment is to provide information on this activity. Specifically, it gives an estimate of the net amount spent as defined below:

> Amount spent on fixed assets
> − Proceeds from sales of fixed assets
> = Net amount spent on fixed assets

Although we would like to know both the amount spent and the proceeds from sales, generally this is not possible from income statement and balance sheet data. We must settle for information on the net amount spent. Moreover, we can only derive an estimate of the net amount spent.

More than one procedure is used for making the adjustment. The one we will rely on should give the best estimate in most instances.

#### Procedure

Add depreciation expense for the period to the change in net fixed assets to obtain an estimate on the net amount spent on fixed assets. This derived quantity replaces the change in net fixed assets on the statement derived in Step 1.

For Andrel, we obtain an estimate of $633,000 as shown below.

| | |
|---|---:|
| Change in net fixed assets | $400,000 |
| + Depreciation expense for Year 2 | 233,000 |
| = Net amount spent on fixed assets | $633,000 |

### Step 3. Incorporating Adjustments

The final step is to prepare a statement incorporating the adjustments. Table 3-2 has the statement for Andrel for Year 2.

We defined flow of funds analysis as the process of constructing and interpreting a flow of funds statement. The discussion of the construction phase is completed and we will now focus on concepts and issues pertaining to interpreting this information.

### Treat the Word Funds with Caution

The word "funds" is used a great deal in business. It's precise meaning will depend on the context in which it is employed. As noted earlier, in the context of flow of funds statements, the word generally refers to net working

**TABLE 3-2**
**ANDREL CORPORATION**
Flow of Funds statement for Year 2
(000 omitted)

*Sources*

| | | |
|---|---|---|
| Net Income | $120 | |
| +Depreciation expense | 233 | |
| +Deferred taxes (noncurrent) | 20 | |
| Net working capital | | $  373 |
| Accounts payable | | 75 |
| Notes payable, bank (short term) | | 597 |
| Accrued income taxes | | 13 |
| Other accrued expenses | | 5 |
| Common stock | | 55 |
| Paid-in capital | | 115 |
| Total sources | | $1,233 |

*Uses*

| | |
|---|---|
| Dividends | $   60 |
| Cash | 15 |
| Accounts receivable | 375 |
| Inventory | 150 |
| Net amount spent on fixed assets | 633 |
| Total uses | $1,233 |

capital or cash. Here are some of the other meanings: (1) cash plus marketable securities, (2) assets and (3) ability to acquire assets. The variation in usage creates errors in financial analyses. Two serious errors are described next.

### Error 1: Funds Provided by Operations

We just explained how to estimate the amount of net working capital generated by operations. This quantity is frequently called funds provided by operations, funds flow or a similar name. The problem is that when it is referred to by a phrase with the word funds in it, many people interpret it as an estimate of the amount of cash produced by operating the business. The fact is that the measure does not represent cash flow and very often it will be quite different from the amount of cash flow.

### *Error 2: Net Income + Depreciation = ?*

Many people add depreciation expense to net income and call the sum cash flow from operations. Moreover, they refer to depreciation as a source of funds. The fact is depreciation is not a source of funds and the sum of net income plus depreciation is an estimate of net working capital from operations, not cash flow from operations.

If depreciation is not a source, why do we add it on the source side of a flow of funds statement? Earlier, we gave the answer. Generally, the only source of net working capital from operating the business is revenues. Some expenses decrease net working capital, others, such as depreciation, do not. Instead of showing revenues that increase net working capital as sources, and expenses that decrease net working capital as uses, we add to net income those expenses that do not decrease net working capital. In other words, it's strictly a format issue.

Sometimes when analysts talk about depreciation being a source of funds, they are referring to the tax shield created by depreciation. A tax shield is a reduction in the dollars of taxes that must be paid because of an expense. It is calculated as follows: tax rate × expense = tax shield. Depreciation like most other expenses creates a tax shield. Still, it is not accurate to call it a source. Here is the precise way to say it: Revenue is the only source of funds from operating a business. This source is reduced by certain expenses, including income taxes. Depreciation like all deductible expenses has the effect of reducing the amount that must be used to pay taxes.

If net income + depreciation is not cash flow, why do so many managers and analysts in the real world call it cash flow? (Students and practitioners like to use the phrase "real world" when talking to professors.) The answer is it's a "quick and dirty" method for deriving an estimate. The trouble is it provides a decent estimate of cash flow from operations *only* when *all* of the following conditions are met.

1. Depreciation expense is the only significant expense that does not decrease net working capital. In other words, expenses such as amortization are minor. (This condition prevails often.)

2. There is no deferred taxes account or the change is not significant. (This condition often is not met.)

3. Sales do not change much and hence the current assets and current liabilities that change almost automatically with sales do not vary considerably. (We are talking about dollar sales levels, so inflation alone can prevent this condition from being satisfied.)

## SALES INDUCED CHANGES IN CURRENT ASSETS AND CURRENT LIABILITIES

Assets are needed to generate sales and most are needed before sales can be generated; others such as accounts receivable are created at the time of sale. Our concern here is with how current assets and current liabilities vary with sales.

Most current assets vary automatically with sales. This means the firm has little or no discretion. Suppose, for example, we sell goods on terms of net 30 days and customers pay on time. If sales are $100 per month, accounts receivable will be $100 at the end of each month. If sales increase to $200 per month, accounts receivable will automatically increase to $200. Most current assets move in the same direction as sales but they do not all change at the same rate as sales. For example, if sales increase by 10% normally we should expect receivables to increase by 10%, but other current assets will often increase at a lower rate.

Accounts receivable and inventory often have a major impact on cash flow from operations and funding requirements. Hence we will focus on these in the ensuing discussion.

Certain current liabilities change automatically with sales, notably accounts payable and accrued expenses. These are major sources of financing for many companies and they are automatically created. For example, suppose we purchase $100 per month on terms of net 30 days and pay on time. Accounts payable would be $100 at the end of each month. If our credit purchases increase to $200 per month, accounts payable will automatically increase to $200 per month.

An accrued expense account is a liability for an expense incurred during the period but not paid as of the end of the period. For example, assume a firm has labor expense of $200 per month and pays 25% of this amount in the next month. At the end of each month, accrued expenses will be $50. If labor expense increases to $400 per month, accrued labor will automatically increase to $100 per month.

Accrued expenses often are substantial amounts and so they are correctly viewed as important sources of funds. However, it is important to realize that this source is fundamentally different from other sources. When a firm issues common stock or borrows from a bank, cash flows into the firm. An accrued expense is not the same kind of liability—cash does not flow into the firm. Rather, it represents the postponement of paying for an expense. Nevertheless, it is properly viewed as an important source because if it did not exist it would have to be replaced by another source. Take the example when monthly labor expense was $200 and the accrued expense account was $50. If the firm began to pay cash for total labor each month, it would need a source of $50 to replace the accrual.

## NET WORKING CAPITAL FROM OPERATIONS

Table 3-2 shows that net working capital from operations for Year 2 was $373,000. This is an estimate of how much net working capital (current assets minus current liabilities) increased because of day-to-day operations. (We must emphasize again that this is not cash flow.)

The concept of net working capital is important because it indicates the extent to which operations can support a firm's financing requirements. For example, if a firm has growing sales, it will need more working capital to support sales increases. If there is no excess capacity, the firm will also need more fixed assets. If net working capital from operations is less than the needed increment to support sales, the remainder must be financed with another source. On the other hand, if the amount generated is greater than the net working capital required for higher sales, the excess can be used to acquire fixed assets, to pay dividends or for some other purpose.

Net working capital from operations is a useful way of thinking about the flow of resources because a firm needs assets to support operations, and cash is only one of many types of assets needed. Finally, we should note that the net change in net working capital for the period normally will not equal the amount of net working capital from operations for the period. The reason is that increases and decreases occur because of other factors. For example, if a firm sells a fixed asset and uses the proceeds to pay a short-term debt, there is an increase in net working capital but it is not due to day-to-day operations.

## CASH FLOW FROM OPERATIONS

Measuring and appraising cash generated or used by a business should be an essential part of a flow of funds analysis. It is quite possible for a firm to have positive, growing profits while its operations consume rather than supply cash. While this is not necessarily a bad sign, especially in the case of a firm with growing sales, it could be a sign of trouble and deserves careful diagnosis. On the other hand, positive cash flow is not necessarily a good sign. For example, a firm with declining sales can produce a substantial cash flow. (This is one reason why an analysis of profitability is so important.)

Cash flow from operations is defined as follows:

> Cash inflows from selling goods and services
> − Cash outlays made in connection with purchasing and/or produc-
>   ing products for sales and for other expenses
> = (net) Cash flow from operations

To calculate the exact amount would require an analysis of a firm's internal accounting records. However, from the data on a firm's published income statements and balance sheets we can generally derive a good estimate. What we do is adjust net working capital from operations for changes in those current assets and current liabilities that vary automatically with sales. We do this by adding increases in liability accounts and subtracting increases in asset accounts and by subtracting decreases in liability accounts and adding decreases in asset accounts. The current accounts normally included are receivables from customers, inventory, prepaid expenses, payables to suppliers, accrued expenses and short-term deferred taxes.

We will illustrate by computing cash flow from operations for Year 2 for Andrel Corporation. Let's first summarize the procedure:

### Procedure for estimating cash flow from operations
> Net working capital from operations for the period
> ± Change in accounts receivable
> ± Change in inventory
> ± Change in prepaid expenses
> ± Change in accounts payable, trade
> ± Change in accrued expenses
> ± Change in short-term deferred taxes
> = Cash flow from operations for the period

For Andrel cash flow from operations for Year 2 was a negative $59,000 as shown below:

| | |
|---|---:|
| Net working capital from operations for Year 2 | $ 373,000 |
| − Increase in accounts receivable | − 375,000 |
| − Increase in inventory | − 150,000 |
| + Increase in accounts payable | + 75,000 |
| + Increase in accrued income taxes | + 13,000 |
| + Increase in other accrued expenses | + 5,000 |
| = Cash flow from operations for Year 2 | $− 59,000 |

The negative figure means that operations used cash.

Notice how important it is not to confuse net working capital from operations, and cash flow from operations. Here we see that Andrel generated $373,000 of net working capital from operations during Year 2 while cash flow was a negative $59,000.

Before proceeding, we should note a limitation on the measure of cash flow from operations. A major purpose of this computation is to help us evaluate if operations generate or consume cash and to determine the size of positive or negative cash flow. Some published flow of funds statements include cash flow from operations along with net working capital from operations. In most instances, the definition used is the one shown above—that is, net working capital from operations is adjusted for changes in the current assets and current liabilities noted above. (In some instances, there are others.) One problem with this measure is that it does not include cash or fixed assets. A firm requires a certain amount of cash to handle day-to-day transactions. If the number or size of transactions changes, then the amount of cash needed may also change. Moreover, if a firm is at or close to capacity, it will need more fixed assets to produce a higher level of sales. Thus, the cash flow from operations figure does not necessarily represent the amount of money available for such purposes as paying off loans or paying dividends. It is left to the analyst to make a judgment on this issue.

## SUITABILITY PRINCIPLE

An important reason for analyzing a flow of funds statement is to judge whether a firm has adhered to the suitability principle also known as the matching or hedging principle. The principle is this: Uses of funds should be financed with the right kind of sources. Permanent or long-term uses should be financed with long term or permanent sources. Temporary uses require temporary sources. For instance, if you lend someone $50 for a week, your increase in accounts receivable is a temporary use. If the loan was for ten years then it is a permanent or long-term use because you would be committing funds for ten years.

Let's look at a similar example. Suppose you and I form a business to undertake one transaction, a five-year loan of $1,000. To finance this, we are considering the following three options.

- Borrow $1,000 from a bank at an interest rate of 10% for 90 days, renewing the loan every 90 days over the five years.

- Borrow $1,000 from a bank at an interest rate of 12% for 2½ years, borrowing again at maturity for the same term.

• Borrow $1,000 from a bank at an interest rate of 14% for five years.

The suitability principle tells us that the first two options are inappropriate because we would be incurring refinancing risk. Specifically, if we cannot obtain new financing when the loans are due, we could encounter serious financial problems. (Obviously, the first option involves more refinancing risk than the second.)

Managers violate the suitability principle all the time and the above example shows why. Very often, short-term interest rates are lower than long-term interest rates and hence it is cheaper to borrow short term. Further, when interest rates are high, financial managers are reluctant to commit to long-term loans. For instance, suppose we started our business at a time when "experts" were predicting a decrease in interest rates. We might decide to borrow for 90 days and then borrow long term three months from now.

The author's view is that generally it is not wise to violate the suitability principle because the refinancing risk is greater than many people think. Sometimes firms have difficulty borrowing money for reasons having little to do with the financial position of the business. For instance, during tight money periods many small businesses have difficulty borrowing money. Furthermore, industrial concerns are not in the business of taking interest rate risk and that's what they do when they borrow short term for permanent requirements. Here's an example of the sort of thing that has happened to many firms. Say the loan we made for five years was at a rate of 15%. At the time of the loan, experts were predicting lower interest rates. So we decided to borrow short term for three or six months until rates are lower. But three months from now interest rates are higher, and in six months they are even higher. To add insult to injury we find six months from now that the experts are predicting even higher interest rates. Let's look at it this way. If we made a list of managers who regret having violated the suitability principle, we would have a very long list. (We should add that the market for financial futures makes it easier to avoid some of the risks we are describing at an acceptable cost.)

Table 3-3 gives some examples of various sources and uses. Notice that we cannot rely on a balance sheet classification of current versus noncurrent to distinguish between permanent and temporary. For example, although accounts payable and accrued expenses are current liabilities, they are often permanent in the sense that they are automatically recreated. Suppose we purchase $100 each month on terms of net 30 days. Accounts payable will be $100 at the end of each month as long as monthly purchases are $100. We do pay $100 each month but this source is automatically renewed. (If

**Table 3-3**  *Examples of Permanent and Temporary Sources and Uses*

*Examples of Permanent Uses*
Fixed asset expenditures
Long-term debt payments
Dividends
Increases in current assets caused by permanent increases in sales

*Examples of Temporary Uses*
Increases in current assets caused by seasonal increases in sales

*Examples of Permanent Sources*
Net working capital from operations
Increases in trade payables and accrued expenses caused by permanent
  increases in sales
Long-term debt
Common stock

*Examples of Temporary Sources*
Short-term bank debt
Commercial paper (short-term unsecured note)
Increases in trade payables and accrued expenses caused by temporary
  sales increases

a firm does not pay its bills on time, the stretched portion of accounts payable and accrued expenses should not be viewed as permanent sources.)

The complicated part of analyzing adherence to the suitability principle is identifying if increases in current assets are temporary or permanent. This in turn depends on the nature of sales increases. Seasonality is the most common reason for temporary increases in current assets. A simple example will help us see the nature of these increases. Firm A has annual sales of $2,700 each year and monthly sales as follows:

| Month | Sales for Month |
|---|---|
| January–September | $100 |
| October | 400 |
| November | 600 |
| December | 800 |

The firm has only two assets (accounts receivable and inventory) and at the end of each month they equal 40% of sales for the month.

*Accounts Receivable + Inventory*

| Month | End of Month |
|---|---|
| January–September | $ 40 |
| October | 160 |
| November | 240 |
| December | 320 |

Let's first look at the $40 level that prevails from January–September. This is a permanent use because the dollar figure never is lower than this amount; thus, a permanent source is required. From the end of September to the end of December, there is an increase of $280. This is a temporary use because the amount will fall to $40 again at the end of January; so a temporary source is in order.

We should mention that Firm A may also have accounts payable and accrued expenses. The amounts of these liabilities when sales are $100 per month would be permanent sources. They would also increase during the busy season but these would be temporary increases and hence temporary sources.

### Analyzing Andrel's Flow of Funds Statement

We will now apply the concepts described above by analyzing Andrel's flow of funds statement for Year 2. Since our primary concern at this juncture is in using the concepts, our treatment of the subject will not be as comprehensive.

A useful starting point is to compute the percentage change in annual sales. They jumped from $4.5 million in Year 1 to $6.75 million in Year 2, an increase of about 50%. Since we are analyzing annual statements and the closing date is the same, we know there is no seasonal influence. This is important because a frequent cause of temporary increases in current assets is seasonality. However, the absence of a seasonal influence does not mean the increase is not temporary. For example, there might have been a one-time contract. Thus, we must look to other sources of information such as management's remarks in the annual report. For purposes of this discussion, let's assume our search reveals that the increase is permanent and annual sales of $6.75 million or more is expected in Year 3.

Next, we can examine the assets and current liabilities that vary automatically with sales. Are the increases in these accounts due to sales? Ratio analysis can help us gain insight into such issues. In this case we would infer that the increases are due to sales.

Net working capital from operations was $373,000 for Year 2 but this amount was not sufficient to support the needed increase in net working capital. This is why cash flow was a negative $59,000. Sales increased substantially causing large increases in accounts receivables and inventory. But this is only part of the reason for the negative cash flow. The firm's net income to total assets ratio for Year 2 was less than 4% (about 4% if we use average assets). If profits were higher, net working capital from operations would have been higher.

Let's now classify the uses and sources according to the guidelines in Table 3-3. All uses are permanent. All sources but the short-term bank debt are permanent. The increase in the short-term note of $597,000 is troublesome. This amount is due in one year. Where will the money come from to pay the loan? Assets will not decrease and operations are not likely to provide the cash. Thus, Andrel will need an external source or it will face financial embarrassment or worse.

We cannot jump to conclusions without further investigation. Sometimes short-term debt is more permanent than it looks. For example, sometimes asset-based financing arrangements are classified as short-term liabilities when in fact they are long term. At any rate, if this is not the case, then we can conclude that Andrel's management does not understand the suitability principle and it could pay a very high price learning it the hard way.

## STATEMENT OF CHANGES IN FINANCIAL POSITION

Firms are required to issue a flow of funds statement in their annual report, so the published statement is often the starting point for the analysis. The format frequently will differ from the one we have been discussing. Many firms include the following in the body of the statement: (net) working capital from operations, the change in each noncurrent account, and only one entry for a change in (net) working capital. In other words, the changes in current assets and current liabilities will appear as one number in the body of the statement. If this format is followed, and it is quite common, then the change in each current asset and current liability account will be shown below the body of the statement. Table 3-4 has an illustration based on Andrel for Year 2.

Table 3-5 summarizes the procedures discussed in the chapter for computing net working capital and cash flow from operations.

**TABLE 3-4**
**ANDREL CORPORATION**
Statement of Changes in Financial Position—Working Capital Basis
for Year 2

| | |
|---|---|
| Resources provided: | |
| Working capital from operations: | |
| Net income | $120,000 |
| Add: Depreciation expense | 233,000 |
| Increase in deferred taxes (noncurrent) | 20,000 |
| Working capital from operations | $373,000 |
| Common stock | 55,000 |
| Paid in capital | 115,000 |
| Total resources provided | $543,000 |
| | |
| Resources applied: | |
| Dividends | $ 60,000 |
| Net additions to fixed assets | 633,000 |
| Total resources applied | $693,000 |
| Decrease in working capital | $150,000 |

**ANDREL CORPORATION**
Composition of Working Capital

| | End of Year 1 | End of Year 2 | Increase (Decrease) in Working Capital |
|---|---|---|---|
| Cash | $ 40,000 | $ 55,000 | $ 15,000 |
| Accounts receivable | 750,000 | 1,125,000 | 375,000 |
| Inventory | 300,000 | 450,000 | 150,000 |
| Total current | $1,090,000 | $1,630,000 | |
| Accounts payable (trade) | $ 150,000 | $ 225,000 | (75,000) |
| Notes payable (bank) | 10,000 | 607,000 | (597,000) |
| Accrued income taxes | 25,000 | 38,000 | (13,000) |
| Other accrued expenses | 10,000 | 15,000 | (5,000) |
| Total current | $ 195,000 | $ 885,000 | ($150,000) |

**Table 3-5** *Procedures for Estimating Net Working Capital and Cash Flow from Operations*

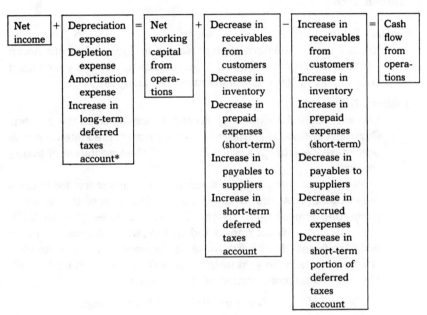

| Net income | + | Depreciation expense Depletion expense Amortization expense Increase in long-term deferred taxes account* | = | Net working capital from operations | + | Decrease in receivables from customers Decrease in inventory Decrease in prepaid expenses (short-term) Increase in payables to suppliers Increase in short-term deferred taxes account | − | Increase in receivables from customers Increase in inventory Increase in prepaid expenses (short-term) Decrease in payables to suppliers Decrease in accrued expenses Decrease in short-term portion of deferred taxes account | = | Cash flow from operations |

* Subtract a decrease

# Problems and Discussion Questions

## A. Solved Problems

### Problem 3-1A

You are given the information presented in Table 3-6 for the Acorn Company. Prepare a flow of funds statement for the year ended December 31, Year 2. Comment on the analysis.

### Solution 3-1A

We will follow the three step procedure explained in the chapter. Our view is that in learning how to construct the statement it is best to rely on this procedure and avoid the temptation of taking shortcuts.

We will not repeat earlier discussions of the importance of carefully reading financial statements other than to note the advice of computing annual sales growth. For Acorn, sales grew by 24% during Year 2. What impact did this growth have on the firm's need for funds? How were these needs met? These are the kind of issues we hope to gain insight about from the analysis. We will now turn to the construction of the statement.

#### Step 1. Compute Balance Sheet Changes
#### (In $ thousands)

| Sources | | Uses | |
|---|---|---|---|
| + Accounts payable | $100 | + Cash | $200 |
| + Long-term debt | 280 | + Accounts receivable | 200 |
| + Deferred taxes | 100 | + Inventory | 400 |
| + Common stock | 20 | + Net fixed assets | 600 |
| + Additional paid-in | | Total | $1,400 |
| capital | 600 | | |
| + Retained earnings | 300 | | |
| Total | $1,400 | | |

#### Step 2. Adjustments

1. We show net income as a source, and dividends as a use. We are not told what dividends are but we can estimate that dividends were zero as follows:

| | |
|---|---|
| Retained earnings at 12/31/Year 1 | $ 950 |
| + Net income for Year 2 | 300 |
| − Dividends | ? |
| = Retained earnings at 12/31/Year 2 | $1,250 |

**TABLE 3-6**
**ACORN COMPANY**
Income Statements
Years Ending December 31
(in $ thousands)

|  | Year 1 | Year 2 |
|---|---|---|
| Net sales | $5,000 | $6,200 |
| Cost of goods sold | 3,500 | 4,000 |
| Gross margin | $1,500 | $2,200 |
| Depreciation expense | 200 | 300 |
| Selling, general and administrative | 1,000 | 1,500 |
| Income before taxes | $ 300 | $ 400 |
| Income tax expense | 75 | 100 |
| Net income | $ 225 | $ 300 |

Balance Sheets
at December 31
(In $ thousands)

|  | Year 1 | Year 2 |
|---|---|---|
| Cash | $ 400 | $600 |
| Marketable securities | 900 | 900 |
| Accounts receivable | 600 | 800 |
| Inventory | 800 | 1,200 |
| Total current | $2,700 | $3,500 |
| Fixed assets (net) | 1,400 | 2,000 |
| Total assets | $4,100 | $5,500 |
| Accounts payable | $400 | $500 |
| Other current | 50 | 50 |
| Total current | $ 450 | $ 550 |
| Long-term debt | 1,500 | 1,780 |
| Deferred income taxes | 100 | 200 |
| Common stock | 200 | 220 |
| Additional paid-in capital | 900 | 1,500 |
| Retained earnings | 950 | 1,250 |
| Total | $4,100 | $5,500 |

2. Estimate net working capital by adding depreciation expense and the increase in long-term deferred taxes to net income.

| | |
|---|---:|
| Net income for Year 2 | $300 |
| + Depreciation expense for Year 2 | 300 |
| + Increase in long-term deferred taxes | 100 |
| = Net working capital from operations for Year 2 | $700 |

3. Estimate net amount spent on fixed assets by adding depreciation expense to the change in net fixed assets.

| | |
|---|---:|
| Change in net fixed assets | $600 |
| + Depreciation expense for Year 2 | 300 |
| = Net amount spent on fixed assets | $900 |

*Step 3. Incorporate Adjustments*
*Acorn Company*
*Flow of Funds Statement*
*Year Ending December 31, Year 2*
*(In $ thousands)*

| | | |
|---|---:|---:|
| *Sources* | | |
| From operations: | | |
| Net income | $300 | |
| + Depreciation expense | 300 | |
| Increase in deferred taxes (noncurrent) | 100 | |
| Total | | $ 700 |
| Accounts payable | | 100 |
| Long-term debt | | 280 |
| Common stock | | 20 |
| Additional paid-in capital | | 600 |
| | | $1,700 |
| | | |
| *Uses* | | |
| Accounts receivable | | $ 200 |
| Inventory | | 400 |
| Net amount spent on fixed assets | | 900 |
| Cash | | 200 |
| Total | | $1,700 |

| | |
|---|---:|
| Let's compute cash flow from operations. | (In thousands) |
| Net working capital from operations | $700 |
| − Increase in accounts receivable | 200 |
| − Increase in inventory | 400 |
| + Increase in accounts payable | 100 |
| Cash flow from operations | $200 |

Receivables and inventory increased at a greater rate than sales, an ominous sign. However, it could be due to the fact that growth in sales occurred during the last part of the year. An examination of quarterly data could provide insight on this matter. In any event, the substantial increases caused cash flow from operations to be much less than net working capital from operations. On the other hand, the positive figure tells us that operations, and the increase in the spontaneous liability, provided the funds to finance the increase in current assets, leaving the $200,000 cash flow available for other purposes. Still, the large increase in fixed assets caused a need for external capital. The firm relied primarily on equity financing and also on long-term debt, which suggests suitability was not violated. Finally, the firm retained all its earnings. One would expect a firm growing at a rapid rate to retain a large portion of its earnings.

## Problem 3-2A

Table 3-7 provides balance sheets at 12/31/Year 1 and 12/31/Year 6 and income statement data for Years 1–6 for the Jones Company. Prepare a flow of funds statement for the five years ended 12/31/Year 6 and cash flow from operations for the five-year period.

## Solution 3-2A

The change in balance sheet accounts are presented below.

| Sources | | Uses | |
|---|---|---|---|
| − Property, plant and | | + Cash | $   500 |
|    equipment (net) | $ 5,000 | + Marketable securi- | |
| + Accounts payable | 1,500 |    ties | 500 |
| + Deferred taxes | | + Accounts receivable | 3,500 |
|    (current) | 1,000 | + Inventory | 1,500 |
| + Deferred taxes (non- | | + Prepaid expense | 700 |
|    current) | 500 | − Long-term debt | 6,000 |
| + Common stock | 500 | Total | $12,700 |
| + Paid-in capital | 1,400 | | |
|    Retained earnings | 2,800 | | |
|    Total | $12,700 | | |

Turning to adjustments, first note that we are preparing a statement for the five years ended 12/31/Year 6, so we need income statement data for Years 2–6 only. We do not need to include the data for

**TABLE 3-7**
**JONES COMPANY**
Balance Sheets as of
12/31 Year 1 and 12/31 Year 6

|  | Year 1 | Year 6 |
|---|---|---|
| Cash | $ 1,000 | $ 1,500 |
| Marketable securities | 3,000 | 3,500 |
| Accounts receivable | 9,000 | 12,500 |
| Inventory | 8,000 | 9,500 |
| Prepaid expenses | 5,400 | 6,100 |
| Total current | $26,400 | $33,100 |
| Property, plant and equipment (net) | 25,000 | 20,000 |
| Total | $51,400 | $53,100 |
| Accounts payable | $ 7,000 | $8,500 |
| Accrued expenses | 5,000 | 5,000 |
| Deferred income taxes | 1,000 | 2,000 |
| Total current | $13,000 | $15,500 |
| Long-term debt | 14,000 | 8,000 |
| Deferred income taxes | 4,000 | 4,500 |
| Total | $31,000 | $28,000 |
| Common stock | 6,000 | 6,500 |
| Paid-in capital | 8,700 | 10,100 |
| Retained earnings | 5,700 | 8,500 |
| Total | $51,400 | $53,100 |

Income Statement Data:

*Years Ended 12/31*

|  | Year 1 | Year 2 | Year 3 | Year 4 | Year 5 | Year 6 |
|---|---|---|---|---|---|---|
| Net income after taxes | 9,000 | 10,000 | 9,500 | 9,500 | 9,000 | 10,000 |
| Dividends | 7,000 | 7,000 | 7,000 | 7,000 | 7,000 | 17,200 |
| Depreciation expense | 1,000 | 1,000 | 1,000 | 1,000 | 1,000 | 1,000 |

the year ended 12/31/Year 1. In other words, we are preparing a statement from the beginning of Year 2 to the end of Year 6, and Year 1 income statement data pertain to a prior period. Here are the adjustments:

1. Remove retained earnings change and show net income of $48,000 as a source, and dividends of $45,200 as a use.

2. Add depreciation expense and increase in long-term deferred taxes to net income to derive net working capital from operations.

| | |
|---|---:|
| Net income for five years | $48,000 |
| + Depreciation expense for five years | 5,000 |
| + Increase in long-term deferred taxes | 500 |
| = Net working capital from operation | $53,500 |

Notice that the increase in short-term deferred taxes is not included.

3. Add depreciation expense to change in net property, plant, and equipment to derive the net amount spent. As shown in Step 1, net property, plant, and equipment decreased, so it is a negative number in the procedure.

| | |
|---|---:|
| Change in property, plant and equipment (net) | ($5,000) |
| + Depreciation expense for five years | 5,000 |
| = Net amount spent on fixed assets | 0 |

The final step is to incorporate the adjustments into a final statement.

*Jones Company*
*Flow of Funds Statement*
*for Five Years Ending 12/31/Year 6*

| | | |
|---|---:|---:|
| *Sources* | | |
| From operations: | | |
| Net income | $48,000 | |
| + Depreciation | 5,000 | |
| + Deferred taxes (noncurrent) | 500 | |
| Total | | $53,500 |
| Accounts payable | | 1,500 |
| Deferred income taxes (current) | | 1,000 |
| Common stock | | 500 |
| Paid-in capital | | 1,400 |
| Total | | $57,900 |
| *Uses* | | |
| Dividends | | $45,200 |
| Marketable securities | | 500 |
| Accounts receivable | | 3,500 |
| Inventory | | 1,500 |
| Prepaid expenses | | 700 |
| Cash | | 500 |
| Long-term debt | | 6,000 |
| Total | | $57,900 |

Cash flow from operations is shown below. Notice that change in short-term deferred taxes is part of the computation.

**Cash Flow From Operations**
**for Five Years Ended 12/31/Year 6**

| | |
|---|---:|
| Net income | $48,000 |
| + Depreciation | 5,000 |
| − Deferred taxes (noncurrent) | 500 |
| Net working capital | $53,500 |
| Accounts receivable | (3,500) |
| Inventory | (1,500) |
| Prepaid expenses | (700) |
| Accounts payable | 1,500 |
| Deferred taxes | 1,000 |
| Cash flow from operations | $50,300 |

This problem was designed to give you practice with mechanics, and only summary income statement data were provided. Because of this it is much more difficult to interpret the flow of funds statement. However, it appears to be a profitable firm that is not growing very rapidly. We are inferring this from the fact that current assets have not increased that rapidly and our estimate of the amount spent on fixed assets was zero. Incidentally, this inference could be totally wrong because we might be missing important activity such as disposal of a segment of the business and an increase of another part. Notice that income statements alone would not enable us to detect such activity. However, it would probably be disclosed in accompanying footnotes.

# B. Discussion Questions

### 3-1B

Explain why the procedures used to compute net working capital and cash flow from operations and the net amount spent on fixed assets give estimates and not exact amounts.

### 3-2B

Explain what the suitability principle is.

### 3-3B

What is an accrued expense? How does it differ from other liabilities? Is it a real source of funds?

**3-4B**

Explain why and how certain current assets and current liabilities change automatically with sales.

**3-5B**

It was Mike's second week at his new job as junior credit analyst at Wheeling Bank. His assignment was to perform an in-depth analysis of a local firm. The firm's net income for the past year was $25,000 and depreciation expense was $15,000. Mike told his boss that the firm's cash flow for the year was $40,000. If you were Mike's boss, how would you respond?

**3-6B**

If a firm had a long-term asset account called long-term deferred taxes, how would a change in this account affect the computation of net working capital and cash flow from operations?

## C. Study Problems

### Problem 3-1C

The chapter explained that many published flow of funds statements present only the net change in net working capital in the body of the statement and separately list the changes in each component. This is often known as a working capital basis. Prepare a flow of funds statement on a working capital basis for the two solved problems—the Acorn Company and the Jones Company.

### Problem 3-2C

Table 3-8 has balance sheets for the Grange Company as of 12/31/Year 1 and 12/31/Year 2. Net income after taxes and depreciation expense for the year ended 12/31/Year 2 were $4 million and $2 million, respectively. Prepare a flow of funds statement for the year ended 12/31/Year 2.

### Problem 3-3C

You are given the financial statements shown in Table 3-9 for the Daly Company. Depreciation expense was $15,000 in Year 1 and $20,000 in Year 2.

1. Prepare a flow of funds statement for the year ended 12/31/Year 2.

2. Compute cash flow from operations for Year 2.

**TABLE 3-8**
**GRANGE COMPANY**
Balance Sheets at 12/31
(in $ thousands)

|  | Year 1 | Year 2 |
|---|---|---|
| Cash | $ 2,000 | $ 5,000 |
| Accounts receivable | 10,000 | 14,000 |
| Prepaid expenses | 15,200 | 19,500 |
| Inventory | 25,000 | 27,200 |
| Total current | $ 52,000 | $ 65,700 |
| Property, plant and equipment (net) | 80,000 | 74,000 |
| Total assets | $132,200 | $139,700 |
| Accounts payable | $ 25,000 | $ 28,500 |
| Accrued expenses | 17,000 | 20,000 |
| Total current | $ 42,000 | $ 48,500 |
| Long-term debt | 35,000 | 30,000 |
| Deferred income taxes | 6,000 | 8,000 |
| Total | $ 83,000 | $ 86,500 |
| Common stock | 20,000 | 20,000 |
| Retained earnings | 29,200 | 33,200 |
| Total | $132,200 | $139,700 |

3. Comment on the reliability of using net income plus depreciation as an estimate of cash flow from operations for this firm for Year 2.

*Problem 3-4C*

Table 3-10 offers income statements and balance sheets for the King Company. Prepare a flow of funds statement for the year ended June 30/Year 2. Also, compute cash flow from operations for Year 2.

*Problem 3-5C*

Table 3-11 has balance sheets and income statement data for the Basden Company. You are to prepare a flow of funds statement for the six years ended 12/31/Year 7. Also, compute cash flow from operations for the six-year period.

*Problem 3-6C*

You are given the income statement and balance sheets shown in Table 3-12 for the Alton Company. Prepare a flow of funds statement for the year ended 6/30/Year 2. For the year ended 6/30/

**TABLE 3-9**
**DALY COMPANY**
Income Statements for Years Ended 12/31
(000 omitted)

|  | Year 1 | Year 2 |
|---|---|---|
| Net sales | $780 | $900 |
| Cost of goods sold | 530 | 620 |
| Gross margin | $250 | $280 |
| Selling, general and administrative | 50 | 70 |
| Income before taxes | $200 | $210 |
| Income tax expense | 100 | 105 |
| Net income | $100 | $105 |

Balance Sheets at 12/31
(000 omitted)

|  | Year 1 | Year 2 |
|---|---|---|
| Cash | $ 50 | $ 30 |
| Accounts receivable | 110 | 140 |
| Inventory | 125 | 155 |
| Deferred charges | 80 | 80 |
| Total current | $365 | $405 |
| Property, plant and equipment (net) | 250 | 280 |
| Total assets | $615 | $685 |
| Accounts payable | $190 | $220 |
| Accrued income taxes | 50 | 75 |
| Total current | $240 | $295 |
| Long-term deferred income taxes | 20 | 100 |
| Total | $260 | $395 |
| Common stock | 10 | 8 |
| Paid-in capital | 270 | 169 |
| Retained earnings | 75 | 113 |
| Total | $615 | $685 |

Year 1 the firm had net sales of almost $900,000 and net income after taxes was $2,000.

*Problem 3-7C*

A firm during its first year of operations had net income of $55,000. Included in expenses were:

| Depreciation expense | $45,000 |
|---|---|
| Amortization expense | 15,000 |
| Labor expense | 255,000 |

**TABLE 3-10**
**KING COMPANY**
Income Statement
for Year Ending 6/30/Year 2

| | |
|---|---|
| Net sales | $2,000 |
| Cost of goods sold | 1,200 |
| Gross margin | $ 800 |
| Operating expenses (including depre- | |
| ciation expense of $55) | 300 |
| Selling, general and administrative | 400 |
| Income before taxes | $ 100 |
| Income taxes | 40 |
| Net income | $ 60 |
| Dividends | $ 30 |

Balance Sheets
at 6/30

| | Year 1 | Year 2 |
|---|---|---|
| Cash | $ 200 | $ 300 |
| Accounts receivable | 400 | 453 |
| Inventory | 325 | 400 |
| Total current | $ 925 | $1,153 |
| Property, plant and equipment | 700 | 780 |
| less accumulated depreciation | 110 | 165 |
| Property, plant and equipment (net) | 590 | 615 |
| Total assets | $1,515 | $1,768 |
| Accounts payable | $ 105 | $ 210 |
| Short-term debt | 250 | 322 |
| Total current | $ 355 | $ 532 |
| Long-term debt | 522 | 582 |
| Deferred income taxes | 118 | 44 |
| Stockholders' equity | 520 | 610 |
| Total liabilities and stockholders' equity | $1,515 | $1,768 |

Of the total labor expense, $215,000 was paid during the year. The remainder was paid in the first month of the second year of operations. Compute net working capital from operations for its first year. (Assume there is no long-term deferred taxes account.)

**TABLE 3-11**
**BASDEN COMPANY**
Balance Sheets
(000 omitted)

|  | at 12/31/Year 1 | at 12/31/Year 7 |
|---|---|---|
| Cash | $ 13 | $ 15 |
| Accounts receivable | 27 | 35 |
| Inventory | 44 | 64 |
| Prepaid expenses | 40 | 37 |
| Total current | $124 | $151 |
| Fixed assets (net) | 72 | 125 |
| Total | $196 | $276 |
| Notes payable (bank) | $ 32 | $ 72 |
| Accounts payable (trade) | 27 | 42 |
| Accrued income taxes | 43 | 64 |
| Other current | 2 | 3 |
| Total current | $104 | $181 |
| Long-term debt | 10 | 5 |
| Deferred income taxes | 15 | 25 |
| Common stock | 35 | 30 |
| Retained earnings | 32 | 35 |
|  | $196 | $276 |

Income Statement Data (000 omitted)

| Year Ended 12/31 | Net Income after Taxes | Dividends | Depreciation Expense |
|---|---|---|---|
| Year 1 | $35 | $40 | $11 |
| Year 2 | 35 | 40 | 12 |
| Year 3 | 45 | 50 | 14 |
| Year 4 | 56 | 61 | 15 |
| Year 5 | 67 | 72 | 17 |
| Year 6 | 71 | 76 | 19 |
| Year 7 | 73 | 45 | 21 |

**TABLE 3-12**
**ALTON COMPANY**
Income Statement for Year Ended 6/30/Year 2
(In $ thousands)

| | |
|---|---|
| Net sales | $952 |
| Cost of goods sold | 756 |
| Gross profit | $196 |
| Selling expense | 167 |
| Administrative* | 60 |
| Income before taxes (loss) | ($ 31) |
| Income taxes | (14) |
| Net loss | ($ 17) |

*Includes depreciation expense of $25,000

Balance Sheets
(In $ thousands)

| | at 6/30/Year 1 | at 6/30/Year 2 |
|---|---|---|
| Cash | $ 65 | $ 15 |
| Accounts receivable | 84 | 94 |
| Inventory | 93 | 147 |
| Total current | $242 | $256 |
| Net fixed asets | 150 | 115 |
| Total | $392 | $371 |
| Accounts payable | $ 87 | $207 |
| Accrued expenses | 10 | 50 |
| Total current | $ 97 | $257 |
| Long-term debt | 195 | 40 |
| Common stock | 50 | 50 |
| Retained earnings | 50 | 24 |
| Total | $392 | $371 |

# Part

# II

# Financial Planning and Control

# 4
# Cost/Volume/Profit Analysis

This chapter discusses cost/volume/profit analysis (CVP), which is concerned with analyzing the interactions among sales, costs and profits. We cover a number of specific applications of CVP such as computing break-even levels and profit targets and evaluating alternative pricing strategies and cost configurations. However, our primary objective is to provide you with a solid grasp of the nature and behavior of costs. This foundation is necessary for most financial analyses, so the basic concepts apply to most topics covered in this book. For instance, after studying CVP you should be more effective in performing ratio analysis. Furthermore, we will see that managers rely on the basic messages of CVP when preparing operating and capital budgets and when developing financial plans. An understanding of the concepts underlying CVP is essential for a proper assessment of a firm's risk and this assessment is part of virtually every business decision.

We begin by discussing breakeven analysis. Then we turn our attention to other applications of CVP. Next we explain operating leverage which helps tie together the basic concepts underlying CVP.

## *Breakeven Analysis*

Breakeven analysis is a handy tool that gives information regarding how much a firm must sell to earn a profit of zero. This analysis is used by managers in profit planning and by external analysts in assessing the financial health of a firm. Suppose, for instance, you work in the credit department of a firm and your boss asks you to assess whether a customer who is currently incurring losses will earn a profit next year. You could rely on breakeven analysis to help make the assessment.

We will begin by explaining two formulas used to compute a firm's breakeven point, that is, the level of sales required to achieve a zero profit. A simple example will help. The data we need are in Table 4-1. The firm sells one product, widgets, purchased for 80¢ and sold for $1. The only other expenses are salaries and rent. There is one employee, a sales clerk,

**Table 4-1**  *Joe Jones Company*

| | |
|---|---|
| Product: | Widgets |
| Selling price: | $1 per unit |
| Cost of widget: | 80¢ per unit |
| Salaries: | 5¢ per unit |
| Rent: | $40,000 per year |

**Table 4-2**  *Breakeven Formulas*

*Breakeven Point—Number of Units*

$$\text{Breakeven Point} = \frac{\text{Fixed Expenses}}{S - V}$$

Where:

S = Selling price per unit
V = Variable expenses per unit

*Breakeven Point—Dollars of Sales*

$$\text{Breakeven Point} = \frac{\text{Fixed Expenses}}{1 - \dfrac{V}{S}}$$

Note: A breakeven computation is made by some analysts as part of a financial statement analysis. Generally, the second formula is used and total variable expenses are substituted for V and total revenues are substituted for S.

who is paid a commission of 5¢ for each widget sold. The rent is $40,000 per year.

To conduct the analysis, expenses must be divided into two categories: fixed and variable. A *fixed expense* is the one that remains the same over a given time period irrespective of volume. In our example, rent is a fixed expense because it will be $40,000 per year no matter how many units are sold. A *variable expense* is one that changes in direct proportion to volume, that is, variable expenses change at the same percentage rate as volume. In our example, commissions and the cost of widgets are variable expenses because they vary at the same rate as sales. For instance, if the firm sells 100 units, cost of goods sold and salary expenses will be $80 and $5, respectively. If sales are twice as large, these expenses will be twice as large as well.

The *breakeven point* is the level of sales at which the firm will earn a profit of zero dollars, that is, it is the sales volume at which total revenues equal total costs. Sometimes we compute a breakeven point in units; at other times the focus is on the dollar level of sales. There is a formula for each and these are defined in Table 4-2. We will illustrate the computations using the data for the Joe Jones Company.

### *Breakeven Point in Units*

$$\text{Breakeven Point} = \frac{\text{Fixed Expenses}}{S - V}$$

Where:

$S$ = Selling price per unit
$V$ = Variable expenses per unit

$$= \frac{\$40,000}{\$1 \text{ per unit} - 85¢ \text{ per unit}}$$

$$= 266{,}667 \text{ units}$$

### *Breakeven Point in Dollars*

$$\text{Breakeven Point} = \frac{\text{Fixed Expenses}}{1 - \dfrac{V}{S}}$$

$$= \frac{\$40,000}{1 - \dfrac{85¢ \text{ per unit}}{\$1 \text{ per unit}}}$$

$$= \$266{,}667$$

Joe must sell 266,667 units to breakeven. Assuming this number is sold the annual income statement would be as follows:

*Joe Jones Company*
*Income Statement*
*for Year 1*

| | |
|---|---:|
| Revenues (266,667 units × $1) | $266,667 |
| Cost of goods sold (266,667 units × 80¢) | 213,334 |
| Commissions expense (266,667 units × 5¢) | 13,333 |
| Rent | 40,000 |
| Net income | $0 |

We can also rely on a breakeven chart to compute a firm's breakeven point. Figure 1 has one for the Joe Jones Company. The fixed expense line is flat depicting these expenses are the same regardless of volume. The toal costs line consists of fixed plus variable expenses. Points on this line are derived by multiplying the number of units by the variable costs (85¢ per unit) and adding to this amount fixed expenses of $40,000. The total revenue line is derived by multiplying the number of units by the selling price ($1 per unit). The intersection point, Point N in Figure 1, is the breakeven level. At sales levels to the right of the intersection point, the firm will earn profits and at sales levels to the left of the point the firm will incur losses.

Information on a firm's breakeven level of sales is useful because it provides insight on profitability and risk. As we will see later, the closer a firm is to its breakeven point, the more variable its profits will be. Moreover, analysts often use these formulas to study the impact of various revenue and cost configurations on a firm's breakeven point, profit levels and/or potential losses. We must keep in mind, however, that expectations regarding sales is also a critical part of an assessment of profitability and risk. Say we expect sales for a firm to be 200,000 units and the breakeven point is 195,000. How likely is it that the firm will incur a loss? It depends on the likelihood of sales falling below 195,000 units. If, for example, there was 100% probability that sales will be 200,000 units then there is a zero chance of a loss.

This analysis is applicable not only to firms but also to individual products, specific services or divisions of firms. For example, when contemplating the introduction of new products, managers typically calculate how many units must be sold to break even. It is not usually the firm's intent to merely break even, but the information is important to know. For one thing, it tells the manager how long it will take for the product to reach breakeven.

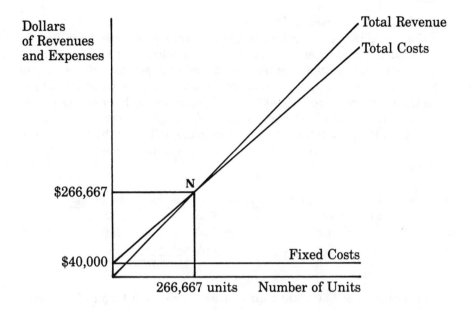

**Figure 4-1   Breakeven Chart for Joe Jones Company**

The breakeven formulas tell us a great deal about the factors affecting profit and loss and the variability of profits. For instance, if fixed expenses are zero, a firm's breakeven level would be zero, that is, there is a zero probability of the firm incurring a loss. But fixed expenses are virtually never zero in business situations. To begin with, a certain level of fixed expenses are inevitable for firms. Moreover, fixed expenses create opportunities which can influence number of units sold, selling price per unit and/ or variable expenses per unit. From the formula we see that a change in any one or a combination of these variables can affect the breakeven point. More importantly for our purposes, it's the interaction among fixed expenses, selling price per unit, and variable expenses per unit that affect breakeven levels and the variability of profits.

# *Other Applications of CVP Analysis*

Breakeven analysis is only one example of the application of CVP. We will now consider three others. These are not only useful on their own but they will also enable you to learn how to apply CVP generally.

### Illustration 1. Profit Targets

Joe Jones is not in business to break even. He wants to earn a profit. How much should he aim for? Answer: He should seek a rate of return on the capital invested that is at least sufficient to compensate him for the risk he would take. Suppose he estimates that to earn a satisfactory rate of return, profits must be $50,000. Should Joe enter the business? One critical issue is evaluating whether he can sell enough units to earn his profit target. CVP can help him estimate how many units must be sold. We can figure this out by adding the profit target to the numerator of the breakeven formula.

$$\frac{\text{Number of Units}}{\text{to Achieve Profit}} = \frac{\text{Fixed Expenses} + \text{Profit Target}}{\text{Selling Price} - \text{Variable Expenses}}$$
$$\text{Target} \qquad \text{per Unit} \qquad \text{per Unit}$$

$$600{,}000 = \frac{\$40{,}000 + \$50{,}000}{\$1 - 85¢}$$

The firm must sell 600,000 units to achieve the profit target of $50,000.

This analysis would be done before entering the business (or introducing a new product or service). Also, we often would test the impact of various profit targets as well as the effects of alternative selling prices and variable expense rates. This kind of analysis is an integral part of a firm's budgeting and planning processes. (Indeed, because of this, CVP is frequently referred to as profit planning and analysis, or some similar name.)

### Illustration 2. Pricing and Cost Decisions

Thus far we have been focusing on required sales and viewing costs and selling prices as given. Often, various cost configurations are possible and options are available for altering the relationship among prices and costs. CVP can help us analyze these alternatives. Let's look at some examples:

Let's alter our example somewhat. Suppose Joe Jones is considering entering the widget business and as before widgets cost 80¢ each, labor is 5¢ per unit and the selling price is $1. Joe wants an annual profit of $50,000 and he estimates that 500,000 units can be sold each year, provided the location is suitable. How much rent can Joe afford to pay? The profit target formula explained in the previous illustration will tell us. Fixed expenses are the unknown. Solving the equation we find that rent must be no more than $25,000 per year.

$$500{,}000 \text{ units} = \frac{\text{Fixed Expenses} + \$50{,}000}{1 - .85}$$

$$\text{Fixed Expenses} = \$25{,}000$$

In this example rent is the only fixed expense. Had there been others, we would still make the calculations shown above. However, when computing maximum fixed expenses, we would subtract fixed expenses other than rent from the total to figure out the maximum rent Joe could pay. Finally, this example dealt with fixed expenses but we can readily see that the above equation can be employed to analyze any one or a combination of variable expenses.

Let's now turn to a pricing decision. We will use Joe Jones again, but this time the per unit selling price and variable expenses are $1 and 85¢, respectively, annual rent is $40,000. Also, let's assume that Joe sets a profit target of $50,000 and that he estimates he can sell 600,000 units, which you may recall produces the desired profit. Suppose he is advised that by cutting the selling price fom $1 to 94¢ he could sell 1.2 million units. Let's look at profits for both prices.

|  | *Price of $1* | *Price of 94¢* |
|---|---|---|
| Revenues | $600,000 | $1,128,000 |
| Variable expenses | 510,000 | 1,020,000 |
| Fixed expenses | 40,000 | 40,000 |
| Profits | $ 50,000 | $ 68,000 |

Should he cut his price? We can't answer this question without additional analysis.

As noted previously, an important financial goal of a firm is to earn a rate of return sufficient to compensate for risk. A reduction in price will increase profits but the firm may need more assets to generate the higher sales. In other words, we must analyze the rate of return on investment, not just the level of profits. Moreover, we must evaluate the impact on risk. CVP can help us analyze risk. Recall that a price of $1, the firm's breakeven point is 266,667 units. At a price of 94¢, the breakeven point is 444,444 units as shown below:

$$444,444 \text{ units} = \frac{\$40,000}{.94 - .85}$$

Cutting the price to 94¢ not only increases the breakeven point but it also makes profits less stable. We will consider the variability issue when we discuss operating leverage.

Let's now look at how CVP can help us with a decision to purchase or produce a product (i.e., a make versus buy decision). Suppose Joe decides not to cut his price and settles for estimated sales of 600,000 units. He is considering making widgets instead of buying them. He estimates that fixed expenses will increase by $60,000 to $100,000 because of new fixed expenses such as depreciation expense and the salary of a production manager. The variable cost of producing a widget is estimated at 50¢, so total variable expense per unit will be 55¢ per unit.

Profits would be $170,000 if the firm makes the widgets, versus $50,000 if the firm buys them as shown below:

|  | *Buy Widgets* | *Make Widgets* |
|---|---|---|
| Revenues | $600,000 | $600,000 |
| Variable expenses | 510,000 | 330,000 |
| Fixed expenses | 40,000 | 100,000 |
| Profits | $ 50,000 | $170,000 |

Should he make or buy widgets? The answer is more analysis is necessary. As we emphasized in the previous example we must figure out the rate of return on the investment required to make widgets and we must also assess risk. With respect to risk, we can analyze the impact on the firm's breakeven point.

$$222{,}222 \text{ units} = \frac{\$100{,}000}{1.00 - .55}$$

The breakeven point declines to 222,222 units. (We can also analyze the impact on profit variability but we are deferring our discussion of this topic to a later section of the chapter.)

Before turning to Illustration 3, let's briefly review what we learned from Illustration 2:

1. We saw that CVP can help analyze pricing and costing decisions. When the decision involves an investment (or disinvestment) we must be concerned about rate of return and risk. To evaluate investments we rely on capital budgeting analysis which is a subject of a later chapter. Notice, however, that an understanding of CVP is essential for effective capital budgeting analyses.

2. An earlier example showed that when fixed expenses are zero a firm's breakeven point is zero, so positive fixed expenses are necessary for the breakeven point to be greater than zero. Given the existence of fixed expenses, however, a change in any one (or combination) of the variables in the formula—fixed expenses, selling price per unit, variable expenses per unit—can produce a change in a firm's breakeven point.

3. Many people assume that whenever fixed expenses increase, a firm's breakeven point increases as well. Our example of make versus buy should dispel that notion. Fixed expenses increased from $40,000 to $100,000 but the breakeven point decreased because the increase in fixed expenses caused an increase in the difference between selling price per unit and variable expense per unit and the latter increase more than offset the higher fixed expenses. More generally, the effect on risk of a change in fixed expenses depends on the impact of the change on the relationship between selling price per unit and variable expenses per unit.[1]

### *Illustration 3. Contribution Analysis*

Contribution analysis is an application of CVP that focuses on analyzing the impact of various actions on the coverage of fixed expenses and profits. Before illustrating what a handy tool contribution analysis is, we must introduce some new terms.

*Contribution margin,* also known as *marginal income,* is defined as the difference between revenues and variable expenses. The following three versions are used in practice:

1. Total contribution margin is equal to total revenues minus total variable expenses. If Joe's firm sells 100 units, revenues will be $100 and total variable expenses will be $85, so total contribution margin will be $15.

2. Per unit contribution margin is equal to selling price per unit minus variable expenses per unit. For the Joe Jones Company, it's 15¢.

3. Contribution margin ratio is equal to one minus the ratio of total variable expenses to total revenue, or one minus the ratio of variable expenses per unit to selling price per unit. For the Joe Jones Company, it's 15%.[2]

The word contribution in this context must be clearly understood. Contribution to what? The answer is contribution to fixed expenses and profits. To see this and how useful this application of CVP can be, let's again rely on Joe Jones. We will assume he has decided to make widgets, so fixed expenses will be $100,000 and per unit variable expenses will be 55¢.

---

[1] Actually, it's a bit more complex. The effect on risk of a change in fixed expenses depends on the impact noted plus the effect, if any, of the change on the demand curve for the product or service being considered.
[2] If you look back at Table 4-2, you will see that the denominator for the breakeven formula in units is equal to per unit contribution margin and the denominator of the dollar version is equal to the contribution margin ratio. We point this out because you may see the breakeven formulas presented with the contribution terms in them.

Further, the per unit selling price is $1 and Joe anticipates annual sales of 600,000 units.

Suppose it turns out that Joe's estimate of sales was much too optimistic, and as the year progresses it appears that annual sales will be only 200,000 units. Finally, let's assume that a wholesaler contacts Joe and offers to purchase 150,000 units at 60¢ each. In deciding whether to accept the order, it is informative to study the impact of accepting or rejecting the order. One way to do this is to compute an estimated income statement for the year without the order, and another income statement assuming the order is accepted. These are presented next:

### Estimated Annual Income Statements

|  | Reject Order | Accept Order |
|---|---|---|
| Estimated sales in units | 200,000 units | 350,000 units |
| Revenues | $200,000 | $290,000 |
| Variable expenses | 110,000 | 192,500 |
| Fixed expenses | 100,000 | 100,000 |
| Profits (losses) | ($ 10,000) | ($ 2,500) |

The loss would be $7,500 less by accepting the order. (We could have derived the $7,500 figure by multiplying the 5¢ per unit contribution margin by the size of the order.)

To see the importance of contribution margin, let's restate the two income statements as follows:

|  | Reject Order | Accept Order |
|---|---|---|
| Revenues | $200,000 | $290,000 |
| Variable expenses | 110,000 | 192,500 |
| Contribution margin | 90,000 | 97,500 |
| Fixed expenses | 100,000 | 100,000 |
| Profits (losses) | ($ 10,000) | ($ 2,500) |

As long as the total contribution margin increases, profits will improve. Notice that the emphasis is on the short run. Even with the order, Joe will incur a loss of $2,500. The business is not viable if he continues to incur losses. He must either make it profitable by earning a satisfactory return on investment or cease operations.[3]

---

[3] Some small businesses continue to operate even though profits are not large enough to provide an adequate return for the risk assumed. Apparently, the owners of these firms derive other benefits. In any event, investors normally demand a rate of return sufficient to compensate for risk.

Generally a business, product line or division must cover both fixed and variable expenses. If profitability is unlikely, then a decision to withdraw is in order. When losses are being incurred but profits are expected, then the issue is: Do we continue in business in the meantime and/or accept special orders such as the one described above? CVP provides the following guidance.

1. If the selling price per unit is less than variable expenses per unit, each additional dollar of sales will magnify the firm's loss. In that case, operations should cease unless there is some overriding consideration such as trying to maintain a skilled work force.

2. If selling price is higher than variable costs but lower than total costs, operate because losses will be lower in the short run. (In other words, operating helps to pay overhead.) This action gives the firm the time necessary to make the product (or service) profitable or to find an alternative product that can cover both fixed and variable expenses plus a suitable profit.

3. If the firm has a chance for a special order such as the one described above, the issue is more complex. Short-term profits will improve as long as selling price per unit is greater than variable expenses per unit. However, sometimes it is worthwhile to sacrifice a short-term profit improvement to achieve another objective such as maintaining the integrity of a firm's pricing policy.

We will now turn our attention to the difficulties that arise in applying CVP.

## PROBLEMS IN APPLYING CVP

When applying CVP in practice, you will become painfully aware of the critical assumptions underlying many of the applications as well as the inherent limitations of these analyses. This section discusses some of these.

### Linear Assumption
Look back for a moment at the breakeven chart in Figure 1 to remind yourself that it consists of three straight lines. The straight line for revenues

implies that selling price per unit is the same no matter how many units are sold. Frequently, a firm can sell only so many units at a given price. Also, it is quite common for variable expenses per unit to depend on the level of volume. Further, fixed expenses are not nearly as fixed as they look. Often, above some volume, fixed expenses increase because of factors such as capacity limits; below some level, fixed expenses decrease because of such actions as the elimination of a production shift. It's also important to keep in mind that fixed expenses vary over time and in the long run no expenses are fixed. For example, the salary of a financial analyst is normally fixed for a given period of time, but the amount changes when the analyst gets a raise. Finally, management action can change an expense classified as fixed. In the case of the analyst, if management fires this person, the salary is not a fixed expense any more.

Because of the above complexities, breakeven and similar analyses are easier to apply in the short-run context, say one year or less. Also, it's important to recognize that breakeven and similar calculations are not as precise as they look. Finally, it is probably best to think in terms of a breakeven range rather than a point, and the same advice applies to other estimates (e.g., sales required to achieve a profit target) as well.

### Semi-Variable Expenses

All the illustrated analyses required that we classify expenses into fixed and variable categories. Many expenses are semi-variable, which means they are partially fixed and partially variable. An example is telephone expense which usually involves a basic (fixed) charge plus a charge that depends on usage. To conduct CVP analyses, we must subdivide semi-variable expenses into their fixed and variable components. Typically it is not possible or feasible to separate the fixed and variable components as precisely as we would like, so the resulting analyses are not as accurate as we might like. Now while the task of subdividing semi-variable expenses can be frustrating, the process itself can be valuable. Analysts often learn a great deal about the nature of specific costs and the firm in general when performing this task.

### Alternative Views of Variable Expenses

For the purpose of the analyses we performed, we defined a variable expense as one that varies directly with sales. Some expenses will vary with some other measure of activity. An example is the telephone expense we just discussed. The variable portion varies with the number and type of telephone calls. Another example is payroll taxes which vary with the dollar level of labor. A final example is heating expense that varies with the price of energy and the weather. Thus, whenever we see the phrase variable expense we should ask: varies with what?

To deal with expenses that vary with an activity other than sales when conducting CVP analyses, we must (somehow) relate this other activity to sales. As we will see below, this is necessary in order to classify the expense as fixed, variable or semi-variable.

## Alternative Definitions of Breakeven

All sorts of breakeven computations are made in practice. Let's look at the following income statement for Saskel Company.

| | |
|---|---:|
| Net sales | $1,000 |
| Cost of goods sold | 500 |
| Gross profit | $500 |
| Selling, general and administrative expenses | 300 |
| Earnings before interest and taxes (EBIT) | $200 |
| Interest expense | 50 |
| Earnings before taxes | $150 |
| Income taxes | 50 |
| Net income | $100 |

Depending on the purpose of the analysis, we may focus on net income, earnings before taxes, EBIT, or all three of them. Let's illustrate by computing the breakeven point in dollars for EBIT, EBT, and net income for Saskel.

The first step is to subdivide the two expense categories into fixed and variable components. Let's say that cost of goods sold is 80% variable and 20% fixed, and selling, general and administrative expenses are 50% fixed and 50% variable.

| Semi-Variable Expense | Fixed Portion | Variable Portion | Total |
|---|---:|---:|---:|
| Cost of goods sold | $100 | $400 | $500 |
| Selling, general and administrative | 150 | 150 | 300 |
| Totals | $250 | $550 | $800 |

Variable operating expenses are $550, or 55% of net sales of $1,000. Hence, given the fixed operating expenses of $250 and the variable rate, we can compute the EBIT breakeven of $555.56 as shown on the next page.

$$\text{EBIT Breakeven} = \frac{250}{1-55\%}$$
$$= \$555.56$$

If sales are $555.56,[4] EBIT would be zero. However, the firm would incur a loss because of interest. Let's compute EBT breakeven. To do this we must classify interest expense. Let's assume that in this instance it is fixed. As shown below, EBT breakeven is $666.67.

$$\text{EBIT Breakeven} = \frac{300}{1-55\%}$$
$$= \$666.67$$

If sales are $666.67, earnings before taxes would be zero. If this is so, then taxes would be zero and thus the breakeven point for net income would also be $666.67.

In the above example, interest expense was assumed to be a fixed expense. Interest expense could be fixed, variable or semi-variable depending on the relationship between the amount of debt outstanding and sales. Suppose a firm borrows $10 million on January 1 to buy fixed assets and this is the only debt it will use for the current year. Interest expense on this debt will be a fixed expense because debt outstanding for the year will be $10 million regardless of sales volume.[5] Now, assume another firm borrows $5 million on January 1 from an insurance company to buy fixed assets, and the firm also plans to rely on bank debt to finance seasonal working capital needs. The level of working capital, and hence the bank debt, would vary with sales, although not necessarily at the same rate as sales. Thus, in this case interest expense would be semi-variable.

Before proceeding, we should point out that lenders, credit analysts and security analysts generally have access only to income statement data. Thus, they must work with the dollar version of the breakeven formula. Further, they encounter much more difficulty in classifying expenses than an analyst working for the firm. Nevertheless, usually reasonable estimates can be derived. Hence, it is feasible to compute a firm's breakeven point and also perform other kinds of CVP analyses. Our own view is that more

[4] As noted earlier, because of various complexities, we cannot compute breakeven points as precisely as we would like. Hence, rounding to the nearest penny, or dollar, for that matter, is generally not a good idea because it implies a false precision. However, this specificity is useful for illustrating computations and that is why we sometimes round to the nearest penny.

[5] Notice that classification as fixed does not imply the interest rate is fixed for the life of the loan. As you may know, some loans carry a variable rate which means the interest rate varies with a benchmark rate like the prime. Let's say that is the case for this $10 million loan. What we would do is estimate an average interest rate for the year and multiply it by $10 million to compute interest expense for the year. This amount would be classified as a fixed expense in conducting CVP analyses.

of this type of analysis should be performed by external analysts. For instance, we think it is a good idea to compute a breakeven point as part of a financial statement analysis especially when there is concern regarding whether the firm in question will be profitable.

### Product Mix

To illustrate breakeven analysis, we relied on the Joe Jones Company that had only one product. When a firm has more than one, a new complexity arises because the analysis must assume something about sales mix. To see the added difficulty, we will rely on an example of computing the breakeven point when a firm has two products.

Assume that Firm N had the following results for its most recent fiscal year:

|  | Product A | | Product B | Total |
|---|---|---|---|---|
| Sales 1,000 units @ $1 | $1,000 | 500 units @ $2 | $1,000 | $2,000 |
| Variable expenses, 50¢ per unit | 500 | 60¢ per unit | 300 | 800 |
| Fixed expenses | 200 | | 600 | 800 |
| Net income | $ 300 | | $ 100 | $ 400 |

Suppose we wanted to calculate Firm N's breakeven point in units. Typically, we would proceed as follows:

*Step 1. Calculate average sales per unit*

$$\frac{\text{Total Revenue}}{\text{Total Units}} = \frac{2,000}{1,500} = \$1.33$$

*Step 2. Calculate average variable expenses per unit*

$$\frac{\text{Total Variable Expenses}}{\text{Total Units}} = \frac{\$800}{1,500} = 53¢$$

*Step 3. Compute the breakeven point using averages*

$$\frac{\$800}{1.33 - .53} = 1,000 \text{ units}$$

The breakeven point for Firm N is 1,000 units. But this calculation assumes a certain sales mix. In this case we calculated an average (weighted) of per unit selling prices and variable expenses based on the most recent year's sales. Other weights could be employed, but to calculate the breakeven point for the firm as a whole, a weighted average must be used based on some sales mix assumption. If the actual sales mix differs, then the break-even point will be different. Thus, it is possible for Firm N to sell less than 1,000 units and earn a profit. Alternatively, if the actual sales mix is different from the one assumed, it is possible for Firm N to sell more than 1,000 units and still incur a loss.

There is a related issue which many people find confusing. Before we can discuss it, we must compute the breakeven point for each of Firm N's two products:

$$\textit{Product A}$$
$$\frac{\$200}{1 - .50} = 400 \text{ units}$$
$$\textit{Product B}$$
$$\frac{\$600}{2 - .60} = 429 \text{ units}$$

Notice that the sum of the two breakeven points does not equal the total breakeven point of 1,000 units calculated earlier. The reason for the difference is that the per unit contribution margin of each product differs. In calculating the breakeven point for the firm as a whole, we used the previous year's sales to compute the weighted average. Specifically, we gave Product A a weight of 2/3 and B a weight of 1/3 which means that we assumed that 2/3 of each total unit sales will be for A and 1/3 will be for B. If actual sales were 400 and 429, respectively, then the weights would be different and so would our calculation of the breakeven point for the firm as a whole.

# Operating Leverage

Because of fixed expenses, profits are more variable than sales. This principle is known as leverage. It is useful to divide leverage into two categories: operating and financial. Operating leverage is concerned with the effects of fixed operating expenses on the variability of operating profits (EBIT). Financial leverage is concerned with the effect that fixed financial charges (interest expense and preferred dividends) have on the relationship between operating profits (EBIT) and earnings per share (EPS) and/or the relationship between rate of return on assets and rate of return on equity.

The following income statement format shows the different focus of operating and financial leverage:

$$\text{Operating Leverage} \begin{cases} \textit{Sales} \\ - \text{ Cost of goods sold} \\ = \text{ Gross profits} \\ - \text{ Selling expenses} \\ - \text{ General expenses} \\ = \text{ Operating profits (EBIT)} \end{cases}$$

$$\text{Financial Leverage} \begin{cases} - \text{ Interest expense} \\ = \text{ Earnings before taxes} \\ - \text{ Taxes} \\ = \text{ Net income} \\ - \text{ Preferred dividends} \\ = \text{ Earnings for common stock} \\ \div \text{ Common shares outstanding} \\ = \text{ EPS} \end{cases}$$

In this chapter we will focus on operating leverage. (Financial leverage is considered further in the last chapter which discusses the analysis of financing decisions.)

Operating leverage helps us assess operating or business risk. When we apply the principle of operating leverage, we are trying to come to grips with the following kinds of issues: What is the probability that the firm will incur an operating loss? How much will operating profits change if sales change by a certain amount? How can we reduce the inherent variability of operating profits?

To explain the principle of operating leverage, we will rely on the original version of the Joe Jones Company. Recall that Joe's company sells widgets for $1 each, per unit variable expenses are 85¢ each, and the only fixed expense is rent of $40,000 per year. Suppose that Joe's landlord makes the following offer: Instead of $40,000 per year, Joe can pay rent equal to 7% of sales. Let's first look at what the alternative arrangement would do to his firm's breakeven point.

$$\begin{aligned} \text{Breakeven} &= \frac{\text{Fixed Expenses}}{1-92\%} \\ &= \frac{0}{1-92\%} \\ &= \text{Zero} \end{aligned}$$

This illustrates what we explained earlier: When a firm has no fixed expenses, the breakeven point will be zero and hence there will be no chance of incurring a loss. Here we refocus the point as follows: When a firm has no fixed operating expenses, there is no chance that operating profits (EBIT) will be below zero.

Let's now assume that Joe takes the rent offer and sales are 600,000 units the first year and 1,200,000 units the second year. The income statements for the first two years are as follows:

|  | Year 1 | Year 2 |
|---|---|---|
| Sales | $600,000 | $1,200,000 |
| Operating expenses (92% of sales) | 552,000 | 1,104,000 |
| Operating profit | $ 48,000 | $ 96,000 |

Notice that both sales and operating profits doubled. This same rate of change is not unique to this example and we can make the following general statement: In the absence of fixed operating expenses, operating profits (EBIT) will always change at the same rate as sales.

Let's now see what would happen if Joe rejects the offer and decides to pay a fixed rent of $40,000 per year.

|  | Year 1 | Year 2 |
|---|---|---|
| Sales | $600,000 | $1,200,000 |
| Variable operating expenses (85% of sales) | 510,000 | 1,020,000 |
| Fixed operating expenses (rent) | 40,000 | 40,000 |
|  | $ 50,000 | $ 140,000 |

If sales double (i.e., increase by 100%), operating profits will increase by 180%. Fixed operating expenses lever operating profits and we can reach the following general conclusion: When a firm has fixed operating expenses, operating profits (EBIT) will always change at a greater rate than sales.

Why would Joe reject the offer of variable rent? After all, he can't incur an operating loss if he accepts the offer. We can see from the above example that there is an opportunity to earn more (i.e., he gets more return for more risk). Notice that at a sales level of 600,000 units, profits are higher with fixed rent. Furthermore, if sales grow, profits grow at a greater rate with the fixed rent option. On the other hand, we must keep in mind that leverage is a two-edged sword. Should sales decrease in the second year, operating profits would decline at a greater rate with fixed rent. How does Joe make the choice? There is no formula to guide him. He has to make a judgment. CVP and knowledge of the principle of operating leverage help him make that judgment. (We should mention that Joe's assessment of demand for the firm's products is a critical factor in making the final decision.)

## DEGREE OF OPERATING LEVERAGE (DOL)

The degree of operating leverage (DOL) is a sensitivity measure. Specifically, it is defined as follows: The degree of operating leverage is the percentage change in operating profits produced by a given percentage change in sales. We can rely on two different formulas to calculate it.

$$DOL = \frac{\text{Total Revenues} - \text{Total Variable Expenses}}{\text{Total Revenues} - \text{Total Variable Expenses} - \text{Fixed Operating Expenses}}$$

For the Joe Jones Company at the $600,000 sales level

$$DOL = \frac{\$600,000 - \$510,000}{\$600,000 - \$510,000 - \$40,000} = 1.8$$

We will interpret the meaning of 1.8 after we present the second formula.

$$DOL = \frac{Q(S - V)}{Q(S - V) - F_o}$$

Where:

Q = Sales volume in units
S = Per unit selling price
V = Per unit variable expenses
$F_o$ = Fixed operating expenses

Using Joe Jones to illustrate:

$$DOL = \frac{600,000\,(1.00 - .85)}{600,000\,(1.00 - .85) - \$40,000} = 1.8$$

The DOL is a measure of the sensitivity of profits at a given sales level. The DOL of 1.8 for Joe Jones means that for any percentage change in sales from the sales level of 600,000 units, operating profits will change by 1.8 times that percentage change. For instance, if sales increase by 10% from the 600,000-unit level, operating profits will increase by 18% and if sales decrease by 10% from this level, operating profits will decrease by 18%.

The second formula enables us to review some important characteristics of operating leverage. To begin, note that if fixed operating expenses are zero the DOL will always equal one, signifying that in the absence of fixed operating expenses, sales and operating profits would change at the same rate. However, given the existence of fixed operating expenses, the DOL can change if any one or a combination of variables in the equation change. The Q in the formula, sales volume in units, tells us that the DOL measure pertains to a given level of sales. Thus, it would be incorrect, for example, to say that the Joe Jones Company has a DOL of 1.8. The correct statement is that the Joe Jones Company has a DOL of 1.8 at a sales level of 600,000 units. At different sales levels, the DOL would be different. Table 4-3 has the DOL for Joe Jones Company at various sales levels. This table will give you a chance to practice the computations. Moreover, the table illustrates a point we mentioned earlier which is that the closer a firm is to its breakeven point, the more variable its profits will be (i.e., the DOL is higher).

Suppose we are told that Firm A has a DOL of 5.0 and Firm B has a DOL of 1.5 at their respective sales levels. Will Firm A's operating profits vary more than Firm B's next year? It depends on how much sales change. Say Firm A's sales increase by 2% and Firm B's sales increase by 50%. Firm A's operating profits will increase by 10% and Firm B's operating profits will increase by 75%. The point is that the DOL alone does not determine variability. Sales must change to begin with and it is the variability rate of sales together with the DOL that determines variability of operating profits.

**Table 4-3** *Joe Jones Company—DOL Calculations for Varying Sales Levels*

*Assume*

| | |
|---|---|
| Fixed expenses | = $40,000 |
| Per unit selling price | = $1.00 |
| Per unit variable expense | = .85 |

*Formula*

$$DOL = \frac{Q\,(S - V)}{Q\,(S - V) - F_o}$$

| Sales (units) | DOL |
|---|---|
| 300,000 | 9.0 |
| 400,000 | 3.0 |
| 500,000 | 2.1 |
| 600,000 | 1.8 |
| 700,000 | 1.6 |
| 800,000 | 1.5 |

Before closing, we will describe one practical application of DOL. In the chapter on ratio analysis, we explained that analysts compare ratios over time to help identify trends. Say we find that a firm's net income to sales ratio increases. This improvement could be due to actions by management to control costs (or raise prices) or it could be due to operating leverage. Computing the DOL for this firm would help us assess the impact of leverage. Because of the complexities described earlier with respect to classifying expenses, we would not be able to derive an exact DOL. Nevertheless, we normally would be able to derive a reasonable estimate and would find this information useful.

This chapter explained various applications of CVP and the principle of operating leverage. Throughout the chapter the focus was on explaining the nature and behavior of costs and studying the impact of various factors and choices on the level and movement of costs and profits.

Finally, we should stress again the importance and pervasiveness of the concepts covered in this chapter. They help with planning and control and assist in a fundamental way in assessing the risk involved in most financial decisions.

# Problems and Discussion Questions

## A. Solved Problems

### Problem 4-1A

John Martin plans to open a record store. He estimates the following for the first year of operations.

- Sales will be 100,000 units and selling price per unit will be $6.

- All records will be purchased for $3.75 each.

- Annual amounts for salaries, rent, and depreciation are estimated at $50,000, $40,000 and $10,000, respectively, and these amounts will not be affected by sales volume—that is, they are fixed expenses.

- All other operating expenses are variable and will be equal to 5% of sales.

- There will be no interest expense and the income tax rate is estimated at 40%.

1. Prepare an estimated income statement for the first year of operations.

2. Calculate the breakeven point in units and dollars.

3. Compute the number of units that must be sold for Mr. Martin's firm to earn a profit before taxes of $120,000.

### Solution 4-1A

1. The estimated income statement is as follows:

Record Store<br>Projected Income Statement<br>for Year 1

| | |
|---|---:|
| Net sales (100,000 @ $6) | $600,000 |
| Cost of goods sold (100,000 @ $3.75) | 375,000 |
| Gross profit | $225,000 |
| Salaries, rent and depreciation | 100,000 |
| Other operating expenses (5% of sales) | 30,000 |
| Profit before taxes | $ 95,000 |
| Income taxes @ 40% | 38,000 |
| Net income | $ 57,000 |

How would you rate this performance? While earning profits in the first year of operations is an encouraging sign, we cannot answer this question without an assessment of risk and return. To illustrate, let's assume that there is no risk and we are 100% sure that profits will be $57,000 every year. Assume further that Mr. Martin must invest $2 million to operate the business. This is a rate of return of about 3%, which is less than he could earn by putting his money in an insured savings account.

2. Relying on the formulas in Table 4-2, we can compute the breakeven points as shown below:

   *Raw Data*

   | | | |
   |---|---|---|
   | Selling price per unit | | $6.00 |
   | Variable expenses per unit | | |
   |    Product cost | $3.75 | |
   |    Other variable (5% × 6.00) | .30 | 4.05 |
   | Fixed expenses | | 100,000 |

   $$\text{Breakeven in Units} = \frac{\$100,000}{\$6.00 - \$4.05} = 51,282 \text{ units}$$

   $$\text{Breakeven in Dollars} = \frac{\$100,000}{1 - \dfrac{4.05}{6.00}}$$

   $$= \frac{\$100,000}{1 - 67^{1}/_{2}\%} = \$307,692$$

   Notice that this is the pretax breakeven point, but given a pretax profit of zero net income also will be zero. There is a difference, however, when we compute profit targets as we will see next.

3. We are asked to compute sales required for pretax profit of $120,000. We simply add this figure to the fixed expenses number in the formulas.

   $$\frac{\$100,000 + \$120,000}{6.00 - 4.05} = 112,820 \text{ units}$$

   $$\frac{\$100,000 + \$120,000}{1 - 67^{1}/_{2}\%} = \$676,923$$

   If you multiply $6 times the 112,820 unit figure shown above, you will get $676,920. The difference is due to rounding out numbers.

   Suppose we were asked to compute the sales in units required to produce a net income after taxes of $120,000. What we do is add to the numerator the amount that must be earned before taxes to give $120,000 after taxes. A little algebra will help:

Earnings Before Taxes (EBT) − Taxes = Earnings After Taxes (EAT)

But we know taxes equals EBT times the tax rate (TR). Hence,
$$EBT - EBT \,(TR) = EAT$$
Remember how to factor?
$$EBT \,(1 - TR) = EAT$$
$$EBT = \frac{EAT}{1 - TR}$$
Let's plug in the numbers:
$$EBT = \frac{120,000}{1 - 40\%}$$
$$= \$200,000$$

So we must earn $200,000 before taxes to have net income of $120,000. Now we can derive the target.

$$\frac{\$100,000 + \$200,000}{6.00 - 4.05} = 153,846 \text{ units}$$

### Problem 4-2A

You are given the following information for a firm:

| | |
|---|---|
| Estimated sales | 70,000 units |
| Selling price per unit | $4 |
| Variable expense per unit | $2.50 |
| Fixed expenses | $60,000 |
| Income taxes | zero tax rate |

1. Compute the breakeven point in units.

2. Calculate the DOL at 70,000 units.

3. Assume fixed expenses increase to $75,000, and variable expenses per unit fall to $2.30. Compute the breakeven point in units and the DOL at 70,000 units.

### Solution 4-2A

1. The breakeven point is 40,000 units.

$$\frac{\$60,000}{\$4.00 - \$2.50} = 40,000 \text{ units}$$

2. We will rely on the unit version of the formula for DOL which was described in the chapter.

$$\text{DOL} = \frac{Q(S-V)}{Q(S-V) - F_o}$$

$$= \frac{70,000 (4.00 - 2.50)}{70,000 (4.00 - 2.50) - \$60,000} = 2.33$$

For any change in sales from the 70,000 unit level, operating profits will change by 2.33 times the percentage change in sales. For instance, if sales decrease by 10% from the 70,000 unit level, profits would decrease by 23.3%.

3. The breakeven point and DOL both change as shown below.

*Breakeven*

$$\frac{\$75,000}{4 - 2.30} = 44,118 \text{ units}$$

*DOL*

$$\frac{70,000 (4 - 2.30)}{70,000 (4 - 2.30) - 75,000} = 2.71$$

They both increase because the increase in fixed expenses more than offsets the accompanying decrease in variable expenses per unit.

### Problem 4-3A

Look back at the information in problem 4-1A for the record store Mr. Martin plans to open. As noted there, he expects to sell 100,000 units the first year. Suppose a radio station offers to buy 50,000 records during the first year at $4.50 each. Assuming he will still sell the 100,000 units at $6 and per unit variable expenses will be $4.05 for all units, should he accept this offer?.

### Solution 4-3A

Let's first restate the projected income statement shown in the answer to Problem 4-1A as follows:

*Projected Income Statement*
*for Year 1*

| | |
|---|---|
| Net sales (100,000 units @ $6) | $600,000 |
| − Variable expenses (100,000 units @ $4.05) | 405,000 |
| = Contribution margin | $195,000 |
| Fixed expenses | 100,000 |
| Profit before taxes | $ 95,000 |
| Income taxes | 38,000 |
| Net income | $ 57,000 |

Let's now compute the projected income statement using the above format, assuming the order is accepted.

*Projected Income Statement*
*for Year 1*
*with Order*

| | |
|---|---|
| Sales (100,000 units @ $6 and 50,000 units @ $4.50) | $825,000 |
| Variable expenses (150,000 @ $4.05) | 607,500 |
| Contribution margin | 217,500 |
| Fixed expenses | 100,000 |
| Profit before taxes | $117,500 |
| Income taxes | 47,000 |
| Net income | $ 70,500 |

Since the selling price per unit for the order is greater than the variable expenses per unit, there is an increase in the contribution margin. The increase in contribution margin tells us how much profit before taxes will increase because of the order. Specifically, the per unit contribution margin is 45¢ ($4.50 − $4.05) and multiplying this by the size of the order (50,000 units) gives $22,500, which is the increase in total contribution margin and hence the increase in profit before taxes. Of course, we must pay more taxes, so the effect on net income is less as shown. Now we can't conclude the firm should accept the order until we evaluate the impact on rate of return and risk.

We should add a caveat about fixed expenses. We assumed above that fixed expenses would not change. For a relatively large order like the one described above, fixed expenses likely would change and this example provides an opportunity to discuss why. If the store is no longer large enough and/or more fixed assets are needed, rent and depreciation would increase. Further it is likely that salaries would increase because there would be 50% more volume and normally we would expect an increase such as this to affect the amount of labor needed.

## B. Discussion Questions

### 4-1B
Define the following:
Variable Expense
Semi-Variable Expense
Breakeven Point
Degree of Operating Leverage
Total Contribution Margin

### 4-2B
Explain how the principle of operating leverage can help the analyst assess risk.

### 4-3B
Distinguish between operating leverage and financial leverage.

### 4-4B
Evaluate the following statement:
"An increase in fixed expenses will always increase a firm's break-even point and its DOL."

### 4-5B
Do you agree that since a firm will not incur a loss if there are no fixed expenses that firms should try to avoid fixed expenses whenever possible?

### 4-6B
Suppose you were told that a firm has a DOL of 1.8 at a given sales level. Assuming no changes in fixed expenses, selling price per unit, and variable expenses per unit, in what direction would you expect its DOL to change if sales decrease?

## C. Study Problems

### Problem 4-1C
Below are estimates for the Greenburg Company for the coming year.

- Annual sales will be $110,000 and the selling price per unit will be 80¢ for all units.

- All goods will be purchased ready for sale at 50¢ apiece.

- Fixed expenses for the year are: depreciation, $1,600; rent, $7,300; salaries, $14,500.

- All other expenses are variable and are equal to four cents per unit.

- There are no income taxes.

1. Calculate the breakeven point in units and in dollars.

2. Calculate the total contribution margin, the contribution margin ratio and the per unit contribution margin.

3. Compute the DOL at the expected sales level relying on the dollar version of the formula explained in the chapter. Then compute the DOL at the same sales level, relying on the unit version of the formula.

### Problem 4-2C

Relying on the data for the Greenburg Company in Problem 4-1C, compute the breakeven point in units and dollars, and the DOL assuming the changes below. Treat each change independently.

- Total fixed expenses are $18,200.

- Variable expenses decrease by 4¢ per unit.

- Total fixed expenses are $18,200 and variable expenses decrease by 2¢ per unit.

- Selling price per unit is 60¢.

- Selling price per unit is 90¢.

- Selling price per unit is 90¢, variable expenses per unit decrease by 50%, and total fixed expenses are $18,200.

- Volume is 120,000 units.

- Volume is 150,000 units.

### Problem 4-3C

The Axton Company sells one product and expects sales will be 300,000 units for the coming year. Selling price per unit and per unit variable expenses are $2.50 and $1, respectively. Total fixed expenses will be $400,000, and the income tax rate is 40%. Management has set $75,000 as the target for net income after taxes. Management would like your advice on a number of matters. Will the profit target be achieved next year under current plans? If not, management will consider lowering the price to $2.20 and spending $50,000 on advertising next year to increase demand. Management estimates these actions would increase expected sales to 540,000 units. Would the profit target be achieved with these actions and sales of 540,000 units? If so, should management take these actions? Do other factors need to be considered as well? What are some of these factors?

### Problem 4-4C

You are given the following information for the Knight Company.

- Expected sales for next year are 30,000 units, but management believes that actual sales might be 20% higher or 20% lower than this expected amount. The selling price per unit will be $10 irrespective of what actual sales are for the year.

- Total fixed expenses are $25,000 and variable expenses are 88% of sales. Taxes are zero.

Included in the variable expense percentage is 12% for rent. The owner of the property has offered to accept a fixed rent of $34,000 per year instead of the 12% of sales. Should Knight accept the offer? Provide numerical support for your answer.

### Problem 4-5C

Mr. Hogan has been selling handcrafted pottery at the local fair for the past five years. During the most recent year the selling price per unit was $22, variable expenses per unit were $14, total fixed expenses were $7,000, and 1,000 units were sold. Mr. Hogan is pessimistic about the coming year. He plans to lower his price to $20 but he thinks that even with this action he would be lucky to sell 1,000 units next year. Fortunately, he has figured a way to reduce expenses and is considering the following two options:

- If fixed expenses are kept at $7,000, variable expenses can be reduced to $11 per unit.

• If fixed expenses are reduced to $5,000, variable expenses can be lowered to $12 per unit.

1. Compute the breakeven point in units and the DOL at 1,000 units for each option.

2. At what sales level would profit be the same for each option? (You may ignore income taxes.)

3. What would you recommend?

### Problem 4-6C

The Rothco Company which manufactures and sells two products, Product A and Product B, has developed the following projections for the coming year.

|  | Units | Product A | Units | Product B | Totals |
|---|---|---|---|---|---|
| Sales | 10,000 | $15,000 | 7,500 | $18,000 | $33,000 |
| Variable expenses |  | 13,000 |  | 5,400 | 18,400 |
| Fixed expenses |  | 1,000 |  | 9,000 | 10,000 |
| Profit before taxes |  | $ 1,000 |  | $ 3,600 | $ 4,600 |

1. Compute the pretax breakeven point in dollars for Product A and Product B.

2. Suppose you were just given the totals shown in the third column above. Compute the pretax breakeven in dollars for the firm as a whole. Does this breakeven point equal the sum of the breakeven levels for Products A and B? If so, why? If not, why not?

3. What implications, if any, does your answer to part two have for the use of breakeven computations in conducting financial statement analyses?

### Problem 4-7C

Joan Williams is going to form a firm to distribute an industrial product to manufacturing firms. She expects to sell 300,000 units the first year at $50 per unit. The cost to purchase a unit is $45. All other costs are fixed and are estimated to be $600,000 per year. Operations proceeded as planned and after the first three months Ms. Williams concludes that sales, costs and profits for the year would be as expected. Shortly thereafter, the largest manufacturer in the industry, who was not expected to do business with the firm and hence was not included in the sales estimate, offers to purchase 100,000 units at the price of $47 per unit.

1. Compute what profits before taxes would be with and without the large order.
2. Compute the breakeven point for the firm with and without the order.
3. Should Ms. Williams accept the offer? Why?

## Problem 4-8C

The Buten Company purchases its products ready for sale. Selling price per unit is $40, variable expenses per unit are $30 and total fixed expenses are $40,000. Management expects to sell 8,000 units during the coming year. For some time, consideration has been given to doing some assembly work in-house. No investment would be required because it is a manual process and there would be no need to carry more inventory. Because of the additional labor required to assemble the product, total fixed expenses would increase to $100,000. On the other hand, per unit variable expenses would decrease from $30 to $20. The decision to assemble would not affect estimated sales levels or the per unit selling price. Finally, assume a zero tax rate.

1. Compute profits for each alternative (i.e., to assemble or to continue to purchase products fully assembled).
2. Calculate the breakeven point for each alternative.
3. Compute the DOL for each alternative at the estimated sales level of 8,000 units.
4. What would you recommend if you were told that the expected sales level of 8,000 units would likely be achieved? What would you recommend if you were told that there is a 25% chance sales would be 5,000 units, a 50% chance they would be 8,000 units and a 25% chance they would be 11,000 units?

# 5
# Cash Budgeting

This chapter explains how to prepare and use a cash budget, which is a statement of estimated cash inflows and cash outflows for some future period. A cash budget is a tool used by managers and analysts to help plan and control the flow of cash. Employed most often for short-term planning and control, cash budgeting assists managers in addressing issues such as the following:

- Will the firm need to raise cash during the next year? If so, how much and when? How should the need be financed?

- Why did actual cash inflows and cash outflows differ from budgeted amounts?

- Will the firm generate excess cash during the coming year? If so, how much and when? How should the anticipated surplus be employed?

The chapter begins with an overview of cash budgeting to demonstrate that it is an essential ingredient of short-term planning and control. Then we discuss planning and control and explain in detail the process of developing an operating budget. This discussion is useful on its own and it is also necessary to enable you to fully appreciate the crucial role of cash budgeting and to understand how the numbers on a cash budget are derived. Next we show how to construct a cash budget and how to use it as a management tool. To insure that you will not get bogged down in details, we will avoid a number of mechanical issues and computational complexities. These are covered in the appendix to this chapter.

# Overview of Cash Budgeting

The process of cash budgeting includes the following:

- Selecting time horizon.
- Developing estimates.
- Constructing a cash budget and taking appropriate action.
- Monitoring the cash budget, that is, comparing actual cash flows to budgeted amounts and taking necessary action.

We can prepare a cash budget for a day, a week, a month, a quarter, a year or some combination of the foregoing. Generally, the maximum is one year or less, and the intervals within the planning horizon depend on the needs of the firm. For instance, a firm might prepare estimates of daily cash flows for the next 30 days and estimates of monthly inflows and outflows for the subsequent eleven months.

Let's assume a firm, whose sales are seasonal, decides to prepare a monthly cash budget for the next year. The analyst would estimate cash inflows and outflows for the next year and prepare a schedule such as the following:

| Month | Cash Inflows | Cash Outflows | Net Cash Flows |
|---|---|---|---|
| January | 42,500 | 44,000 | (1,500) |
| February | 46,000 | 47,000 | (1,000) |
| March | 39,000 | 41,000 | (2,000) |
| April | 33,000 | 36,000 | (3,000) |
| May | 53,000 | 56,000 | (3,000) |
| June | 70,000 | 76,000 | (6,000) |
| July | 59,000 | 66,000 | (7,000) |
| August | 70,000 | 62,000 | 8,000 |
| September | 80,000 | 71,000 | 9,000 |
| October | 80,000 | 70,000 | 10,000 |
| November | 53,000 | 47,000 | 6,000 |
| December | 44,000 | 43,000 | 1,000 |

Normally a cash budget would include a detailed list of cash inflows and outflows for each period (each month in our example). As we will see later these specifics are important for judging the reliability of estimates and for making comparisons between actual and budgeted amounts. For discussion purposes let's assume we analyzed the detailed lists of cash inflows and cash outflows and concluded that the estimates are reasonable.

What does the information tell us? The firm is expecting negative cash flows for the first seven months of the year and positive amounts for the last five. This pattern is not unusual. In fact, it is typical in a seasonal business to have several consecutive months of negative cash flows during the "busy season," when receivables and inventory are high, and positive amounts at other times during the year. What if all the amounts were negative? This would indicate a more permanent need for cash instead of a temporary requirement.

Practice varies with respect to funding seasonal shortages of cash. Some firms rely on short-term debt either from a bank or from another source such as issuing commercial paper to finance the temporary asset increases caused by seasonally higher sales. Other firms rely on their own cash. What these firms do is to keep money temporarily invested in marketable securities like Treasury bills and to liquidate these investments when they need the cash to finance the temporary build-up in receivables and inventory.

Chapter 3 explained the suitability principle, which tells us that temporary needs require short-term sources and permanent or long-term needs require permanent or long-term sources such as equity financing or long-term debt. Does the above cash budget signal a temporary or permanent requirement? It appears to be temporary but to be sure it would help to compute a cumulative sum of the net cash flow figures. This additional information is shown below along with the net cash flow figures already presented.

| Month | Net Cash Flows | Cumulative Amount |
|---|---|---|
| January | (1,500) | (1,500) |
| February | (1,000) | (2,500) |
| March | (2,000) | (4,500) |
| April | (3,000) | (7,500) |
| May | (3,000) | (10,500) |
| June | (6,000) | (16,500) |
| July | (7,000) | (23,500) |
| August | 8,000 | (15,500) |
| September | 9,000 | (6,500) |
| October | 10,000 | 3,500 |
| November | 6,000 | 9,500 |
| December | 1,000 | 10,500 |

The cumulative amount column is simply a running total of the net cash flow figures. For instance, February's negative $2,500 is derived by adding the negative net cash flow amounts for January and February.

Is the need for cash temporary or permanent? The three consecutive positive amounts signal a temporary need. However, we can't be sure because all the figures are estimates. There is no simple rule or formula for making decisions based on figures such as these because it requires a judgment based on one's confidence in the estimates. We should point out, however, that some people do rely on simple rules. For example, you might encounter a guide like the following: For a cash shortage to be considered temporary, there must be at least two consecutive positive amounts and one must be at least 25% greater than the maximum estimated need, that is, the largest negative number in the cumulative amount column.

For purposes of discussion, let's suppose that we are going to borrow to finance the need and our assessment of the estimates leads us to conclude that the need is temporary.[1] We still must resolve two issues: How much money should we borrow? When should we borrow the money? The cumulative amount column shows a maximum need of $23,500 in July. Normally, we would plan to arrange financing for more than the maximum negative figure and the extra amount is called a cushion or margin of safety. Later in the chapter we discuss how to set an appropriate margin of safety and we will only mention here that often it is a substantial sum such as 40% to 50% or more of the maximum need.

Suppose we decide to arrange for $35,000 of financing. The next issue is when to borrow. If we borrow the total amount in January, we will be paying interest on money we don't require because the expected shortage in January is $1,500. We could try for a separate loan each month but this is a risky strategy because we may be turned down. Fortunately, there are lending arrangements which resolve this dilemma. For example, a line of credit permits one to borrow all or part of a predetermined amount (the line) over a specific period of time, typically one year, and to repay all or part of the line at any time. Hence, a line of credit is a viable option for financing the firm's seasonal cash requirements for the coming year.

If we knew the sales of the firm in our example were seasonal, why did we bother to perform an analysis? Why didn't we simply conclude that a short-term financing source was in order? The reason is that many firms have both temporary and permanent requirements and so a careful appraisal of the information contained in the cash budget is necessary to distinguish between the two types of need. For instance, in our example, had all the cumulative amounts been negative, we likely would have concluded that a short-term and a long-term source of funds were required.

With respect to the positive cumulative amounts, the same kind of analy-

---

[1] As explained later, we likely would perform additional analysis to help make this assessment. For instance, we might revise the cumulative amounts based on the assumption that customers will take longer to pay.

sis is necessary to decide what to do with the money. If the positive amounts are temporary, then investment in marketable securities may be in order. Further, the cash budget can help us choose the appropriate maturity for the marketable security. For instance in our example, the positive amounts likely will be needed early in the next year, so we should plan to invest these amounts for several months. Had our example shown mostly positive cumulative amounts, we likely would have concluded that this indicated a more permanent build-up in cash. Thus, we probably would plan to do something more permanent with the money like acquiring additional fixed assets.

Once the year begins, the analysts should record actual cash inflows and outflows and compare them to budgeted amounts. All substantial variances should be investigated and corrective action should be taken, if necessary. For example, customers might take longer to pay than anticipated and this will cause cash inflows to be below budgeted figures. By making comparisons on a timely basis—monitoring the budget—we would learn about this right away. Suppose we find that slower collections are due to inefficiencies in the credit department. We could take steps to correct the problem and reverse the situation. Had we not monitored the budget, we probably would have learned about the credit department inefficiencies at a later date and we likely would be facing a more serious problem. Keep in mind that major crises usually start out as manageable problems that have not been dealt with in the right way and/or at the right time.

# Cash Budgeting: An Integral Part of Planning and Control Functions

Well-managed firms have effective planning and control systems for both the long term (e.g., five years or longer) and the short term (e.g., next year). Cash budgeting is generally an essential part of short-term planning and control. This section briefly describes these functions.

Before proceeding, we should note that there are no universally accepted definitions of the terms we will employ. For instance, a cash budget is frequently referred to as a cash forecast or a cash plan. Our purpose here is not to present ideal definitions; rather it is to describe terms and functions in a way that allows you to appreciate the environment in which cash budgeting takes place. With this in mind, we will begin our discussion with a description of strategic planning.

*Strategic planning* may be viewed as the process of setting objectives, designing strategies and formulating policies. The word "process" is used to emphasize that planning is an ongoing activity. It is not a document. Moreover, strategic planning is an integrated activity in the sense that one part of the process is not finalized until all the elements are in place. For instance, consideration of policies can influence objectives and strategies.

An *objective* or *goal* is an expression of what a firm wants to accomplish. For example, a primary financial objective for most firms is to increase the market value of its common stock, although this goal may be stated another way such as attaining certain rate of return targets. A nonfinancial objective might be that the firm will be a responsible corporate citizen. Strategies provide an answer to the following question: How will we accomplish our objectives? Policies flow from strategies and provide guidelines for managers and other employees. For example, a strategy for increasing market share might be to offer more generous credit terms and this would be translated into a specific set of credit terms like net 90 days. In this example, increasing market share is an objective, more generous credit terms is a strategy, and credit terms of net 90 days is a policy.

*Financial planning* is one component of strategic planning. It is concerned with providing insight on the profitability of various objectives, estimating the funds needed to implement strategies, and designing financial policies. For example, suppose we wish to start a new business. We would have to estimate the profitability of the venture, how much capital is required, and how to raise the needed capital. This is financial planning.

At the end of the strategic planning process in a given year, a financial plan is prepared which includes projected financial statements. For instance, a financial plan might consist of estimated annual income statements and balance sheets for each of the next five years.[2] These statements represent what the firm intends to accomplish in terms of sales, profits, etc., and the proposed financial policies such as how much long-term debt will be employed. A financial plan normally is somewhat tentative and it is during the budgeting process (described below) that financial targets are finalized. Moreover, as noted, strategic planning is an ongoing activity which is undertaken on an annual basis in many firms. Financial planning is part of this and the financial plan typically is updated and revised on an annual basis.

Finally, many people refer to financial planning (and budgeting) as financial forecasting. For our purposes, when we discuss forecasting we mean predicting something that is beyond management's control like the level of

---

[2] The preparation of these statements is covered in the next chapter. There we show that monthly income statements and balance sheets convey the same information on cash needs and surpluses as a cash budget. Thus, when we say cash budgeting is essential, we are talking about the process. The specific tool employed depends on the preference of managers.

interest rates and inflation. When we use the terms planning and budgeting, we are talking about making something happen. Forecasting is needed to do planning and budgeting but it is not the same thing.

*Management control* is a system or process which motivates people who work for the company to achieve the goals of the organization. Control is also concerned with the evaluation process which addresses issues such as the following: Were actual results different from what was planned? If so, why? What should we do about it? Planning and control are related in a fundamental way. Productive planning requires an effective control system and vice versa.

We will now turn our attention to short-term planning and control systems. The discussion will show how cash budgeting is part of both short-term planning and control and also explain how the basic estimates for a cash budget are derived. To illustrate, we will describe a system that is based on one used by a small firm which we will call the Eftco Company. For reasons that will be obvious, facts and figures will be disguised. Moreover, in the interest of clarity we will omit a number of details.

### Eftco Company

Eftco has formal short-term planning and control systems. The tools of the system are an operating budget and a cash budget. We will discuss the process in the context of these two budgets which are interrelated in that they are parts of the overall budgeting process. We should mention that the firm does strategic planning and a financial plan is revised each year in late summer. The first year of the plan becomes the starting point for the budget process which begins in October with the preparation of an operating budget.

# Operating Budget

The operating budget at Eftco is the key tool of its short-term planning and control system. It contains the firm's targets (goals for the next year) and is the device used to help insure that targets are met. It is also the starting point for the preparation of the cash budget, but we should note that the operating budget is not approved until the cash budget is approved. More precisely they are approved at the same time.[3]

---

[3] Look at it this way. The cash budget tells managers if they can afford the targets shown in the operating budget. Say the initial attempt shows a substantial cash need and the firm cannot raise the money at an acceptable cost. The firm would have to revise its targets.

Table 5-1 has part of the operating budget for the Eftco Company for a recent year. It has been simplified. For example, the last expense, "other," is for $40,300. Actually, this represents about ten items on the firm's budget. We summarized them into one number for convenience but it is important to note how detailed the actual budget was. It is also important to keep in mind that Table 5-1 has only part of the budget. The remainder includes targets for capital expenditures, dividends, accounts receivable amounts, inventory levels and similar items. As we will see, these other targets are needed to derive the figures for a cash budget.

The portion of the budget shown in Table 5-1 looks like an income statement but it is not the same thing. It was prepared and issued prior to the start of the year. Moreover, it was a summary of targets for revenues and expenses for the next year. The word "target" means something very

### TABLE 5-1
### EFTCO COMPANY
Operating Budget
Year Ended December 31,19X6
(In $ thousands)

| | |
|---|---:|
| Net sales | $1,300.0 |
| Cost of goods sold | 910.0 |
| Gross margin | $ 390.0 |
| Selling, general and administrative | |
| Salaries | $ 188.9 |
| Payroll taxes | 16.1 |
| Advertising | 2.3 |
| Auto expense | 13.1 |
| Lease expenses | 3.6 |
| Commissions | 7.1 |
| Professional | 8.7 |
| Depreciation | 10.3 |
| Freight | 7.1 |
| Heat, light and power | 3.7 |
| Interest | 4.5 |
| Insurance | 14.1 |
| Office supplies | 8.4 |
| Rent | 9.6 |
| Telephone | 7.6 |
| Other | 40.3 |
| Total | $ 345.4 |
| Profit before income taxes | $ 44.6 |

specific. A target is not a forecast or an "educated guess," although both are used to develop targets. A target represents the amount that management has decided is reasonable and has committed to achieve. We will now explain how some of the targets in Table 5-1 were set. At the same time, we will describe how a larger firm might set them, to give you a broader view of the process.

### Sales Target

In most instances, a firm should rely on both an external and an internal analysis in setting a sales target. The external analysis might proceed in the following way: We could relate sales of the industry to some economic indicator like Gross National Product or Disposable Income. Statistical techniques, like regression analysis, are available to help determine if a relationship exists and what the relationship is. Next, we would obtain an estimate of the relevant economic indicator for the next year which likely would be available from some government agency and/or private organization to forecast industry sales. Then, based on the firm's historical market share adjusted for a planned change in market share, if any, we would compute the sales estimate for the coming year.

The internal analysis might consist of a target developed by the marketing personnel based on an evaluation of the sales potential of each product and/or service. Basically, this approach relies on the knowledge, experience and judgment of the people responsible for achieving the sales target.

The sales figures produced by the external and internal analyses must be reconciled. If the analyses are carefully performed, the two figures probably will not be too different. If they are, the entire process might begin over again. In any event, a sales target is ultimately set. (Keep in mind that no target is finalized until all targets are approved.)

At Eftco, there was no formally separate internal and external analyses. The external analysis consisted of the managers' assessments of the state of the economy, the prospects for the industry and the nature of the competitive environment. These assessments were based on knowledge gained through reading business and trade publications, attending meetings, etc. and on their experience in the business.

The sales manager was responsible for developing the sales target. He analyzed past sales data and other information. For instance, he examined monthly sales data for the past several years, past sales of key product lines, annual sales data for each salesperson for the last several years and the general sales objectives set at prior planning sessions. He then discussed this information with each salesperson and asked these people to think about their sales quota for the coming year. At a subsequent meeting, a tentative quota for each sales person was set. The sales manager then discussed the information with the president and other key people and after several iterations, the sales target was set.

### Cost of Goods Sold/Gross Profit Target

As Table 5-1 shows, cost of goods sold is the largest expense for Eftco and this is the case at many firms. Hence, this item typically receives considerable attention. Although we are separating the sales and gross profit targets for purposes of discussion, they are viewed as inseparable at Eftco and this is also the case at many firms. The reason is that the gross profit and sales levels both are affected by a firm's pricing policy.

Eftco purchased its products ready for sale and did no manufacturing. In setting this target, the first issue addressed was sales mix.[4] Earlier we explained that the sales manager reviewed sales by product category. When he did this he also reviewed gross margin differences. He concluded from this analysis that the variation in sales mix would have no effect on the gross margin target for the coming year.

After reviewing sales mix, the manager dealt with the effects of inflation and competiton. With respect to inflation, he had to figure out when and if suppliers would increase prices. For several years prior to the one we are studying, inflation rates had varied a great deal. This further complicated an already difficult task. What the sales manager did that year was rely on the advice of the firm's suppliers. They were quite helpful but they had no special insight. (Many large firms rely on the services of professionals for forecasts of inflation, interest rates, etc.)

We must keep in mind that inflation's impact on cost of goods sold expense may not be the same as its effect on other expenses. Typically, people talk about "the inflation rate." However, the impact of inflation is not identical for all expense categories. Thus, when we talk about a firm being able to pass on cost increases in the form of higher prices, we are not referring just to product cost increases.

In the year we are studying, management was particularly concerned about inflationary cost increases because of recent changes in the competitive environment. Competition had intensified and no letup was in sight. Hence, management decided on a gross profit target of 30% (cost of goods sold of 70%) which was less than the prior year's target of 30.5%. This was a significant decision because given the need to earn an acceptable level of net income this target put pressure on other expense targets.

---

[4] Products have varying gross margins. Hence, if there is a change in the mix of products sold, there can be a change in gross margin even if there are no changes in prices or volume. Chapter 4 shows how to analyze the impact of variations in sales mix on profit margins.

Before continuing, we should note that many manufacturing firms maintain production schedules and have excellent cost accounting systems. These can be quite helpful for setting a gross profit target (and for developing estimates for a cash budget).

### Other Expenses

We will now discuss how some of the remaining expense targets in Table 5-1 were set.

The target for salaries was set at $188,900 as shown in Table 5-1. Each manager was responsible for submitting figures for people under his or her supervision. Managers were given guidelines with respect to how much to include for cost of living and for merit. At this time managers also requested new positions if they wanted them. All submissions were reviewed by the president.

How likely is it that actual salaries will be close to budget? The answer is the actual amount will be very close to the target of $188,900. The reason for this is that once the salary levels are approved, managers normally are not allowed to spend more. For example, suppose a manager did not request a new position and after the start of the year decided one was needed. The request most likely would not be approved. Of course, a budget is not fixed in cement. Sometimes the environment changes unexpectedly and unanticipated expenditures are permitted. For example, after the start of the year Eftco might uncover an unusual opportunity to do more business. This likely would require unplanned increases in salaries and other operating expenses.

Advertising expense will underscore the point about control and give a capsule view of developing targets for operating expenses. The sales manager was responsible for advertising. Traditionally, the firm had done little advertising and the sales manager wanted to institute a new program that called for much more advertising. Thus, he submitted a request that was much larger than the previous year's level. The president had serious reservations and persuaded the sales manager that it would not be a productive use of funds. The initial submission was revised and ultimately the target was set at $2,300 as shown in Table 5-1.

Notice that the target was agreed to by the sales manager. The president did not simply cut the figure; instead there was a discussion to resolve differences in point of view. This process is necessary to gain commitment from operating managers. Also, note that once the figure was set this amount was all the sales manager would be allowed to spend. Finally, we should add that the president's point of view did not always prevail. For instance, in another year the sales manager had persuaded the president to add a new salesperson.

Some expenses were not as easy to control as salaries and advertising. For example, heat, light, and power depend on the weather and the price of energy and Eftco could not control either of these factors. Nevertheless, based on an analysis of past data generally a reasonable target was established. Moreover, a manager was assigned the task of controlling this expense.

A similar procedure was used for setting all other expense targets and targets for other items such as capital expenditures. Once the final budget was approved it was carefully monitored. At Eftco, each month an income statement was prepared and actual revenues and expenses were compared to budgeted amounts, and corrective action was taken, whenever necessary. For example, suppose in the first month there had been more overtime in the warehouse than expected. The controller would alert the warehouse manager to the possible problem. The warehouse manager would be expected to take action to correct the situation. What if the warehouse manager believed it would be unproductive to reduce labor costs in future months to make up for the average in January? He would request an allocation from the contingency. Included in "other" expenses in Table 5-1 is an amount for cost overruns in various expense categories. Only the president could approve expenditures from the contingency.

Budget systems like the one described above can help in a significant way to achieve short-term profit goals. We have noted some of the key characteristics for an effective system. Let's briefly summarize some of them:

1. Generally an individual's name must be associated with each line on the budget. In other words, someone must be responsible for achieving the figure.

2. The person responsible for achieving the budgeted item must have a role in setting the target and must believe it is reasonable. If either of these elements is missing, then the system most likely will produce suboptimal performance.

3. Actual results must be compared against budgeted figures on a timely basis. For example, a sales target for the year may be divided into monthly (or even weekly) quotas. Each week or month actual sales should be compared against the target for the period, variances should be carefully analyzed, and necessary corrective action should be taken. This activity ought to take place as soon after the end of the period as possible.

4. Sometimes differences between actual and budgeted amounts are due to factors beyond the control of the person responsible. If so, the individual should not be penalized or rewarded for the actual result.

5. The individual who has the responsibility for achieving the budgeted figure must have an appropriate level of authority. Now a fact of management life is that rarely does one have as much authority as responsibility—that is, one almost never has total control. Still, without the requisite authority the system just will not work.

6. Corrective action must be taken. Once a problem is detected, one should move quickly to solve it. Monitoring a budget—that is, comparing and analyzing actual and budgeted amounts—will tell us something is wrong and might even give a clue as to what ought to be done. However, management must be ready to act.

Cash budgeting is part of the overall budgeting process. Before the operating budget is approved, a cash budget should be prepared to ensure that the short-term plan is financially feasible. One example will show why. The sales target in Table 5-1 is $1.3 million, which represented a substantial increase over the previous year. This likely means more financing. How much? When? What kind of financing is necessary? Can the firm raise the money? Cash budgeting helps us deal with these kinds of issues.

We will now turn our attention to Eftco's cash budget. Our primary purpose for discussing it is to explain how to construct and use a cash budget. For the sake of clarity and to prevent you from getting bogged down in details, we will avoid a number of mechanical matters and computational complexities. These issues are addressed in the appendix to this chapter.

# How To Construct and Use a Cash Budget

To illustrate how to construct and use a cash budget, we will rely on the Eftco Company for the budget year discussed above. Recall that at the beginning of the chapter, we explained that the cash budgeting process includes the following:

• Selecting time horizon.

• Developing estimates.

- Constructing a cash budget and taking appropriate action.

- Monitoring the cash budget, that is, comparing actual cash flows to budgeted figures and taking necessary action.

We will now discuss each of these elements in the context of Eftco.

Before continuing we should note a subtle difference between operating and cash budgeting. As we saw above, all the key players of the firm were actively involved in the preparation and monitoring of the operating budget. This broad involvement is quite common. For cash budgeting, however, nonfinancial managers are not as actively involved in the preparation and use of the cash budget.

### Selecting Time Horizon

The time horizon selected depends on the needs of the firm. Eftco prepared a monthly cash budget for the year. Many large firms do something like this but in addition, they often prepare a daily or weekly breakdown for the next month or two. For example, a firm which generates substantial cash surpluses during certain times in a month might rely on a daily cash budget for the next 30 days to help maximize the return on temporary investments.

### Developing Estimates

The estimates for the cash budget are derived from the operating budget and information on payment patterns. In addition to the targets described above, Eftco had targets for capital expenditures and dividends. Capital expenditures for the year in question were budgeted at $12,000 ($4,000 in June and $8,000 in July) and management planned to make two equal dividend payments of $5,000 in January and in August. The firm also had targets for receivables and inventory levels and we will see shortly how they are needed to derive cash flow figures.

With respect to payment information there are several items that affect Eftco's cash budget. These are discussed below in outline form:

1. *Managers' bonuses.* Managers received a bonus each year if profits exceeded a predetermined level. The amount was expensed in December and paid in January. For the year we are studying, a payment of $12,500 was anticipated for January.

2. *Tax payments.* The firm was required to make estimated payments for State and Federal income taxes at various points during the year. For the year in question, there would be a payment of $2,500 in January and $1,500 in March. (As explained below, we will illustrate the detailed

computations only for January to March so we don't need tax payment figures for other months.)

3. *Long-term debt.* Eftco had a long-term debt arrangement that required principal payments of $7,500 each in January, April, July and October. (Interest also would be paid but amounts for interest are included with operating expenses.)

4. *Credit terms for purchases of inventory.* Terms for purchases of products for resale were net 30 days which means purchases in one month were paid for in the next month. Eftco's policy was to pay for purchases when due.

5. *Payment of expenses.* Operating expenses may be paid for in the month incurred (i.e., recorded as an expense), in a subsequent or prior month, or some combination. Hence, in addition to estimating the monthly expense we must also figure out when the expense will be paid. Let's look at some examples from Table 5-1:

   - Salaries. Generally 75% to 100% was paid in the month incurred with the remainder paid in the next month.

   - Lease expense. Paid for in the month of incurrence.

   - Payroll tax. Most of the expense for one month was paid the next month.

   - Office supplies. Most of the expense for one month was paid for in a prior month but a portion in some months was paid for in the same and/or subsequent months.

   - Rent expense. The expense for one month was paid in the prior month.

These examples show how varied payment pattern for operating expenses can be. We should point out, however, that usually the challenging task is estimating the monthly expense. Given monthly expense estimates, estimating the timing of payments is generally a simple matter.

## CONSTRUCT CASH BUDGET AND TAKE APPROPRIATE ACTION

We will now explain how to construct a cash budget and discuss further how the information is used. As noted above, we will compute detailed inflows and outflows for Eftco for only three months instead of the full year because this is sufficient to explain the basic mechanics. For the sake of clarity we will not dwell on the many refinements involved in computing inflows and outflows. These are addressed in the appendix to this chapter.

Table 5-2 outlines the procedure for preparing a cash budget. As shown, there are four steps: (1) compute cash inflows for the period, (2) calculate cash outflows for the period, (3) compute net cash flow for each period and (4) calculate a summary. To explain each step, we will rely on Eftco's monthly cash budget for that year which is presented in Table 5-3. The detail is shown for January to March only but it is important to keep in mind that specific information on inflows and outflows for each month is needed to interpret the cash budget. (Eftco's cash budget that was distributed to the firm's managers did have all the detail.)

### *Step 1. Computing Cash Receipts*

Table 5-3 shows that cash inflows are anticipated from cash sales, collections of credit sales, and the sale of a vehicle. We can see that the major source of cash is from the sale of products. This is usually the case for Eftco and many other firms, but keep in mind that all cash inflows are included.

**Table 5-2**   *Procedure for Constructing Cash Budget*

1. Cash Receipts
   Cash sales
   Collection of accounts receivable
   Interest income
   Other cash inflows

2. Cash Disbursements
   Payment of purchases
   Payment of salaries
   Cash outlays for operating expense
   Capital expenditure
   Long-term debt payments
   Dividends
   Other cash outlays

3. Net Cash Flow

4. Summary

**TABLE 5-3**
**EFTCO CO.**
**for Year Ended 12/31/19X6**

| | January | February | March | April | May | June | July | August | September | October | November | December |
|---|---|---|---|---|---|---|---|---|---|---|---|---|
| **I. Cash Receipts** | | | | | | | | | | | | |
| Cash sales and collections of accounts receivable | $111,200 | $109,500 | $101,200 | | | | | | | | | |
| Sale of vehicle | | | 1,500 | | | | | | | | | |
| Total inflow | $111,200 | $109,500 | $102,700 | | | | | | | | | |
| **II. Cash Disbursements** | | | | | | | | | | | | |
| Payment of purchases | $ 75,600 | $ 66,700 | $ 73,000 | | | | | | | | | |
| Salaries | 13,200 | 13,200 | 16,500 | | | | | | | | | |
| Payroll taxes | 1,500 | 1,200 | 1,300 | | | | | | | | | |
| Advertising | 1,500 | — | — | | | | | | | | | |
| Auto expense | 1,100 | 1,000 | 1,200 | | | | | | | | | |
| Lease expense | 300 | 300 | 300 | | | | | | | | | |
| Commissions | 600 | 600 | 600 | | | | | | | | | |
| Professional | 500 | 500 | 600 | | | | | | | | | |
| Freight | 600 | 600 | 600 | | | | | | | | | |
| Heat, light and power | 700 | 700 | 500 | | | | | | | | | |
| Interest expense | 200 | 200 | 300 | | | | | | | | | |
| Insurance | 2,000 | — | 1,500 | | | | | | | | | |
| Office supplies | 800 | — | 700 | | | | | | | | | |
| Rent | 800 | 800 | 800 | | | | | | | | | |
| Telephone | 600 | 600 | 600 | | | | | | | | | |
| Tax payments | 2,500 | — | 1,500 | | | | | | | | | |
| Other | 3,500 | 3,500 | 3,500 | | | | | | | | | |
| Bonus | 12,500 | | | | | | | | | | | |
| Dividends | 5,000 | — | — | | | | | | | | | |
| Debt payments | 7,500 | | | | | | | | | | | |
| Total cash disbursements | $131,000 | $ 89,900 | $103,500 | | | | | | | | | |
| **III. Net Cash Flow** | ($ 19,800) | $ 19,600 | ($ 800) | ($ 2,000) | $6,000 | $4,000 | ($1,000) | $6,000 | $5,000 | $1,500 | $500 | ($5,000) |
| Cash on hand $30,000 | | | | | | | | | | | | |
| Desired cash $45,000 | | | | | | | | | | | | |
| **IV. Cumulative Cash** | ($ 34,800) | ($ 15,200) | ($ 16,000) | ($18,000) | ($12,000) | ($8,000) | ($9,000) | ($3,000) | $2,000 | $3,500 | $4,000 | ($1,000) |

Examples are proceeds from issuing stock or long-term debt, selling fixed assets, and interest income.[6]

To compute cash inflows from sales, the controller needed monthly sales targets and end of month accounts receivable balances. These were derived from the operating budget and are shown below:

| Month | Total Sales | Accounts Receivable Balance—End of Month |
|---|---|---|
| December | (not needed) | $150,300 |
| January | $ 95,000 | 134,100 |
| February | 105,000 | 129,600 |
| March | 112,500 | 140,900 |

Given these amounts, we can compute monthly cash inflows from sales by relying on the following procedure:

> Accounts receivable, beginning of month (BOM)
> + Sales for month
> = Maximum inflow possible from sales
> − Accounts receivable, end of month (EOM)
> = Cash inflows from sales for month

Let's apply this procedure for January to March for Eftco:

| | January | February | March |
|---|---|---|---|
| Accounts receivable, BOM | $150,300 | $134,100 | $129,600 |
| + Sales | 95,000 | 105,000 | 112,500 |
| = Maximum possible | $245,300 | $239,100 | $242,100 |
| − Accounts receivable, EOM | 134,100 | 129,600 | 140,900 |
| = Cash inflows from sales | $111,200 | $109,500 | $101,200 |

To see the logic, let's talk our way through January. Eftco is owed $150,300 at the start of January and expects sales of $95,000 for the month. The total of these two amounts is the most that could come in during the month. Think of it this way. If Eftco's customers don't owe any money at the end of January, then the inflow for the month would be $245,300. But we expect $134,100 to be owed from customers at the end of January and so the difference of $111,200 is what we expect the cash inflow from sales to be during January.

---

[6] One of the purposes of a cash budget is to estimate additional financing required. Most firms do not include proceeds from this additional financing in the cash receipts sections. Instead, they show these proceeds as part of the summary section. We will illustrate the format later in the chapter.

Notice that the above procedure gives cash inflows from sales each month regardless of the proportions of sales that are for credit and cash. What if we wanted to list cash sales and collections of accounts receivable separately on a cash budget? We would divide the monthly sales target into cash and credit sales. This gives us the cash sales figure, and to compute collections of receivables we rely on the following altered version of the procedure just described.

> Accounts receivable, BOM
> + Credit sales
> = Maximum collections possible
> − Accounts receivable, EOM
> = Collections of accounts receivable for month

Eftco did not separate credit and cash sales because over 95% of its sales were on credit. However, firms with a substantial amount of cash sales typically show both cash sales and collections of receivables on a cash budget.

We did not show how Eftco's controller computed the accounts receivable balances because the calculations were detailed and we are saving this sort of detail for the appendix. However, we should point out the basic approach. Suppose a firm has credit sales of $100 in January and $150 in February and that sales are spread evenly during the month. If the collection period is 30 days, the accounts receivable balance at the end of February will be $150. (For simplicity, we are assuming 30-day months.) If the firm collects in 45 days, the accounts receivable balance at the end of February will be $200 which is the total of credit sales for February plus one-half of January's credit sales. We can also see from this simple example that we don't have to rely on the procedure described to compute collections. If credit terms are net 30 days and customers pay on time, this means that credit sales in one month are collected in the next month. What if the collection period is 45 days? Given that sales are spread evenly during the month, one-half of credit sales are collected in the next month and the other one-half is collected in the second month. For instance, in our simple example, $75 of February's credit sales will be collected in March and the other $75 will be collected in April.

## Step 2. Compute Cash Disbursements

Table 5-3 shows individual cash disbursements for January to March. We will discuss selected items.

Payment of purchases is the largest disbursement in each of the three months. To derive the amounts, we proceed in two steps: (1) compute purchases for the month and (2) compute when purchases will be paid. Note that since we want the payment for January and purchases are on credit, we must include data on the previous year's purchases. To see how purchases are derived, let's first review how cost of goods sold is computed for a firm that purchases products ready for sale, which we label a merchandising firm, and for a manufacturer.

> *Cost of Goods Sold Expense—Merchandising Firm*
>   Beginning inventory
> + Purchases
> − Ending inventory
> = Cost of goods sold expense

> *Cost of Goods Sold Expense—Manufacturing Firm*
>   Beginning inventory of finished goods
> + Cost of goods manufactured
> − Ending inventory of finished goods
> = Cost of goods sold expense

Eftco did no manufacturing so we can rely on the first relationship.

Cost of goods sold expense for each month is derived by multiplying the target of 70% described earlier times the sales estimate for the month. (This assumes the 70% target applies to each month's sales. This was true for Eftco but in some firms the percent differs by month.) Given the sales figures shown earlier and the 70% target, the cost of goods sold amounts are computed as follows:

| Month | Sales | | Cost of Goods Sold | | Cost of Goods Sold Expense |
|---|---|---|---|---|---|
| January | $ 95,000 | × | 70% | = | $66,500 |
| February | 105,000 | × | 70% | = | 73,500 |
| March | 112,500 | × | 70% | = | 78,750 |

You may recall that one version of the inventory turnover ratio is the following:

$$\text{Inventory Turnover Ratio} = \frac{\text{Cost of Goods Sold Expense}}{\text{Ending Inventory}}$$

With the targets for inventory turnover and cost of goods sold expense, the following inventory figures were derived.[7]

---

[7] We are not illustrating Eftco's actual computations because they involve more detail than we need. The controller computed an annualized cost of goods sold figure based on cumulative cost of goods sold expense for the previous two months. This figure was divided by the turnover target to obtain the inventory figures shown.

| Month | Inventory—End of Month |
|---|---|
| December | $300,800 |
| January | 301,000 |
| February | 300,500 |
| March | 300,450 |

Given the inventory and cost of goods sold figures, the purchase figures can be derived by relying on the following restated accounting relationship.

Cost of goods sold expense
+ Ending inventory
− Beginning inventory
= Purchases

For Eftco for January to March,

| | January | February | March |
|---|---|---|---|
| Cost of goods sold | $ 66,500 | $ 73,500 | $ 78,750 |
| + Ending inventory | 301,000 | 300,500 | 300,450 |
| − Beginning inventory | 300,800 | 301,000 | 300,500 |
| = Purchases | 66,700 | 73,000 | 78,700 |

Goods purchased in one month were paid for in the next month. This means that January's purchases of $66,700 will be paid in February and February's $73,000 will be paid in March. The cash budget shows a payment of $75,600 for purchases in January which is December's amount.

Some firms maintain detailed purchase schedules and part of the short-term planning process includes budgeting monthly purchases. In such a situation it would not be necessary to derive the purchase figures as shown above. Also, if a firm manufactures products, we would need to compute cost of goods manufactured for each month. You may recall that cost of goods manufactured includes raw materials used, direct labor and overhead. (See Chapter 1 for a discussion of cost of goods manufactured.) Raw materials used can be derived as follows:

Beginning inventory of raw materials
+ Purchases of raw materials
− Ending inventory of raw materials
= Raw materials used

Relying on this relationship we can derive purchases of raw materials and then figure out the timing of payments.

We discussed payments for other expenses earlier. Recall that we explained how we must first estimate the monthly amount and then figure when the expense would be paid. This is what the controller did to get the numbers shown in Table 5-3. Notice that all the expenses from Table 5-1 are included, except for depreciation expense. As you know, depreciation is a non-cash expense and so no cash outlay is required.

Payments for items besides expenses are also included. For instance, Table 5-3 shows a dividend and debt payment in January. Frequently, we will also see cash outflows for capital expenditures. In any event, after all cash outflows are listed, total disbursements are computed as shown in Table 5-3.

### Net Cash Flow

The next step is to compute net cash flow for each month. If inflows are greater than outflows, there is a net inflow for the month and we signify this by listing a positive number. If outflows are greater than inflows, there is a net outflow for the month and we either put a minus sign before the number or place the number in parentheses. Table 5-3 shows a net outflow for January and March and a net inflow for February.

Cash flow should not be confused with profit and loss. The fact that a firm experienced a negative cash flow for the month does not imply a loss. Positive cash flow does not indicate profit, nor does a net profit for the month signal a positive cash flow. For example, Eftco expects a negative cash flow of $19,800 in January. A profit for the month was expected. Why was there a difference? The reason is that there would be substantial cash outflows for non-expense items like dividends and principal payments on debt and for expenses incurred in a previous period like the bonus.

One final point about cash flow. In Chapter 3 the important notion of cash flow from operations was explained. There we noted that cash flow from operations does not include all the cash inflows and outflows for the period. Net cash flow on a cash budget does include all cash inflows and cash outflows; so we rely on this concept when we want to analyze all sources and uses of cash and not only those related to generating revenues and incurring expenses. Moreover, it's important to keep in mind that net cash flow for the period and cash flow from operations for the period are not the same thing.

### Cumulative Amount

The final step to complete the cash budget is to compute a summary which is given a variety of names such as cumulative amount, need/surplus, and cumulative cash. It is called cumulative cash in Table 5-3. Parentheses indicate a need for cash and positive amounts signal excess cash available over and above the minimum desired cash balance. We will review how to compute the figures in this row but we must first explain cash on hand of $30,000 and desired cash of $45,000. (These are shown between the net cash flow and cumulative cash rows in Table 5-3.)

Cash on hand of $30,000 represents the actual cash balance on January 1. (Actually, it was the controller's estimate of what the balance would be at that time. Recall that the cash budget was being prepared in December.) Desired cash of $45,000 represents the amount of cash the controller wanted to have on hand at the start of each month. Why did he want to have this amount? The reason is to help finance intra-month cash requirements. The negative $19,800 for January, for example, was an estimate of the net amount for the month but at various times during the month at Eftco cash outflows exceeded cash inflows by a much greater amount. The primary cause of this was the fact that collections from credit sales were received evenly through the month but about 90% of the purchase payments were made on the tenth of the month. Now Eftco could have borrowed to finance all of these intra-month needs. However, its policy was to rely partially on its own cash, and the controller decided that $45,000 was the appropriate amount for the year we are studying.

Another reason for having a minimum or desired cash balance is to compensate banks for services. Often a firm does not pay a direct fee for services such as processing checks but pays for them indirectly by keeping a certain amount in its checking account. Balances kept to pay for services are called compensating balances.

Now we can show how the cumulative cash figures are computed. Given the desire to have $45,000 on hand at the beginning of each month and actual cash of $30,000, Eftco will need $15,000 to bring cash up to the desired level. Thus, the total estimated need for January is $15,000 plus the negative net cash flow of $19,800 for a total of $34,800. The other figures are calculated in the manner explained earlier in the chapter. The computations for February and March are shown below:

|  |  |
|---|---:|
| Cumulative cash, end of January | ($34,800) |
| + Net cash flow for February | 19,600 |
| = Cumulative cash, end of February | ($15,200) |
|  |  |
| Cumulative cash, end of February | ($15,200) |
| + Net cash flow for March | (800) |
| = Cumulative cash, end of March | ($16,000) |

Some people find it difficult to work with the summary format used in Table 5-3. (We like it because it results in fewer numbers on the page.) To see if you can follow it see if you can answer the following by looking at Table

5-3. How much will the firm's cash balance be at the end of February, March and September? The answer is $45,000 at the end of February and March, and $47,000 at the end of September. Once we adjust the cash figure for the desired amounts, the negative amounts in the cumulative cash row tell us what we need to maintain cash at $45,000. The positive amounts tell us how much extra we expect over and above the minimum desired. If you have trouble following this approach, you may prefer to work with the format shown in Table 5-4.

## INTERPRETING INFORMATION AND TAKING APPROPRIATE ACTION

As the controller was making the computations described above, he was evaluating accuracy. For instance, he was confident that payments for expenses were reasonable because the firm's budgeting system helped keep expenses on target. He was less sanguine, however, about the payment of purchases because of previous experience. Eftco's track record with respect to achieving targets was excellent except for inventory. The result of this was that actual purchase payments could be substantially different from the amounts shown in Table 5-3. In any event, the uncertainty of estimates influence the amount and type of financing to arrange as we will see below:

Eftco had a line of credit which was renegotiated each December. At the time the budget was being prepared, the line was $50,000 which meant that the firm could borrow up to this amount at any time during the year. Further, Eftco could repay borrowings at any time. For instance, say the balance was zero on January 1. The firm could borrow $34,800 for January and then repay $19,600 in February. There are two other features of the line worth noting. First, the line had to have a zero balance (i.e., no borrowings) for 60 consecutive days. This is known as a clean-up provision. For the year prior to the one we are discussing, the controller paid off the line for the first time in October and did not borrow again for the rest of the year. (Incidentally, he had to let the firm's cash balance fall below the desired amount to accomplish this.)

The second feature is the compensating balance requirement. Eftco was expected to keep an average balance in its checking account equal to 10% of the total line plus 10% of amounts borrowed. For example, if the firm borrowed $30,000 when the line was $50,000, the average deposit balance to pay for the line would be $8,000 (10% × $50,000 plus 10% × $30,000). Of course, the firm also paid interest on any amounts borrowed on the line.

## TABLE 5-4
## EFTCO CO.
### Alternative Cash Flow Summary

| | January | February | March | April | May | June | July | August | September | October | November | December |
|---|---|---|---|---|---|---|---|---|---|---|---|---|
| Beginning cash | $30,000 | $45,000 | $45,000 | $45,000 | $45,000 | $45,000 | $45,000 | $45,000 | $45,000 | $47,000 | $48,500 | $49,000 |
| Net cash flow | (19,800) | 19,600 | (800) | (2,000) | 6,000 | 4,000 | (1,000) | 6,000 | 5,000 | 1,500 | 500 | (5,000) |
| Balance | $10,200 | $64,600 | $44,200 | $43,000 | $51,000 | $49,000 | $44,000 | $51,000 | $50,000 | $48,500 | $49,000 | $44,000 |
| Desired cash | 45,000 | 45,000 | 45,000 | 45,000 | 45,000 | 45,000 | 45,000 | 45,000 | 45,000 | 45,000 | 45,000 | 45,000 |
| Borrowing required for month | $34,800 | — | $ 800 | $ 2,000 | — | — | $ 1,000 | — | — | — | — | $ 1,000 |
| Excess cash available | — | $19,600 | — | — | $ 6,000 | $ 4,000 | — | $ 6,000 | $ 5,000 | $ 3,500 | $ 4,000 | — |
| Use of excess cash | | | | | | | | | | | | |
|   1. Repay debt | | $19,600 | | | $ 6,000 | $ 4,000 | | $ 6,000 | $ 3,000 | | | |
|   2. Increase minimum balance | | | | | | | | | $ 2,000 | $ 3,500 | $ 4,000 | |
| Total borrowing required | | | | | | | | | | | | |
| End of month | $34,800 | $15,200 | $16,000 | $18,000 | $12,000 | $8,000 | $ 9,000 | $ 3,000 | 0 | 0 | 0 | $ 1,000 |

Does a compensating balance have a cost? The answer is that it depends on the firm's normal cash balance. If it is larger than the amount needed for compensating balances, there is no cost. On the other hand, if a firm has to maintain a balance larger than it otherwise would, there is a cost. Eftco maintained normal working balances that were much larger than those required to compensate the bank for the line and for other services. Hence, the cost for these services was zero.

One final point before returning to our discussion of how the controller used the information in the cash budget. The line of credit we just discussed is an informal arrangement. This means the bank could cancel the line of credit at any time, although banks rarely do this. This arrangement should not be confused with a revolving line of credit ("revolver") which is a formal arrangement generally lasting several years. Here the bank is making a legal commitment to lend money for the period. Generally, there is a fee involved, say 1% of the total line, and the firm may also have to maintain compensating balances. (The reason there is confusion is that both kinds of arrangement are referred to as a line of credit.)

The controller at Eftco had to resolve two issues: (1) Should the line of credit be relied upon to finance all requirements for the coming year? (2) What should be the size of the line? We will discuss each of these but we should note that the controller sought the advice of other key people at Eftco, particularly the president and the firm's banker, in arriving at these decisions.

The cumulative cash row of the cash budget in Table 5-3 shows three consecutive months of excess cash, starting in September. The amounts are:

| Month | Cumulative |
|-----------|------------|
| September | $2,000 |
| October | 3,500 |
| November | 4,000 |

In your opinion, can the firm meet the clean-up provision? The controller decided not to risk it and to arrange for some permanent financing. (Specifically, he decided to finance the $12,000 capital expenditures scheduled for June and July with a term loan from the bank.) Do not infer that this was necessarily the right answer because it is a matter of judgment. The controller reached this decision for three reasons. First, the positive amounts were relatively small and occurred later in the year. Second, as noted earlier, he was confident about the accuracy of most estimates except for purchases. If actual purchases were higher than the targeted figures, then the actual cumulative cash figures for September–November likely would be negative.[8] Finally, if Eftco could not meet its clean-up provision, it would, in the controller's opinion, strain relations between the firm and its bank.

With respect to the size of the line, the cash budget shows a maximum need of $34,800 in January and this peak need declines rapidly, as shown in Table 5-3. To this amount we must add a margin of safety because all the cumulative cash figures are summaries of estimates. Table 5-5 has a list of some of the factors normally considered when deciding on a margin of safety. After considering factors like these the controller decided to request an increase in the line from $50,000 to $60,000.

**Table 5-5**   *Factors to Consider in Choosing Margin of Safety To Add to Maximum Expected Need*

---

1. *Assessment of Estimates.* An assessment of the reasonableness of estimates is a key factor in deciding on size of margin. For instance, if we believe that there is a high probability that actual cash flows will be close to budget then we need only a small margin of safety.
2. *When during the year does the maximum need occur?* Generally, the further in the future the maximum occurs, the less confident we are in the accuracy of this estimate. So, a larger cushion is in order.
3. *Cost.* Keep in mind that compensating balances are often required. If there is a cost to maintaining these balances, as described earlier, then the greater the margin, the greater the cost.
4. *Attitude of Lender.* What if we have to request an increase in the line during the year? What if we can't meet the clean-up provision? Generally, lenders view requests to increase the amount or change terms as signs of poor management. Of course, if something totally unexpected happens, most lenders are quite understanding and support their customers.
5. *Liquid Reserves.* Many firms maintain liquid reserves—funds invested in marketable securities—to fund unexpected needs. If we have a healthy reserve, then we don't need a large cushion.
6. *Access to External Sources of Cash.* Some firms have ready access to several external sources of funds. In this fortunate environment a large margin is not needed.

---

[8] We should point out that the controller performed additional financial analyses. For instance, he revised the cash flow figures assuming purchases in several months were 20% higher than anticipated. Testing the impact of alternative estimates is frequently referred to as sensitivity analysis.

## MONITORING THE CASH BUDGET

The final part of the process is to monitor cash flows. That is, we compare actual cash flows to budgeted amounts, investigate differences, and take appropriate action. For instance, as soon as possible after the end of January, the controller of Eftco should list actual cash flows beside the budgeted amounts and compute the difference. He should then investigate variances and take action, if necessary.

For example, suppose the controller found that the actual cash inflow for January was below the budgeted amount. This could be due to failure to reach the sales targets during previous months and/or a problem with collections. Say it was due to a longer than anticipated collection period for some customers. He would talk to the individuals responsible for these customers to resolve the matter.

It's imperative to stress the importance of monitoring on a timely basis. Suppose the collection lag described in the previous paragraph was one or two large customers who paid in 60 days instead of 30 days as they normally did. Very often if you allow a customer to get away with this sort of thing for several months, you will have a tough time effecting a reversion to normal terms. More generally, major problems and crises start as small problems. Timely monitoring of budgets enables us to identify problems when they are small and easier to solve.

# Appendix to Chapter 5
# Constructing A Cash Budget

The appendix elaborates on the chapter's discussion of how to construct a cash budget. The primary purposes are to provide drill on the basic mechanics covered in the chapter and to explain how to handle more complex calculations. Another important objective is to make the appendix a handy reference on how to construct cash budgets. We start with basic computations and move to more complex situations. This approach not only will make it easier for you to learn the complex computations but it also will enable you to refer to this appendix in the future without having to review the chapter.

Let's assume we were asked to prepare a monthly cash budget for October through March for the Mardo Company. The following estimates and actual information were gathered for this purpose.

### Mardo Company

| Actual Sales | | Estimated Sales | | | |
|---|---|---|---|---|---|
| July | $30,000 | October | $12,000 | January | $30,000 |
| August | 10,000 | November | 20,000 | February | 20,000 |
| September | 20,000 | December | 30,000 | March | 30,000 |

1. All sales are on terms of net 30 days, sales are spread evenly during each month, customers pay on time, and there are no bad debts. (For simplicity, we will assume that each month has 30 days.)

2. Cost of goods sold expense is 50% for all sales. Other expenses are: depreciation, $2,000 per month; labor, $3,000 per month; income taxes, rate is 50%; interest expense, the annual interest rate is 12% on the debt that will discussed below.

3. Labor is a cash expense. Taxes due through the end of September were paid in September, income taxes for October through December will be paid in December, and the amount due for January through March will be paid at the end of March.

4. The 12% interest rate mentioned above refers to a $100,000 loan that the firm arranged on September 30th. A principal payment of $2,000 is due at the end of each month. Interest due for the month will also be paid at the end of each month. There is no other interest bearing debt and for simplicity, we will ignore interest on any new debt that may be required during the period.

5. All goods are purchased ready for sale. Goods needed for one month are purchased in the preceding month on terms of net 60 days. For example, the amount that the firm expects to sell in October was purchased in September and payment for these purchases are due in November.

6. A cash purchase of $15,000 for equipment will be made in November. (This expenditure was taken into account in deriving the depreciation expense estimate of $2,000 per month.)

7. The firm will issue common stock in December. It is anticipated that the net proceeds from the issue will be $40,000 and it will be received in December.

8. Cash on hand on October 1st is $10,000. The firm's desired cash balance is $25,000—that is, the firm wants to maintain a cash balance of $25,000 and so it is short $15,000.

9. Finally, the firm will pay cash dividends of $1,000 each month.

Table 5-6 presents the monthly cash budget and we will now explain how the numbers are derived.

### Cash Inflows

The firm expects inflows from two sources: collections of accounts receivable and the proceeds from the sale of stock. The latter is estimated at $40,000 for December and it is simply listed as an inflow for that month.

To compute inflows from sales one needs information on the following:

1. Estimate of sales by month.

2. Estimate of the proportions that will be cash and credit sales.

3. Estimate of how long it will take to collect sales made on credit.

For Mardo, we were given the monthly estimates of sales and were told that all sales will be on terms of net 30 days, which means that all sales

**TABLE 5-6**
**MARDO COMPANY**
Monthly Cash Budget
October to March

| | October | November | December | January | February | March |
|---|---|---|---|---|---|---|
| **Cash Inflows:** | | | | | | |
| Collections of receivables | $20,000 | $12,000 | $20,000 | $30,000 | $30,000 | $20,000 |
| Stock issue | | | 40,000 | | | |
| Total | $20,000 | $12,000 | $60,000 | $30,000 | $30,000 | $20,000 |
| **Cash Disbursements:** | | | | | | |
| Payment of purchases | $10,000 | $ 6,000 | $10,000 | $15,000 | $15,000 | $10,000 |
| Labor | 3,000 | 3,000 | 3,000 | 3,000 | 3,000 | 3,000 |
| Interest | 1,000 | 980 | 960 | 940 | 920 | 900 |
| Income taxes | | | 6,530 | | | 11,120 |
| Equipment | | 15,000 | | | | |
| Loan payment | 2,000 | 2,000 | 2,000 | 2,000 | 2,000 | 2,000 |
| Dividends | 1,000 | 1,000 | 1,000 | 1,000 | 1,000 | 1,000 |
| Total | $17,000 | $27,980 | $23,490 | $21,940 | $21,920 | $28,020 |
| Net Cash Flow (deficit) | $ 3,000 | ($15,980) | $36,510 | $ 8,060 | $ 8,080 | ($ 8,020) |

Beginning cash   $10,000
− Desired cash    25,000
= Amount available
  (required)     ($15,000)

| | October | November | December | January | February | March |
|---|---|---|---|---|---|---|
| Cumulative Cash (deficit) | ($12,000) | ($27,980) | $ 8,530 | $16,590 | $24,670 | $16,650 |

are credit sales. If all customers pay in 30 days, which is expected, then sales in one month will be collected in the next month. September's sales of $20,000 will be collected in October, October's sales of $12,000 will be collected in November and so forth.

### Cash Disbursements

Since many payments relate to income statement items, it is often useful to begin by preparing estimated income statements by month. Table 5-7 presents these statements. Let's take a moment to explain the numbers. The sales figures are the estimates provided, cost of goods sold expense is 50% of sales, and labor and depreciation expense estimates are given. To derive interest expense we multiply the interest rate of 12% times the amount of the loan outstanding for the month and then divide the result by 12. We divide by 12 because 12% is an annual rate. Table 5-8 presents the interest rate calculations for each month. Finally, the income tax figures were derived by multiplying the pretax profit numbers by the income tax rate of 50%.

Before proceeding we should make an observation. The estimated net income figures and the estimated net cash flow numbers are different, which should not be surprising. The point is that net income and net cash flow are two different concepts. When interpreting net cash flow amounts, you should not infer that positive amounts mean the firm is profitable and that negative figures mean the firm is incurring losses.

Turning to the disbursements, the first item is payment of purchases. To derive these figures we need to know purchases by month and payment terms. We are told that products needed in one month will be purchased

### TABLE 5-7
### MARDO COMPANY
Estimated Monthly Income Statements
October to March

|  | October | November | December | January | February | Marc |
|---|---|---|---|---|---|---|
| Net sales | $12,000 | $20,000 | $30,000 | $30,000 | $20,000 | $30,00 |
| Cost of goods sold | 6,000 | 10,000 | 15,000 | 15,000 | 10,000 | 15,00 |
| Gross profit | $ 6,000 | $10,000 | $15,000 | $15,000 | $10,000 | $15,00 |
| Labor | 3,000 | 3,000 | 3,000 | 3,000 | 3,000 | 3,00 |
| Depreciation | 2,000 | 2,000 | 2,000 | 2,000 | 2,000 | 2,00 |
| Interest | 1,000 | 980 | 960 | 940 | 920 | 90 |
| Profit before taxes | $    0 | $ 4,020 | $ 9,040 | $ 9,060 | $ 4,080 | $ 9,10 |
| Income taxes | 0 | 2,010 | 4,520 | 4,530 | 2,040 | 4,55 |
| Net income | $    0 | $ 2,010 | $ 4,520 | $ 4,530 | $ 2,040 | $ 4,55 |

**TABLE 5-8**
**MARDO COMPANY**
Calculation of Monthly Interest

| Month | Loan Balance Beginning of Month | Interest | Principal Payment | Loan Balance End of Month |
|-------|-------------------|----------|-------------------|---------------------|
| October | $100,000 | $1,000 | $2,000 | $98,000 |
| November | 98,000 | 980 | 2,000 | 96,000 |
| December | 96,000 | 960 | 2,000 | 94,000 |
| January | 94,000 | 940 | 2,000 | 92,000 |
| February | 92,000 | 920 | 2,000 | 90,000 |
| March | 90,000 | 900 | 2,000 | 88,000 |

in the preceding month. The amount needed for October was purchased in September, the amount needed for November will be purchased in October and so forth. Given this policy and the cost of goods sold estimate, we can compute monthly purchases as shown below:

| Month | Amount Needed | Month Purchased |
|-------|---------------|-----------------|
| September | $10,000 | August |
| October | 6,000 | September |
| November | 10,000 | October |
| December | 15,000 | November |
| January | 15,000 | December |
| February | 10,000 | January |
| March | 15,000 | February |

The figures in the amount needed column were derived by multiplying sales for the month by the cost of goods sold rate of 50%. For example, it is estimated that sales will be $20,000 in November. The products needed to support this level of sales will cost Mardo $10,000. This amount will be purchased in October. (Note that all goods are purchased ready for sale, which means Mardo does not produce the products it sells. As we will see later, deriving purchases for a manufacturing company involves a different procedure.)

All purchases are on terms of net 60 days, which means there are no cash purchases. Also, these terms mean that what is purchased in one month is paid for two months later. Thus purchases in August will be paid in October, purchases in September will be paid in November and so forth.

The following information is needed to derive payment of purchases:

1. Estimate of purchases by month.

2. Estimate of the proportions that will be cash and credit purchases.

3. Estimate of how long it will take to pay for purchases.

If you look back at cash inflows from sales, you will see that the information requirements are similar. However, normally the firm will be more certain of its payment of purchases estimates because it can exert a greater degree of influence than for collections. For example, a firm can take action to encourage customers to pay on time, but this does not always work. On the other hand, it has direct control over purchases.

The next three disbursements: labor, interest and income taxes are for expenses. In dealing with these items, we need to know three things:

1. How much is the expense?

2. When will the expense be incurred? That is, when will it be recognized for accounting or tax purposes?

3. When will payments be made?

The amount for labor was given and we discussed interest expense earlier. These two items are cash expenses which mean payment is made when the expense is incurred. With respect to taxes, we are told that income taxes due through the end of September were paid in September. Tax expense for October through December, which is estimated at $6,530, will be paid in December. The total for January through March is estimated at $11,120, to be paid in March. We did not include depreciation expense as a cash outflow because it is a noncash expense. However, noncash expenses like depreciation cannot be ignored in cash budgeting because they may affect the amount of income taxes that will be paid. The amount and timing of the final three disbursements: payment for new equipment, the loan and dividends were given. After listing all the cash outlays, we compute a total for each month. This computation completes the second step.

### Net Cash Flows

The next step is to compute the net cash flow for each month by subtracting outflows from inflows. If total inflows for the month are greater than total outflows, this means an excess is expected and it is listed as a positive number. For example, for October total inflows are $20,000 and total outflows are $17,000, producing a positive net cash flow of $3,000. If total outflows for a month are greater than the inflows then a cash shortage is anticipated for the month and it is listed as a negative number. For

November, for example, outflows of $27,980 and inflows of $12,000 are expected, indicating the firm expects a cash shortage of $15,980.

### Cumulative Cash

The final step is to summarize the first three to facilitate the interpretation of the information. We first adjust for the difference, if any, between the desired and actual cash balances. In our example, Mardo wants a cash balance of $25,000 and it has $10,000 on hand. The firm needs $15,000 more. Since we expect October to provide $3,000, the net need is $12,000. This is shown as a negative number for October in the cumulative cash row.

Once the cumulative cash flow figure for the first month is computed, the remaining numbers are derived by summing the net cash flow figures. Specifically, the net cash flow for the month is added to the cumulative cash figure at the end of the preceding month. The necessary computations for November to January are shown below:

|  | *November* |
|---|---|
| Cumulative cash (end of October) | ($12,000) |
| + Net cash flow for November | (15,980) |
| = Cumulative cash (end of November) | ($27,980) |
|  | *December* |
| Cumulative cash (end of November) | ($27,980) |
| + Net cash flow for December | 36,510 |
| = Cumulative cash (end of December) | $ 8,530 |
|  | *January* |
| Cumulative cash (end of December) | $ 8,530 |
| + Net cash flow for January | 8,060 |
| = Cumulative cash (end of January) | $16,590 |

For the most part, the above discussion reviewed mechanical topics covered in the chapter. Now we will turn our attention to refinements.

## REFINEMENTS

We will begin by considering more complex computations for cash inflows. We will again rely on the Mardo Co. Recall that we were given the following information on monthly sales.

| *Actual Sales* | | | *Estimated Sales* | | |
|---|---|---|---|---|---|
| July | $30,000 | October | $12,000 | January | $30,000 |
| August | 10,000 | November | 20,000 | February | 20,000 |
| September | 20,000 | December | 30,000 | March | 30,000 |

Let's suppose that credit terms are net 45 days for all sales. We will continue to assume that customers pay on time, that sales are spread evenly during the month and that there are no bad debts.

Given the above, we can figure out that one-half of sales in one month will be collected in the next month and the other half will be collected in the second subsequent month. For example, sales for the first half of September will be collected in October and sales for the second half will be collected in November. Will Mardo collect just one-half of September's sales in October? The answer is "no." One-half of August's sales will also be collected in October. Below are the calculations of collections for the six months:

| *October* | | | *November* | |
|---|---|---|---|---|
| $\frac{1}{2}$ August Sales | $ 5,000 | | $\frac{1}{2}$ September Sales | $10,000 |
| $\frac{1}{2}$ September Sales | 10,000 | | $\frac{1}{2}$ October Sales | 6,000 |
| Collections | $15,000 | | Collections | $16,000 |

| *December* | | | *January* | |
|---|---|---|---|---|
| $\frac{1}{2}$ October Sales | $ 6,000 | | $\frac{1}{2}$ November Sales | $10,000 |
| $\frac{1}{2}$ November Sales | 10,000 | | $\frac{1}{2}$ December Sales | 15,000 |
| Collections | $16,000 | | Collections | $25,000 |

| *February* | | | *March* | |
|---|---|---|---|---|
| $\frac{1}{2}$ December Sales | $15,000 | | $\frac{1}{2}$ January Sales | $15,000 |
| $\frac{1}{2}$ January Sales | 15,000 | | $\frac{1}{2}$ February Sales | 10,000 |
| Collections | $30,000 | | Collections | $25,000 |

Net 45 days or any other collection period, for that matter, is not complex, provided you learn to reason out the cash inflow pattern instead of memorizing a formula. For terms of net 45 days, what is sold on the 1st of the month will be collected on the 16th of the next month; what is sold on the 2nd of the month will be collected on the 17th of the next month; and so forth. Continuing with this reasoning we arrive at a pattern of one-half in the next month and one-half in the second subsequent month.

There is an alternative procedure for calculating monthly cash inflows. Let's first see how it works by relying on a simple example. Suppose you are owed $100 from customers at the beginning of January (which is the same as the end of December) and you have credit sales of $50 during

January. What is the most that cash inflows from sales can be during January? The answer is $150, the $100 owed you at the beginning of the month plus sales of $50 during the month. Now suppose you were told customers owed you $25 at at the end of January. How much did you collect during January? The answer is $125, derived as follows:

| | |
|---|---:|
| Accounts receivable—beginning of January | $100 |
| + Credit sales during January | 50 |
| = Most that can be collected | $150 |
| − Accounts receivable—end of January | 25 |
| = Collections during January | $125 |

In general, collection of credit sales can be computed by relying on the following relationship.

Accounts receivable—beginning of month
+ Credit sales during month
= Most that can be collected during month
− Accounts receivable—end of month
= Collections of credit sales during month

Let's try it for Mardo assuming terms are net 75 days. All the other conditions are the same—that is, sales are spread evenly during each month, customers pay on time, and there are no bad debts. A collection period of net 75 days means that at any time the firm will have the last 75 days sales outstanding. Putting it another way, at the end of any month the accounts receivable balance will consist of sales for the preceding $2^{1}/_{2}$ months. For example, at the end of September, sales for September, August and one-half of July will be outstanding. The calculations for October to March for Mardo are presented below. (The accounts receivable balance at the beginning of a month is the same as the balance at the end of the preceding month.)

| | October | November | December | January | February | March |
|---|---:|---:|---:|---:|---:|---:|
| Beginning AR | $45,000 | $37,000 | $42,000 | $56,000 | $70,000 | $65,000 |
| + Credit Sales | 12,000 | 20,000 | 30,000 | 30,000 | 20,000 | 30,000 |
| − Ending AR | 37,000 | 42,000 | 56,000 | 70,000 | 65,000 | 65,000 |
| = Collections | $20,000 | $15,000 | $16,000 | $16,000 | $25,000 | $30,000 |

We will conclude our discussion of cash inflows with a test. You are given the following information for the Zado Co.

| *Month* | *Sales* |
|---|---|
| December | $1,500 |

| | |
|---|---|
| January | 1,800 |
| February | 2,100 |

In addition, you are told that all sales are on terms of 2/10 net 30 which means that customers who pay in 10 days can deduct a cash discount of 2% from the invoice; if the customer does not take this option, full payment must be made within 30 days. Assume that all customers pay in ten days and take the 2% discount, that sales are spread evenly during each month, and to simplify the calculations, that each month has 30 days.

Given the above information, compute collections for January and February.

The answer is $1,666 for January and $1,960 for February. It is derived in two stages. Since a cash discount is involved, we must first compute the proportion of sales that will actually be collected. In this example, all customers will take the 2% discount and so only 98% of sales will be collected as shown below:

| Month | Sales | Amount To Be Collected |
|---|---|---|
| December | $1,500 | $1,470 |
| January | 1,800 | 1,764 |
| February | 2,100 | 2,058 |

Once we have the amount to be collected, we must derive the collection pattern. Given that customers will pay in 10 days, sales on the 1st of the month, less the discount, will be collected on the 11th of the same month; sales on the 2nd of the month, less the discount, will be collected on the 12th; and so forth. This reasoning will lead us to conclude that $2/3$ of sales for the month, less the discount, will be collected in the same month; and $1/3$, less the discount, will be collected in the next month.

# Computing Payment of Purchases and Expenses

Some computational complexities can arise when computing payment of purchases and expenses. To begin, suppose we were given the following information and asked to compute monthly purchase payments for January to March:

| Month | Estimated Sales |
|---|---|
| January | $80,000 |
| February | 60,000 |
| March | 90,000 |
| April | 50,000 |
| May | 75,000 |

We are also given the following:

1. All goods are purchased ready for sale on terms of net 15 days. (The phrase "ready for sale" tells us that the firm does no manufacturing.) Purchases in December were $40,000. Purchases are spread evenly during each month, the firm will pay on time and 30-day months will be assumed for all calculations.

2. Cost of goods sold is 60% for all sales.

3. Inventory on hand at January 1 is $40,000. A new inventory policy will be established so that at the end of January and each subsequent month there will be enough inventory on hand to support sales for the next two months.

To calculate monthly payments we must first compute purchases for each month. Recall that cost of goods sold expense for a firm which does no manufacturing is derived in the following manner:

    Beginning inventory
    + Purchases
    − Ending inventory
    = Cost of goods sold expense

The information we were given enables us to compute cost of goods sold and beginning and ending inventory for each month, making it possible for us to "back into" purchases.

Cost of goods sold expense for each month is 60% of sales as shown below:

| Month | Sales | | Cost of Goods Sold Rate | | Cost of Goods Sold Expense |
|---|---|---|---|---|---|
| January | $80,000 | × | 60% | = | $48,000 |
| February | 60,000 | × | 60% | = | 36,000 |
| March | 90,000 | × | 60% | = | 54,000 |
| April | 50,000 | × | 60% | = | 30,000 |
| May | 75,000 | × | 60% | = | 45,000 |

Next, we must determine inventory balances. We are told that the amount on January 1 was $40,000, but we must derive the balance for the other periods of interest. We are told that at the end of January the firm will have enough to support sales for February and March, which means that $90,000 will be on hand at the end of January. This amount was obtained by adding the cost of goods sold figures for February and March. The inventory balance at the end of February is estimated at $84,000, derived by adding cost of goods sold expense for March and April. The end of March balance will be $75,000, the sum of cost of goods sold for April and May.

We can now calculate purchases for each month:

|  | *January* | *February* | *March* |
|---|---|---|---|
| Beginning inventory | $40,000 | $90,000 | $84,000 |
| + Purchases | ? | ? | ? |
| − Ending inventory | 90,000 | 84,000 | 75,000 |
| = Cost of goods sold | $48,000 | $36,000 | $54,000 |
| Purchases | $98,000 | $30,000 | $45,000 |

The beginning inventory balance for January 1 is given. February's beginning balance is January's ending amount and the beginning figure for March is the ending balance for February.

What we have done thus far is to derive the estimates for purchases from given estimates. Had we been told what the purchases would be, we could have avoided the above procedure and proceeded immediately to the calculation of payments discussed next.

Purchase terms are net 15 days. As was the case for collections, a pattern must be developed. (Since the process was discussed in some detail above it will not be repeated here.) Given that purchases are spread evenly during each month and payment in 15 days, one half of purchases for the month will be paid in the same month and one half will be paid in the next month. Monthly payments for January–March are shown below. (The one half in the following schedule refers to one half of monthly purchases. For example, one half December means one half of purchases for December.)

| *Month* | *Payments* | |
|---|---|---|
| January | $\frac{1}{2}$ December + $\frac{1}{2}$ January | = $69,000 |
| February | $\frac{1}{2}$ January + $\frac{1}{2}$ February | = 64,000 |
| March | $\frac{1}{2}$ February + $\frac{1}{2}$ March | = 37,500 |

When collection of receivables was discussed, we considered the alternative procedure of taking the beginning balance of receivables, adding sales and deducting the ending balance. Relying on the same logic you can employ the following alternative procedure for purchase payments.

    Accounts payable trade (beginning of month)
    + Credit purchases for the month
    − Accounts payable trade (end of month)
    = Payment for purchases

The word trade means that the accounts payable balance consists only of what is owed for purchases of inventory. Usually, a separate accounts payable account is maintained for goods purchased for sale (or for manufacturing products). If a separate account is not used, then one cannot rely on this procedure.

If terms are net 15 days, at any point in time the accounts payable balance will equal the total of purchases for the previous 15 days. Thus, the accounts payable balance at the end of each month is derived as follows:

| Month | Purchases | Accounts Payable (End of Month) |
|---|---|---|
| December | $40,000 | $20,000 |
| January | 98,000 | 49,000 |
| February | 30,000 | 15,000 |
| March | 45,000 | 22,500 |

We can now compute payments:

| | January | February | March |
|---|---|---|---|
| Beginning accounts payable | $20,000 | $49,000 | $15,000 |
| + Credit purchases | 98,000 | 30,000 | 45,000 |
| − Ending accounts payable | 49,000 | 15,000 | 22,500 |
| = Payments | $69,000 | $64,000 | $37,500 |

So far we have been discussing calculating purchase payment for firms which do not engage in manufacturing. For firms that do, the computations can be more complex if one has to "back into" the purchase estimates. Cost of goods sold expense for a manufacturing company is calculated as follows:

    Beginning inventory of finished goods
    + Cost of goods manufactured
    − Ending inventory of finished goods
    = Cost of goods sold expense

Cost of goods manufactured includes raw material, direct labor and overhead. Thus, one has to develop a cost of goods manufactured schedule and separate the component for raw materials. Purchases can then be computed in the following manner:

> Beginning inventory of raw materials
> + Purchases of raw materials
> − Ending inventory of raw materials
> = Raw materials used

Once the purchase figure is derived the rest of the process is the same as described above.

Turning to other disbursements, there will be cash outlays for expenses and for other items like fixed assets, loans and dividends. The other items are straightforward in the sense that normally the amount and timing of payments will be established when the estimates are developed. Often this will be the case for expenses also. However, sometimes one will have to derive payments from other estimates, so we should briefly discuss how one would do it.

A firm might pay for an expense in the same month that it is incurred— that is, recognized and recorded on its income statement. For this type of expense, there is no added complexity because payments are obtained directly from the estimated income statements. (Recall that this was the case for certain expenses for the Mardo Co., which was the example employed to demonstrate the construction of a cash budget.) However, a firm might pay for an expense in a period prior to or subsequent to the one in which it is recognized on the income statement. It is for this type of expense that the computations are more complex if payments are derived from other estimates. We will look first at expenses paid in prior periods and then at those paid in subsequent periods.

If a firm pays for an expense in a prior period, this fact will be reflected by the existence of a prepaid expense account on the asset side of the balance sheet. (The asset might be called prepaid expenses, deferred charges or some similar name.) Given information on prepaid expenses and the expense, you can derive the payment. For example, suppose we were given the following information:

1. A firm's balance sheets include the following asset:

|  | *End of Year 1* | *End of Year 2* |
|---|---|---|
| Prepaid rent | $1,000 | $600 |

2. This firm's income statement for Year 2 has rent expense of $1,500.

With this information, we can figure out that the total of payments for rent expense during Year 2 was $1,100. This amount was computed by using the following procedure:

> Prepaid expense at the end of the period
> + Expense incurred during the period
> − Prepaid expense at the beginning of the period
> = Payments for expense during the period

We will explain the logic for the procedure using the above example. The asset prepaid rent was $1,000 at the end of Year 1. This tells us that $1,000 was already paid for rent expense to be incurred subsequent to the end of Year 1. (It is most likely for Year 2's expense but it does not have to be for the procedure to work.) Thus, only $500 of Year 2's rent expense of $1,500 must be paid in Year 2. The asset prepaid rent of $600 at the end of Year 2 tells us that the amount was paid prior to the end of Year 2 for rent expense that will be incurred in a subsequent period. Hence, total payments must have been $1,100.

If a firm pays for an expense in a period subsequent to the one in which it is incurred, this fact will be reflected by the existence of an accrued expense account on the liability side of the balance sheet. (The liability might be called accrued expenses or a more specific name like wages payable.) Given information on accrued expenses and the expense, you can derive the payment. For example, suppose we were given the following information:

1. A firm's balance sheets include the following liability:

|  | End of Year 1 | End of Year 2 |
|---|---|---|
| Accrued wages | $750 | $1,300 |

2. This firm's income statement for Year 2 has a labor expense of $2,850.

With this information, we can figure out that the total of payments for labor expense for Year 2 was $2,300. This amount was computed by using the following procedure:

> Accrued expenses at the beginning of the period
> + Expense incurred during the period
> − Accrued expenses at the end of the period
> = Payment for expense during the period

We will explain the logic of the procedure by relying on the example for wages. The liability accrued wages of $750 at the end of Year 1 tells us that this amount will be paid subsequent to the end of Year 1. (The amount most likely will be paid in Year 2 but it does not have to be paid then for the procedure to work.) The expense for Year 2 is $2,850. Thus, the most that can be paid during Year 2 is this amount plus the beginning of the year balance of $750 or a total of $3,600. However, the accrued wages balance of $1,300 at the end of Year 2 tells us that this amount was incurred prior to the end of Year 2 but will be paid after that point in time. Thus, the total of payments for Year 2 must be the difference of $2,300.

One final point is in order. It's important to keep in mind that a cash budget is the tool of the processes described in the chapter. However, it's possible to rely on other techniques. For example, some firms rely on a set of projected financial statements as the tool for short-term planning and control. This tool is explained in the next chapter.

# Problems and Discussion Questions

## A. Solved Problems

### Problem 5-1A

You are given the following information for the Pentron Company:

| Actual Sales | | Estimated Sales | |
|---|---|---|---|
| January | $100 | April | $120 |
| February | 90 | May | 80 |
| March | 70 | June | 150 |

All sales are on credit, customers pay on time, there are no bad debts, and sales are spread evenly through the month. Assume 30-day months.

1. Calculate monthly collections of accounts receivable for April to June, assuming each of the following sets of credit terms:

    (a) Net 15 days
    (b) Net 45 days

### Solution 5-1A

1(a) *Net 15 days*

Given that sales are spread evenly through the month and the other conditions noted, one half of sales for the month will be collected in the same month and the other one half will be collected the next month.

#### Monthly Collections

| | | | | |
|---|---|---|---|---|
| Collected in April | $= \frac{1}{2}$ March | $+ \frac{1}{2}$ April | $=$ | $ 95 |
| Collected in May | $= \frac{1}{2}$ April | $+ \frac{1}{2}$ May | $=$ | 100 |
| Collected in June | $= \frac{1}{2}$ May | $+ \frac{1}{2}$ June | $=$ | 115 |

1(b) *Net 45 days*

Given that sales are spread evenly and the other conditions noted, one half of sales for the month will be collected in the next month and the other one half will be collected in the second month.

#### Monthly Collections

| | | | | |
|---|---|---|---|---|
| Collected in April | $= \frac{1}{2}$ February | $+ \frac{1}{2}$ March | $=$ | $ 80 |
| Collected in May | $= \frac{1}{2}$ March | $+ \frac{1}{2}$ April | $=$ | 95 |
| Collected in June | $= \frac{1}{2}$ April | $+ \frac{1}{2}$ May | $=$ | 100 |

We can see that at the end of any month sales for the last 45 days are outstanding. For instance, note that at the end of June the second half of May's sales plus all of June's sales are outstanding.

|  | April | May | June |
|---|---|---|---|
| Accounts receivable BOM | $115 | $155 | $140 |
| + Sales | 120 | 80 | 150 |
| = Maximum possible | $235 | $235 | $290 |
| − Accounts receivable EOM | 155 | 140 | 190 |
| = Collections | $ 80 | $ 95 | $100 |

We should note the similarity between computing collections of receivables and payments for purchases. Suppose the above information had pertained to monthly purchases. We would have computed payments in the same basic way. For instance, we can derive the beginning of the month accounts payable trade balance, add purchases for the month, and subtract the end of month payables balance to compute the payment of purchases for that month.

## Problem 5-2A

You are given the following information for the Lanser Company:

| Actual Sales | | Estimated Sales | |
|---|---|---|---|
| July | $250 | October | $375 |
| August | 350 | November | 290 |
| September | 400 | December | 430 |

All products are sold during the first 10 days of each month on terms of net 45 days, customers pay on time, and there are no bad debts. Assuming 30-day months, compute monthly collections for October to December.

## Solution 5-2A

Given that all sales are made during the first ten days on terms of net 45 days and the other conditions noted, all sales in one month are collected in the next month. Hence monthly collections will be $400 in October, $375 in November and $290 in December.

We included this problem primarily to allow you to test yourself with respect to understanding procedures versus simply memorizing formulas. The previous problem included terms of net 45 days and collections were spread over two months. Here terms are also net 45 days but collections are all in one month. The reason is due to the different sales patterns.

## Problem 5-3A

You are given the following information for Farnwood, Inc.

| Actual Sales | | Estimated Sales | |
|---|---|---|---|
| January | 10,000 | April | $25,000 |
| February | 20,000 | May | 40,000 |
| March | 30,000 | June | 60,000 |

Thirty percent of sales are for cash and 70% are on terms of net 30 days. Customers pay on time, sales are spread evenly during the month and there are no bad debts. (You may assume 30-day months for all calculations in this problem.)

• The firm sells a service and the labor cost to provide this service is equal to 60% of sales. This labor cost is paid in the month of sale. The only other expenses are depreciation of $8,000 per month and income taxes. The firm's income tax rate is 40%. Income taxes due through the end of March were paid in March. Income taxes for April to June will be paid in June.

• A cash dividend on common stock of $15,000 will be paid in May.

• Equipment costing $10,000 will be purchased for cash in June.

• The firm will issue stock in April and receive the proceeds of $5,000 in that month.

• The cash balance is $20,000 on April 1 and a minimum balance of $38,000 is desired.

Prepare a monthly cash budget for April to June.

## Solution 5-3A

Table 5-9 has the cash budget. All the receipts and disbursements except for sales and income taxes are taken directly from the information provided. Cash sales are derived by multiplying 30% times sales for the month and collections are gotten by multiplying 70% times sales for the previous month. To derive the income tax figure of $10,400 we need to prepare an income statement for the quarter.

|  | Income Statement for April to June |
|---|---|
| Sales | $125,000 |
| Labor expense | 75,000 |
| Depreciation expense | 24,000 |
| Profit before taxes | $26,000 |
| Income taxes @ 40% | 10,400 |
| Net income | $15,600 |

Some of you may have included the equipment purchase and/or the dividends with the expenses. (Another common error is to include principal payments on the debt as an expense.) Keep in mind that these are not expenses. Also, keep in mind that proceeds from debt and stock issues are not revenues.

The net cash flow is $18,500 for April as shown. Given the desired balance of $38,000 and the fact that the firm has only $20,000 on hand at the end of March, only $500 of the $18,500 is excess in the sense of being available for another purpose. This amount is shown as cumulative cash at the end of April. The cumulative cash at the end of May is computed by adding the cumulative amount of $500 at the end of April to May's net cash flow of minus $9,500. The cumulative cash at the end of June is calculated by adding June's net cash flow of minus $10,400 to the cumulative cash of minus $9,000 at the end of May. The negative figures indicate that $9,000 must be raised in May and another $10,400 is needed for June to maintain a cash balance of $38,000 at the end of each of these months.

## B. Discussion Questions
### 5-1B
How is a cash budget used by managers? What information does a cash budget provide that an operating budget does not?

### 5-2B
Explain how cash budgeting is an essential part of a firm's short-term planning and control functions.

### 5-3B
In preparing a cash budget what is the purpose of computing a cumulative amount row?

### 5-4B
Suppose accounts receivable balances at the end of June and July

**TABLE 5-9**
**FARNWOOD, INC.**
Monthly Cash Budget*
April to June

|  | *April* | *May* | *June* |
|---|---|---|---|
| **Cash Receipts** | | | |
| Cash sales | $ 7,500 | $12,000 | $18,000 |
| Collections | 21,000 | 17,500 | 28,000 |
| Stock issue | 5,000 | | |
| Total cash receipts | $33,500 | $29,500 | $46,000 |
| **Cash Disbursements** | | | |
| Labor | $15,000 | $24,000 | $36,000 |
| Income taxes | | | 10,400 |
| Dividends | | 15,000 | |
| Equipment | | | 10,000 |
| Total disbursements | $15,000 | $39,000 | $56,400 |
| **Net Cash Flow** | $18,500 | ($ 9,500) | ($10,400) |
| Cash balance $20,000 | | | |
| Desired balance 38,000 | | | |
| Increase in cash balance | (18,000) | | |
| **Cumulative Cash** | $   500 | ($ 9,000) | ($19,400) |

*Negative amounts are shown in parentheses.

---

were $23,700 and $26,500, respectively. Sales during July were $28,500. Do we need to know what portions of sales are cash and credit to compute cash inflows from sales for July? If so, why? If not, what is the total inflow from sales for July?

**5-5B**

Suppose a firm relies on a line of credit to finance seasonal cash requirements. Would it need to maintain a minimum cash balance? Why?

**5-6B**

Mr. Anderson, owner of an antique shop, was upset to discover that for the third consecutive month his firm had been pressed for cash and had to pay bills late. This puzzled him because sales had increased steadily and his accountant prepared monthly income statements which showed substantial profits in each month. Be prepared to explain to Mr. Anderson what might be causing the cash shortages and why these can occur in spite of substantial profits.

## C. Study Problems
### Problem 5-1C
You are given the following information for the Talon Company.

| Actual Sales | | Estimated Sales | |
|---|---|---|---|
| May | $150 | August | $170 |
| June | 200 | September | 220 |
| July | 180 | October | 280 |

All sales are on credit, customers pay on time, there are no bad debts and sales are spread evenly during the month. Assume 30-day months.

Compute monthly collections of accounts receivable for August to October for each of the following sets of credit terms:

Net 75 days
Net 45 days
Net 15 days
Net 10 days

### Problem 5-2C
Information on actual and estimated purchases are presented below for the GAR Company.

| Actual Purchases | | Estimated Purchases | |
|---|---|---|---|
| January | $300 | April | $320 |
| February | 260 | May | 410 |
| March | 290 | June | 370 |

All purchases are made in the last ten days of each month, purchases for the month are spread evenly during the ten days, and the firm pays on time.

Assuming 30-day months, compute monthly purchase payments for April to June for each of the following sets of credit terms.

Net 10 days
Net 30 days
Net 45 days
Net 75 days

## Problem 5-3C

You are given the following information from Roscoe, Inc.'s cash budget.

|  | January | February | March | April |
|---|---|---|---|---|
| Cash receipts | $62,500 | $79,000 | $88,000 | $74,000 |
| Cash disbursements | 72,000 | 74,500 | 78,500 | 75,000 |
| Net cash flow | ($9,500) | $ 4,500 | $ 9,500 | ($1,000) |

The cash balance on January 1 is $10,000 and the minimum desired cash balance is $8,000.

Compute the cumulative amount row of the cash budget.

## Problem 5-4C

You are given the following information for Swingto, Inc.

• Actual Sales

| April | $50,000 |
|---|---|
| May | 55,000 |
| June | 50,000 |

• Estimated Sales

| July | $70,000 | October | $55,000 |
|---|---|---|---|
| August | 85,000 | November | 48,000 |
| September | 62,000 | December | 40,000 |

• All sales are on terms of net 75 days. Assume that sales are spread evenly through the month, that customers pay on time and that there are no bad debts. Assume 30-day months for all computations in this problem.

• All goods are purchased ready for sale on terms of net 30 days. Goods needed to support sale are purchased in the month of sale. For instance, inventory needed for sales in July will be purchased in July.

• Cost of goods sold is 70% for all sales. Selling and administrative expenses are equal to 10% of sales each month and these are cash expenses. Depreciation expense is $2,500 per month. The only other expenses are interest of $2,000 per month and income taxes. Interest for July to September will be paid in September and interest for October to December will be paid in December. The income tax rate is 46%. (Payment of income taxes is discussed next.)

• Income taxes due through the end of June was paid in June. Taxes for July to September will be paid in September. Income taxes for October to December will be paid in January.

• No principal payments on long-term debt will be made during the period.

• There will be a $2,000 dividend payment in August and a $3,000 dividend payment in November.

• Equipment with a book value of $10,000 will be sold for $10,000 in August. This will be a cash sale. (This transaction was considered in deriving the depreciation expense estimate noted above.)

• On June 30th the cash balance was $5,000 and the minimum desired balance is $10,000

Prepare a monthly cash budget for July to December.

### Problem 5-5C

You are given the following information for the Doral Company

| Actual Sales | | Estimated Sales | |
|---|---|---|---|
| June | $200,000 | September | $280,000 |
| July | 225,000 | October | 260,000 |
| August | 210,000 | November | 230,000 |
| | | December | 240,000 |

• All sales are credit sales and terms are net 60 days. Customers pay on time and there are no bad debts. The firm purchases all products ready for sale (i.e., it does no manufacturing).

• The gross margin is 30% for all sales and inventory needed to support sales for a month is purchased in the preceding month on terms of net 10 days. Purchases are spread evenly during the month. Assume 30-day months for all calculations in this problem.

• Labor expense is $20,000 per month and selling expense equals 2% of sales for the month. These are cash expenses. Depreciation expense is $10,000 per month. The only other expenses are for interest and income taxes and these are discussed below.

• The firm borrowed $500,000 from a life insurance company on the last day of August. The annual interest rate is 15%. Interest must be paid quarterly starting in November. The first principal payment on the debt is not due until next August.

• The income tax rate is 50% and taxes are paid monthly.

• The minimum desired cash balance is $50,000 and cash on hand at the end of August is $35,000.

Prepare a monthly cash budget for September to November.

**Problem 5-6C**

You are given the following information for Delicious Products, Inc.

| Actual Sales | | | | Estimated Sales | |
|---|---|---|---|---|---|
| January | $18,000 | April | $22,000 | July | $37,000 |
| February | 17,000 | May | 24,000 | August | 38,000 |
| March | 20,000 | June | 34,000 | September | 40,000 |

• Seventy-five percent of sales each month are for cash and the remainder are on terms of 2/10 net 30 (which means customers can deduct 2% from the invoice if paid in ten days, otherwise, the full amount must be paid in 30 days). All credit customers pay in ten days, there are no bad debts, and sales are spread evenly during the month. Assume 30-day months for all calculations in this problem.

• Estimates of cost of goods sold expense for each month are as follows:

| Cost of Goods Sold | | | |
|---|---|---|---|
| March | $12,500 | July | $23,000 |
| April | 13,200 | August | 21,000 |
| May | 15,100 | September | 24,000 |
| June | 20,300 | | |

• Cash operating expenses are 10% of sales each month. Depreciation expense is $1,500 per month. The only other expense is income taxes. The tax rate is 45% and taxes for April to June will be paid in June and taxes for July through September will be paid in September. (Taxes due through the end of March were paid for in March.)

• Dividend payments of $1,000 each will be made in June and September.

• Cash purchases of equipment of $12,000 and $10,000 will be made in May and August, respectively. These purchases were taken into account in deriving the depreciation expense estimates noted above.

• The firm plans an $8,000 stock issue in September. The $8,000 will be received in September.

• All goods are purchased ready for sale on terms of net 20 days. Purchases are spread evenly during the month and the company pays on time. Estimated end of month inventory balances are:

| | | | |
|---|---|---|---|
| February | $ 9,500 | June | $13,500 |
| March | 10,000 | July | 11,800 |
| April | 14,200 | August | 20,000 |
| May | 15,100 | September | 18,000 |

• The cash balance on April 1 is $17,000 and the minimum desired balance is $14,000.

Prepare a monthly cash budget for April through September.

### Problem 5-7C

You are given the following information for Jermal, Inc.

| *Actual Sales* | | | *Estimated Sales* | | |
|---|---|---|---|---|---|
| July | $40,000 | October | $180,000 | January | $70,000 |
| August | 20,000 | November | 40,000 | February | 30,000 |
| September | 60,000 | December | 30,000 | March | 20,000 |

All sales are made on terms of net 75 days, sales are spread evenly during the month, customers pay on time and there are no bad debts. (Assume 30-day months for all calculations in this problem.)

• Cost of goods sold expense is 80% for all sales. All goods are purchased ready for sale and purchases are made in the month preceding sale. All purchases for the month are made on the tenth of the month on terms of net 75 days.

• The only expenses besides cost of goods sold expense are:

| | |
|---|---|
| Depreciation expense | $2,000 per month |
| Labor | $10,000 per month |
| Income tax | Tax rate is 40%. |

Labor is a cash expense. Taxes due through the end of September were paid in September. Taxes due for October through March will be paid in March.

• A cash purchase of $15,000 for equipment will be made in November. The $40,000 proceeds from a common stock issue will be received in December.

• Cash on hand on October 1 exceeds the minimum desired balance by $5,000.

Prepare a monthly cash budget for October through March.

### Problem 5-8C

You are given the following information for the Calico Manufacturing Company.

| Actual Sales | | Estimated Sales | |
|---|---|---|---|
| April | $300,000 | July | $300,000 |
| May | 180,000 | August | 320,000 |
| June | 250,000 | September | 350,000 |
| | | October | 300,000 |

### Balance Sheet
### at June 30

| | | | |
|---|---|---|---|
| Cash | $ 50,000 | Accounts payable, | |
| Accounts receivable | 258,000 | trade | $40,000 |
| Inventories: | | Accrued expenses | 4,000 |
| Raw materials | 50,000 | Mortgage debt | 200,000 |
| Work in process | 107,000 | Common stock | 30,000 |
| Finished goods | 95,000 | Paid in capital | 500,000 |
| Net fixed assets | 600,000 | Retained earnings | 386,000 |
| Total assets | $1,160,000 | Total | $1,160,000 |

• Forty percent of sales are for cash and 60% are on terms of net 60 days. Sales are spread evenly during the month, customers pay on time and there are no bad debts. (Assume 30-day months for all calculations in this problem.)

• The gross margin for all sales is 50%.

• The cost of goods manufactured schedule for the next three months is as follows:

*Cost of Goods Manufactured*

| | |
|---|---|
| July | $160,000 |
| August | 150,000 |
| September | 170,000 |

• The components of cost of goods manufactured are the same each month and are equal to the following:

| | |
|---|---|
| Raw material | 30% |
| Direct labor | 50% |
| Overhead | 20% |

• Purchases of raw materials in June were $40,000 and this amount will be paid in July. Raw material purchases will continue to be paid in 30 days and estimated end of month raw materials inventory balances are:

| | | | |
|---|---|---|---|
| July | $55,000 | September | $65,000 |
| August | 60,000 | | |

• No changes are expected in the work in process or finished goods inventory balances.

• Direct labor is a cash expense. Overhead includes depreciation expense of $2,000 per month. Remaining overhead expenses are cash expenses.

• Other expenses include:

| | |
|---|---|
| Depreciation on office furniture | $ 1,000 per month |
| Selling and administrative expenses | 75,000 per month |
| Interest expense | 2,000 per month |

• The income tax rate is 40%. Taxes through the end of June were paid in June. Taxes for July to September will be paid in September.

• Accrued expenses of $4,000 on the above balance sheet pertain to selling and administrative expenses. The estimated balances at the end of each of the next three months for this liability are:

| July | $6,000 |
|------|--------|
| August | 3,000 |
| September | 3,000 |

- Interest expense of $2,000 per month noted above is on the mortgage debt. Interest is paid monthly. A principal payment on this debt was paid at the end of June and the next payment is due in December.

- Cash dividends will be $10,000 per month.

- There will be a cash purchase of equipment of $100,000 in September.

- The cash balance is $50,000 on June 30 and the minimum desired balance is $60,000.

Prepare a monthly cash budget for July to September.

# 6

# Projected Financial Statements

This chapter explains how to prepare and use projected income statements and balance sheets. These statements are prepared to help analysts address issues such as the following: How much money will the firm need to finance growth? Can the company pay its debts on time? Will the firm be profitable in the future? Will earnings per share increase? Will the rate of return on equity increase? Are the firm's financial policies realistic?

The chapter begins with an overview of the process of preparing and using projected financial statements. Then we focus on developing estimates from publicly available information. After that we explain the mechanics of constructing the statements. Next we briefly illustrate how these statements can be used for long-term financial planning and control purposes and conclude with a short discussion of the use of a growth model.

The previous chapter included an overview of planning and control and showed how cash budgeting is an essential element. We explained how a controller of a firm relied on a monthly cash budget to estimate how much cash would be needed, when it would be needed and how to control its flow. We noted, however, that more than one tool is available for planning and controlling cash and we mentioned projected financial statements as an alternative. For instance, instead of preparing a monthly cash budget, the controller could have constructed a set of projected income statements and balance sheets to estimate cash requirements and to control the flow of cash. In other words, a cash budget and a set of projected financial statements give the same information regarding the amount of timing of estimated cash flows, so either tool can be used to help plan and control the flow of cash.

The process of preparing and using projected financial statements is known by a variety of names. For example, it is frequently called pro forma analysis, and projected statements are known as pro forma statements. Instead of preparing projected income statements and balance sheets some analysts prepare projected flow of funds statements. While this is a format issue and not a conceptual matter, it is worthwhile to keep in mind as we proceed that we are projecting sources and uses of funds.

# Overview of the Process

In this overview of the process of preparing and using projected financial statements, we will rely on a simple example. Suppose that Gloria Stine formed a company one year ago to sell a single product. The financial statements for the first year are presented below:

*Stine Company*
*Income Statement for Year 1*

| | |
|---|---|
| Net sales | $600,000 |
| Cost of goods sold | 480,000 |
| Gross profit | $120,000 |
| Rent expense | 30,000 |
| Labor | 60,000 |
| Profit before taxes | $30,000 |
| Income taxes | 15,000 |
| Net income | $ 15,000 |

*Balance Sheet at the End of Year 1*

| | | | |
|---|---|---|---|
| Cash | $ 15,000 | Accounts payable | $ 40,000 |
| Accounts receivable | 50,000 | Common stock | 50,000 |
| Inventory | 40,000 | Retained earnings | 15,000 |
| Total | $105,000 | Total | $105,000 |

Here are the facts that produce the above financial results.

1. The firm purchases 50,000 units each month for 80¢ each and sells them for $1 each. All sales are on terms of net 30 days and all customers pay on time. Hence, at the end of each month the accounts receivable balance is $50,000.

2. The firm needs a one month's supply of inventory to support operations, and purchases are on terms of net 30 days. Thus, at the end of each month the inventory balance is $40,000 and the accounts payable balance is also $40,000.

3. A cash balance of $15,000 is needed to support a sales volume of 50,000 units per month. Ms. Stine originally invested $50,000 to start the business and decided to retain all profits. Hence, the common stock and retained earnings balances at year end are $50,000 and $15,000, respectively.

4. The firm rents all its fixed assets. That is why there are no fixed assets on the balance sheet. The rental rate is $2,500 per month or $30,000 for the year. The only other operating expense is labor of $5,000 per month and the tax rate is 50%. Finally, rent, labor and tax expense are paid monthly.[1]

Now let's suppose that Ms. Stine on the first day of Year 2 realizes that she can double monthly sales and decides to do it. She estimates that the gross margin of 20% will be maintained. Twice as many employees will be needed and the firm will have to double the fixed assets it rents, but there will be no change in wage or rental rates. So, annual rent expense and annual labor expense will double to $60,000 and $120,000, respectively. The firm will continue to offer credit terms of net 30 days and all customers will pay on time. Further, the policy of a one month's supply of inventory and purchase terms of net 30 days will continue. Finally, a cash balance of $20,000 will be needed to support the higher level of activity and the firm will continue its policy of retaining all profits.

Ms. Stine believes she will need external financing to fund the growth. Let's suppose she is a relative of yours and asks you for an interest free loan of $20,000 which she will repay at the end of Year 2.[2] A number of questions come to mind but we will focus on two. Can she pay back the $20,000 at the end of Year 2? Will $20,000 be enough? Projected financial

---

[1] As you know, generally firms do not pay income taxes monthly. We make the assumption of monthly tax payments here (and elsewhere in the chapter) only to keep the explanation as simple as possible.

[2] For purposes of discussion, we are violating one of the most basic laws of the management of a small business. It is: Don't borrow money from relatives! Those who have violated this law will know what we mean and, unfortunately, many other readers will learn the hard way.

statements will help us answer these questions. Below is a projected income statement and balance sheet based on the estimates described above.

*Stine Company*
*Projected Income Statement*
*For Year 2*

| | |
|---|---:|
| Net sales | $1,200,000 |
| Cost of goods sold | 960,000 |
| Gross margin | $ 240,000 |
| Rent expense | 60,000 |
| Labor expense | 120,000 |
| Profit before income taxes | $ 60,000 |
| Income taxes | 30,000 |
| Net income | $ 30,000 |

*Projected Balance Sheet at the*
*End of Year 2*

| | | | |
|---|---:|---|---:|
| Cash | $ 20,000 | Accounts payable | $ 80,000 |
| Accounts receivable | 100,000 | Common stock | 50,000 |
| Inventory | 80,000 | Retained earnings | 45,000 |
| Total | $200,000 | Total | $175,000 |

The balance sheet does not balance! Did we make an error? The answer is "no." What the statement tells us is that a shortage of $25,000 is projected at year end. This is the difference between total assets and the total of liabilities plus owners' equity. The statement is also telling us that the Stine Company cannot wait until the end of Year 2 to figure out what to do. It must raise funds *before* the end of Year 2. If this is not possible, then the firm will not be able to attain the desired sales growth. Finally, it's important to keep in mind that the projected statement is a compilation of estimates. Hence, $25,000 is an estimate of how much is needed at year end.

Let's look at the shortage another way. The asset side of the firm's balance sheet represents a firm's uses of funds and the liabilities and owners' equity side represents a firm's sources of funds. Obviously, you cannot spend money you do not have, that is, sources and uses must balance. In this example, uses are projected at $200,000 and sources are estimated to be $175,000 at year end, indicating that an additional $25,000 will be needed at that time. We must emphasize that Ms. Stine cannot wait until the end of Year 2 to figure out what to do. The money is needed before then.

The sources and uses context enables us to generalize the interpretation of the information on a projected balance sheet with respect to estimating cash needs and surpluses.

*Interpretation Guide For Projected Balance Sheet*
If total estimated sources (i.e., the total of liabilities plus owners' equity) are greater than total estimated uses (i.e., total assets), the difference is an estimate of the cash surplus at that point in time. If the estimated uses exceed the estimated sources, the difference is an estimate of the resources required to arrive at that point in time.

Later we will explain the various formats used for showing needs and surpluses.

Returning to our example, let's address the two questions posed earlier. Can the Stine Company pay you back the $20,000 at the end of Year 2? Will $20,000 be enough? The analysis indicates that the answer to each question is "no." Of course, we must keep in mind that the projected statements are summaries of estimates and so we must assess the reasonableness of the estimates. For the sake of discussion, let's assume we are confident that actual amounts will be close to the estimates.

How much will the Stine Company need to double sales? The projected balance sheet indicates a need of $25,000 at the end of Year 2. But it does not tell us: (1) whether $25,000 is the maximum amount needed for Year 2 and (2) when the maximum need will occur. To obtain information on the amount and timing of the maximum need during the year, we could prepare projected balance sheets at the end of each month. Alternatively, we could figure out when during the year the maximum need will occur and prepare a balance sheet as of that date. Let's try this second approach. Can you figure out when the maximum need will occur? Think about the timing for a moment and then read on to check your answer.

You might recall that increases in assets and decreases in liabilities are uses of funds. So, if either or both of these are causing the need, we must estimate when during the year the total uses will be the greatest. For the Stine Company, the increase in assets needed to generate higher sales is causing the need. The higher level of sales will occur in the first month of Year 2. So more inventory will be needed right away and accounts receivable will double by the end of the first month, given the term of net 30 days. Hence, the maximum need will occur during the first month and so a projected balance sheet at the end of Month 1, Year 2, will give us the desired information.[3] Below is a projected balance sheet at this date. (Net

[3] To be precise, we should consider when during January the maximum need will occur. However, generally end-of-month statements will be sufficient to gain the desired information, especially when there are no substantial timing differences of cash inflows and outflows during the month or when needs created by timing differences during the month are funded by credit lines and/or liquidity reserves.

income for Month 1 will be $2,500, so the retained earnings balance will equal the end of Year 1 balance of $15,000 plus $2,500.)

*Stine Company*
*Projected Balance Sheet*
*End of Month 1, Year 2*

| Cash | $ 20,000 | Accounts payable | $ 80,000 |
|---|---|---|---|
| Accounts receivable | 100,000 | Common stock | 50,000 |
| Inventory | 80,000 | Retained earnings | 17,500 |
| Total | $200,000 | Total | $147,500 |

| | |
|---|---|
| Total estimated assets (uses) | $200,000 |
| Total estimated liabilities and owners' equity (sources) | 147,500 |
| Need | $ 52,500 |

The above statement shows that $52,500 will be needed to double sales growth. We know this is the maximum need because given the estimates, the assets will be at the same level of $200,000 at the end of each subsequent month. In other words, no further uses are expected. However, there will be sources and so the need will decline. Specifically, operations will provide $2,500 per month, all of which will be retained in the business. The balance sheet at the end of Year 2 indicates a need of $25,000. Hence, we can conclude that if debt financing is employed to finance the need of $52,500, part but not all of the debt can be repaid during the second year.

Before proceeding, a further comment is in order regarding the interpretation guide for a projected balance sheet. The last sentence of the guide tells us that if uses exceed sources, this is an estimate of the resources required to arrive at that point in time. Note that we said, "resources required"—instead of—"cash required." The reason is that locating a source of cash is not the only way to finance the need. For instance, suppose Ms. Stine persuades the trade creditors to give terms of net 60 days instead of net 30 days. This would solve the financing problem but the trade creditors would not be giving the firm cash. Look back for a moment at the end of Year 2's projected balance sheet and analyze the impact of terms of net 60 days. Accounts payable would be $160,000 instead of $80,000, total sources would be $255,000, and there would be a cash surplus of $55,000 rather than a need of $25,000. Notice that the trade creditors do not provide cash directly to the firm in the sense that they do not write a check for $80,000. However, permitting terms of net 60 days instead of net 30 days has the same effect as writing the firm a check.

# *Elements of the Process*

The above overview illustrated four of the five elements of the process of preparing and using projected financial statements. Below is a list of all five followed by a brief discussion of each.

• Selecting time horizon.

• Developing estimates.

• Constructing statements.

• Interpreting information and taking appropriate action.

• Comparing actual statements with projections and taking necessary action.

The time horizon selected depends on the purpose of the analysis. For the Stine Company, we needed projected balance sheets at the end of Month 1, Year 2, and at the end of Year 2 to address the two issues of interest. Had the example been more complex, we might have needed monthly projections for all 12 months. Further, had we wanted to focus on longer term issues, we likely would have needed annual projections for a number of years.

In our examples, all the estimates were given but this is a key task in the process and we will turn our attention to it shortly. Regarding mechanics, given the nature of the example, the preparation of the statements was fairly simple. In practice, the computations are generally more complex, and we discuss this aspect further later in the chapter.

Once the statements are prepared, we must assess the information and act. In our example, the statements told us that about $50,000 would be needed right away and that a short-term source would not be appropriate. We will discuss the interpretation of the information further but we will not stress all the subtleties because these have been discussed at length in the chapters on cash budgeting and flow of funds analysis. Finally, we will not stress comparing actual figures with projected amounts because this phase also was emphasized in the prior chapter on cash budgeting.

Before moving on, we should address a format issue. It concerns how analysts list a need or surplus on a projected balance sheet. One way is to present the amount needed (or surplus) just below the balance sheet as we did for the Stine Company. Another way is to rely on a "plug" figure. The projected balance sheet at the end of Month 1, Year 2 is presented below in this format. The estimated need of $52,500 is shown as "Notes payable (plug)."

*Stine Company*
*Projected Balance Sheet*
*End of Month 1, Year 2*

| | | | |
|---|---|---|---|
| Cash | $ 20,000 | Notes payable (plug) | $ 52,500 |
| Accounts receivable | 100,000 | Accounts payable | 80,000 |
| Inventory | 80,000 | Common stock | 50,000 |
| Total | $200,000 | Retained earnings | 17,500 |
| | | Total | $200,000 |

When there is an estimated cash surplus, analysts usually show either a negative notes payable plug account, lump the surplus in with the cash figure, or show a separate asset account under the cash account called excess cash or something similar.

Many analysts prefer using a plug figure so the balance sheet will balance. This approach is more convenient if further analysis based on the statement will be performed such as ratio analysis. In any event, if you use this approach be sure to clearly identify the plug figure and make sure there is only one plug figure on each projected balance sheet.

We will now turn our attention to developing estimates.

## DEVELOPING ESTIMATES

The previous chapter explained how to develop estimates for a cash budget. We described how one firm did it and saw that the estimates were fairly accurate. The reason for this was that the estimates flowed from targets for revenues and expenses and other items affecting cash flows, and managers of that firm worked hard to achieve the established targets. Moreover, we noted that the estimates used to prepare the cash budget also could be employed to prepare a set of projected income statements and balance sheets. Hence, the entire discussion in the last chapter pertaining to developing estimates is relevant for projected income statements and balance sheets. Obviously we will not repeat that discussion. Instead, we will explain how someone outside the firm, such as a trade creditor or security analyst, with access only to publicly available information might develop estimates. Please keep in mind that we are providing a general guide and that the ideal approach will depend on the purpose of the analysis, specific circumstances and the particular firm.

The analyst might begin by collecting data on the firm, the industry (or industries) in which it operates, and the economy. The firm's annual or 10-K report normally will include summary annual financial data for the last 10 years and quarterly data for the previous eight quarters. While these data will suffice in a pinch, we should normally work with complete financial statements for say the past five or 10 years and quarterly financials for the previous eight quarters. Moreover, there should be a search for articles written about the firm in publications like the *Wall Street Journal* and for reports prepared by analysts. Industry information would include items like average ratios, relative market shares of all or the major participants, and reports written about the industry by other analysts. Finally, the information on the economy would include items like historical and forecasted data on inflation and interest rates, Gross National Product and various economic indicators.

### Sales

Deriving an estimate of sales normally deserves the most attention because it is most critical in the sense that other estimates are based on it. One approach is to relate sales for the industry to some economic indicator like Gross National Product. Statistical procedures are available to help determine if a relationship exists and what the relationship is. Once an estimate of industry sales is derived, the analyst must estimate the firm's market share for the next year. Historical data on market share might help to detect trends and/or the firm's annual report might provide a clue. For example, it might be stated that one of the firm's goals is to increase or maintain its existing market share.

For a small firm, the above procedure would not work. Even if the firm is large enough, the scope of the analysis might not justify such an elaborate effort and we probably would do something much less sophisticated. For example, we might calculate the annual percentage change in sales for each of the past five or ten years and make a judgment based on these data, the prospects for the economy and the industry for the coming year, and any hints that may be provided in the firm's annual report.

### Expenses

A useful starting point for estimating expenses is to construct 100% income statements for several previous periods, which means listing each expense as a percentage of net sales. As noted in the chapter on ratios, we compute these percents by dividing each expense, except income taxes, by net sales. (Income tax expense is normally listed as a percent of pretax income.) Circumstances will determine how many periods in the past 100% income statements are constructed and whether one relies on annual or quarterly data, or both. In any event, if the 100% income statements show a stable pattern for a particular item and a reading of the annual report and other sources gives no reason to expect a change, then this figure could be used. For example, if cost of goods sold expense was 50% of sales for each of the past several years, this could be employed as the forecast of the cost of goods sold rate. On the other hand, if there was an upward or downward drift, we might rely on the most recent figure or continue the trend. For instance, say that we found the following for selling, general and administrative expenses for each of the last five years: 18%, 19%, 20%, 21% and 22%. We might use 22% or a percent higher like 23%. The choice is a judgment based on the historical ratios, industry averages, and information contained in the annual report and/or other reports.

When reviewing 100% income statements, we frequently will find an expense category which is not stable and displays no trend. For instance, we might find the following historical ratios for an expense: 18%, 22%, 19%, 21%, 20%. As discussed in the chapter on cost-volume-profit analysis, a number of factors such as changing sales mix, fixed expenses and varying inflation rates can cause a trendless pattern. When this occurs, some analysts like to be conservative and choose the rate that produces the lowest profit figure. At any rate, we should look closely at information in annual and other reports to help make the estimates (or guesstimates) more reasonable and less arbitrary.

### Assets

Cash plus marketable securities, which we will refer to as cash, represent the firm's liquid balances. Generally, the firm holds cash for a combination of reasons which may include the following: to compensate banks for services, to support day-to-day operations, to provide a cushion or reserve for unexpected emergencies and opportunities and to help finance major expenditures. Calculating the ratio of cash to net sales for each of the past several years might help but because of the various motives for holding cash, we will often find a pattern that is not stable and displays no trend. Hence, in situations like this we will have to rely on an assumption that may be somewhat arbitrary like assuming that cash will increase at the same rate as sales or at a somewhat lower rate.[4]

To estimate accounts receivable balances, we need the sales estimates and information on the firm's collection experience. Historical information on the receivable turnover ratio or the days' sales outstanding ratio can be quite helpful. We must keep in mind, however, that the state of the economy can affect the collection rate. For example, there is often a lengthening of

---

[4] Very often there are economies with respect to the amount of cash needed to support normal operations (often referred to as transaction balances). Hence, in these cases, we would expect cash to increase at a lower rate than sales.

the collection period during recessions and periods of high interest rates. Furthermore, as explained in the chapter on ratio analysis, turnover ratios, and the days' sales outstanding ratio (a turnover ratio stated another way), can give a distorted view when a firm's sale pattern changes and/or when sales are growing rapidly. Consequently, care must be exercised in examining historical turnover ratios. Usually it helps to work with quarterly data.[5]

To estimate inventory we can rely on the projection for cost of goods sold (discussed above) plus an estimate of what the firm's inventory turnover will be. In the absence of better information, we might rely on an analysis of past inventory turnover ratios to develop an estimate. Some analysts rely on an analysis of past ratios of inventory to sales to derive an estimate of inventory. This will give essentially the same amount as working with cost of goods sold when a firm's gross margin is stable. When the gross margin varies, we will get a different answer and, in these instances, it is usually better to work with cost of goods sold.

Providing guidance on other current assets is difficult. Sometimes these assets vary with sales, other times they vary with the passage of time, and in certain instances, they will change in no particular pattern or not change at all. In any event, we must make an assessment of what these assets consist of and work from there.

Turning to long-term assets, often the major portion will consist of fixed assets. Firms add fixed assets to replace worn out equipment and/or to support expansion plans. Although the fixed asset balance typically changes with volume over time, often the relationship will not be direct—that is, fixed assets will not change at the same percentage rate as sales. Thus, we may have difficulty deriving a decent estimate. Hopefully, information in the annual or 10-K report will provide insight. If not, we will have to do something that is somewhat arbitrary like increase the net fixed asset balance at the same rate as sales or rely on an average of past percentage increases. Finally, although it is sometimes helpful to derive separate estimates for gross fixed assets and accumulated depreciation, generally this is not necessary and we can work just with the net fixed asset balance.

The appropriate method for estimating other long-term assets will depend on what these assets represent. For instance, for an intangible asset like goodwill declining over time, we might continue the reduction. Past statements likely will help us judge what the reduction (amortization) rate should be.

---

[5] This caveat applies to other turnover ratios such as inventory turnover and also to ratios designed to provide insight on how long it takes the firm to pay for purchases such as the days' purchases outstanding ratio. See chapter on ratio analysis for a discussion of the analytical difficulties involved and how to deal with them.

## Liabilities and Owners' Equity

Turning our attention to the estimates of liabilities and owners' equity, we begin with current liabilities. You likely will encounter the following current liabilities: trade accounts payable, accrued liabilities (accrued expenses), loans due in one year, current maturities of long-term debt and other current liabilities. We will discuss each type.

With respect to trade payables, we could rely on historical ratios of accounts payable to sales to derive an estimate. Usually, it's safer to derive a purchase figure,[6] and then try to figure out the firm's payment policy. Information on payments of purchases may be readily available. If not, we could rely on historical days' purchases outstanding ratios to derive an estimate.

Recall that accrued expenses are liabilities for expenses that have been incurred but not paid as of the balance sheet date. They might be for wages, utilities, interest, taxes, and/or other expenses. Thus, the method we employ will be dictated by the nature of the expenses that make up the account(s). Often it will be safe to assume that accrued expenses will vary with volume. This assumption can be tested by looking at historical accrued expenses to sales ratios. If a stable pattern does not exist, one must look to other information in the annual report to help derive a reasonable estimate.

Short-term loans are debts due within one year, typically, to a bank or finance company or to the public via the commercial paper market. These can represent four different items and normally the footnotes to the financial statements will enable us to judge which of the four it is. The first is a temporary loan which is not recurring in nature. Hence, the balance would be zero one year in the future. The second is a line of credit which is for seasonal needs. If the line is indeed used for seasonal financing requirements and the basic seasonality of the firm's sales does not change substantially, then we would expect the balance to vary at the same rate as sales. The third type is not really a short-term loan but because of the nature of the agreement it is listed as a current liability. An example is a loan secured by and based on the size of the firm's receivables. The fourth is the current portion of long-term debt. For the third and fourth types, generally, information in the annual or 10-K reports will help us develop reasonable estimates.

It is hard to provide guidance for other current liabilities. Some vary with sales, others vary with another index and others do not vary at all. All we can do is look to other information to make a reasonable as-

---

[6] In the last chapter we explained a procedure for deriving a purchase figure from cost of goods sold and inventory. We will explain the procedure again a little later.

sumption. If such information is not available, an "educated guess" is necessary.

Turning to long-term liabilities, long-term loans are debts with a maturity of more than one year. Examples are bonds and term loans from banks. Generally, information in the firm's annual or 10-K report will help us derive a decent estimate. Another long-term liability that we frequently encounter is deferred income taxes. Recall that this account represents a timing difference between income tax expense recorded on the firm's income statement and its actual tax liability for the period. At any rate, often an examination of the firm's financial statements (including accompanying footnotes) will enable us to derive reasonable figures. Finally, there may be other long-term liabilities besides long-term loans and deferred income taxes. If so, generally information in the annual or 10-K report will enable us to make a good estimate.

Preferred and common stock issues are typically planned well in advance so it will normally not be too difficult to get information concerning these plans. In most instances, especially for small firms, there will be only minor changes in these two accounts (for something like the exercise of stock options) or no change at all.

The final item is the retained earnings account which is calculated as follows:

> Retained earnings at the beginning of the period
> + Net income after taxes
> − Dividends on common and preferred
> = Retained earnings at the end of the period

Since the beginning balance is known and the estimate of net income has already been derived, all that must be estimated is dividends. Many firms have a clearly articulated dividend policy. Hence there should not be any difficulty obtaining a reasonable estimate. Sometimes there will be other items besides net income and dividends which are included in the computation of retained earnings. Generally, these will be relatively small and, in addition, the information in the annual report will enable one to derive a good estimate.

To develop estimates for projected financial statements, assumptions are often necessary. Often analysts prepare multiple sets of projected financial statements relying on different assumptions for each. Financial planning models are available to perform the arithmetic, so preparing multiple projections is a simple task. This kind of analysis is known as sensitivity analysis or financial modeling.

# Constructing Projected Financial Statements

The overview presented earlier showed how to prepare projected financial statements. We will now discuss this element in a bit more detail. Before proceeding we should note that many of the computations discussed below were explained in the appendix to the previous chapter. If you have difficulty with some of the derivations, particularly accounts receivable, inventory and accounts payable, we suggest that you refer to that appendix.

Table 6-1 outlines the procedure for preparing projected financial statements. To illustrate we will rely on the following figures for the Bedco Company:

*Bedco Co.*
*Balance Sheet at June 30*

| | | | |
|---|---|---|---|
| Cash | $ 29,000 | Accounts payable | $ 25,000 |
| Accounts receivable | 160,000 | Accrued wages | 40,000 |
| Inventory | 80,000 | Long-term debt | 360,000 |
| Net fixed assets | 600,000 | Common stock | 1,000 |
| Total | $869,000 | Paid-in capital | 99,000 |
| | | Retained earnings | 344,000 |
| | | Total | $869,000 |

| *Actual Sales* | | *Estimated Sales* | |
|---|---|---|---|
| April | $ 40,000 | July | $180,000 |
| May | 60,000 | August | 210,000 |
| June | 100,000 | September | 220,000 |
| | | October | 300,000 |

---

**Table 6-1**   *Procedure for Constructing Projected Financial Statements*

---

• Prepare the projected income statement.

• List and total projected asset balances.

• List and total projected liability and owners' equity balance.

• Compare the two totals and compute need or surplus.*

• Insert plug figure.

---

*If the total assets (uses) exceed the total of liability plus owners' equity balances, a need is indicated. If the total of liability and owners' equity balances exceed the total assets, a surplus is indicated.

1. Through the end of June all sales were on terms of net 60 days. Commencing July 1 terms will be net 20 days for all sales. Assume that sales are spread evenly throughout each month, customers pay on time, and there are no bad debts. (For simplicity we will assume 30-day months for all calculations.)

2. Cost of goods sold expense is 60% for all sales, and other estimated expenses are as follows: (1) rent, $2,000 per month (all cash), (2) depreciation, $4,000 per month, (3) wages, $50,000 per month, wages for one month are paid in the next month, (4) interest, annual rate on long-term debt (discussed below) is 12% and (5) income taxes, rate is 50% (payments discussed below).

3. All goods are purchased ready for sale. It is estimated that purchases will be $100,000 per month starting in July. The accounts payable balance of $25,000 shown on the end of the June balance sheet represents purchases for June, which were on terms of net 45 days. Terms for purchases in July will be net 40 days and terms for purchases in August and September will be net 15 days. Finally, there are no cash purchases and it will be assumed that purchases are spread evenly during the month.

4. Interest and principal due on the long-term debt through the end of June was paid on June 30th. A principal payment of $20,000 is due at the end of August and at that time interest for July and August will be paid. After that, no payments of interest and principal are required until the end of October.

5. Income taxes will be paid in the month of incurrence except for September's amount which will be paid on October 5th.

6. Cash purchases of fixed assets will be $2,000 per month and the firm will not sell or retire any fixed assets.

7. Finally, cash dividends will be $8,000 per month and the firm's minimum desired cash balance is $15,000.

Table 6-2 presents projected income statements for July, August and September, and projected balance sheets at the end of each of these months. We will now explain how the numbers were derived.

The income statements are straightforward and require little explanation. The figures for sales are the estimates given, cost of goods sold is 60% of sales, and rent, wages and depreciation were given. Interest expense is derived by multiplying the loan balance outstanding by the annual interest

**Table 6-2**  *Monthly Pro Forma Income Statements*

|  | For July | For August | For September |
|---|---|---|---|
| Net sales | $180,000 | $210,000 | $220,000 |
| Cost of goods sold | 108,000 | 126,000 | 132,000 |
| Gross profit | $ 72,000 | $ 84,000 | $ 88,000 |
| Rent | 2,000 | 2,000 | 2,000 |
| Depreciation | 4,000 | 4,000 | 4,000 |
| Wages | 50,000 | 50,000 | 50,000 |
| Interest | 3,600 | 3,600 | 3,400 |
| Profit before taxes | $ 12,400 | $ 24,400 | $ 28,600 |
| Income taxes | 6,200 | 12,200 | 14,300 |
| Net income | $  6,200 | $ 12,200 | $ 14,300 |
| Dividends | 8,000 | 8,000 | 8,000 |
| To retained earning | ($1,800) | $  4,200 | $  6,300 |

*Pro Forma Balance Sheets*

|  | End of July | End of August | End of September |
|---|---|---|---|
| Cash | $ 15,000 | $ 15,000 | $ 15,000 |
| Accounts receivable | 220,000 | 140,000 | 146,667 |
| Inventory | 72,000 | 46,000 | 14,000 |
| Net fixed assets | 598,000 | 596,000 | 594,000 |
| Total uses | $905,000 | $797,000 | $769,667 |
| Notes payable (plug) | ($  63,300) | ($122,733) | ($140,733) |
| Accounts payable | 112,500 | 83,333 | 50,000 |
| Accrued wages | 50,000 | 50,000 | 50,000 |
| Accrued interest | 3,600 | 0 | 3,400 |
| Accrued income taxes | 0 | 0 | 14,300 |
| Long-term debt | 360,000 | 340,000 | 340,000 |
| Common stock | 1,000 | 1,000 | 1,000 |
| Paid-in capital | 99,000 | 99,000 | 99,000 |
| Retained earnings | 342,200 | 346,400 | 352,700 |
| Total | $905,000 | $797,000 | $769,667 |

rate of 12% and dividing the total by 12 for the number of months in a year, as shown below:

| Month | Balance Outstanding For the Month | | Annual Interest Rate | | Annual Interest |
|---|---|---|---|---|---|
| July | $360,000 | × | 12% | = | $43,200 |
| August | 360,000 | × | 12% | = | 43,200 |
| September | 340,000 | × | 12% | = | 40,800 |

| Month | Annual Interest | | | | Monthly Interest |
|---|---|---|---|---|---|
| July | $43,200 | ÷ | 12 | = | $ 3,600 |
| August | 43,200 | ÷ | 12 | = | 3,600 |
| September | 40,800 | ÷ | 12 | = | 3,400 |

We were told that a principal payment of $20,000 will be made at the end of August, leaving a loan balance of $340,000. (Another way of deriving monthly interest is as follows: Divide annual interest rate of 12% by 12 to get a monthly interest rate of 1%; then multiply the monthly rate of 1% by the loan balance for the month.)

Income tax expense is obtained by multiplying pretax income by the tax rate of 50%. The "To retained earnings" line shows how much the retained earnings balance will *change* for the month because of income and dividends. It is derived by subtracting dividends for the month from that month's net income after taxes. (Sometimes analysts do not show dividends and to retained earnings numbers on the projected income statements. While these are not necessary, they do make the statements more informative.)

Turning to the assets, cash is the minimum desired balance. (The format used here is to rely on "notes payable-plug" as the balancing figure.) For accounts receivable, we were told that terms were net 60 days through the end of June and that they will change to net 20 days on July 1. Thus, at the end of July, June's sales of $100,000 will be outstanding because they will be collected in August. Terms of net 20 days mean that one-third of a month's sales will be collected in the same month and two-thirds will be received in the next month. Thus, two-thirds of July's sales of $180,000, which is $120,000, will be outstanding at the end of July, so the total balance at that time will be $220,000.

By the end of August, all of June and July's sales will be collected as well as one-third of the sales for August. Thus, two-thirds of the August sales of $210,000, which is $140,000, will be outstanding at the end of August. At the end of September, two-thirds of September's sales of $220,000, which is $146,667, will be outstanding at the end of September.

The figures for inventory were derived by relying on the relationship for computing cost of goods sold. Recall that for a merchandising firm, cost of goods sold is computed as follows:

> Beginning inventory
> + Purchases
> − Ending inventory
> = Cost of goods sold expense

The end of June balance sheet shows an inventory figure of $80,000, which is also beginning inventory for July. We were given estimates for purchases and cost of goods sold so we can derive ending inventory for July and for the next two months as shown below. (Note that we are rearranging the relationship for cost of goods sold.)

|  | July | August | September |
|---|---|---|---|
| Beginning inventory | $ 80,000 | $ 72,000 | $ 46,000 |
| + Purchases | 100,000 | 100,000 | 100,000 |
| − Cost of goods sold expense | 108,000 | 126,000 | 132,000 |
| = Ending inventory | $ 72,000 | $ 46,000 | $ 14,000 |

The final asset, net fixed assets, represents the sum of the book values of the firm's property, plant and equipment. The net amount is computed as follows:

> Gross fixed assets
> − Accumulated depreciation
> = Net fixed assets

Gross fixed assets, also referred to as just fixed assets, and accumulated depreciation accounts are affected by the purchase and sale of fixed assets, the retirement of fixed assets and depreciation expense. We can approximate the computation of the fixed asset balance by relying on the following relationship.

> Net fixed asset balance, beginning of period
> + Purchases of fixed assets during period
> − Sales of fixed assets during the period
> − Depreciation expense for the period
> = Net fixed assets balance, end of period

This relationship gives an approximation and not an exact figure because it assumes that retired assets are fully depreciated and sales of fixed assets occur at a price equal to the asset's book value. However, the procedure normally gives a good approximation and so we will not deal with additional refinements.

The end of June balance sheet shows a net fixed asset balance of $600,000. To this amount we add the estimate for purchases of $2,000 and subtract the depreciation estimate of $4,000 to derive the end of July balance. From there we can derive the balances for the next two months. The calculations are presented below:

|  | July | August | September |
|---|---|---|---|
| Net fixed assets, beginning of month | $600,000 | $598,000 | $596,000 |
| + Purchases for month | 2,000 | 2,000 | 2,000 |
| − Sales of fixed assets during month | 0 | 0 | 0 |
| − Depreciation expense for month | 4,000 | 4,000 | 4,000 |
| = Net fixed assets, end of month | $598,000 | $596,000 | $594,000 |

The reader should note that it is not necessary that the purchases or sales of fixed assets be for cash. The same procedure is used for cash and credit transactions. If the transaction involves credit, however, a liability account will be affected.

Turning to the other side of the balance sheet we will save "notes payable (plug)" for last because it is computed last. To derive the accounts payable we need historical and estimated data on purchases and credit terms. We were told that all purchases were on credit and were spread evenly during the month. June's purchases were $25,000 and terms were net 45 days. Hence, one-half of this amount, which is $12,500, will be outstanding at the end of July. Also outstanding at the end of July will be total purchases for July of $100,000 because terms will be net 40 days. So the total amount owed at the end of July will be $112,500.

Purchases for August and September will be $100,000 per month on terms of net 15 days. Given that purchases are spread evenly during the month, terms of net 15 days tell us that one-half of purchases for a month will be outstanding at the end of the month. So 50% of August's purchases, which is $50,000, will be owed at the end of August. Will any of June or July's purchases still be outstanding? All of June's purchases and all but one-third of July's purchases, which is $33,333, will be paid by the end of August. Hence the total owed at the end of August will be $83,333. This amount will be paid by the end of September, so all that will be owed at that point will be one-half of September's purchases, which is $50,000.

The next three liabilities are accrued expenses representing expenses that have been incurred but not yet paid. We were told that wage expense of $50,000 each month would be paid in the next month. Hence, accrued wages will be $50,000 at the end of each month. Interest due through the end of June was paid. That is why there is no accrued interest on the end of June balance sheet. Interest for July and August will be paid at the end of August. So interest expense for July will be owed on that date as shown and the liability will be zero at the end of August. Since no further payments will be made until October, interest expense for September will be a liability at that time.

We were told that income tax expense will be paid in the month of incurrence for July and August, and September's amount will be paid on October 5th. Recall that payment for an expense in the month of incurrence means that it is a cash expense. Thus, we are being told that income tax expense is a cash expense for July and August, but September's amount will be paid in the next month. Thus, there is a zero liability at the end of July and August, and September's balance will be $14,300, the tax expense for that month.

When dealing with accrued expenses, some people ask: Why do we bother with accounting rules if we are concerned with cash flows? There are two parts to the answer. First, projected financial statements are prepared for reasons other than estimating cash needs and surpluses. Examples are for estimating profitability and for evaluating future financial position. Second, these liabilities are real sources in the sense that they reflect the fact that the firm is postponing payment of expenses.

The long-term debt balances reflect the information provided about payment of principal. The common stock and paid-in capital accounts in July, August and September are the same as the end of June because no transactions involving stock are anticipated. Finally, the retained earnings balances were derived as follows:

|  | July | August | September |
|---|---|---|---|
| Retained earnings, beginning of month | $344,000 | $342,200 | $346,400 |
| + Net income after taxes for month | 6,200 | 12,200 | 14,300 |
| − Dividends for the month | 8,000 | 8,000 | 8,000 |
| = Retained earning, end of month | $342,200 | $346,400 | $352,700 |

(The retained earnings balance at the beginning of July is taken from the end of June balance sheet.)

Now that we have listed all the liabilities and owners' equity accounts, we compute the total for each month, compare the totals to the total assets for each month and derive the estimate of the amount needed or the surplus generated for each month. This is shown below:

|  | *July* | *August* | *September* |
|---|---|---|---|
| Total estimated assets | $905,000 | $797,000 | $769,667 |
| Total estimated liabilities and owners' equities | 968,300 | 919,733 | 910,400 |
| Surplus (need) | $ 63,300 | $122,733 | $140,733 |

There is a projected surplus for each month, and these amounts are shown as negative numbers for notes payable (plug).

In interpreting need or surplus figures, inexperienced analysts frequently make the error of cumulating the amounts. For instance, the projected balance sheets in our example show an estimated surplus at the end of July and an estimated surplus at the end of August. Since these are totals for certain points in time, it would be incorrect to add them together.

In our example, we saw three consecutive surpluses. Are these permanent or temporary? What should we do with the money? There was not enough information given in the example to deal effectively with these questions, but these are the kinds of issues we address in actual situations. Furthermore, we should emphasize the importance of comparing actual statements with projections, investigating differences and taking appropriate action. As discussed in the last chapter, this is an essential part of the control process.

# Use of Projected Financial Statements In Long-Term Financial Planning

The previous chapter included a brief discussion of long-term financial planning. It is beyond our scope to delve much further into this topic. However, we will discuss a simple example so you may gain additional insight on the importance of long-term planning and the use of projected financial statements. Suppose we are given the following information for the J Company.

### J Company
### Balance Sheet, End of Year 1
### (000 omitted)

| Cash | $ 50 | Accounts payable | $ 50 |
|---|---|---|---|
| Accounts receivable | 100 | Long-term debt | 150 |
| Inventory | 200 | Common stock | 400 |
| Net fixed assets | 300 | Retained earnings | 50 |
| Total | $650 | | $650 |

- Sales were $1 million during Year 1 and net income after taxes was $50,000.

- Management wants to establish the following financial policies and targets: (1) sales growth of 25% per year for the next five years, (2) net profit margin of 5% each year, (3) dividend distribution equal to 50% of net income for the year and (4) long-term debt to equity ratio of one-third.

- Given the cash needed to support operations and credit terms, management estimates that year-end cash and receivable levels will equal 5% and 10%, respectively, of sales for that year.

- A new inventory policy will be implemented in Year 2 and it is anticipated that the level of inventory at the end of each year will equal 19% of sales for that year. Despite this change, year-end accounts payable balances will continue to equal 5% of sales for the year.

- Management estimates that net fixed assets will increase at the same rate as sales. In other words, the net fixed asset balance at the end of each year will equal 30% of annual sales.

- The owners do not want to delete their ownership nor invest additional money so there will be no common stock issued; nor will there be any preferred stock issued.

Table 6-3 has projected income data and annual balance sheets for five years based on the above information.

The projected financial statements show that the desired sales growth of 25% per year cannot be achieved given the profit level, the asset increases due to higher sales, and the desired debt, stock and dividend policies. The "notes payable (plug)" figures show a continuous and growing need for funds. Management can consider altering its financial policies with respect to debt, stock and dividends, lowering its sales growth target or a combination of both. The firm may be able to alter asset levels but often these are primarily sales driven, which means that once you commit to a sales level, you are also committing to specific asset levels. In any event, it is necessary to construct projected financial statements when considering

**TABLE 6-3**
**J COMPANY**
Estimated Income Data
For Year Ended 12/31
(000 omitted)

|  | Year 2 | Year 3 | Year 4 | Year 5 | Year 6 |
|---|---|---|---|---|---|
| Net sales | $1,250 | $1,563 | $1,954 | $2,443 | $3,054 |
| Net income | 63 | 78 | 98 | 122 | 153 |
| Dividends | 31 | 39 | 49 | 61 | 76 |
| To retained earnings | 32 | 39 | 49 | 61 | 77 |

Pro Forma Balance Sheets
at 12/31
(000 omitted)

|  | Year 2 | Year 3 | Year 4 | Year 5 | Year 6 |
|---|---|---|---|---|---|
| Cash | $ 63 | $ 78 | $ 98 | $ 122 | $ 153 |
| Accounts receivable | 125 | 156 | 195 | 244 | 305 |
| Inventory | 238 | 297 | 371 | 464 | 580 |
| Net fixed assets | 375 | 469 | 586 | 733 | 916 |
| Total | $801 | $1,000 | $1,250 | $1,563 | $1,954 |
| | | | | | |
| Notes payable (plug) | $ 95 | $ 227 | $ 392 | $ 600 | $ 857 |
| Accounts payable | 63 | 78 | 98 | 122 | 153 |
| Long-term debt | 161 | 174 | 190 | 210 | 236 |
| Common stock | 400 | 400 | 400 | 400 | 400 |
| Retained earnings | 82 | 121 | 170 | 231 | 308 |
| Total | $801 | $1,000 | $1,250 | $1,563 | $1,954 |

alternatives because it makes little sense to consider options that would not solve the funds shortage problem. For instance, suppose management of the J Company wants to consider a long-term debt to equity ratio of 40% and a dividend payout ratio of 25%. The first step would be to construct a set of projected financial statements incorporating these changes. (The analysis would show that these financial policies would not enable the firm to increase sales by 25% per year.)

Altering assumptions about financial policies, sales growth, profit levels or some other factor is known as sensitivity analysis, scenario forecasting or a similar name. Basically, the analyst asks a series of "What if?" questions and tests the impact. Computer-based planning models are available for performing this analysis so it is a fairly simple task, which generally provides considerable insight.

# Growth Models

Instead of developing sets of projected financial statements, the analyst can rely on one of a number of growth models. These models enable us to gain the same kind of insight as the sensitivity analysis just described.

We will rely on a model based on the one developed by Robert Higgins that appeared in the Fall 1977 issue of *Financial Management*. It is presented below.

$$g = \frac{MRL}{A - MRL}$$

Where:

g = Sales growth in dollars possible without reliance on external equity

M = Net profit margin

R = The retention rate which is one minus the ratio of dividends to earnings

L = One plus the ratio of total liabilities, excluding spontaneous liabilities, to total owners' equity

A = Total assets minus spontaneous liabilities to total sales

Spontaneous liabilities are those which move directly with sales.

We will illustrate the computation of g by relying on the J Company. Recall that we just saw that the firm could not achieve sales growth of 25% per year given a net profit margin of five percent, a dividend payout ratio of 50% and a long-term debt to the owners' equity ratio of one-third. What sales growth can the J Company achieve without relying on external equity? Figures from the above model are as follows: M is 5%, R is 50% and L is 1⅓. The end of Year 1 balance sheet shows total assets to sales of 65%, but we are told that in the future that total of assets would equal 64% of sales as shown in Table 6-3. Hence, given that accounts payable will be 5% of sales and that it is the only spontaneous liability, A equals 59%, the difference between total assets of 64% and spontaneous liabilities of 5%. We can now compute g.

$$g = \frac{(5\%)\,(50\%)\,(1\tfrac{1}{3})}{59\% - (5\%)\,(50\%)\,(1\tfrac{1}{3})}$$

$$g = 6\%$$

The J Company's sales can grow at 6% per year without raising external equity.

It is important to keep the underlying assumptions of the model in mind when applying it. The model assumes that total assets change in direct proportion to sales and that liabilities either vary directly with sales or bear a constant relationship to owners' equity. Now these assumptions almost never hold exactly in practice. However, often they are reasonable enough to produce a rough estimate and to allow a useful analysis, particularly when you only have enough time for a "quick and dirty analysis."

In closing, we should mention that our experience is that many people have difficulty learning how to prepare projected financial statements. Very often the difficulty is due to failure to recall specific financial accounting principles and procedures. Hence, if you should encounter serious difficulty in solving the end-of-chapter problems, we suggest you review the chapter on financial accounting. Projected financial statements have many applications and it is important that you learn how to work with them.

# Problems and Discussion Questions

## A. Solved Problems

### Problem 6-1A

In December, Mackie Company's gross sales were $95,500, and gross sales for the next three months were:

| Month | Gross Sales |
|---|---|
| January | $85,400 |
| February | 83,900 |
| March | 92,300 |

All sales are made on terms of 2/10, net 30, which means customers can deduct 2% from the price if paid within 10 days, otherwise, the full amount must be paid in 30 days. It is estimated that 30% of sales volume will be discounted each month and the remainder will be paid in 30 days. You may assume that sales are spread evenly during each month, that all customers pay on time, that bad debts are zero and that there are 30-day months. Compute the accounts receivable balances at the end of January, February and March.

### Solution 6-1A

Below is the portion that will be discounted each month, the amount to be collected and the portion that will be collected in 30 days.

| Month | Discounted Portion 30% of Total | | Amount to be collected 98% | Undiscounted portion 70% of Total |
|---|---|---|---|---|
| January | $25,620 × 98% | = | $25,108 | $59,780 |
| February | 25,170 × 98% | = | 24,667 | 58,730 |
| March | 27,690 × 98% | = | 27,136 | 64,610 |

The final column shows the amounts that will be collected in 30 days. These amounts will be outstanding at the end of each month. To these amounts we add the portion of discounted sales that will be owed, which is one-third of the discounted portion given that they are paid in 10 days. This is shown next along with computations of the accounts receivable balances.

| Month | Amount to be Collected | | Amount Owed from Discounted Sales | | Amount Owed from Undiscounted Sales | | Accounts Receivable balance, EOM |
|---|---|---|---|---|---|---|---|
| January | $25,108 × ⅓ = | | $8,369 | + | $59,780 | = | $68,149 |
| February | 24,667 × ⅓ = | | 8,222 | + | 58,730 | = | 66,952 |
| March | 27,136 × ⅓ = | | 9,045 | + | 64,610 | = | 73,655 |

## Problem 6-2A

You are given the following information for the Decker Company, Inc.

| • Actual Sales | | Estimated Sales | |
|---|---|---|---|
| April | $60,000 | July | $75,000 |
| May | 40,000 | August | 70,000 |
| June | 50,000 | September | 64,000 |

Twenty-five percent of sales each month is for cash and 75% is on terms of net 45 days. Assume sales are spread evenly during each month, all credit customers pay on time and no bad debts. Finally, assume 30-day months for all calculations in this problem.

| • Actual Purchases | | Estimated Purchases | |
|---|---|---|---|
| April | $35,000 | July | $40,000 |
| May | 30,000 | August | 52,000 |
| June | 28,000 | September | 36,000 |

All goods are purchased ready for sale on terms of net 60 days.

• Cost of goods sold is 60% for all sales. Operating expense estimates are: rent, $4,000 per month; salaries and wages, $5,400 per month; and depreciation expense, $1,500 per month. The firm's income tax rate is 50% and taxes are paid monthly.

• Not all operating expense will be paid by the end of the month. Management estimates that the accrued expenses balance at the end of each month will equal 2% of sales for the month. (The accrued expenses account is the liability account that reflects the unpaid portion of rent, salaries and wages.)

• The firm does not plan to purchase or sell or retire fixed assets during the period. Also, no transactions involving stock or long-term debt are anticipated.

**Decker Company, Inc.**
**Balance Sheet**
**at June 30**

| | | | |
|---|---|---|---|
| Cash | $ 32,000 | Accounts payable | $ 58,000 |
| Accounts receivable | 52,500 | Accrued expenses | 1,000 |
| Inventory | 15,000 | Common stock and | |
| Net fixed assets | 67,000 | paid-in capital | 50,000 |
| Total | $166,500 | Retained earnings | 57,500 |
| | | Total | $166,500 |

• Finally, the desired cash balance is $40,000 and the firm will pay dividends of $1,000 per month

Prepare projected income statements for the months of July, August and September, and projected balance sheets at the end of each of these months. If there is a need in any month, list it as "notes payable (plug)." If there is a surplus in any month, list it as "excess cash" right beneath the cash account.

## Solution 6-2A

Table 6-4 has the projected statements. The income statement needs little explanation since the sales and operating expenses were given and we were told that cost of goods sold will be 60% for all sales, and income taxes will be 50% of pretax income. Finally, we list the dividend estimates and a line for "to retained earnings," which is how much the retained earnings balance will increase each month.

On the balance sheets, since the plug figures are computed last we will discuss them last. The cash balance of $40,000 is the desired amount. (Note that some analysts use cash as a plug figure.) Accounts receivable balances are computed in two steps.

### Step 1. Compute Monthly Credit Sales

| Month | Total Sales | | Percent on Credit | | Credit Sales |
|---|---|---|---|---|---|
| June | $50,000 | × | 75% | = | $37,500 |
| July | 75,000 | × | 75% | = | 56,250 |
| August | 70,000 | × | 75% | = | 52,500 |
| September | 64,000 | × | 75% | = | 48,000 |

**TABLE 6-4**
**DECKER COMPANY**
Projected Income Statements and
Balance Sheets

| | July | August | September |
|---|---|---|---|
| Net sales | $ 75,000 | $ 70,000 | $ 64,000 |
| Cost of goods sold | 45,000 | 42,000 | 38,400 |
| Gross profit | $ 30,000 | $ 28,000 | $ 25,600 |
| Rent | 4,000 | 4,000 | 4,000 |
| Salaries and wages | 5,400 | 5,400 | 5,400 |
| Depreciation | 1,500 | 1,500 | 1,500 |
| Profit before taxes | $ 19,100 | $ 17,100 | $ 14,700 |
| Income taxes | 9,550 | 8,550 | 7,350 |
| Net income | $ 9,550 | $ 8,550 | $ 7,350 |
| Dividends | 1,000 | 1,000 | 1,000 |
| To retained earnings | $ 8,550 | $ 7,550 | $ 6,350 |
| | | | |
| Cash | $ 40,000 | $ 40,000 | $ 40,000 |
| Surplus cash | 0 | 12,375 | 24,880 |
| Accounts receivable | 75,000 | 80,625 | 74,250 |
| Inventory | 10,000 | 20,000 | 17,600 |
| Net fixed assets | 65,500 | 64,000 | 62,500 |
| Total | $190,500 | $217,000 | $219,230 |
| Notes payable (plug) | $ 4,950 | 0 | 0 |
| Accounts payable | | | |
| (trade) | 68,000 | 92,000 | 88,000 |
| Accrued expenses | 1,500 | 1,400 | 1,280 |
| Common stock and | | | |
| paid-in capital | 50,000 | 50,000 | 50,000 |
| Retained earnings | 66,050 | 73,600 | 79,950 |
| Total | $190,500 | $217,000 | $219,230 |

*Step 2. Compute Month End Accounts Receivable*

| Month | Amount Owed, EOM | Accounts Receivable |
|---|---|---|
| July | all of July + ½ June | $75,000 |
| August | all of August + ½ July | 80,625 |
| September | all of September + ½ August | 74,250 |

Terms of sale are net 45 days. We are told that sales are spread evenly during the month and all customers pay on time. Hence, credit sales for the previous 45 days (i.e., previous 1½ months) will be outstanding at the end of each month.

Purchase and cost of goods sold estimates are provided along with the inventory balance at the end of June. From this information and the fact that all goods are purchased ready for sale, we can compute ending inventory balances as follows:

|  | July | August | September |
|---|---|---|---|
| Beginning inventory | $15,000 | $10,000 | $20,000 |
| + Purchases | 40,000 | 52,000 | 36,000 |
| − Cost of goods sold | 45,000 | 42,000 | 38,400 |
| = Ending inventory | $10,000 | $20,000 | $17,600 |

The chapter gave the following procedure for calculating net fixed assets estimates.

Net fixed assets balance beginning of period
+ Purchases of fixed assets during period
− Sales of fixed assets during the period
− Depreciation expense for period
= Net fixed asset balance, end of period

There will be no purchases or sales of fixed assets so we simply subtract depreciation expense of $1,500 from the balance at the beginning of the month (i.e., end of previous month) to compute the figure at the end of the month. As noted in the chapter, the above procedure gives an approximation not an exact answer, but generally relying on it will produce a good approximation.

Purchase terms are net 60 days, so at the end of each month accounts payable (trade) will equal the sum of purchases for the previous two months. Accrued expenses balances are derived by multiplying monthly sales by 2%. There will be no transactions involving stock, so common stock plus paid-in capital will be $50,000 at the end of each month. Finally, retained earnings figures are derived by adding the increase for the month to the balance at the end of the previous month.

Once we list all the assets and liabilities and equities, we total them to figure out the surplus and/or need as of the end of the month.

|  | July | August | September |
|---|---|---|---|
| Total assets | $190,500 | $204,625 | $194,350 |
| Total liabilities plus owners' equity | 185,550 | 217,000 | 219,230 |
| Surplus (need) | ($4,950) | $ 12,375 | $ 24,880 |

These amounts are listed as plug figures as shown.

# B. Discussion Questions

### 6-1B

You are given all the estimates of assets, liabilities and owners' equity accounts for a firm at a given future point in time. Suppose you compute a total of the estimated assets and a total of the estimated liabilities plus owners' equity accounts and you find that the two totals do not balance. What does this inequality indicate?

### 6-2B

Say a firm is relying on projected financial statements to estimate cash needs and surpluses. Why should it worry about an estimate of depreciation expense since this is a noncash expense?

### 6-3B

Accrued expense accounts are liabilities that represent the unpaid portion of expenses incurred up to that point. Why is it necessary to include accrued expense accounts on the projected balance sheet when we are trying to figure cash requirements?

### 6-4B

Should a principal payment on debt be included as an expense on a projected income statement? If so, why? If not, why not? If your answer is "no" also explain how this expenditure is reflected on the projected financial statements.

### 6-5B

Should a cash purchase of fixed assets be included as an expense on a projected income statement? If so, why? If not, why not? If your answer is "no'" also explain how this expenditure is reflected on projected financial statements. Assume the fixed asset is purchased on credit. How does this change affect your answer?

### 6-6B

Assume a projected balance sheet shows a need for funds. Is this a sign of weakness? Explain.

# C. Study Problems

### Problem 6-1C

You are given the following estimates and actual information for the Crypto Company.

### Balance Sheet
### End of September

| | | | |
|---|---|---|---|
| Cash | $ 35,000 | Accounts payable | |
| Accounts receivable | 150,000 | (trade) | $ 45,000 |
| Inventory | 95,000 | Accrued wages | 10,000 |
| Net fixed assets | 500,000 | Long-term debt | 410,000 |
| Total | $780,000 | Common stock and | |
| | | paid-in capital | 100,000 |
| | | Retained earnings | 215,000 |
| | | Total | $780,000 |

| *Actual Sales* | | *Estimated Sales* | |
|---|---|---|---|
| July | $60,000 | October | $100,000 |
| August | 75,000 | November | 120,000 |
| September | 75,000 | December | 160,000 |
| | | January | 150,000 |
| | | February | 200,000 |

• Through the end of September all goods were sold on terms of net 60 days. Starting October 1 terms will be net 45 days for all sales. Assume sales are spread out evenly during the month, customers pay on time and zero bad debts. Also assume 30-day months for all calculations in this problem.

• All goods are purchased ready for sale (i.e., the firm does no manufacturing). Cost of goods sold will be 50% of sales each month. Wages will be $10,000 per month and wage expense for the month is paid for in the subsequent month. Depreciation expense will be $5,000 per month. The only other expenses are for interest and taxes and these are described below.

• The income tax rate is 40%. Taxes due through the end of September were paid for in September. Taxes for October and November will be paid in December and the next tax payment after that will be in February. (Hint: There is no liability for accrued income taxes on the September 30 balance sheet because all taxes due through that date were paid.)

• The interest rate on the long-term debt is 12%. A payment of principal and interest was made on September 30. A principal payment of $40,000 will be made on November 30 and interest for October and November will also be paid on that date. No further interest or principal payments will be due until February.

• A new inventory system designed to reduce inventory levels will be implemented on October 1. It is anticipated that because of the new system, inventory on hand at the end of each month will be just enough to support sales for the next month. For instance, say sales of $100 was expected for November. Inventory of $50 would be needed to support this level and this would be the inventory balance at the end of October.

• The "accounts payable (trade)" balance of $45,000 listed on the September 30 balance sheet will be paid in October. Starting October 1, purchase terms will be net 15 days for all purchases. Assume that purchases are spread evenly during the month and that the firm will pay in a timely fashion.

• Fixed asset expenditures will be $5,000 per month. Expenditures for October and November will be for cash. The $5,000 expenditure of fixed assets in December will be on December 27 on terms of net 10 days. These transactions were taken into account in deriving the depreciation expense estimates noted above.

• The firm will declare a cash dividend of $25,000 and pay the dividend on December 20. There will be no other dividends during the period.

• There will be no transactions involving stock. Finally, management has concluded that it does not need to maintain a cash balance of $35,000 and that a balance of $20,000 would be sufficient to support operations.

1. Prepare projected income statements for October, November and December and projected balance sheets at the end of each of these months. Be sure to identify clearly projected needs and/ or surpluses.

2. Suppose you were not told what the firm's minimum desired cash balance was. What would you have done?

**Problem 6-2C**

You are given the following information for Chamberlain Plastics, Inc.

*Balance Sheet*
*at December 31, Year 1*

| | | | |
|---|---|---|---|
| Cash | $15,000 | Notes payable (bank) | $19,400 |
| Accounts receivable | 25,600 | Accounts payable | 7,300 |
| Inventory | 67,300 | Total current | $26,700 |
| Total current | $107,900 | Common stock and | |
| Property, plant & | | paid-in capital | 55,900 |
| equipment (net) | 111,100 | Retained earnings | 136,400 |
| Total | $219,000 | Total | $219,000 |

Sales for Year 1 were $282,500 and the net profit margin was 5%. Sales for Year 2 are expected to be $350,000 and the net profit margin is expected to remain at 5%. Cash, accounts receivable, inventory and accounts payable are expected to change at the same rate as sales. Further, there will be no other current assets or current liabilities on the end of Year 2 balance sheet except perhaps for a "notes payable (bank)" account. Expenditures on fixed assets for the year will exceed depreciation expense for the year by $50,000. The firm anticipates no transactions involving long-term debt or stock. Finally, the firm will pay dividends during Year 2 equal to one-half of the net income for Year 2.

1. Prepare a projected balance sheet at the end of Year 2. If there is a need rely on the "notes payable (bank)" account as the plug figure. If there is a surplus create an account called "excess cash."

2. Be prepared to explain what the projected balance sheet you construct does and does not indicate regarding needs and/or surpluses.

### Problem 6-3C

Suppose Rita Long is seeking your advice regarding a new business she plans to form on January 1, Year 1. She gives you the following information:

• Sales will be 100,000 units per month for the first six months and 200,000 units for each of the last six months. Selling price per unit will be $2 for all sales.

• All sales will be credit sales. Terms will be net 60 days, customers will pay on time, and there will be no bad debts.

• All goods will be purchased ready for sale and the cost per unit will be $1. Units sold in one month will be purchased in the prior month on terms of net 30 days.

- The firm will rent all its fixed assets, and rent expense will be $10,000 per month regardless of the number of units sold each month. The only other expenses are labor of 20¢ per unit and income taxes. The tax rate is 30%. Rent, labor and income tax expense are paid for in the month of incurrence.

- In years subsequent to Year 1 monthly sales will be 200,000 units per month.

- Selling price and costs will not change in years subsequent to Year 1. There will be no change in the 30% income tax rate in later years. Finally, there will be no change in credit terms, purchase terms or inventory policy in later years.

- A cash balance of $10,000 is needed to support sales of 100,000 units per month and $15,000 is required for monthly sales of 200,000 units.

- Ms. Long has $25,000 to invest in the common stock of the new business and all profits will be retained.

  Ms. Long's parents will give her an interest-free loan to finance the business if she will need more than the $25,000 she has already. Here are the questions Ms. Long wants you to help her answer:

1. Will she need more than $25,000 to finance the anticipated level of operations? If so, how much and when will she need the money?

2. If she borrows the amount needed from her parents when can she pay them back?

3. Suppose she does not want to borrow from her parents. Assume further that her investigation reveals that no one else will lend her money or invest in the stock of her firm. Does she have other options? If so, what are they and what would you recommend?

### Problem 6-4C

The Eastlake Company had sales of $1 million for the year ended 12/31/Year 1. The net profit margin was 5% and is expected to remain at this level in the future. Assets needed to support sales will be 80% of sales and spontaneous liabilities will be equal to 10% of sales in future years. Liabilities, excluding spontaneous liabilities, will equal 50% of net worth in subsequent years. Eastlake is considering the following dividend payout ratios (i.e., div-

idends divided by net income): 0%, 25%, 50%, 75% and 100%.
Compute the annual rate of sales growth that the firm can sustain
without relying on external equity for each of the contemplated
dividend policies. Be prepared to comment on the relationship
between dividend policy and growth.

### Problem 6-5C

You are given the following information for the Belton, Inc.

*Balance Sheet*
*at December 31/Year 1*

| | | | |
|---|---|---|---|
| Cash | $40,000 | Accounts payable | $20,000 |
| Accounts receivable | 30,000 | Accrued expenses | 10,000 |
| Inventory | 50,000 | Long-term debt | 70,000 |
| Net fixed assets | 100,000 | Common stock | 70,000 |
| Total | $220,000 | Retained earnings | 50,000 |
| | | Total | $220,000 |

• The firm is anticipating much higher sales as shown by the following estimates:

| Month | Gross Sales |
|---|---|
| January | $150,000 |
| February | 270,000 |
| March | 350,000 |
| April | 400,000 |
| May | 500,000 |

• Sales in December were $30,000 on terms of net 30. Starting
January 1, Year 2, all sales will be on terms of 2/10 net 30 and
it is estimated that one-half of sales will be discounted (e.g., customers purchasing $75,000 in January will take the discount) and
the other half will not. Assume that sales are spread evenly during
the month, that there are no bad debts and that customers pay
on time (i.e., those taking discounts pay in 10 days and others
pay in 30 days). Assume 30-day months for all calculations. Keep
in mind that cash discounts and sales returns and allowances are
deducted from gross sales in deriving net sales. Finally, assume
there are no sales returns and allowances.

• All goods are purchased ready for sale and cost of goods sold
expense is 50% of net sales for all sales. The firm has normally
maintained a relatively low level of inventory and starting Jan-

uary 1, Year 2, a new policy will be implemented so that at the end of January there will be an amount on hand sufficient to support sales for the next month. This will increase to one and a half months' supply by the end of February and two months' supply at the end of March.

• Purchases are made in three equal installments each month on the 10th, 15th and 25th of the month. Terms are net 45 days for all purchases and the firm pays on time.

• Other expenses are as follows:

| | |
|---|---|
| Administrative | $30,000 per month |
| Depreciation | $10,000 per month |
| Selling | $10,000 per month |
| Other | $5,000 per month |
| Interest | Discussed below |
| Income taxes | 50% tax rate |

• The interest rate on the long-term debt is 10%. A payment of principal and interest was made at 12/31/Year 1. The next principal payment will be $30,000 on 6/30/Year 2. The next interest payment will be on 4/30/Year 2.

• Fixed asset expenditures will be $5,000 per month. These were taken into account in deriving the depreciation expense estimates noted above.

• The accounts payable balance of $20,000 on the 12/31/Year 1 balance sheet pertains to purchases of inventory. Credit terms were different in the year from those described above. You may assume that this $20,000 will be paid in January, Year 2.

• The accrued expenses balance of $10,000 on the 12/31/Year 1 balance sheet pertains to administrative expenses and selling expenses. You may assume that in the future, 10% of these expenses for the month will be outstanding at the end of the month and that the 12/31/Year 1 balance will be paid in early January, Year 2.

• Income taxes due through the end of December, Year 1, were paid at the end of December. The next income tax payment is due in March but only taxes due through the end of January will be paid at that time. The next tax payment after March will be made in May but only the amount due for February will be paid at that time.

• There will be no transactions involving common stock, the desired cash balance is $30,000, and dividends will be $5,000 per month.

Prepare projected income statements for January, February and March, and projected balance sheets at the end of each of these months.

### Problem 6-6C

You are given the following information for the Drexler Manufacturing Company.

•
### Balance Sheet
### at December 31, Year 1

| Cash | $ 25,000 | Notes payable (bank) | $ 20,000 |
|---|---|---|---|
| Accounts receivable | 250,000 | Accounts payable | 25,000 |
| Inventories: | | Accrued income taxes | 15,500 |
| Raw materials | 50,000 | Current portion | |
| Work in process | 10,500 | of long-term debt | 20,000 |
| Finished goods | 80,000 | Total current | $ 80,500 |
| Other current | 9,500 | Long-term debt | 200,000 |
| Total current | $ 425,000 | Common stock and | |
| Fixed assets (net) | 685,000 | paid-in capital | 350,000 |
| Other long term | 5,500 | Retained earnings | 485,000 |
| Total | $1,115,500 | Total | $1,115,500 |

| • | *Actual Sales* | | *Estimated Sales* | |
|---|---|---|---|---|
| November | $200,000 | January | $300,000 |
| December | 250,000 | February | 400,000 |
| | | March | 600,000 |

All sales are on terms of net 30 days, customers pay on time and there are no bad debts. You may assume 30-day months for all calculations in this problem.

• Cost of goods sold is 50% of sales for all sales. Other expenses are:

| | |
|---|---|
| Selling and administrative | 20% of sales |
| Depreciation on office equipment | $3,000 per month |
| Interest expense | Discussed below |
| Income taxes | Tax rate is 40% |

Selling and administrative are cash expenses.

• The interest rate on the long-term debt is 14%. A payment of principal and interest was made on 12/31/Year 1. Interest for January and February will be paid at the end of February and at that time a principal payment of $5,000 will be made. The next payment of interest and principal after that will occur in May. (Interest on the short-term note is included in selling and administrative expenses.)

• At the end of January income taxes due through the end of January will be paid. Income taxes for February to April will be paid in April.

• Although sales are seasonal, the firm follows a level production policy. Cost of goods manufactured will be $250,000 per month and it consists of the following each month:

|  |  |
|---|---|
| Raw materials used | 20% of total |
| Direct labor | 50% of total |
| Overhead | 30% of total |

Direct labor is paid monthly. Overhead includes depreciation expense of $15,000 per month. The remaining portion of overhead is paid monthly.

• At the end of each month raw materials on hand will equal the amount needed for the next month's production. All raw materials are purchased on terms of net 15 days and purchases are spread evenly during the month.

• The balance of work-in-process inventory will be $10,500 at the end of each month.

• There will be no changes in the following accounts during the next three months: "Other" current assets, "other" long-term assets, common stock and paid-in capital.

• Cash purchases of fixed assets will be $10,000 per month for each of the next three months. These purchases were considered in estimating depreciation. The firm will pay its normal quarterly dividend in March. The amount of the dividend will be $40,000. Finally, the desired cash balance is $25,000.

Prepare projected income statements for January, February and March, and projected balance sheets at the end of each of these months. Use the short-term bank note as the plug figure and ignore the possible impact changes in this account may have on the selling and administrative expense estimates.

## Problem 6-7C
You are given the following information for Inselcon, Inc.

- 

*Balance Sheet*
*at August 31, Year 1*

| Cash | $ 25,000 | Accounts payable | |
|---|---|---|---|
| Accounts receivable | 45,000 | (trade) | $ 30,000 |
| Inventory | 30,000 | Long-term debt | 26,000 |
| Fixed assets (net) | 80,000 | Common stock and | |
| Total | $180,000 | paid-in capital | 80,000 |
| | | Retained earnings | 44,000 |
| | | Total | $180,000 |

- 

| *Actual Purchases* | | *Actual Sales* | |
|---|---|---|---|
| June | $10,000 | June | $30,000 |
| July | 10,000 | July | 30,000 |
| August | 10,000 | August | 30,000 |

*Estimated Sales*

| September | $80,000 | December | $ 40,000 |
|---|---|---|---|
| October | 70,000 | January | 105,000 |
| November | 85,000 | February | 75,000 |

- All sales are credit sales, sales are spread evenly during the month, customers pay on time and there are no bad debts. Assume 30-day months for all calculations in this problem.

- Through the end of August all sales were on terms of net 45 days. Effective September 1 there will be a change in credit terms for each of the firm's two product lines. Sales for the first line, which accounts for 40% of monthly sales, will be on terms of net 15 days. Sales for the second line, which accounts for 60% of monthly sales, will be on terms of net 75 days.

- All products are purchased ready for sale. On September 1 the firm will institute a new inventory policy so that at the end of September there will be an amount on hand sufficient to support sales for the next month. At the end of October and November there will be enough inventory on hand to support sales for the next 45 days.

• Through the end of August, all purchases were on terms of net 90 days. Goods purchased in September will be on terms of net 45 days. Purchases in October will be on terms of net 20 days and purchases in November will be on terms of net 10 days. Purchases are spread evenly during the month and the firm pays for all purchases on the due date.

• Expenses are as follows:

| | |
|---|---|
| Cost of goods sold | 50% of sales for all sales |
| Depreciation | $6,000 per month |
| Selling | $20,000 per month |
| Interest | 12% interest rate on long-term debt |
| General and administrative | $10,000 per month |
| Income taxes | 50% income tax rate |

• Selling and general and administrative expenses are cash expenses. A payment of interest and principal on the long-term debt is made every six months. A payment was made on the last day of August. The next payment of interest and principal payment will be made at the end of February.

• Income taxes due through the end of August were paid at the end of August. The next income tax payment is due on December 15.

• Cash expenditures for fixed assets will be $4,000 in September, $7,000 in October and $7,000 in November. These expenditures were considered in deriving the above depreciation estimates.

• There will be no transactions involving stock. Finally, dividends will be $4,000 per month and the desired cash balance is $20,000.

Prepare projected income statements for September, October and November, and projected balance sheets at the end of each of these months.

# Part

# III

# Investment and Financing Decisions

# 7
# The Time Value of Money

Suppose you were offered a choice between one dollar today or one dollar in a year. You would always choose today's dollar and here are some reasons why.

- You need the money now to pay bills or to make purchases.

- If someone gives you one dollar now, you have it. There may be some uncertainty regarding whether you actually would receive the dollar one year from now.

- Inflation. If there is inflation, and there usually is, one dollar a year from now will buy less.

- Money can earn interest. That is, you always have the opportunity to put the dollar in an interest-bearing account, so it would be worth more than one dollar in a year.

All four of these reasons may be relevant to your choice and perhaps you can think of others. However, the last one alone—the fact that money can earn interest—is sufficient to prove that one dollar today is worth more than one dollar one year from now.

Actually, the result is more general. Because money can earn interest, there is a time value of money which means that dollars received or paid out at different points in time have different values (i.e., they are not worth the same amount). Hence, every business decision that involves dollars at different points in time must take the time value of money into account. This chapter explains how to do that.

Suppose instead of the above offer, you were given a choice between $1 today or $1.10 one year from now. To take the time value of money into account, you could figure out what today's dollar would be worth in a year if invested at a certain interest rate. You would be making a *future value* calculation and we show how to make these computations in the first part of this chapter. Another way of taking the time value of money into account in your choice is to figure out what $1.10 in a year is worth today at a given interest rate. In this instance, you would be making a *present value* calculation and we show how to make these computations in the second part of this chapter. We should add that we also discuss a number of practical applications including an analysis of retirement planning, the internal rate of return and the analysis of various facets of loans.

We will rely on tables of factors to make present and future value computations. Most people find the tables useful for learning the concepts. Once you are satisfied you understand the principles, no doubt you will rely on calculators and computers to make the calculations.

# *Future Value*

In this section we will compute the future value of an amount invested today and the future value of a number of investments made at different points in time. We begin by developing a future value formula.

Suppose your aunt gives you $100 but insists that you put the money in a savings account paying interest of 5% per year compounded annually. What would this amount be worth if you left it in the bank for three years? During the first year you would earn interest of $5 ($100 times five percent) and the total value of your account would be $105 ($100 plus $5) at the end of the first year. In the second year, you would earn interest of $5.25 ($105 times five percent) and the total value of your account would be $110.25. Interest for the third year would be $5.51 ($110.25 times five percent) and the balance in the account at the end of the third year would be $115.76 ($110.25 plus $5.51).

Let's go through the example again, only this time let's summarize the figures in equation format. To begin, the value at the end of the first year can be computed as follows:

$$FV_1 = Po + I_1$$

Where:

    $FV_1$ = total balance at the end of the first period
    $Po$ = amount deposited at the beginning of the first period
    $I_1$ = dollar amount of interest earned during the first period

The amount at the end of the first year ($FV_1$ = \$105) can be derived by adding the dollar amount of interest earned during the Year ($I_1$ = \$5) to the amount deposited at the start of the year ($Po$ = \$100). The interest earned was derived by multiplying the interest rate by the principal as shown below.

$$I_1 = Po \times i$$

Where:

    $i$ = Interest rate

$$\$5 = 100 \times 5\%$$

By substituting $Po \times i$ for I, we can rewrite the equation as follows:

$$FV_1 = Po \times (Po \times i)$$

or

$$FV_1 = Po (1 + i)$$

The value of the account at the end of the second year ($FV_2$ = \$110.25) equals the value at the end of the first year ($FV_1$ = \$105) plus the interest earned during the second year ($I_2$ = \$5.25).

$$FV_2 = FV_1 + I_2$$

Since $I_2$ equals $FV_1$ times i (\$105 times five percent) we can write the equation for the second year as follows:

$$FV_2 = FV_1 + (FV_1 \times i)$$

or

$$FV_2 = FV_1 (1 + i)$$

From the earlier equation, we know that $FV_1 = Po (1 + i)$, so we can substitute and rewrite the equation as follows:

$$FV_2 = Po (1 + i) (1 + i)$$

or

$$FV_2 = Po (1 + i)^2$$

The balance in the account at the end of the third year ($FV_3 = \$115.76$) equals the amount at the end of the second year ($FV_2 = \$110.25$) plus interest earned during the third year ($I_3 = \$5.51$).

$$FV_3 = FV_2 + I_3$$

Since $I_3$ equals $FV_2$ times i, we can substitute as shown below:

$$FV_3 = FV_2 + (FV_2 \times i)$$
or
$$FV_2 (1 + i)$$

We know that $FV_2$ equals Po $(1 + i)^2$, so we can substitute as follows:

$$FV_3 = Po (1+i)^2(1+i)$$
or
$$Po (1 + i)^3$$

Let's summarize our findings.
$$FV_1 = Po (1 + i)^1$$
$$FV_2 = Po (1 + i)^2$$
$$FV_3 = Po (1 + i)^3$$

We can see that a pattern is developing. The general equation for computing the future value of a single amount is shown below:

*Future Value of Single Amount (Annual Compounding)*
$$FV_n = Po (1 + i)^n$$

Once we know the rate of interest and the amount invested we can figure out the future value for any number of years in the future. We must add that this equation as stated assumes annual compounding. Later we will explain how to adjust it for compounding at more frequent intervals.

Suppose we want to compute the value of $1 in two years at a rate of interest of 10% per year compounded annually. As shown below, $1 would grow to $1.21.

$$FV_2 = \$1 (1 + .10)^2$$
$$= \$1 (1.210)$$
$$= \$1.21$$

Now suppose we want to compute the value of $150 in two years at 10% per year compounded annually.

$$FV_2 = \$150 \ (1 + .10)^2$$
$$= \$150 \ (1.210)$$
$$= \$181.50$$

Notice that we multiplied $1 times 1.210 and $150 times 1.210. No matter what the beginning amount is, we would multiply it times 1.210 to compute the future value of that amount in two years at 10% per year compounded annually.

The 1.210 is called a factor. Since we will be working with several kinds of factors, it helps to have a shorthand expression for each type. For this type we will use the following:

$$(FV\$1, \ i, \ n)$$

Where:

FV$1 = Future value of $1 in hand today
i      = Interest rate
n      = Period

Period could be any time interval such as one year or one six month time period.[1] Given this shorthand, we can refer to our factor of 1.210 as follows:

$$(FV\$1, \ 10\%, \ 2) = 1.210$$

Appendix F-1 at the end of the book has a table of future value factors, FV$1, for various interest rates and periods. Part of the table is shown in Table 7-1 for illustrative purposes. First, go across the top of the table to 10% and down to two periods (n = 2). We see 1.210, the factor derived earlier. All the factors in the table were derived the same way. That is, the future value formula was solved for all the values of i and n shown. Let's now rely on the table to solve a problem.

Suppose we have $500 and want to figure out how much it would grow to in 25 years at a rate of 6% per year, compounded annually. In learning how to use tables of factors, many people find it helpful to first list the expression and then the specific items as shown below.

$$(FV\$1, \ i, \ n)$$
$$(FV\$1, \ 6\%, \ 25)$$

---

[1] For a while we will be discussing only annual periods so n will stand for year. It may be easier for you to think of n this way for now.

**Table 7-1**   *Future Value $1 at Various Interest Rates and Periods.*

| n | 1% | 2% | 3% | 4% | 5% | 6% | 7% | 8% | 9% | 10% |
|---|-----|-----|-----|-----|-----|-----|-----|-----|-----|-----|
| 1 | 1.0100 | 1.0200 | 1.0300 | 1.0400 | 1.0500 | 1.0600 | 1.0700 | 1.0800 | 1.0900 | 1.1000 |
| 2 | 1.0201 | 1.0404 | 1.0609 | 1.0816 | 1.1025 | 1.1236 | 1.1449 | 1.1664 | 1.1881 | 1.2100 |
| 3 | 1.0303 | 1.0612 | 1.0927 | 1.1249 | 1.1576 | 1.1910 | 1.2250 | 1.2597 | 1.2950 | 1.3310 |
| 4 | 1.0406 | 1.0824 | 1.1255 | 1.1699 | 1.2155 | 1.2625 | 1.3108 | 1.3605 | 1.4116 | 1.4641 |
| 5 | 1.0510 | 1.1041 | 1.1593 | 1.2167 | 1.2763 | 1.3382 | 1.4026 | 1.4693 | 1.5386 | 1.6105 |
| 6 | 1.0615 | 1.1262 | 1.1941 | 1.2653 | 1.3401 | 1.4185 | 1.5007 | 1.5869 | 1.6771 | 1.7716 |
| 7 | 1.0721 | 1.1487 | 1.2299 | 1.3159 | 1.4071 | 1.5036 | 1.6058 | 1.7138 | 1.8280 | 1.9487 |
| 8 | 1.0829 | 1.1717 | 1.2668 | 1.3686 | 1.4775 | 1.5938 | 1.7182 | 1.8509 | 1.9926 | 2.1436 |
| 9 | 1.0937 | 1.1951 | 1.3048 | 1.4233 | 1.5513 | 1.6895 | 1.8385 | 1.9990 | 2.1719 | 2.3579 |
| 10 | 1.1046 | 1.2190 | 1.3439 | 1.4802 | 1.6289 | 1.7908 | 1.9672 | 2.1589 | 2.3674 | 2.5937 |
| 11 | 1.1157 | 1.2434 | 1.3842 | 1.5395 | 1.7103 | 1.8983 | 2.1049 | 2.3316 | 2.5804 | 2.8531 |
| 12 | 1.1268 | 1.2682 | 1.4258 | 1.6010 | 1.7959 | 2.0122 | 2.2522 | 2.5182 | 2.8127 | 3.1384 |
| 13 | 1.1381 | 1.2936 | 1.4685 | 1.6651 | 1.8856 | 2.1329 | 2.4098 | 2.7196 | 3.0658 | 3.4523 |
| 14 | 1.1495 | 1.3195 | 1.5126 | 1.7317 | 1.9799 | 2.2609 | 2.5785 | 2.9372 | 3.3417 | 3.7975 |
| 15 | 1.1610 | 1.3459 | 1.5580 | 1.8009 | 2.0789 | 2.3966 | 2.7590 | 3.1722 | 3.6425 | 4.1772 |
| 16 | 1.1726 | 1.3728 | 1.6047 | 1.8730 | 2.1829 | 2.5404 | 2.9522 | 3.4259 | 3.9703 | 4.5950 |
| 17 | 1.1843 | 1.4002 | 1.6528 | 1.9479 | 2.2920 | 2.6928 | 3.1588 | 3.7000 | 4.3276 | 5.0545 |
| 18 | 1.1961 | 1.4282 | 1.7024 | 2.0258 | 2.4066 | 2.8543 | 3.3799 | 3.9960 | 4.7171 | 5.5599 |
| 19 | 1.2081 | 1.4568 | 1.7535 | 2.1068 | 2.5270 | 3.0256 | 3.6165 | 4.3157 | 5.1417 | 6.1159 |
| 20 | 1.2202 | 1.4859 | 1.8061 | 2.1911 | 2.6533 | 3.2071 | 3.8697 | 4.6610 | 5.6044 | 6.7275 |
| 21 | 1.2324 | 1.5157 | 1.8603 | 2.2788 | 2.7860 | 3.3996 | 4.1406 | 5.0338 | 6.1088 | 7.4002 |
| 22 | 1.2447 | 1.5460 | 1.9161 | 2.3699 | 2.9253 | 3.6035 | 4.4304 | 5.4365 | 6.6586 | 8.1403 |
| 23 | 1.2572 | 1.5769 | 1.9736 | 2.4647 | 3.0715 | 3.8197 | 4.7405 | 5.8715 | 7.2579 | 8.9543 |
| 24 | 1.2697 | 1.6084 | 2.0328 | 2.5633 | 3.2251 | 4.0489 | 5.0724 | 6.3412 | 7.9111 | 9.8497 |
| 25 | 1.2824 | 1.6406 | 2.0938 | 2.6658 | 3.3864 | 4.2919 | 5.4274 | 6.8485 | 8.6231 | 10.835 |
| 26 | 1.2953 | 1.6734 | 2.1566 | 2.7725 | 3.5557 | 4.5494 | 5.8074 | 7.3964 | 9.3992 | 11.918 |
| 27 | 1.3082 | 1.7069 | 2.2213 | 2.8834 | 3.7335 | 4.8223 | 6.2139 | 7.9881 | 10.245 | 13.110 |
| 28 | 1.3213 | 1.7410 | 2.2879 | 2.9987 | 3.9201 | 5.1117 | 6.6488 | 8.6271 | 11.167 | 14.421 |
| 29 | 1.3345 | 1.7758 | 2.3566 | 3.1187 | 4.1161 | 5.4184 | 7.1143 | 9.3173 | 12.172 | 15.863 |
| 30 | 1.3478 | 1.8114 | 2.4273 | 3.2434 | 4.3219 | 5.7435 | 7.6123 | 10.063 | 13.268 | 17.449 |

To locate this factor we go across the top of the table to 6% and look down to n = 25. The factor is 4.2919. We then multiply this factor times the present amount of $500 to compute the future value as shown next.

$$\begin{array}{ccccc} FV & & \text{Present Amount} & & (FV\$1,\ 6\%,\ 25) \\ \$2{,}146 & = & \$500 & \times & 4.2919 \end{array}$$

This amount, $2,146, is the future value of $500 invested today at a rate of 6% per year, compounded annually.

See if you can rely on Table 7-1 to answer the following question: If you invest a given amount today at 5% per year compounded annually, about how long would it take you to double your money? The answer is approximately 14 years. We solved this by going across the top of the table to 5%. We then looked down that column until we came to the factor that was closest to 2.0000. This is 1.9799 which is at n = 14. As it turns out there is a simple rule of thumb for approximating this answer, and while we generally don't like simple rules, we think you might find this one useful. It's called the Rule of 72.

### Double Your Money. Rule of 72

Let's look at how long it would take a sum to double at several different interest rates.

| i | n | Factor |
|---|---|--------|
| 5% | 14 | 1.9799 |
| 6% | 12 | 2.0122 |
| 7% | 10 | 1.9672 |
| 8% | 9 | 1.9990 |

We found the factors for 6%, 7%, 8%, the same way we did for the 5% rate described above. Notice what happens if we divide 72 by each interest rate.

| 72 | i | Result |
|----|---|--------|
| 72 ÷ | 5 = | 14.4 |
| 72 ÷ | 6 = | 12.0 |
| 72 ÷ | 7 = | 10.3 |
| 72 ÷ | 8 = | 9.0 |

Look at how close the result figures are to the values of n shown above. This finding is not unique to this example and generally dividing 72 by an interest rate will give a pretty good estimate of about how long it will take a sum to double if invested at that rate compounded annually.

## COMPOUNDING INTERVALS

Thus far we have been focusing on annual compounding but compounding occurs at more frequent intervals such as semi-annually (every six months) or monthly. When we are working with intervals other than one year we must rely on the following version of the future value equation.

*Future Value of Single Amount (Any Compounding Interval)*
$$FV_n = Po \left(1 + \frac{i}{m}\right)^{mn}$$

Where:

  m = number of times per year that compounding takes place. Notice that if there is annual compounding, m equals one and the equation reduces to the version presented earlier.

Suppose we wanted to compute how much $100 would grow into in one year at an interest rate of 8% per year compounded quarterly.

$$FV = 100 \left(1 + \frac{.08}{4}\right)^{4 \times 1}$$
$$= 100 (1 + .02)^4$$
$$= \$108.24$$

One hundred dollars will grow to $108.24 in one year at 8% per year compounded quarterly. The table of FV$1 factors can be used to solve this.

  Given quarterly compounding, we let n equal a three-month interval. We go across the top of the table to 2% because 8% per year compounded quarterly is the same as 2% per quarter. Looking down to n = 4, the factor is 1.0824 and this figure is multiplied by $100 as shown below.

| FV | Present Amount | | (FV$1, 2%, 4) |
|---|---|---|---|
| $108.24 = | $100 | × | 1.0824 |

If we invest $100 at 8% per year compounded annually, it would grow into $108 in one year which is less than the $108.24 for quarterly compounding. Why is there a difference? The answer is the effect of compounding, or stated another way interest earning interest. Say you put $100 in a bank that pays interest of 8% per year compounded annually. One year from now the bank would credit your account for $8 interest. Now suppose you put your $100 in a bank that pays interest of 8% per year compounded quarterly. Three months from now the bank would credit your account with interest of $2. Hence in the second quarter you would earn interest on the total balance of $102. Here are the computations for the year.

| Quarter | Balance Start of Quarter | | Interest Rate for Period | | Interest | Balance End of Quarter |
|---|---|---|---|---|---|---|
| 1 | $100.00 | × | 2% | = | $2.00 | $102.00 |
| 2 | 102.00 | × | 2% | = | 2.04 | 104.04 |
| 3 | 104.04 | × | 2% | = | 2.08 | 106.12 |
| 4 | 106.12 | × | 2% | = | 2.12 | 108.24 |

The more frequent the compounding interval, the greater the future value for a given interest rate and a given terminal date such as one year from now. For instance, $100 would grow to $108.33 in one year at a rate of 8% per year compounded daily.

You might think that the difference is not worth worrying about since we got numbers that differ only by pennies (i.e., $108.00 versus $108.24 versus $108.33). However, the difference can be substantial, especially when there are a series of investments for a large number of years.[2]

Before proceeding, let's try a short quiz. Compute how much $100 will grow to in ten years at an interest rate of 10% per year compounded semi-annually. Our answer is presented in three steps.

*Step 1. Set Up Problem in Equation Format*

$$FV = P_o \left(1 + \frac{i}{m}\right)^{mn}$$

$$= \$100 \left(1 + \frac{.10}{2}\right)^{2 \times 10}$$

$$= \$100 (1 + .05)^{20}$$

*Step 2. Locate Factor*

Go across the top of the table to 5% and down to $n = 20$. The factor is 2.6533. (Interest is 5% per period and there are 20 periods.)

*Step 3. Compute Future Value*

| FV | Present Amount | (FV$1, 5%, 20) |
|----|----------------|----------------|
| $265.33 = | $100 × | 2.6533 |

Many of you probably could go to step three directly and others will be able to after a little practice. The above format is suggested only to help you avoid errors while learning how to work with various compounding intervals.


## FUTURE VALUE OF ANNUITIES

An annuity is a series of equal amounts at regular intervals like every year or every six months. We will now describe how to make computations for the future value of annuities. Let's start with an example:

---

[2] The most frequent compounding possible is continuous compounding. (Think of it as more frequent than every second.) This is computed by allowing m, the compounding interval, to approach infinity. The term $(1 + i)^{mn}$ in the future value equation approaches $e^{in}$ as m approaches infinity, where e is the base of the natural logarithm. Many banks offer interest rates that are continuously compounded. Say two banks offer the same interest rate but one has continuous compounding and the other has a less frequent interval like monthly. We would choose the continuous compounding alternative.

Suppose your aunt will give you $100 one year from now, $100 two years from now and $100 three years from now. You put the three amounts in a bank that pays interest of 10% per year compounded annually. How much would these amounts grow to at the end of the third year? We can rely on the factors in Table 7-1 to help compute the value. The $100 received one year from now would grow to $121 by the end of the third year because it would be invested for two years.

$$FV \qquad Amount \qquad (FV\$1, \ 10\%, \ 2)$$
$$\$121.00 = \quad \$100 \quad \times \quad 1.2100$$

The end of Year 2 receipt of $100 would be invested for one year and grow into $110 by the end of the third year.

$$FV \qquad Amount \qquad (FV\$1, \ 10\%, \ 1)$$
$$\$110.00 = \quad \$100 \quad \times \quad 1.1000$$

The end of Year 3 receipt obviously would not earn any interest by the end of the third year. So the total is $331 as shown below:

*End of Year*

| 1 | 2 | 3 |
|---|---|---|
| $100 $\longrightarrow$ | | $\longrightarrow$ $121.00 |
| | $100 $\longrightarrow$ | 110.00 |
| | | 100.00 |
| | | $331.00 |

(Some people find it useful to rely on a diagram, often called a time line, when solving time value of money problems.)

We multiplied each of the first two receipts by a factor. Suppose for consistency we wanted to multiply the third receipt by a factor. What would the factor be? The factor would be 1.0000 because no interest is earned on the third receipt. Let's now multiply each of the receipts by the appropriate factor.

| End of Year | Receipt | | Factor | | Values End of Year 3 |
|---|---|---|---|---|---|
| 1 | $100 | × | 1.2100 | = | $121.00 |
| 2 | 100 | × | 1.1000 | = | 110.00 |
| 3 | 100 | × | 1.0000 | = | 100.00 |
| | | | | | $331.00 |

Notice that we can add up the factors and multiply by the amount of the annuity.

*Factor*
1.2100
1.1000
<u>1.0000</u>
3.3100 × \$100 = \$331.00

We can compute the future value three years from now at 10% per year compounded annually of any three-year annuity by multiplying by 3.3100. Say we will receive \$500 one year from now, \$500 two years from now and \$500 three years from now. What will this stream be worth in three years at 10% per year compounded annually? The answer is \$1,655 derived as follows:

$$\$1,655 = \$500 \times 3.3100$$

In other words, 3.3100 is a factor.

Recall that the factors in Table 7-1 were derived by solving the future value equation for various values of i and n. Well there is a general equation for the future value of annuities and we can derive factors from it. Here is the equation:

*Future Value of Annuity (First Amount in One Year—Annual Compounding)*

$$\text{FV annuity} = A \sum_{T=1}^{n} (1+i)^{n-T}$$
$$= A\left[\frac{(1+i)^n - 1}{i}\right]$$

Where:
  A = Annual amount one year from now
  n = Number of annual periods
  i = Interest rate
Let's apply the equation to our two examples:

*Example 1. \$100 per year for three years at 10% per year compounded annually.*

$$FV = \$100\left[\frac{(1+.10)^3 - 1}{.10}\right]$$
$$= \$100\,[3.3100]$$
$$= \$331.00$$

*Example 2. $500 per year for three years at 10% per year compounded annually.*

$$FV = \$500 \, \frac{[(1+.10)^3 - 1]}{.10}$$

$$= \$500 \, [3.3100]$$

$$= \$1655$$

These two computations show more formally that no matter what the value of A, the term in brackets would be 3.3100 given i is 10% and n equals 3.

Appendix F-2 has a table of factors for annuities. It was derived by solving the above equation for A = 1 for various values of i and n. We will rely on the following shorthand expression to refer to these factors:

$$(FVA\$1, i, n)$$

Where:

FVA$1 = Future value of a stream of $1, with the first occurring one period from now

i = Interest rate

n = Period

Let's rely on the table to compute the future value of $1,000 per year, starting one year from now, for ten years at 20% per year compounded annually. The answer is $25,959 as shown below:

| *Future Value* | | *Equal Amount* | | *(FVA$1, 20%, 10)* |
|---|---|---|---|---|
| $25,959 | = | $1,000 | × | 25.959 |

For compounding intervals other than one year we would make the same adjustments described earlier, which is to divide the interest rate by m, the compounding interval, and to multiply m times n. Suppose in our previous example, the $1,000 would be received every six months, starting six months from now, for five years. What would this annuity grow into in five years at 20% per year compounded semi-annually? We go across the top of the table of annuity factors to 10% and down to n = 10 to locate the factor. We then compute the future value which is $15,937.

| *FV* | | *Equal Amount* | | *(FVA$1, 10%, 10)* |
|---|---|---|---|---|
| $15,937 | = | $1,000 | × | 15.937 |

Some of you may be surprised that here we got $15,937 and for the annual compounding example the answer was $25,959. Didn't we say earlier that the more frequent the compounding interval, the greater the future value? This will always be true for a given interest rate and for a given terminal date. The terminal dates differ for these two annuities (i.e., 10 years from now versus five years from now). The annual annuity is worth so much more because compound annual interest is earned for 10 years.

### Practical Application: Retirement Planning

There is a provision of the tax law that allows an individual to establish an IRA,[3] an Individual Retirement Account and invest up to $2,000 per year tax deferred. You can deduct the $2,000 on your tax return. Tax deferred means that you will pay taxes on this amount at a later date when you withdraw the funds. (Interest earned also is tax deferred.)

Let's assume you turned 25 today. You plan to put $2,000 in an IRA today plus $2,000 each year starting one year from now until you reach age 65. You will make your last investment on your 65th birthday. This is a total of 41 investments of $2,000. To simplify matters, we will initially assume that you can earn interest of 10% per year compounded annually for the entire period and beyond that as well. How much will your IRA be worth on your 65th birthday? Let's begin by specifying the timing of the cash flows.

| End of Year | Cash Flows |
|---|---|
| 0 | $2,000 |
| 1–40 | 2,000 |

Our objective is to compute the future value of this stream at 10% per year compounded annually.

The table in Appendix F-1 can be used to compute the future value of the $2,000 invested today and Appendix F-2 can be relied upon to solve for the future value of the annuity. These computations follow:

| FV | | Present Amount | | (FV$1, 10%, 40) |
|---|---|---|---|---|
| $90,518 | = | $2,000 | × | 45.259 |
| FV | | Equal Amount | | (FVA$1, 10%, 40) |
| $885,180 | = | $2,000 | × | 442.59 |

The sum of these two is $975,698 ($90,518 + $885,180) which is what your IRA would be worth on your 65th birthday.

---

[3] We are giving a simplified description of a provision that was in effect when this chapter was being written. As you know, tax provisions are frequently modified and so you should be aware that the actual provision in effect now may be different.

Let's pause for a moment and analyze the power of compounding. Note that the $2,000 invested today will grow to $90,518 in 40 years at an interest rate of 10% per year compounded annually. Suppose you put another $2,000 in a bank that pays the same rate. You decide to withdraw interest each year and stuff it in your mattress. Assuming you don't have to pay taxes on the withdrawn interest, how much would be in your mattress 40 years from now? Well, you would put $200 of interest each year in your mattress and so there would be $8,000 there 40 years from now. This together with the $2,000 balance in the account gives a total of $10,000. This amount is very different from $90,518 and the difference is due to the effect of compounding (i.e., earning interest on interest).

Suppose you decide on your 65th birthday to work until age 70. You won't make any more investments but you will have the $975,698 in the account earning 10% per year compounded annually until your 70th birthday. How much will the account be worth at that time? It will earn interest for five more years and we can compute the value as follows:

| *Value on 70th Birthday* | | *Value on 65th Birthday* | | *(FV$1, 10%, 5)* |
|---|---|---|---|---|
| $1,571,362 | = | $975,698 | × | 1.6105 |

Notice again the power of compounding and congratulations on being a millionaire.

Although some investment alternatives are available which promise a fixed interest rate for many years, most people choose to commit to a fixed interest rate for a much shorter period. It is beyond our scope to delve into the pros and cons of the various alternatives. However, we must point out that in analyzing what a long series of investments will be worth in the future, it makes sense to try a variety of rates. Below is what your IRA would be worth on your 65th birthday at various interest rates.[4]

| *Interest Rate* | *Value in 40 Years* |
|---|---|
| 6% | $   330,095 |
| 8% | 561,562 |
| 10% | 975,698 |
| 12% | 1,720,285 |
| 16% | 5,478,956 |
| 20% | 17,627,259 |

[4] Each illustration assumes a fixed rate over the 40-year period. While this is appropriate for our purposes, sometimes it is useful to vary the rate over the period. For example, you may assume you will earn a certain rate for the next several years and then different interest rates after that time.

The figure at 10% is the $975,698 we derived earlier. The other figures were calculated the same way. (We used a financial calculator and it took a few seconds to get the answers. If you check these figures, you likely will get slightly different answers because of rounding differences.)

Earlier we noted the dramatic impact of leaving the money invested for five more years. Here we see the effect of the interest rate on future values. At a rate of 6% the future value is a little more than $330,000; at 20% the future value is greater than $17.6 million. Besides seeing the importance of investing wisely, the point is that both n and i in the future value equation affect the future value of a single amount and/or a series of investments. The higher these variables, the greater the future value and vice versa.

# *Present Value*

In this section we explain the notion of present value and show how to make present value calculations. You will see that we have already covered many of the principles and so we are not really changing topics.

We began our discussion of future value with a simple example. Recall your aunt who gave you $100 and insisted you place it in a savings account paying interest of 5% per year compounded annually for three years. We saw that the $100 would grow to $115.76 in three years. Let's assume that instead of giving you $100 today, your aunt decides to give you $100 three years from now. To assure your gift, your aunt will invest an amount today that will be worth $100 three years from now. The amount will be put in a savings account that pays interest of 5% per year compounded annually. How much must she place in the account today to have $100 three years from now? Should she put $100 in the account? The answer is "no" because we know that $100 would grow into $115.76 in three years. Thus, she must put in some amount less than $100. While this is obvious, it does illustrate the following important point: at any rate of interest above zero, $1 in the future is worth less than $1 today.

Let's see if the equation for the future value of a present amount can help us figure out how much your aunt must put in the bank today:

$$FV = P_o (1 + i)^n$$

We know the rate of interest is 5%, the number of years is three, and the desired amount at the end of the period (i.e., future value) is $100. Let's insert these values in the equation.

$$\$100 = P_o (1 + .05)^3$$

Solving for Po we get $86.38 as shown below:

$$Po = \frac{\$100}{(1+.05)^3}$$

$$\$100 \quad [\frac{1}{(1+.05)^3}]$$

$$= \$100 \quad [.8638]$$

$$= \$86.38$$

A deposit of $86.38 invested at 5% per year compounded annually will grow into $100 in three years. We can also state this as follows: The present value of $100 three years from now at 5% per year compounded annually is $86.38. Let's look at a diagram.

*End of Year*

| 0 | 1 | 2 | 3 |
|---|---|---|---|
| $86.38 ←——————————— $100 | | | |

Note that for present value the arrow points to time zero as compared to future value where the arrows point to some future period.

All the comments made in the previous section regarding the general nature of the equation apply to present value. Let's first rewrite the equation in the present value format and then briefly review some of the points.

*Present Value of Future Amount (Annual Compounding)*

$$\text{Present Value} = \text{Future Value} \; [\frac{1}{(1+i)^n}]$$

To compute the present value of $100 in three years at 5% per year compounded annually, we multiplied $100 by .8638 in the last step. We would multiply by .8638 to compute the present value of any amount in three years at this rate. In other words, .8638 is a factor. Thus, by solving for various values of i and n we can generate a table of factors. Appendix P-1 has a table of present value factors and a portion of this table is shown in Table 7-2.

Notice in Table 7-2 that all the factors are less than 1.0000, illustrating that the present value of $1 in the future at any positive interest rate is

**Table 7-2**    *Present Value $1 at Various Interest Rates and Periods.*

| n | 1% | 2% | 3% | 4% | 5% | 6% | 7% | 8% | 9% | 10% |
|---|------|------|------|------|------|------|------|------|------|------|
| 1 | .9901 | .9804 | .9709 | .9615 | .9524 | .9434 | .9346 | .9259 | .9174 | .9091 |
| 2 | .9803 | .9612 | .9426 | .9246 | .9070 | .8900 | .8734 | .8573 | .8417 | .8264 |
| 3 | .9706 | .9423 | .9151 | .8890 | .8638 | .8396 | .8163 | .7938 | .7722 | .7513 |
| 4 | .9610 | .9238 | .8885 | .8548 | .8227 | .7921 | .7629 | .7350 | .7084 | .6830 |
| 5 | .9515 | .9057 | .8626 | .8219 | .7835 | .7473 | .7130 | .6806 | .6499 | .6209 |
| 6 | .9420 | .8880 | .8375 | .7903 | .7462 | .7050 | .6663 | .6302 | .5963 | .5645 |
| 7 | .9327 | .8706 | .8131 | .7599 | .7107 | .6651 | .6227 | .5835 | .5470 | .5132 |
| 8 | .9235 | .8535 | .7894 | .7307 | .6768 | .6274 | .5820 | .5403 | .5019 | .4665 |
| 9 | .9143 | .8368 | .7664 | .7026 | .6446 | .5919 | .5439 | .5002 | .4604 | .4241 |
| 10 | .9053 | .8203 | .7441 | .6756 | .6139 | .5584 | .5083 | .4632 | .4224 | .3855 |
| 11 | .8963 | .8043 | .7224 | .6496 | .5847 | .5268 | .4751 | .4289 | .3875 | .3505 |
| 12 | .8874 | .7885 | .7014 | .6246 | .5568 | .4970 | .4440 | .3971 | .3555 | .3186 |
| 13 | .8787 | .7730 | .6810 | .6006 | .5303 | .4688 | .4150 | .3677 | .3262 | .2897 |
| 14 | .8700 | .7579 | .6611 | .5775 | .5051 | .4423 | .3878 | .3405 | .2992 | .2633 |
| 15 | .8613 | .7430 | .6419 | .5553 | .4810 | .4173 | .3624 | .3152 | .2745 | .2394 |
| 16 | .8528 | .7284 | .6232 | .5339 | .4581 | .3936 | .3387 | .2919 | .2519 | .2176 |
| 17 | .8444 | .7142 | .6050 | .5134 | .4363 | .3714 | .3166 | .2703 | .2311 | .1978 |
| 18 | .8360 | .7002 | .5874 | .4936 | .4155 | .3503 | .2959 | .2502 | .2120 | .1799 |
| 19 | .8277 | .6864 | .5703 | .4746 | .3957 | .3305 | .2765 | .2317 | .1945 | .1635 |
| 20 | .8195 | .6730 | .5537 | .4564 | .3769 | .3118 | .2584 | .2145 | .1784 | .1486 |
| 21 | .8114 | .6598 | .5375 | .4388 | .3589 | .2942 | .2415 | .1987 | .1637 | .1351 |
| 22 | .8034 | .6468 | .5219 | .4220 | .3418 | .2775 | .2257 | .1839 | .1502 | .1228 |
| 23 | .7954 | .6342 | .5067 | .4057 | .3256 | .2618 | .2109 | .1703 | .1378 | .1117 |
| 24 | .7876 | .6217 | .4919 | .3901 | .3101 | .2470 | .1971 | .1577 | .1264 | .1015 |
| 25 | .7798 | .6095 | .4776 | .3751 | .2953 | .2330 | .1842 | .1460 | .1160 | .0923 |
| 26 | .7720 | .5976 | .4637 | .3607 | .2812 | .2198 | .1722 | .1352 | .1064 | .0839 |
| 27 | .7644 | .5859 | .4502 | .3468 | .2678 | .2074 | .1609 | .1252 | .0976 | .0763 |
| 28 | .7568 | .5744 | .4371 | .3335 | .2551 | .1956 | .1504 | .1159 | .0895 | .0693 |
| 29 | .7493 | .5631 | .4243 | .3207 | .2429 | .1846 | .1406 | .1073 | .0822 | .0630 |
| 30 | .7419 | .5521 | .4120 | .3083 | .2314 | .1741 | .1314 | .0994 | .0754 | .0573 |

less than $1. We will rely on the following shorthand expression to refer to the factors for the present value of a single future amount.

$$(PV\$1, i, n)$$

Where:
$$PV\$1 = \text{Present value of \$1 at some future time}$$
$$i = \text{Interest rate}$$
$$n = \text{Period}$$

As was the case for future value, n could be any period such as a year or a six-month interval. Of course, as we will see later, we would have to adjust the equation for m, compounding intervals just as we did for future values. Let's practice using the table to solve a problem.

Suppose we want to compute what $175 ten years from now is worth today at 8% per year compounded annually. We go across the top of the table to 8% and down to n = 10 to locate the factor which is .4632. Multiplying this factor by $175 gives us the answer.

| PV | Future Amount | | (PV$1, 8%, 10) |
|---|---|---|---|
| $81.06 = | $175 | × | .4632 |

This amount, $81.06, is the present value of $175 ten years from now at 8% per year compounded annually. (We can turn this around and say the following: $81.06 will grow to $175 in ten years at 8% per year compounded annually. In other words, as noted earlier, the present value of a future amount is simply the reciprocal of the future value of a present amount.)

To see the kinship to future value, see if you can answer the following: How much is $175 in ten years worth today at 8% per year compounded semi-annually? We adjust the present value equation just as we adjusted the future value equation. That is, we divided i by m, the compounding interval, and multiply m times n. For this example we get 4% per period and 20 six-month periods. We go across the top of Table 7-2 to 4% and down to n = 20 to locate the factor, .4564, and then we compute the present value which is $79.87.

| PV | Future Amount | | (PV$1, 4%, 20) |
|---|---|---|---|
| $79.87 = | $175 | × | .4564 |

Notice that the present value of $79.87 is less than the $81.06 we got for annual compounding. Recall that earlier we saw that the more frequent the compounding interval, the greater the future value for a given rate and terminal date. Well it's just the opposite for present value, that is, for a given rate and terminal date the more frequent the compounding interval the lower the present value. We should add that in present value instead of referring to compounding it is fairly common to refer to discounting. Present value is often called discounted value, the interval m is called the discounting interval, and the rate used to compute present value is known as the discount rate. In any event below is the general form of the present value equation.

*Present Value of Future Amount (Any Discounting Interval)*

$$PV = FV \left[ \frac{1}{(1 + i)^{\frac{mn}{m}}} \right]$$

## PRESENT VALUE OF ANNUITIES

Many financial analyses involve computing the present value of annuities (i.e., a series of equal amounts). Here we show how to make these calculations and we begin by referring to your aunt again. Suppose she is going to give you $100 at the end of each year for three years starting one year from now. What is the present value of this annuity at 10% per year compounded annually? We can use the present value equation to solve this problem.

$$\text{Year 1 Po} = \$100 \left[ \frac{1}{(1 + .10)^1} \right] = \$\ 90.91$$

$$\text{Year 2 Po} = \$100 \left[ \frac{1}{(1 + .10)^2} \right] = \ 82.65$$

$$\text{Year 3 Po} = \$100 \left[ \frac{1}{(1 + .10)^3} \right] = \ \underline{75.13}$$
$$\$248.69$$

The present value of $100 per year for three years at 10% per year compounded annually is $248.69. (We could have used the factors in Appendix P-1 but we did it this way to illustrate a point and to emphasize again that factors are derived from an equation. Incidentally, the factor in the table for n = 2 at 10% is .8264 which is different from the .8265 derived here. This difference is due to rounding.)

Instead of listing three separate equations, we can solve one as shown below.

$$P_o = \$100[\frac{1}{(1 + .10)^1}] + \$100[\frac{1}{(1 + .10)^2}] + \$100[\frac{1}{(1 + .10)^3}]$$

$$= \$100[\frac{1}{(1 + .10)^1} + \frac{1}{(1 + .10)^2} + \frac{1}{(1 + .10)^3}]$$

$$= \$100[2.4869]$$

$$= \$248.69$$

Notice that no matter what the equal annual amount is for three years, we would multiply by 2.4869 to compute the present value at 10% per year compounded annually. In other words, 2.4869 is a factor. Further we can compute the present value of any annuity where the first periodic receipt or payment begins one period from now by solving the following equation.

*Present Value of Annuity (Annual Discounting—First Amount Occurs One Year from Now)*

$$\text{Present Value of Annuity} = A \sum_{T=1}^{n} \frac{1}{(1+i)^T}$$

$$= A[\frac{1 - \frac{1}{(1+i)^n}}{i}]$$

Where:

A = Equal annual amount

Appendix P-2 has a table of factors for computing the present value of annuities. These were derived by solving the above equation for various values of i and n. When referring to these factors we will use the following shorthand expression.

(PVA$1, i, n)

Where:

PVA$1 = Present value of a series of $1, with the first dollar one period from now

i = Interest rate

n = Period

Let's rely on the table to compute the present value of a three-year annuity of $200, with the first amount due one year from now at 14% per year compounded annually. We will first specify the cash flows in a diagram and then list them.

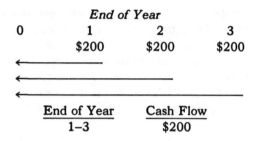

We observe from the diagram that (1) the amounts are the same, (2) they occur at the same regular interval like every year, (3) and the first amount occurs one period from now. If any one of these three elements is missing, we cannot go directly to the factors in Appendix P-2 to solve the problem. For this problem we can, so we go across the top of the table to i = 14% and down to n = 3 to locate the factor which is 2.3216. We multiply the factor by $200, the equal annual amount, and get $464.32 which is the present value of the stream at the given rate.

> **Present Value**     **Equal Amount**     **(PVA$1, 14%, 3)**
> $464.32     =     $200     ×     2.3216

For discounting intervals other than every year we make the familiar adjustments of dividing the rate by m, the discounting interval, and multiplying m by n. For instance, suppose we want to compute the present value of $100 received every six months, starting six months from now, for three years at 14% per year compounded semi-annually. We go across the top of the table to 7% and down to n = 6 to locate the factor which is 4.7665. The present value of this stream is $476.65.

> **Present Value**     **Equal Amount**     **(PVA$1, 7%, 6)**
> $476.65     =     $100     ×     4.7665

## POWER OF DISCOUNTING AND INFINITE ANNUITIES

Earlier we saw that when the funds are invested for a long time the effect of compounding is quite substantial. Now we will explain this effect on present value which we are calling the power of discounting. In the process we will explain how to compute the present value of infinite annuities which are important for analyses described in later chapters.

Say your aunt decides to give you $100 per year, starting one year from now, for 50 years. She is going to set aside an amount today in a savings account that will be sufficient to cover the 50 payments. Finally, we will assume that this savings account will pay interest of 10% per year compounded annually for the entire period. How much must your aunt put in the savings account today? The answer is the present value of the annuity at 10% per year compounded annually, which is $991.48.

| *Present Value* | | *Equal Amount* | | *(PVA$1, 10%, 50)* |
|---|---|---|---|---|
| $991.48 | = | $100 | × | 9.9148 |

If she put $991.48 in this savings account today she could withdraw $100 per year, starting in one year, and there would be a zero balance in the account 50 years from now after the 50th withdrawal.

Let's say your aunt is superstititous and thinks that if she gives you a 100-year annuity, you will live for another 100 years. How much must she put in the savings account to fund a 100-year annuity of $100 per year? The answer is $999.93, given a rate of 10% per year compounded annually for the entire period.

| *Present Value* | | *Equal Amount* | | *(PVA$1, 10%, 100)* |
|---|---|---|---|---|
| $999.93 | = | $100 | × | 9.9993 |

This annuity will cost your aunt $8.45 more (i.e., $999.93 − $991.48 = $8.45).

Notice the power of discounting, or saying it another way note how little the dollars received many years from now are worth today. In this example, $100 at the end of years 51 to 100 is worth only $8.45 today at a rate of 10% per year compounded annually. To be more complete, we should emphasize that both the rate and the years involved have an effect on present value. For instance, if the rate were 5% instead of 10%, the 100-year annuity would require $159.20 more today than the 50-year annuity. If the rate were 20% instead of 10%, the 100-year annuity would require about five cents more today than the 50-year annuity.

Suppose your aunt wanted $100 per year to go to your family for generations. How much must she set aside today to fund this assuming a rate of 10% per year compounded annually? There is no need to figure out how many years are involved. We just figured out that $999.93 will fund an annuity of $100 per year for 100 years. By putting $1,000 in the bank at 10% per year compounded annually she can fund an annuity of $100 per year forever, that is, at the end of years one to infinity. The reason is that $100 will be the interest earned each year on the $1,000 balance. For our present purposes, the important implication is that $1,000 is the present value of an infinite (or perpetual) stream of $100 per year at 10% per year compounded annually. Furthermore, we can compute the present value of any infinite annuity by following the same logic which translates into the equation presented below:

*Present Value of Infinite Annuity (Annual Compounding)*
$$\text{Present Value} = A_{1-\infty} \left[\frac{1}{i}\right]$$

Where:
$\infty$ = Infinity
$A_{1-\infty}$ = Amount at end of years $1-\infty$
$i$ = Compound annual rate

Let's compute the present value of the infinite annuity of $100 at compound annual rates of 5% and 20%.

*5%*
$$\text{Present Value} = \$100 \left[\frac{1}{.05}\right]$$
$$= \$100 \, [20.000]$$
$$= \$2,000$$

*20%*
$$\text{Present Value} = \$100 \left[\frac{1}{.20}\right]$$
$$= \$100 \, [5.0000]$$
$$= \$500$$

The large difference in the two present values illustrates again the impact of the interest rate on present values.

Before proceeding to other kinds of annuities, we should note that the present value of infinite annuities was explained for reasons other than showing the power of discounting. In later chapters we will rely on this tool in performing various kinds of financial analysis. For instance, we will see how it can be used to estimate the required rate of return on investments.

## UNEVEN SERIES

In performing financial analyses, you will often encounter an unequal series of cash flows and annuities that begin in periods subsequent to the end of the first year and be required to compute the present value of these streams. Here we look at several examples to show how these computations are made. To begin, let's assume that we want to compute the present value of the following stream at 6% per year compounded annually.

| End of Year | Cash Flow |
|:---:|:---:|
| 1 | $100 |
| 2 | 100 |
| 3 | 200 |
| 4 | 200 |
| 5 | 200 |

One way of deriving the present value of this stream is to rely on the factors in Appendix P-1 as shown below:

| End of Year | Cash Flow | | $(PV\$1, 6\%, n)$[5] | | Present Value |
|:---:|:---:|:---:|:---:|:---:|:---:|
| 1 | $100 | × | .9434 | = | $ 94.34 |
| 2 | 100 | × | .8900 | = | 89.00 |
| 3 | 200 | × | .8396 | = | 167.92 |
| 4 | 200 | × | .7921 | = | 158.42 |
| 5 | 200 | × | .7473 | = | 149.46 |
| | | | | | $659.14 |

To reduce the number of computations, we can rely on the annuity table. Let's first restate the problem as follows:

| End of Year | Cash Flow |
|:---:|:---:|
| 1–2 | $100 |
| 3–5 | 200 |

We see we have two annuities. The factor for the first can be obtained directly from Appendix P-2. It is 1.8334. For the second, we have an annuity for three years, but the first amount occurs at the end of Year 3. Thus, we have to derive an annuity factor as shown below.

---

[5] When the computations involve several different factors we will not specify the various values for n.

| End of Year | (PVA$1, 6%, n) |
|:-----------:|:--------------:|
| 1–5 | 4.2124 |
| − 1–2 | 1.8334 |
| = 3–5 | 2.3790 |

We can now solve the problem.

| End of Year | Cash Flow | | (PVA$1, 6%, n) | | Present Value |
|:-----------:|:---------:|:-:|:--------------:|:-:|:-------------:|
| 1–2 | 100 | × | 1.8334 | = | $183.34 |
| 3–5 | 200 | × | 2.3790 | = | 475.80 |
| | | | | | $659.14 |

Try to apply the procedure to the following example. Compute the present value of the following stream at a rate of 10% per year compounded annually.

| End of Year | Cash Flow |
|:-----------:|:---------:|
| 5 | $500 |
| 6 | 500 |
| 7 | 500 |
| 8 | 500 |
| 9 | 500 |
| 10 | 500 |

We must first derive a factor for a six-year annuity with the first amount at the end of Year 5.

| End of Year | (PVA$1, 10%, n) |
|:-----------:|:---------------:|
| 1–10 | 6.1446 |
| − 1–4 | 3.1699 |
| = 5–10 | 2.9747 |

The next step is to compute the present value.

| End of Year | Cash Flow | | (PVA$1, 10%, n) | | Present Value |
|:-----------:|:---------:|:-:|:---------------:|:-:|:-------------:|
| 5–10 | $500 | × | 2.9747 | = | $1,487.35 |

Let's apply this procedure to the following example.

| End of Year | Cash Flow |
|:---:|:---:|
| 1 | 0 |
| 2 | 0 |
| 3 | 0 |
| 4–∞ | $100 |

We want to compute the present value of this stream at 20% per year compounded annually. The first step is to compute the factor.

| End of Year | (PVA$1, 20%, n) |
|:---:|:---:|
| 1–∞ | 5.0000[6] |
| − 1–3 | 2.1065 |
| | 2.8935 |

$$2.8935 \times \$100 = \$289.35$$

The present value of an infinite annuity of $100, starting at the end of Year 4, at 20% per year compounded annually, is $289.35.

Sometimes it's convenient to use an alternative procedure to compute the present value of an annuity where the first annual amount occurs at the end of a year subsequent to one year from now. We will rely on the previous example of $100 per year for years 4–∞ at 20% to illustrate it. We first compute the present value assuming the series of $100 amounts begins one year from now. This is $500 as shown below.

$$PV = A \left[\frac{1}{i}\right] = 100 \left[\frac{1}{.20}\right] = \$500$$

Five hundred dollars is the present value at the end of Year 3 of an infinite annuity of $100, where the first periodic amount occurs at the end of Year 4. In other words, the following two streams are equivalent at a rate of 20% per year compounded annually.

| End of Year | Cash Flow |
|:---:|:---:|
| 1 | 0 |
| 2 | 0 |
| 3 | 0 |
| 4–∞ | $100 |

---

[6] Recall that the factor for an infinite annuity at a given compound annual interest rate is derived as follows:
$$\frac{1}{i} = \frac{1}{.20} = 5.0000$$

This series is the same as the following at 20%.

| End of Year | Cash Flow |
|:-:|:-:|
| 1 | 0 |
| 2 | 0 |
| 3 | $500 |

In effect we have a single future amount and we can compute the present value by relying on the factors in Appendix P-1.

| End of Year | Cash Flow | | (PV$1, 20%,3) | | Present Value |
|:-:|:-:|:-:|:-:|:-:|:-:|
| 3 | $500 | × | .5787 | = | $289.35 |

This completes our discussion of the concept of present value and our explanation of how to make present value computations. Before closing we will discuss two practical applications. First we will show how the above principles and calculations are needed to compute an important measure called the internal rate of return and after that we will show how they are essential for analyzing various facets of a loan.

## INTERNAL RATE OF RETURN

The Internal Rate of Return (IRR) is the rate that makes the present value of an investment's cash inflows equal to the present value of an investment's cash outflows. Here we show how to compute the IRR and the next section and later chapters show its many practical applications. We should point out, however, that it is known by a variety of names such as yield, yield to maturity, discounted cash flow (DCF), and the marginal efficiency of capital.

Suppose we are given the following cash flows for an investment.

| End of Year | Cash Flow |
|:-:|:-:|
| 0 | ($100) |
| 1 | 40 |
| 2 | 80 |

The investment requires an immediate (i.e., at time zero) cash outlay of $100 and promises to return $40 one year from now and $80 two years from now.[7] This investment has a life of two years which means there are no cash flows beyond the end of the second year. The internal rate of return for the above investment is the rate that makes the present value of $40 one year from now plus the present value of $80 two years from now equal to $100 which is the present value of the investment's cash outflows.

One way of solving for the internal rate of return is by a trial and error method, which means we pick a rate and see if it works. Let's try 15%.

*Trial 1. 15%*

| End of Year | Cash Flow | | (PV$1, 15%, n) | | Present Value |
|---|---|---|---|---|---|
| 1 | $40 | × | .8696 | = | $34.78 |
| 2 | 80 | × | .7561 | = | 60.49 |
| | | | | | $95.27 |

Is this investment's IRR 15%? The answer is "no" because by definition it is the rate that makes the present value of the cash inflows equal to $100. Earlier we saw that there is an inverse relationship between the rate and present value, that is, the higher the rate, the lower the present value and vice versa. Hence, since $95.27 is less than $100, we need a lower rate for our second trial because we want to make the present value of the inflows larger. Let's try 10%.

*Trial 2. 10%*

| End of Year | Cash Flow | | (PV$1, 10%, n) | | Present Value |
|---|---|---|---|---|---|
| 1 | $40 | × | .9091 | = | $ 36.36 |
| 2 | 80 | × | .8264 | = | 66.11 |
| | | | | | $102.47 |

Let's try 11% since 10% is too low.

*Trial 3. 11%*

| End of Year | Cash Flow | | (PV$1, 11%, n) | | Present Value |
|---|---|---|---|---|---|
| 1 | $40 | × | .9009 | = | $ 36.04 |
| 2 | 80 | × | .8116 | = | 64.93 |
| | | | | | $100.97 |

Not quite, let's try 12%.

*Trial 4. 12%*

| End of Year | Cash Flow | | (PV$1, 12%, n) | | Present Value |
|---|---|---|---|---|---|
| 1 | $40 | × | .8929 | = | $35.72 |
| 2 | 80 | × | .7972 | = | 63.78 |
| | | | | | $99.50 |

The internal rate of return is between 11% and 12%. There is a way of computing a more precise rate by hand. We won't illustrate it, however,

---

[7] In analyzing investments, we generally will distinguish between inflows and outflows by inserting outflows in parentheses.

because most financial calculators and computers provide a more precise figure and you can see from the above trial and error procedure why you will want to rely on these tools in computing the IRR in practice. We should add that for many investments there is considerable uncertainty regarding how much the cash flows actually will be. Hence, for this type, stating the IRR to one or more decimal places like 14.67% implies a precision that does not exist. In other words, if our example was an actual capital investment (e.g., introducing a new product) being considered by a firm, it probably would be good enough to say that the IRR is between 11% and 12%.

Notice the similarity and difference between computing the IRR and the calculation of the present value of a series of cash flows. In the present value examples, we were given future amounts and a rate and we computed the present value. Here we have the amount at time zero, which is the present value, and the future amounts and we want to compute the rate. This analogy has several practical uses. One is a shortcut procedure for computing the IRR when all the future amounts are the same. Let's look at an example:

Suppose we want to compute the IRR for the following investment.

| End of Year | Cash Flow |
|:---:|:---:|
| 0 | ($10,000) |
| 1–5 | 3,054 |

Recall that we computed the present value of a stream of equal annual cash flows starting one year from now as follows:

Present Value = Equal Amount × (PVA$1, i, n)

Given that we know i or n in the last term, this is an equation with three variables and knowing two of them allows us to solve for the third. To see how, let's put the data for this investment in the present value format.

| Present Value | | Equal Amount | (PVA$1, i, 5) |
|:---:|:---:|:---:|:---:|
| $10,000 | = | $3,054 | × (PVA$1, i, 5) |

Let's solve for (PVA$1, i, 5).

$$(\text{PVA\$1, i, 5}) = \frac{\$10,000}{\$3,054} = 3.2744$$

The answer, 3.2744, is a PVA$1 factor for an unknown interest rate for n = 5. All we have to do to solve for the IRR is turn to Appendix P-2 and locate this factor. Specifically, we go down the table to n = 5 and read across until we find the factor closest to 3.2744. It is 3.2743 which is the factor for 16%, that is, (PVA$1, 16%, 5) is 3.2743. Hence, this rate, 16%, is the internal rate of return for this investment.

If you have trouble seeing this result think of it in the following way: Say we were asked to compute the present value of a five-year annuity of $3,054 at 16% per year compounded annually. We would derive the answer as follows:

*Present Value*      *Equal Amount*      *(PVA$1, 16%, 5)*
$9,999.71    =    $3,054    ×    3.2743

The present value is almost $10,000. So, if $10,000 is the present value of an investment's cash outflows and the annual inflows are $3,054 for five years, then 16% must be the rate that makes the present value of the cash inflows equal to the present value of the cash outflows.

As noted, the IRR has many practical applications. We will see one in a moment and others in later chapters.

## ANALYZING LOANS

The interest rate that a bank or any financial institution charges on a loan is conceptually equivalent to the internal rate of return. It is computed the same way.[8] Let's assume you borrow $10,000 from a bank today. The loan requires five equal annual payments of $3,054, with the first payment due one year from now. The interest rate on this loan is 16% which is the IRR we just computed for an investment. Look at it this way. The bank is making an investment of $10,000 and in return is getting annual cash inflows of $3,054 for five years. This is an internal rate of return of 16% on this investment.

Equal annual payments are quite common. Although the dollar amount paid each year is fixed, the portions devoted to interest and principal will vary each year. No matter what the payment stream, interest is always computed as follows:

Principal Amount             Annual             Fraction of           Interest
Beginning of Period  ×  Interest Rate  ×  Year in Period  =  for Period

(There are other ways of computing interest but they are all consistent with the above procedure.) We will illustrate with our example.

[8] Sometimes an add-on or discount method is used to compute the interest amount but even in these instances we would compute the internal rate of return to convert to a true interest rate.

| Year | Loan Balance Beginning of Year | Payment End of Year | Interest | Principal | Loan Balance End of Year |
|------|-------------------------------|---------------------|----------|-----------|--------------------------|
| 1 | $10,000 | $3,054 | $1,600 | $1,454 | $8,546 |
| 2 | 8,546 | 3,054 | 1,367 | 1,687 | 6,859 |
| 3 | 6,859 | 3,054 | 1,097 | 1,957 | 4,902 |
| 4 | 4,902 | 3,054 | 784 | 2,270 | 2,632 |
| 5 | 2,632 | 3,054 | 421 | 2,633 | (1) |

(The loan balance at the end of Year 5 differs from zero because of rounding.)

The interest for the first year was calculated by multiplying $10,000 by 16%. So $1,600 of the $3,054 payment was for interest, the remaining $1,454 went toward principal, leaving a loan balance of $8,546 at the end of the first year. Interest for the second year of $1,367 was derived by multiplying the loan balance of $8,546 by 16%. So $1,367 of the second year's payment of $3,054 was for interest, the remaining $1,687 went toward principal, leaving a loan balance of $6,859 at the end of the second year. The reader should be able to derive the other figures.

Suppose the banker in our example decided to charge an interest rate of 14% instead of 16%. How much would the five equal annual payments be for the $10,000 loan? Let's state the procedure for computing the present value of an annuity and put in the data we know.

$$\underset{\$10,000}{Present\ Value} = \underset{Equal\ Amount}{Equal\ Amount} \times \underset{3.4331}{(PVA\$1,\ 14\%,\ 5)}$$

Now let's solve for the unknown which in this instance is the equal annual amount.

$$\frac{\$10,000}{3.4331} = Equal\ Amount = \$2,913$$

A loan of $10,000 at 14% would require five equal payments of $2,913 with the first payment due one year from now.

This chapter explained the notion of the time value of money and showed how to make present value and future value computations. It is essential that you have a solid grasp of these principles and computations because most of the topics in subsequent chapters build on them. Finally, the chapter also illustrated a number of practical applications including an analysis of retirement planning, the internal rate of return and analyzing various features of loans.

# Problems and Discussion Questions

## A. Solved Problems

### Problem 7-1A

You are going to receive $1,000 today, $1,000 one year from now, $1,000 two years from now and $1,000 three years from now. You will place these amounts in a savings account that pays interest of 10% per year compounded annually and make no withdrawals during the three-year period.

1. How much are the four receipts worth today?

2. What will be the balance in your savings account three years from now?

### Solution 7-1A

1. When solving a time value of money problem you should first make sure you understand whether it is a present value problem, a future value problem, or one that involves both present and future values. Further, you must specify whether an annuity is involved and what the compounding (discounting) interval is so you will know which table of factors to use and how to use them. To sort this out, it often helps to prepare a diagram like the following

End of Year

| 0 | 1 | 2 | 3 |
|---|---|---|---|
| $1,000 | $1,000 | $1,000 | $1,000 |

The arrows indicate that our goal is to compute present value and the heading, end of year, clarifies that it is annual discounting.

There are four equal receipts. Do we turn to Appendix P-2 to obtain a factor for a four-year annuity? The answer is "no" because the factors in Appendix P-2 are for annuities whose first cash flow occurs one year from now. We can see from the diagram that the first of the four equal cash flows occurs at time zero. Leaving that one aside for a moment, we can compute the present value of the next three by relying on the factor for a three-year annuity as shown next:

| Present Value | | Equal Amount | | (PVA$1, 10%, 3) |
| --- | --- | --- | --- | --- |
| $2,486.90 | = | $1,000 | × | 2.4869 |

To this amount we add the present value at 10% of $1,000 today. The present value of $1,000 today at 10%, or any rate for that matter, is $1,000. In other words, the present value of $1 today is $1 regardless of the rate and so no calculation is required. Hence, the present value of the four cash receipts is $3,486.90, which is the present value of the three-year annuity, $2,486.90, plus $1,000.

2. Again we begin with a diagram.

|  | | End of Year | | |
| --- | --- | --- | --- |
| 0 | 1 | 2 | 3 |
| $1,000 | $1,000 | $1,000 | $1,000 |

The arrows point to the end of Year 3 indicating we want to compute the value three years from now of the four cash flows. Note that there is no arrow under the cash flow for the end of Year 3 cash flow. This shows that the last receipt will not earn interest.

With respect to which table of factors (or future value equation) to use, we must recall that the factors in Appendix F-2 assume that the first amount occurs one period from now. Hence, we must again separate the present amount and the annuity. However, in this instance a computation is required to compute the future value of the remaining receipt.

| Future Value | | Equal Amount | | (FVA$1, 10%, 3) |
| --- | --- | --- | --- | --- |
| $3,310.00 | = | $1,000 | × | 3.3100 |

| Future Value | | Present Amount | | (FV$1, 10%, 3) |
| --- | --- | --- | --- | --- |
| $1,331.00 | = | $1,000 | × | 1.3310 |

We now add these two amounts to get the answer.

$$\$4,641.00 = \$3,310.00 + \$1,331.00$$

The $1,000 received today and at each of the next three years will grow into $4,641 in three years at 10% per year compounded annually. Hence, this will be the balance in your savings account three years from now.

We recommend that you make sure you understand the scope of the problem and suggest a diagram. Our experience is that laying out the problem, either in diagram form or some other convenient format, helps people avoid errors when learning the time value of money. This advice applies whether you are working with a table of factors or solving the problems with the use of a financial calculator or computer.

### Problem 7-2A

Compute the present value of the following stream at a rate of 12% per year compounded quarterly.

| End of Quarter | Cash Flow |
| :---: | :---: |
| 0 | $   500 |
| 1–12 | 200 |
| 13–24 | 100 |
| 25 | 1,000 |

### Solution 7-2A

This problem requires that we compute the present value of a series of cash flows and quarterly compounding is involved. We will begin by sorting out the cash flows.

| | | End of Quarter | | | |
| :---: | :---: | :---: | :---: | :---: | :---: |
| 0 | 1............... | 12 | 13 ............. | 24 | 25 |
| $500 | $200 | $200 | $100 | $100 | $1,000 |

There are a number of ways to solve this problem. We will solve it in four parts: (1) the $500 today, (2) the stream for the first 12 quarters, (3) the stream for the next 12 quarters and (4) the final single amount.

1. *$500 at the end of quarter zero*
   The present value of one dollar today is one dollar regardless of the discount rate. Hence, no calculation is required since the present value is $500.

2. *$200 per quarter at the end of quarters 1–12*
   We divide i of 12% by m of 4 to get the interest rate per period of 3%. There are 12 periods of three months (i.e., m × n = 12). So we compute this part as follows:

*Present Value*     *Equal Amount*     *(PVA$1, 3%, 12)*
   $1,990.80     =          $200          ×          9.9540

3. *$100 per quarter at the end of quarters 13–24*
   The chapter explained two methods of dealing with annuities where the first cash flow occurs beyond the end of period one. We will illustrate both here. The first approach is to derive a 13–24 period annuity as shown below.

| *End of Quarter* | *(PVA$1, 3%, n)* |
|---|---|
| 1–24 | 16.9360 |
| − 1–12 | 9.9540 |
| 13–24 | 6.9820 |

$698.20 = $100 × 6.9820

The second approach is to first compute the present value as if the cash flows were occurring at the end of quarters 1–12.

*Present Value*     *Equal Amount*     *(PVA$1, 3%, 12)*
   $995.40     =          $100          ×          9.954

An annuity of $100 at the end of quarters 13–24 is equivalent to the following at 12% per year compounded quarterly.

| *End of Quarter* | *Cash Flow* |
|---|---|
| 12 | $995.40 |

We now compute the present value of this single amount to get the present value of the annuity for quarters 13–24.

*Present Value*     *Future Amount*     *(PV$1, 3%, 12)*
   $698.17     =          $995.40          ×          .7014

The slight difference between the $698.17 and the $698.20 is due to rounding. (We will use $698.20 in the final total.)

4. *$1,000 at the end of quarter 25*
   This is a single future amount and the present value is $477.60 as shown below.

*Present Value*     *Future Amount*     *(PV$1, 3%, 25)*
   $477.60     =          $1,000          ×          .4776

The final step is to add the four parts.

| End of Quarter | Cash Flow | Present Value |
|:---:|:---:|:---:|
| 0 | $ 500 | $ 500.00 |
| 1–12 | 200 | 1,990.80 |
| 13–24 | 100 | 698.20 |
| 25 | 1,000 | 477.60 |
| | | $3,666.60 |

Many people get overwhelmed when a time value problem has many parts. Our advice is to first make sure you understand the scope of the problem and then tackle it one piece at a time.

### Problem 7-3A

You need to borrow $4,000 and you are considering the following two alternatives.

• Borrowing $4,000 from a commercial bank at 12%. The loan would require 12 equal monthly payments starting one month from now.

• Borrowing $4,000 from a finance company. This loan would require payments of $378.24 at the end of each of the next 12 months.

Which financing alternative is cheaper?

### Solution 7-3A

This problem can be solved by comparing rates or cash flows. We will do it both ways but it is much more common to compare rates. First, a word about terminology that might have concerned some of you. Note that we are told that the interest rate on the loan is 12% but we were not told the compounding interval. At the end of each month the bank will multiply the principal outstanding for the month by 12% and then divide by 12 to get interest for the month. This means the interest rate is 1% per month or in the terminology of the chapter, 12% per year compounded monthly.

*Comparing rates.* We know the bank is charging us 12% so we must figure out the interest rate on the finance company loan. The internal rate of return on the finance company's investment is the interest rate. In other words, we solve the IRR for the following:

| End of Month | Cash Flow |
|:---:|:---:|
| 0 | ($4,000) |
| 1–12 | 378.24 |

Recall that when there is only one cash outflow and the inflows are an annuity that IRR can be computed as follows:

*Present Amount*     *Equal Amount*     *(PVA$1, i, n)*
$4,000          =          $378.24       × (PVA$1, i, 12)

$$(PVA\$1, i, 12) = \frac{4,000}{378.24} = 10.575$$

---

We go down to n = 12 in Appendix P-2 and across until we find the factor closest to 10.575. The factor at 2% is 10.575 indicating that the IRR is 2% per month or 24% per year. The interest rate on the finance company loan is 24% versus the 12% offered by the bank. Hence, the bank alternative is cheaper.

*Comparing cash flows.* We know what the loan payments would be for the finance company alternative, so we must figure out what they would be for the bank loan. We can again rely on the procedure for computing the present value of an annuity to solve this.

*Present Amount*     *Equal Amount*     *(PVA$1, 1%, 12)*
$4,000       = Equal Amount ×        11.255

$$\text{Equal Amount} = \frac{4,000}{11.255} = \$355.40$$

The loan payments for the bank alternative would be $355.40 each, which is less than the monthly payments of $378.24 required by the finance company option. Hence, the bank alternative is cheaper.

This problem was designed to give you practice in solving for loan payments and the interest rate on the loan. Note that had we given you the loan payments and the interest rate you could have computed the amount of the loan. You would have done this by solving the above equation for the present amount.

## B. Discussion Questions

### 7-1B

Evaluate the following statement: Because of the impact of compounding, the larger the interest rate, the larger the present value of a given future amount.

*7-2B*

Why are all the factors for n = 1 in Appendix F-2 equal to 1.0000?

*7-3B*

In Appendix P-1 the factor for i = 10%, n = 1, is .9091 and the factor for i = 10%, n = 2, is .8264. If we add these two factors we get 1.7355 which is the factor for i = 10%, n=2, in Appendix P-2. Is this a coincidence? Why or why not?

*7-4B*

In Appendix F-1, the factor for i = 10%, n = 1, is 1.1000 and the factor for i = 10%, n = 2, is 1.2100. If we add these together we get 2.3100. How come this is different from the factor of 2.1000 for i = 10%, n = 2, in Appendix F-2?

*7-5B*

What impact does the frequency of the compounding interval, m, have on the future value of a present amount for a given interest rate and terminal date? Why?

*7-6B*

Which of the options below would you choose? Why?

• $100 one year from now at 14% per year compounded annually.

• $100 one year from now at 14% per year compounded monthly.

## C. Study Problems

### Problem 7-1C

If you were to deposit $1,000 today in a savings account and leave it there for 20 years what would be the balance in your account at the end of 20 years if the interest rate is:
1. 10% per year compounded annually?
2. 10% per year compounded semi-annually?
3. 12% per year compounded quarterly?
4. 12% per year compounded monthly?
5. 12% per year compounded semi-annually, for the first eight years, then 16% per year compounded quarterly for the last 12 years?

### Problem 7-2C

In problem 7-1C assume the interest rate is 10% per year compounded annually. What would be the balance in your account, assuming no withdrawals, five years from now? 10 years from now? 30 years from now? 50 years from now? 100 years from now?

**Problem 7-3C**

You have won a prize and have been given the choice of receiving one of the following payment streams:

• $1,000 per year at the end of years 1–40.

• $1,000 per year at the end of years 21 to infinity.

• $10,000 per year at the end of years 16–50.

Assuming you have the opportunity to earn interest of 8% per year compounded annually from now to infinity, which option would you choose?

**Problem 7-4C**

Suppose you just won a prize that will pay you $1,000 on every December 31st with the first payment on December 31, 1987, and the last payment on December 31, 1992. Assuming you can earn interest of 10% per year compounded annually through December 31, 1992, what is the prize worth on December 31, 1982? On December 31, 1989? On December 31, 1990?

**Problem 7-5C**

$50,000 from your late uncle's trust will be available to you exactly five years from now, but you need some money today. A bank is willing to lend you money at 12% per year compounded annually, with all principal and interest payable at the end of five years. What maximum amount can you borrow today such that proceeds from the trust will completely cover your future obligations associated with the loan?

**Problem 7-6C**

Your aunt bought a painting 16 years ago for $252 and just sold it for $6,000. What compound annual rate of return did she earn?

**Problem 7-7C**

The following cash inflows are expected from an investment that requires an immediate outlay of $400.

| End of Year | Cash Flow |
| --- | --- |
| 1–3 | $100 |
| 4–8 | 50 |

What is the internal rate of return on this investment?

### Problem 7-8C

Joe is going to borrow $12,000 to buy a new car and he is considering the following two alternatives.

- Borrowing $12,000 from a bank at a rate of 14%. The loan would require three equal annual payments with the first payment due one year from now.

- Borrowing $12,000 from a finance company. This loan would require annual payments of $4,825 at the end of years 1–3.

1. What are the equal annual loan payments on the bank alternative?

2. What is the interest rate on the finance company loan?

3. Which would you choose?

4. Did you have to solve both 1 and 2 to answer 3? Why or why not?

### Problem 7-9C

Carla just borrowed the purchase price of a new car from a bank at an interest rate of 12%. The loan requires payments of $350 at the end of each of the next 36 months. What is the purchase price of Carla's car?

### Problem 7-10C

Anthony wants to have $1,000 saved to purchase a Christmas gift next year for his favorite nephew. His bank pays 12% per year compounded monthly. What equal monthly amounts must he save if his first deposit is on January 1 and his last deposit is on November 30th (12 deposits in all) such that he has $1,000 in his account on December 1.

### Problem 7-11C

Alicia Marston just celebrated her 40th birthday and needs your advice regarding a savings program. She plans to retire on her 65th birthday and would like an income of $10,000 per year from this savings program for 20 years thereafter (starting on her 66th birthday and ending on her 85th birthday). She will be able to earn interest of 10% per year compounded annually from now until her 85th birthday on a savings account. Her program involves an equal annual amount being deposited in the savings account starting on her 41st birthday and ending on her 65th birthday. What equal annual amount must she deposit in her savings account to achieve her retirement income goal from the savings program?

**Problem 7-12C**

Sam Soares has taken out a $10,000 loan from his bank today with the following provisions: interest of 12% per year compounded quarterly for the entire term of the loan; repayments of principal and interest due in ten equal quarterly payments starting one year from today. How much will each equal quarterly payment be?

**Problem 7-13C**

Little Joe is only one year old but his uncle already is starting a college savings program for him. Tuition at the uncle's alma mater, where Joe will, of course, attend, is now $7,000 but is expected to increase at 6% per year compounding annually over the next 25 years. If all goes according to schedule, Joe will enter college 17 years from today, so annual tuition payments will be due starting on that date and continuing for each of the three years after that. Joe's uncle plans to begin the savings program by depositing an equal annual amount into a savings account starting today and ending on the day Joe enters college, 17 years from now (18 deposits in all). If the savings account earns interest of 8% per year compounded annually for the entire period, what equal annual amount must the uncle deposit to meet Joe's expected tuition costs?

**Problem 7-14C**

Your fun-loving cousin, Paul, has just received an inheritance from his late aunt's estate. It provides for an immediate bequest of $325,000 plus an income of $10,000 per year for 20 years with the first $10,000 received one year from today. All the funds—the immediate bequest plus annual payments—will go directly into a savings account that will pay interest of 12% per year compounded annually for as long as there is money in the account. Paul believes his inheritance should set him up for life so he has quit his job and is relying solely on the proceeds from the inheritance for his support. If Paul spends $50,000 per year (assume, for simplicity, that he withdraws all his spending money at one time at the end of each year starting one year from now), how many years will this inheritance last?

**Problem 7-15C**

You are going to make three equal annual deposits in a savings account. The first will be made today, the second will be made one year from now and the final deposit will be made two years from now. The account will pay interest of 8% per year compounded annually for the next three years. Assuming you want $15,000 in the account three years from now, compute the size of each of the three deposits.

### Problem 7-16C

Compute the internal rate of return for the following investment.

| End of Year | Cash Flow |
|:---:|:---:|
| 0 | ($27,420) |
| 1–10 | 0 |
| 11–50 | 50,000 |

### Problem 7-17C

In problem 7-15C, compute the IRR assuming cash inflows of $50,000 per year will be received at the end of Years 11 to infinity instead of 11–50.

# 8

# Valuation and Required Rates of Return

The previous chapter explained that one dollar in the future is worth less than one dollar today and showed how to compute the present value of future amounts. The primary intent of this chapter is to discuss the valuation of uncertain (i.e., risky) cash flows, that is, to explain how one can estimate the present value of uncertain cash flows.

We will focus on two of the most important ideas in finance. They are:

1. The value of investment is the present value of the cash flows that the investment will generate discounted at an appropriate risk-adjusted discount rate.

2. The risk of an investment determines the appropriate risk-adjusted discount rate that should be used to compute the value of the investment.

It's important to keep in mind as we proceed that we can only estimate the value and the risk-adjusted rate for many investments. Thus, while we may round figures to the nearest dollar (or penny) and rates to the nearest tenth or one-hundredth of a percent, this will be for clarity only. Do not infer a precision that does not exist.

The chapter begins with a brief discussion of discount rates used in valuation. After that we explain two valuation principles and then turn our attention to valuing bonds and stocks. Then we discuss the notion of the firm's cost of capital and the selection of required rates for evaluating capital investments. We conclude with a brief discussion of the relationship between value and market price.

## A WORD ABOUT RATES

We will frequently refer to risk-free or riskless rates and risk-adjusted discount rates. Hence, we need to begin by describing what we mean by these terms.

The United States Government borrows money and like anyone else must pay interest and principal at specified times. These borrowings are called either Treasury bills, Treasury notes or Treasury bonds depending on the maturity of the financial instrument. For instance, Treasury securities issued with a maturity of one year or less are called Treasury bills, or simply T bills. Since the Government is guaranteeing interest and principal payments on these securities, and presumably won't default, the interest rate on them is known as the risk-free or riskless rate. Typically, these rates are used to compute the present value of certain future cash flows, that is, when there is 100% chance that the future cash flow will occur.[1]

Suppose you can buy a Treasury security today for $1,000 that promises $1,100 one year from now. An industrial firm offers you a debt instrument for $1,000 today and will pay interest one year from now plus repay the $1,000 at that time. Now you would not purchase this security unless it promised to pay more than $100 of interest next year. Why? The industrial firm may not be able to make the promised payment and the Treasury security gives a definite return of $100. In other words, since you are incurring risk when you buy an industrial bond you would require a rate of return greater than the risk-free rate. The greater the risk involved the greater the rate of return you would require.

The extra rate of return investors require over the risk-free rate is called the risk premium. Obviously the size of the risk premium depends on the amount of risk. The total of the risk-free rate plus the risk premium is frequently referred to as the required rate or the risk-adjusted discount rate.

[1] A more precise term than risk-free rates is default-free rate meaning the Government will pay interest and principal when due. As we will see later, prices on fixed income securities, including Treasury securities, vary inversely with changes in open market interest rates. For instance, suppose you purchased a newly issued Government bond for $10,000 that matures in ten years. A year later you had an unexpected need for cash and had to sell the bond. If interest rates had increased during the year, you would have received less than $10,000 when the bond was sold and you would have incurred a capital loss.

Risk-Adjusted Discount Rate = Risk-Free Rate + Risk Premium

One final point before we proceed. When there is a 100% probability that a cash flow will occur, we will typically refer to it as a certain cash flow. A less than 100% probability of occurrence will be referred to as uncertainty or risk. We should add that for some analyses, it is useful to make a distinction between risk and uncertainty. This distinction is not necessary for our purposes so we will use the two terms interchangeably throughout the chapter.

# *Valuation Principles*

We will now explain two principles that will serve as our guide for valuing future cash flows. A simple example will show that we have already relied upon these principles. Assume we are analyzing two United States Government bonds—Bond A and Bond B—that were issued at different times many years ago and will mature in one year. Bond A will pay interest of $100 plus $1,000 principal in a year and Bond B will pay interest and principal of $150 and $1,000, respectively, at the same time.[2] Finally, the rate today on one-year Treasury securities is 10%. How much is each bond worth today? The answer is the present value of the remaining cash flow that each will generate discounted at 10%.

|  | Bond A |  |  |
|---|---|---|---|
| *Present Value* | *Future Amount* |  | *(PV$1, 10%, 1)* |
| $1,000.00 = | $1,100 | × | .9091 |

|  | Bond B |  |  |
|---|---|---|---|
| *Present Value* | *Future Amount* |  | *(PV$1, 10%, 1)* |
| $1,045.47 = | $1,150 | × | .9091 |

As shown, Bond A's cash flow is worth $1,000 today and Bond B's cash flow is worth $1,045.47 today. Stating this another way, Bond A's value is $1,000 and Bond B's value is $1,045.47. Now would you pay $1,025 for Bond A? No, because the bond is worth only $1,000 (i.e., its value is $1,000). This example illustrates the following two valuation principles:

[2] The interest rate on a Government bond depends on prevailing market rates when the bond is issued. So it's not unusual to see two different interest rates on Government bonds that mature at the same time. What is a bit unusual is to see interest paid annually because semi-annual interest is more common. We do this to minimize details; the point of the illustration is in no way affected by this simplifying assumption.

*Valuation Principle 1*
The value of an investment is the present value of the cash flows that the investment will generate discounted at an appropriate risk-adjusted discount rate. (When the investment's cash flows are certain, they are discounted at a suitable risk-free rate.)

*Valuation Principle 2*
The present value of the cash flows of an investment discounted at an appropriate risk-adjusted discount rate is the maximum price that one should be willing to pay for that investment. (When the investment's cash flows are certain, they are discounted at a suitable risk-free rate.)

These two principles apply to any investment, including bonds and stocks and other financial instruments, and capital investments made by firms acquiring assets to introduce a new product line. Because valuation provides the conceptual framework for financial decision making, it is frequently referred to as the central and unifying theme in finance.

To explain the logic of the principles, we relied on an example of two investments with certain cash flows. As you can imagine, applying these principles to investments that have risky cash flows is much more difficult. Nevertheless, they still apply. In other words, when valuing risky investments we need a conceptual framework and the valuation principles provide a framework that is based on sound economic reasoning. Furthermore, any procedure for valuing investments that is not consistent with these principles is flawed.

Risky investments also raise the issue of the relationship between values and prevailing market prices. In our example, we noted with confidence that you would not pay $1,025 for Bond A. Later we will see why we can be confident that the price on the open market would be $1,000. Now for risky investments, it's not so clear that the price investors should be willing to pay is indeed the price investors would pay. We address this issue later in the chapter and until then we will not be concerned about the possible difference between value and price.

Although it is the mission of the next two chapters to show how the valuation principles can be used by firms to help make capital investment decisions, it would be worthwhile to look at one example here. Suppose the management of Ablco Inc. sought our advice on a capital investment. The firm is considering purchasing new equipment for $100,000 that is designed to reduce labor costs. Management wants to know if it's a good investment. To make this assessment we must do the following:

1. Estimate the amount and timing of the (after tax) cash flows that the savings in labor will generate.

2. Estimate an appropriate risk-adjusted discount rate.

3. Compute the present value of the cash flows at the rate selected.

Assume we estimate that the savings will produce the following cash flows over the equipment's ten-year life.

| End of Year[3] | Cash Flow |
|---|---|
| 1 | $17,000 |
| 2 | 18,000 |
| 3 | 18,000 |
| 4 | 18,000 |
| 5 | 18,000 |
| 6 | 16,000 |
| 7 | 15,000 |
| 8 | 14,000 |
| 9 | 13,000 |
| 10 | 9,000 |

We then estimate an appropriate risk-adjusted discount rate. This depends on the risk involved, that is, the likelihood that the firm will actually receive the expected cash flows. Let's assume that our assessment indicates that a rate of 15% is appropriate for evaluating this investment. Given this we compute the present value of the cash flows at 15% as shown below:

| Year | Cash Flow | | (PV$1, 15%, n) | | Present Value |
|---|---|---|---|---|---|
| 1 | $17,000 | × | .8696 | = | $14,783 |
| 2 | 18,000 | × | .7561 | = | 13,610 |
| 3 | 18,000 | × | .6575 | = | 11,835 |
| 4 | 18,000 | × | .5718 | = | 10,292 |
| 5 | 18,000 | × | .4972 | = | 8,950 |
| 6 | 16,000 | × | .4323 | = | 6,917 |
| 7 | 15,000 | × | .3759 | = | 5,639 |
| 8 | 14,000 | × | .3269 | = | 4,577 |
| 9 | 13,000 | × | .2843 | = | 3,696 |
| 10 | 9,000 | × | .2472 | = | 2,225 |
| | | | | | $82,524 |

[3] To simplify the example, it is assumed that the cash flows occur once each year at the end of the year.

Should the firm purchase the new equipment? The answer is "no" unless there is some important factor that offsets the economics of the venture. The machine costs $100,000 and the present value of the inflows is only $82,524. This tells us that the savings are not worth the cost. In other words, the maximum price that the firm should be willing to pay for this investment is $82,524.

Say we invest $100,000 to start a new firm. The manager we hired takes the $100,000 and invests in the asset described above. We would view this as a bad investment decision because the value of our firm would decrease from the initial $100,000 invested to $82,524, the value of the cash flows we expect to receive. In other words, we suffer a loss of wealth. Viewing the example in this context shows the centrality of valuation for business finance. Managers make decisions all the time and value should serve as the guide because owners want managers to make decisions that increase the value of the firm.

# *Valuation of Bonds*

This section applies the valuation principles to bonds, also known as fixed income securities. We begin with a brief description of some of the features of bonds.

When one party borrows from another, normally there is a legal obligation to pay interest and to repay principal. Frequently, the obligation is in the form of a written contract which is known as a debt instrument. A bond is one type of debt instrument. A bond's face value, also referred to as par value, is the principal amount that will be paid at maturity—the date that the principal must be paid. Often, the face value of a bond is $1,000. The face value should not be confused with the bond's market value, which is the price at which the bond can be purchased or sold on the open market.

The coupon rate on the bond is the rate that is multiplied by the face value to compute the dollars of interest that will be paid each year. For instance, suppose a firm issues a bond with a face value of $1,000 and a coupon rate of 15%. This means the firm will pay interest of $150 per year on this bond. Typically, interest is paid every six months, so in this illustration $75 would be paid every six months and the interest rate would be 15% per year compounded semi-annually. In any event, the dollar amount of interest is fixed, meaning that even if interest rates on the open market change, the firm still will pay $150 per year. Sometimes bonds are issued with "floating coupons" or "variable interest rates." This means that the coupon rate on the bond will change periodically. In other words, for these bonds, the dollar amount of interest paid each year is not fixed for the life of the bond. The adjustment to the coupon rate is based on some benchmark rate such as the rate on a specific U.S. Treasury security.

A bond's current yield is the dollars of interest paid each year divided by the bond's market value. For example, suppose a bond has a market value of $950, a face value of $1,000, and pays interest of $100 each year. The current yield on this bond is 10.5% as shown below:

$$\text{Current Yield} = \frac{\text{Annual Interest}}{\text{Market Value}} = \frac{\$100}{\$950} = 10.5\%$$

While the current yield is used by some analysts, the most commonly-employed measure is yield to maturity (YTM). Yield to maturity is the rate that makes the present value of the cash inflows that the bond will generate (i.e., interest and principal payments) equal to the market price of the bond. This is the definition of the internal rate of return described in the last chapter. Indeed, yield to maturity is simply another name for internal rate of return. Since we have already explained the trial and error procedure for computing the YTM, we will focus here on why it is a useful measure.

Suppose you put $1,000 in a bank that pays interest of 10% per year compounded annually. You plan to withdraw interest one year from now, and interest plus the $1,000 deposited two years from now. Your cash flow stream would be as follows:

| End of Year | Cash Flow |
|:-----------:|:---------:|
| 0 | ($1,000) |
| 1 | 100 |
| 2 | 1,100 |

Now assume you purchased a Government bond for $1,000 which has two years remaining until maturity. The face value of the bond is $1,000, the coupon rate is 10% and the interest is paid once each year. The cash flows from this investment are:

| End of Year | Cash Flow |
|:-----------:|:---------:|
| 0 | ($1,000) |
| 1 | 100 |
| 2 | 1,100 |

The yield to maturity on this bond is 10% as is the coupon rate and the current yield. This is not unique to this example and these three rates will be equal whenever a bond's market value equals its face value. Further, when face and market value are equal, all three rates are comparable to rates on other financial instruments as well as interest rates offered on savings accounts.

Suppose the price of the Government bond was $950 instead of $1,000. The cash flows would be:

| End of Year | Cash Flow |
|:-----------:|:---------:|
| 0 | ($  950) |
| 1 | 100 |
| 2 | 1,100 |

The coupon rate is 10%, the current yield is 10.5% and yield to maturity is 13%. Which of the three rates is most useful? The answer is yield to maturity and to see why let's assume the following facts: You place $950 in a bank that pays a compounded annual interest rate. One year from now you withdraw $100. Two years from now you close the account and on that date the balance is $1,100. The compound annual interest rate that the bank is paying is 13%. The cash flows here are the same as the bond and the rate is the same as the bond's YTM. Thus, in comparing the rate of return on the bond to alternative market rates such as the rate on savings accounts, we must rely on the bond's yield to maturity because this is the only rate that is directly comparable.

To be a useful measure, a rate of return calculation must incorporate the total cash flows from an investment and take into account the time value of money. Yield to maturity meets these criteria but the coupon rate and the current yield do not. Note that these criteria apply to any investment and not just bonds. So whenever you see reference to a rate of return on an investment, you should check to see that it meets these criteria. If it does not, then it likely can give misleading signals.

## MARKET PRICE OF A BOND

Like any investment, the value of a bond is the present value of the cash flows that the bond will generate (i.e., interest and principal payments) discounted at an appropriate risk-adjusted discount rate. The appropriate risk-adjusted discount rate for a bond is its yield to maturity. If a bond is publicly traded this means we know its price and so computing its YTM is a simple matter. We can compute it by the trial and error procedure for deriving the internal rate of return that was explained in the last chapter.

Sometimes we are analyzing a bond (or other debt instrument) that is not publicly traded and we want to estimate its market price. To do this we must estimate the bond's yield to maturity. Then we use this rate to compute the present value of the bond's interest and principal payments to derive an estimate of the bond's value and hence its market price.

It is beyond our scope to explore the process of estimating the yield to maturity on a bond but we should briefly describe one approach. Services like Moody's and Standard & Poor's rate bonds. The rating given to a bond is based on the issuer's ability to meet required interest and principal payments in a timely manner. Now as a starting point, we could estimate the rating for the bond we are studying and then examine yields for publicly traded bonds in the same class. When making this comparison we have to be concerned about maturity and other factors. Bonds in the same rating class will have different yields because of differences in maturity. There is a term structure of interest rates which means that there is not a single interest rate on the open market but a series of rates that are a function of maturity. For instance, we might see that the YTM on a one-year Treasury bill is 9% when the YTM on a ten-year Treasury bond is 11%.

Suppose we find several bonds in the same rating class with identical maturities to the bond we are studying. This eases our task but does not make it that simple because we have to adjust for other factors. There are many such as differences in covenants that can cause variations in yields. In any event, because we can't identify precisely what the yield to maturity is on a private bond, we must recognize that the resulting estimate of value may not be as accurate as we would like.

We will now look at several examples showing how to compute the value of bonds given an estimate of yield to maturity. These examples are designed to show the relationship between market value and face value when the yield to maturity is the same as and different from the bond's coupon rate. They also show the direction and magnitude of a change in market price for a given change in interest rates. Here is a summary of what will be shown:

1. When a bond's YTM equals its coupon rate, market price will equal face value regardless of maturity.

2. When a bond's YTM is greater than its coupon rate, price will be less than face value and vice versa.

3. There is an inverse relationship between bond prices and interest rates. When interest rates increase, bond prices decrease and vice-versa. Further, the longer the term to maturity, the greater the change in price for a given change in yield to maturity.

A bond which will mature eight years from now has a face value of $1,000, a coupon rate of 12%, and a yield to maturity of 14%. Interest is paid once each year and the next payment is due one year from now. The price of this bond can be computed as follows:

| End of Year | Cash Flow | | (PVA$1, PV$1, 14%, 8)[4] | | Present Value |
|---|---|---|---|---|---|
| 1–8 | $ 120 | × | 4.6389 | = | $556.67 |
| 8 | 1,000 | × | .3506 | = | 350.60 |
| | | | | | $907.27 |

The price of this bond is $907.27 which is less than its face value of $1,000. This will always be the case when the yield to maturity of a bond is greater than its coupon rate. The reverse is also true: When the yield to maturity on a bond is less than its coupon rate, its market price will be greater than its face value.

Interest rates on the open market change and when this happens, bond prices change. Suppose you owned the above bond that promises a yield to maturity of 14%. Suppose, for some reason, yields on a new eight-year bond of similar quality suddenly increased to 16%. You and other owners would sell your bond because it yields only 14% and would purchase those that offer 16%. This action would cause the price of the bond to fall. Selling would continue until the price fell from $907.27 to $826.23. At this price, the yield to maturity on this bond would be 16%, the same as the yields on similar bonds. This new price was derived by computing the present value of the bond's cash flows at 16% as shown below:

| End of Year | Cash Flow | | (PVA$1, PV$1, 16%, 8) | | Present Value |
|---|---|---|---|---|---|
| 1–8 | $ 120 | × | 4.3436 | = | $521.23 |
| 8 | 1,000 | × | .3050 | = | 305.00 |
| | | | | | $826.23 |

The above example showed that when the market rate of interest on eight-year bonds of similar quality increased, the market price of the bond decreased. Had the interest rate decreased, the bond price would have increased. In short, there is an inverse relationship between changes in interest rates and changes in bond prices. This inverse relationship holds for all fixed income securities regardless of whether the maturity date is one week from now or 100 years from now. Time to maturity does influence, however,

---

[4] This format signifies that the calculations involve both the present value of an annuity and the present value of a future amount.

the magnitude of the change in price for a given change in interest rates. We will illustrate this impact with a different example:

Assume Bond A and Bond B each has a coupon of 12%, a face value of $1,000, and pays interest once each year. Bond A will mature three years from today and Bond B will mature 30 years from today. Let's compute the price of each assuming three different yields to maturity— 12% (which is also the coupon rate), 10%, and 14%.[5]

### 12%: Bond A

| End of Year | Cash Flow | | (PVA$1, PV$1, 12%, 3) | | Present Value |
|---|---|---|---|---|---|
| 1–3 | $ 120 | × | 2.4018 | = | $ 288.22 |
| 3 | 1,000 | × | .7118 | = | 711.80 |
| | | | | | $1,000.02 |

### 12%: Bond B

| End of Year | Cash Flow | | (PVA$1, PV$1, 12%, 30) | | Present Value |
|---|---|---|---|---|---|
| 1–30 | $ 120 | × | 8.0552 | = | $ 966.62 |
| 30 | 1,000 | × | .0334 | = | 33.40 |
| | | | | | $1,000.02 |

The price of each is $1,000. (The $1,000.02 shown is due to rounding in tables of factors.) When a bond's yield to maturity equals its coupon rate, the market value of the bond will equal its face value. This will be true regardless of the maturity date of the bond.

Below is the price of each at a yield to maturity of 10%:

### 10%: Bond A

| End of Year | Cash Flow | | (PVA$1, PV$1, 10%, 3) | | Present Value |
|---|---|---|---|---|---|
| 1–3 | $ 120 | × | 2.4869 | = | $ 298.43 |
| 3 | 1,000 | × | .7513 | = | 751.30 |
| | | | | | $1,049.73 |

### 10%: Bond B

| End of Year | Cash Flow | | (PVA$1, PV$1, 10%, 30) | | Present Value |
|---|---|---|---|---|---|
| 1–30 | $ 120 | × | 9.4269 | = | $1,131.23 |
| 30 | 1,000 | × | .0573 | = | 57.30 |
| | | | | | $1,188.53 |

[5] Because of the term structure of interest rates, we normally would expect different yields on these bonds assuming similar risk. We assume the same YTM for each to highlight the effect of interest rate changes on market price.

This case illustrates that when the yield to maturity on a bond is less than its coupon rate, the bond's market price will be above its face value. Further, if we view the 10% case versus the 12% case as a decrease in market interest rates, we see that when interest rates decrease, bond prices increase. However, note that the price of the 30-year bond increases much more than the three-year bond. This illustrates that the greater the term to maturity, the greater the price increase for a given decrease in interest rates.

Below is the price of each at 14%:

### 14%: Bond A

| End of Year | Cash Flow | | (PVA$1, PV$1, 14%, 3) | | Present Value |
|---|---|---|---|---|---|
| 1–3 | $ 120 | × | 2.3216 | = | $ 278.59 |
| 3 | 1,000 | × | .6750 | = | 675.00 |
| | | | | | $ 953.59 |

### 14%: Bond B

| End of Year | Cash Flow | | (PVA$1, PV$1, 14%, 30) | | Present Value |
|---|---|---|---|---|---|
| 1–30 | $ 120 | × | 7.0027 | = | $ 840.32 |
| 30 | 1,000 | × | .0196 | = | 19.60 |
| | | | | | $ 859.92 |

This case illustrates that when the yield to maturity on a bond is greater than its coupon rate, the bond's market price will be less than its face value. Further, if we view the 14% case versus the 10% or 12% cases as an increase in market interest rates, we see that when interest rates increase, bond prices decrease. However, note that the price of the 30-year bond decreases much more than the price of the three-year bond. This illustrates that the greater the term to maturity, the greater the price decrease for a given increase in the interest rate.

# Valuation of Common Stock

Common stockholders are the firm's owners. Unlike bondholders, common stockholders are not promised a fixed return. Moreover, usually interest on the firm's outstanding debt must be paid before the common stockholders of the firm can receive any dividends. Further, in the event of liquidation, all the firm's creditors, including bondholders, are entitled to be paid in full before any proceeds can be allocated to common stock. On the other hand, bondholders generally receive a fixed return but there is no limit to how much the common stock can earn. In short, a firm's common stockholders take more risk than its bondholders in the hope of earning a greater return.

Common stock can receive a return in one of two ways: (1) cash dividends; (2) price appreciation on the stock. Say you buy a share of stock for $20 today, receive a dividend of $1 one year from now and after receiving the $1 sell the stock for $23. Here is how you can compute your rate of return for the year.

$$\text{Rate of Return} = \frac{D + (P_{T+1} - P_T)}{P_T}$$

Where:

$$D = \text{Dividend}$$
$$P_T = \text{Price at period t}$$
$$P_{T+1} = \text{Price at period t} + 1$$

$$20\% = \frac{\$1 + (\$23 - 20)}{\$20}$$

This method is quite common for computing the annual rate of return on common stock. Earlier we established two criteria for a rate of return measure: (1) the measure must incorporate all the cash flows from the investment and (2) it must take into account the time value of money. Does this measure meet the criteria? The answer is "yes" provided the dividend is received one year from now. Putting it another way, given that the dividend is received one year from now, the above equation is the same as the internal rate of return.[6]

The valuation principles apply to common stock, that is, the value of a share, and hence the price one should be willing to pay, equals the present value of the cash flows that the common stock will generate discounted at an appropriate risk-adjusted discount rate. To illustrate, suppose we estimate that a share of stock will receive a cash dividend of $5 one year from now, $6 two years from now and its price will be $40 two years from now. Further, assume we estimate that 16% is an appropriate risk-adjusted discount rate for this investment. We can compute its estimated value as follows:

---

[6] Many analysts use the equation to compute an annual rate of return when the dividend for the year is paid in several installments during the year. Thus, they are not obtaining a rate of return that is as useful for comparison purposes as they would if they computed the internal rate of return.

| End of Year | | Cash Flow | | (PV$1, 16%, n) | | Present Value |
|---|---|---|---|---|---|---|
| 1 | | $ 5 | × | .8621 | = | $ 4.31 |
| 2 | 6+40 = | 46 | × | .7432 | = | 34.19 |
| | | | | | | $38.50 |

Our estimate of the stock's value is $38.50. In security analysis this amount is frequently referred to as the stock's "intrinsic value."

The valuation principle in the context of common stock is known as the dividend valuation model. We will discuss this model after we say more about intrinsic value. Security analysts estimate intrinsic value, computed as shown or another way, and then compare this value to the market price of the stock. If the intrinsic value is more, the stock is undervalued and hence is a candidate for purchase. If intrinsic value is less than the market price, the stock is overvalued and hence should be sold. Whether it is possible to locate securities that are substantially undervalued or overvalued is a matter of considerable dispute because it assumes that market prices will be substantially different from values.

If it is reasonable to assume that value and market price will be equal, we can rely on the above approach to estimate the appropriate risk-adjusted discount rate for common stock. Specifically, given the price of a share and an estimate of future dividends and price, we can derive the required rate by computing the internal rate of return. We will illustrate how to do this later in the chapter.

## DIVIDEND VALUATION MODEL[7]

The dividend valuation model (DVM) says that the value of a share of stock is equal to the present value of all future dividends discounted at a suitable required rate of return. For the above example, we saw that the value of a share equals:

$$\text{Value} = \frac{\text{Present Value of}}{\text{Future Dividends}} + \frac{\text{Present Value of}}{\text{Future Price}}$$

We will see in a moment that this equation is equivalent to the following:

Value = Present Value of Future Dividends to Infinity

[7] M.J. Gordon and J.B. Williams working at different times developed this model. Much of what we know about valuation is due to their path-breaking contributions. For an in-depth treatment of their work see: M.J. Gordon, *The Investment, Financing and Valuation of the Corporation* (Irwin, 1962) and J.B. Williams, *The Theory of Investment Value* (Harvard University, 1938).

We will present the DVM in a formal manner shortly but first recall from the last chapter that we compute the present value of an infinite annual annuity as follows:

$$PV = A_{1-\infty} \left[\frac{1}{i}\right]$$

Where:

$A_{1-\infty}$ = Equal amount at the end of years one to infinity
  $i$ = Compound annual interest rate

To illustrate, let's assume that a share of stock will pay a dividend of $1 per year forever, starting one year from now and that the appropriate risk-adjusted discount rate for this investment is 15%. Further, let's assume initially that you purchase the stock today and plan to hold it forever. Given these facts, the stock's value, and hence the price you should be willing to pay, is $6.67 as shown below:

| End of Year | Cash Flow | | (PVA$1, 15%, ∞) | | Present Value |
|---|---|---|---|---|---|
| 1–∞ | $1 | × | 6.6667 | = | $6.67 |

Now suppose you plan to sell the stock five years from now. Its value at that time will be $6.67 (explained later) and you would receive the following stream of cash:

| End of Year | Cash Flow |
|---|---|
| 1 | $1.00 |
| 2 | 1.00 |
| 3 | 1.00 |
| 4 | 1.00 |
| 5 | 1.00 + 6.67 = 7.67 |

The present value of this stream at 15% is $6.67, the same answer we got when we assumed an infinite holding period.

How do we know the price will be $6.67 five years from now? It has to be given a constant dividend and a required rate of 15%. Suppose Joe Jones buys it from us five years from now and plans to hold it forever. The present value at the end of Year 5 of an infinite annual stream of $1, starting at the end of Year 6 at 15% is $6.67. So this is the value to him at that time and hence the price he should be willing to pay. Suppose Joe Jones plans to buy it five years from now and sell it to Sally Smith ten years from now. Sally would pay $6.67 because that is the present value at that time of dividends from years 11 to infinity at 15%. Hence, the stream of cash Joe would receive would be the same as the one shown above only the years would be 6–10 and the present value of the end of Year 5 of this stream at 15% is $6.67.

Because we assumed a constant dividend, the price of the stock always was $6.67 in the above example. Had we assumed an increasing dividend, the price of the stock would have increased over time. Nevertheless, we still would have found that the price today is the present value of future dividends to infinity.

What about firms that don't pay dividends? Dividends have to be expected at some future point even if that point is far in the future. Think of it this way: What is the value of stock to you today that will never pay a dividend? The answer is zero because the present value of zero dollars in the future has to be zero. Hence this is the price you should be willing to pay. What if you could sell it on the open market later at a higher price? You should not be able to sell it for more than zero in the future because zero would be the stock's value in the future. In other words, only an irrational person would pay more for an investment than it is worth.[8]

Now we are not saying that it is easy to estimate the value of common stock. Indeed, it is extremely difficult to estimate both future dividends and an appropriate risk-adjusted discount rate. Nevertheless, this does not mean that the valuation principles do not apply.

Let's now look at the dividend valuation model in equation form:

$$P_0 = \sum_{T=1}^{\infty} \frac{D_T}{(1+K_e)^T}$$

Where:

$P_0$ = Market price of stock at time zero
$D_T$ = Dividend at time T
$K_e$ = Risk-adjusted discount rate (also known as cost of equity capital)

When dividends are constant, this equation reduces to:

$$P_0 = \frac{D}{K_e}$$

---

[8] This is a version of the "greater fool theory" which says that only a fool would pay more for a stock than it's worth, thinking that a bigger fool can be found to pay a higher price in the future.

In the above example D was $1 and $K_e$ was 15% and so the price of $6.67 can be derived as follows:

$$P_o = \frac{D}{K_e}$$

$$= \frac{\$1}{15\%}$$

$$= \$6.67$$

When dividends grow at a constant annual rate, the equation reduces to:

$$P_o = \frac{D_1}{K_e - g}$$

Where:

$D_1$ = Annual dividend received one year from now

$g$ = Constant compound annual growth rate in dividends for all subsequent years

Suppose a firm will pay a dividend on each share of $2 one year from now and the dividend will grow at 5% each year after that forever. The risk adjusted discount rate for this stock is 18%. The price is $15.38 as shown below:

$$P_o = \frac{\$2.00}{18\% - 5\%} = \$15.38$$

Notice that $K_e$ must be greater than g for this version to give a meaningful answer.

In most real situations, firms do not pay constant dividends forever, or dividends that will grow at a constant compound annual growth rate. The DVM still can be used to estimate value as the following example illustrates:

Suppose we estimate that per share dividends for a firm will be $4 next year, the per share amount will grow at 25% per year for the next two years, and 15% for the two years after that. Further, we estimate that an appropriate required rate is 18%. Dividends for the next five years are:

| End of Year | Dividend per Share |
|:---:|:---:|
| 1 | $4.00 |
| 2 | 5.00 |
| 3 | 6.25 |
| 4 | 7.19 |
| 5 | 8.27 |

To estimate the value today, we need to estimate the price five years from now, which is function of dividends beyond that time. Usually, estimates for the next five years are questionable enough, never mind dividends beyond that time. In such a situation, we could proceed by judging whether growth beyond Year 5 will be above the average for the economy. If so, we would estimate a rate and a period for above average growth and after that rely on a growth estimate for the economy as a whole. Generally, we can make a reasonable judgment on these matters because the key is the nature of the industry. For instance, when this chapter was written, most analysts agreed that the computer industry would grow at a rate greater than the average of the economy for more than five years.

Let's assume we conclude that the firm in our example will not experience above average growth beyond Year 5 and that 6% is a reasonable guess for how quickly the economy will grow. Once this stable rate is estimated, we can derive a future price for the stock. In this case, we can derive a price at the end of Year 5 by relying on the following:

$$\text{Price, End of Year 5} = \frac{\text{Dividend End of Year 6}}{K_e - g}$$

Above we noted that $K_e$ is 18% and dividend per share in the fifth year will be $8.27. Hence the dividend in the sixth year will be $8.77 (1.06 × $8.27) and we can compute the end of Year 5 price as follows:

$$P_5 = \frac{\$8.77}{18\% - 6\%} = \$73.08$$

Cash flow at the end of Year 5 is $81.35 ($8.27 + $73.08). Now we can compute the present price.

| End of Year | Cash Flow | | (PV$1, 18%, n) | | Present Value |
|---|---|---|---|---|---|
| 1 | $ 4.00 | × | .8475 | = | $ 3.39 |
| 2 | 5.00 | × | .7182 | = | 3.59 |
| 3 | 6.25 | × | .6086 | = | 3.80 |
| 4 | 7.19 | × | .5158 | = | 3.71 |
| 5 | 81.35 | × | .4371 | = | 35.56 |
| | | | | | $50.05 |

We are estimating that the value of the stock today is $50.05

Before concluding this section on valuing common stock, we should note that other valuation methods are used in practice. For example, many analysts estimate earnings per share and a price earnings ratio and estimate value this way. However, this and other methods are in effect designed to be proxies for the dividend valuation model. Whether they will be decent proxies depends on the situation.

# Required Rates of Return

We will now turn our attention to the process of estimating required risk-adjusted discount rates for investments. Our primary intent is to explain how to estimate required rates for evaluating capital investments. These required rates frequently are called "screening rates."

Up to now we have relied on the idea that the greater the risk, the greater the rate of the return. For instance, if we invest in a Government bond we would accept the risk-free rate but we would want this plus a risk premium for riskier investments. How much should the risk premium be? The answer is it depends on the riskiness of the investment. Here we show how to derive specific estimates, but the crucial point to note at the outset is that the risk of an investment determines what the required risk-adjusted discount rate should be. With this in mind, we begin by discussing a firm's cost of capital.

## COST OF CAPITAL OF A FIRM

The cost of capital is defined as the rate of return that must be earned on capital to leave the value of the firm unchanged. If the firm earns more than this rate, its value will increase; and if less is earned, its value will decrease. In other words, it is a breakeven point in value terms. The chapter on cost/volume/profit analysis showed how to compute breakeven in terms of the level of sales that must be achieved to earn a profit of zero. There we noted that we can't obtain a sales breakeven figure that is as precise as we would like and so we must settle for an estimate. Well it's much more difficult to obtain a reasonable estimate for a market value breakeven level. So keep in mind that while we may state percents to the nearest tenth or one-hundredth of a percent, this is for expositional convenience only and not to imply that we can derive precise estimates.

We will begin our discussion of the cost of capital with a simple example designed to give you an intuitive sense of the underlying logic behind its computation. Say a firm is formed to be in business for five years and expects to generate the following cash flows during that period:

| End of Year | Cash Flow |
|:-----------:|:---------:|
| 1 | $100 |
| 2 | 150 |
| 3 | 150 |
| 4 | 150 |
| 5 | 100 |

The firm expects to earn no more and no less than these amounts and, in fact, these precise amounts are guaranteed by the U.S. Government. In other words, these are certain cash flows, that is, there is a 100% chance that the actual amounts will equal the expected amounts. To compute the value of this firm, we would rely on a risk-free rate. In this instance, the risk-free rate would be this firm's cost of capital.

For a firm whose expected returns are not certain, and this is usually the case, it is the extent of variability that influences its cost of capital. What causes a firm's returns to be variable? There are numerous factors including the following:

1. *The state of the economy.* As we will see the relationship between the performance of the economy and a firm's returns has important implications for required rates of return.

2. *The firm's competitive position.* Does it have a dominant position? Is it a price leader or does it follow leaders in setting price?

3. *The firm's cost structure.* As we saw in the chapter on cost/volume/profit analysis, the amount of fixed costs and the relationship among fixed expenses, variable expenses and selling prices are major determinants of how variable a firm's profits will be.

4. *The firm's capital structure.* The amount of debt a firm has affects the firm's solvency and also affects the variability of earnings that are available to common stock. Preferred stock can also affect variability.

To compute a firm's cost of capital, we can assess the above and other relevant factors and make a judgment that way. While this is done in some instances, it is more common to rely on objective data. Specifically, we obtain market prices of the claims to the firm's capital (i.e., stocks and bonds), estimate cash returns accruing to these claims, compute individual rates and combine these into an average. As we shall see, computing rates involves nothing more than applying the valuation principles, only this time we solve for a rate instead of value. Before illustrating this process, however, we must discuss how the various rates are combined into an average and we shall rely on an example to explain how this is done:

The Delden Company was formed last week. The firm issued bonds and sold stock and used most of the proceeds to purchase inventory and fixed assets. The proportions of debt and equity employed to raise capital were considered ideal by management. Below is the balance sheet just prior to the start of operations (the end of the first day of the firm's existence):

*Delden Company*
*Balance Sheet*
*End of First Day*

| | | | |
|---|---|---|---|
| Cash | $ 25,000 | Accounts payable | $ 50,000 |
| Inventory | 175,000 | Long-term debt | |
| Total current | $200,000 | (current portion) | 25,000 |
| Fixed Assets (net) | 350,000 | Total current | $ 75,000 |
| Total | $550,000 | Long-term debt | 175,000 |
| | | Common stock | 300,000 |
| | | Retained earnings | 0 |
| | | Total | $550,000 |

The long-term debt is a bond issue with a 14% coupon rate which we will assume equals its yield to maturity. The common stockholders require a rate of return of 18%, which is the cost of common equity. (Think of 18% as the figure for $K_e$ in the dividend valuation model discussed earlier.) Finally, the firm's income tax rate is 40%.

Delden's total capital is $550,000. To obtain the firm's cost of capital we multiply the required rate of return (i.e., cost) for each source by the weight of that source in the firm's capital structure. In computing weights, analysts usually exclude all current liabilities except the current portion of long-term debt and short-term debt used on a regular basis.[9] For Delden, the total capital structure is $500,000. This consists of $200,000 (or 40%) debt and $300,000 (or 60%) of equity. Using these proportions we can compute the weighted average cost of capital as shown below:

[9] We could compute weights with accounts payable and other current liabilities such as accrued expenses included. This is perhaps a more useful way of thinking of the cost of capital. However, given the way the resulting rate is normally used, this traditional approach is workable. Indeed, if we didn't follow it, as we will see in the next chapter, we would have to alter the way we compute cash flows for analyzing capital investments.

| Source | Weight | | After-Tax Cost | | |
|--------|--------|---|----------------|---|--------|
| Debt | .40 | × | .084 | = | .0336 |
| Common equity | .60 | × | .180 | = | .1080 |
| | 1.00 | | Weighted average | = | .1416 |

Delden's weighted average cost of capital is 14.16%.

The after-tax cost of each source is used because generally the rate is employed to discount after-tax cash flows. For debt, we multiply the interest rate, yield to maturity in this instance, by one minus the tax rate.

$$\begin{array}{ccc} \textit{After-Tax Cost of Debt} & & \textit{Interest Rate } (1-T) \\ 8.4\% & = & 14\% \times (1-40\%) \end{array}$$

We make this adjustment because interest is tax deductible. The cost of equity is the rate the firm must earn *after taxes* to give common stockholders their required rate. In other words, once we know the required rate of return on common stock, no tax adjustment is needed because this is already an after-tax rate.

The above example avoided two issues we will frequently encounter. These are: (1) historical rates versus current rates and (2) book value weights versus market value weights. We will briefly discuss each.

### Current Market Rates Versus Historical Rates

In our example, the firm just issued debt with a coupon rate of 14%, which is also its yield to maturity. Suppose the firm had been in existence for a year and issued debt with a 12% coupon one year ago. What some analysts would do is compute different weights for the new and old debt, and multiply the weight of the old debt by 12%, the coupon rate on the old debt. This is not a useful approach because we want to know what investors are requiring currently. Hence we always use current market rates, that is, the bond's yield to maturity.

### Book Value Weights Versus Market Value Weights

A problem related to the issue of existing versus historical costs is what debt and equity amounts to use in computing weights. In our example, we employed the amounts on the balance sheet known as book value weights. However, in this instance the book values of debt and equity equal their respective market values. Typically, there will be a difference between book and market values. When there is, we should rely on market values because we are trying to compute a breakeven point in terms of value. Suppose a firm reports the following on its balance sheet:

| | |
|---|---|
| Long-term debt | $10,000 |
| Common stock | 1,000 |
| Paid-in capital | 5,000 |
| Retained earnings | 4,000 |
| | $20,000 |

There are no other liability or equity accounts, the market value of the debt is $8,000, the firm has 1,000 common shares outstanding and the market price per share is $20. The market value of the firm's common equity is $20,000, which is derived by multiplying the price per share of $20 by the number of shares outstanding. Given this, the weights are computed as follows:

| | | *Proportion of Total* |
|---|---|---|
| Market value of debt | $ 8,000 | .286 |
| Market value of equity | 20,000 | .714 |
| Total | $28,000 | 1.000 |

Note that the 71.4% for equity is the weight assigned to the total of common stock plus paid-in capital plus retained earnings.

We should point out that despite the theoretical superiority of market value weights, many analysts rely on book value weights. Apparently, they find it convenient to do so and believe that the result is a cost of capital estimate that is reasonable. While book value weights may be suitable in certain instances, this approach can, in our opinion, cause faulty analyses and should be avoided, particularly when market values are readily available.

We should also point out that some analysts rely on a firm's target capital structure to derive weights. Many firms have a target for how much debt and equity to employ. There may be variations from year to year but on average the target weights are the overall goal. Hence, rather than adjust proportions for temporary variations, analysts rely on permanent proportions. If the targets are based on market value weights, we think this is a reasonable approach, but if book values are used we must be aware of the possible problems mentioned above.

We will now turn our attention to the cost of each source. We will refer to them as explicit costs to signify that part of the total cost is not included. To explain, let's review Delden's interest rate of 14%. Debt creates risk and hence increases the return that common stockholders require. The

14% rate does not account for this effect on the cost of equity. So, to be precise, we should make it clear that the interest rate is not the total cost of debt and to accomplish this we will call it the explicit cost. The same is true for other sources. Say a firm issues common stock and investors require a return of 20%. Ordinarily an increase in equity enables a firm to issue more debt and so to make this clear, we will refer to 20% as the explicit cost of equity.

The details of computing the explicit cost of various sources differ, as we shall see. However, we shall also see that the basic concept is the same because the explicit cost of a source is the rate that makes the present value of the cash flows accruing to the source equal to the source's value. Earlier we estimated an investment's cash flows and its required rate to obtain an estimated value. Here we rely on market determined prices (when we can), estimate cash flows accruing to the source and solve for the internal rate of return, that is, the rate that makes the present value of the cash flows equal to the market price.

## EXPLICIT COST OF DEBT

The explicit after-tax cost of debt is the interest rate adjusted for the tax shield created by interest. The calculation is as follows:

$$\text{After-Tax Cost of Debt} = i\,(1 - T)$$

Where:
    $i$ = Interest rate
    $T$ = Tax rate

The interest rate is the rate that makes the present value of the interest and loan payments equal to the market value of the debt. We give this precise definition to avoid confusion that can result from the way terms are used in practice. For instance, we saw that a bond has a coupon interest rate, a current yield and a yield to maturity. It is the yield to maturity that is the true interest rate and so we would multiply the YTM by one minus the tax rate to compute the after-tax explicit cost of a bond.

Many firms have more than one class of debt outstanding. For example, a firm might have $50 million (market value) of mortgage bonds outstanding with a YTM of 12% and $150 million (market value) of debentures with a YTM of 14%. (A mortgage is a debt instrument secured by fixed assets and a debenture is an unsecured bond.) In this kind of situation, we can simply take a weighted average as shown below:

*Market Value Proportion*                              *YTM*

$$\frac{50}{200} \quad = \quad 25\% \quad \times \quad 12\% \quad = \quad .030$$

$$\frac{150}{200} \quad = \quad 75\% \quad \times \quad 14\% \quad = \quad \underline{.105}$$

Weighted Average YTM     =     .135

We then multiply the average yield by one minus the tax rate to get the after-tax cost.

When the firm has debt outstanding that is not publicly traded, we must estimate the interest rate on this debt. Earlier in the chapter we outlined an approach for estimating the yield to maturity on privately-placed bonds. This basic approach can be used for all private debt.

## EXPLICIT COST OF PREFERRED STOCK

Preferred stock is a financial instrument that generally pays the holder a fixed dividend rate each year. The rate is multiplied by the par value to derive the dollars of dividends to be paid to each share. Like common stock it is a perpetual security that has no maturity. However, we shall see in a moment that often in practice it is not a perpetual security and this affects how we compute the cost. Nevertheless, sometimes it is appropriate to view preferred stock as a perpetual security and when it is we compute its cost as shown below:

*Perpetual View*

$$\text{After-Tax Cost} \ = \ \frac{D}{P_o}$$

Where:

$D$ = Dividend per share
$P_o$ = Market price per share

No tax adjustment is needed because preferred dividends are not tax deductible and hence do not create a tax shield.

Most preferred stock issues have a call feature. This means that after a specific date the firm has the option of purchasing the stock at a price specified in the agreement. Very often firms issue preferred with the intent of retiring them at some future date (or reach this decision subsequent to issue). Furthermore, some preferred stock agreements include a provision requiring the firm to call the preferred stock. This type is known as redeemable preferred. In any event, if call is contemplated, we compute the explicit cost of preferred just as we would compute the YTM on a bond. To illustrate, let's assume a firm intends to retire its preferred stock outstanding five years from now at a call price of $108 per share, which is a premium of $8 over the par value of $100.[10] Dividends per share are $8 and the recent market price per share is $85. Let's list the cash flows over the planned time horizon:

| End of Year | Cash Flow |
|:-----------:|:---------:|
| 0 | ($ 85) |
| 1–5 | 8 |
| 5 | 108 |

The internal rate of return (the rate that makes the present value of $8 per year for five years plus $108 in Year 5 equal to $85) is a little less than 14%. This is the explicit cost of this preferred stock.

## EXPLICIT COST OF OWNERS' EQUITY

The cost of owners' equity is very difficult to estimate. The reason is that unlike bonds or preferred stock it is often hard to develop reasonable estimates of the cash flows that will accrue to the owners of common stock and thus difficult to estimate an internal rate of return. We start with this approach, which is nothing more than an alternate view of the dividend valuation model, and then we consider three other methods which are designed to give the same information.

### Approach 1. Dividend Valuation Model
Let's begin by stating again the dividend valuation model in equation form:

$$P_o = \sum_{T=1}^{\infty} \frac{D_T}{(1+K_e)^T}$$

Where:
$P_o$ = Market price per share
$D_T$ = Dividend after share at time T
$K_e$ = Risk-adjusted discount rate

[10] The call price on preferred is typically higher than the par value, at least for a certain number of years. This is also true for the call price on a bond relative to its face value.

Recall that when dividends are constant this equation reduces to:

$$P_o = \frac{D}{K_e}$$

We can solve for $K_e$ instead of $P_o$ which is the cost of equity:

$$K_e = \frac{D}{P_o}$$

When growth, g, is constant the dividend valuation model reduces to:

$$P_o = \frac{D_1}{K_e - g}$$

Again, solving for $K_e$, we have:

$$K_e = \frac{D_1}{P_o} + g$$

Suppose a firm expects to pay a per share dividend of $3 next year and dividend increases of 6% per year are expected after that to infinity. The market price per share is $20. The explicit cost of common equity for this firm is 21% as shown below:

$$21\% = \frac{\$3}{\$20} + 6\%$$

We will not illustrate further because we have already shown several examples of how to apply the dividend valuation model. To see how that discussion applies here, just imagine that in those examples we were given the current price instead of $K_e$. We could have solved $K_e$ by computing the internal rate of return, that is, compute the rate that makes the present value of all future dividends (or future dividends up to a point plus a future price) equal to the current price of the stock. Of course, this assumes that the current price is known and that we can develop reasonable estimates of future dividends. If either of these conditions are not present, then we must use one of the other approaches. This does not mean that the dividend valuation model is incorrect. What it means is that we can't apply the theory very well in such circumstances.

When it is difficult to estimate future dividends, either because a firm pays no dividends or its dividends vary considerably from year to year, analysts rely on different approaches to compute the cost of equity. These other approaches are designed to give the same or similar answers as the dividend model.

## Approach 2. Capital Asset Pricing Model (CAPM)

One of the major contributions in finance in recent years is the Capital Asset Pricing Model (CAPM), a theory of how assets are priced.[11] This theory has many uses including helping analysts estimate a firm's cost of equity capital. Before turning to this use, however, we should comment briefly on the theory because of its importance in finance, though it is well beyond our scope to delve into this matter.

Of the many threads that are needed to tie this theory together, two important ones are the notions that financial markets are efficient and that the right kind of diversification reduces risk. There are many implications that stem from the idea that markets are efficient. A crucial one for our purpose is that market price will equal value. In other words, in a well-functioning market, actual market prices will provide the best estimates of values as defined earlier. We shall discuss this implication further a little later in the chapter.

With respect to diversification, say a share of stock has an expected rate of return of 20% and a standard deviation of 10%.[12] Portfolio theory tells us that by combining this security with others, you likely can obtain the same expected return but with a lower standard deviation, say of 8%.[13] Suppose you are stubborn and insist on holding that one share with an expected return of 20% and risk of 10%. You won't be rewarded for taking this extra risk. The market only pays a return for risks that cannot be diversified away. This is one of the important insights of the CAPM.

Another interesting and important insight can be gleaned from the following example: Suppose the author manages a firm that produces electronic equipment. To benefit his firm's stockholders, the author decides to

---

[11] Professors Lintner and Sharpe, working independently, performed much of the basic theoretical development. Many others have made important contributions as well, particularly with respect to extensions and refinements. See Lintner, "Security Prices, Risk and Maximal Gains from Diversification" *Journal of Finance* December 1965 and Sharpe, "Capital Asset Prices: A Theory of Market Equilibrium under Conditions of Risk" *Journal of Finance* September 1964.

[12] Standard deviation is a measure of variability which provides a quantitative measure of the amount that the actual return can vary from the expected return. For instance, say the mean of a normal probability distribution is 10% and the standard deviation is 2%. The standard deviation tells us that there is about a 95% probability that the actual return will be between 6% and 14%.

[13] Harry Markowitz formalized the basic ideas pertaining to the benefits of diversification. See Harry Markowitz, *Portfolio Selection: Efficient Diversification of Investments* (Wiley, 1959).

diversify, so he acquires a supermarket chain. Will investors view this as a good move and bid up the price of the firm's stock? The answer is probably not. If the result is simply to have two separate firms under one umbrella, we would not expect anyone to pay a premium for this. After all, investors can diversify on their own by buying shares of a producer of electronic equipment and the shares of a supermarket chain. In other words, investors will not pay a firm a premium to do something they can do on their own. What if the combined firms can earn more together than either can alone? This is a different story and investors would pay for this. This is another important message derived from the CAPM.

For the purposes of this chapter, the most relevant insight pertains to the nature of risk premium on common stock. Recall that earlier we specified the following relationship.

**Risk-Adjusted Discount Rate = Risk-Free Rate + Risk Premium**

The risk premium for an investment is a function of the expected variability in rate of return. There are two types of factors that cause the rate of return on a firm's common stock to vary. These are:

1. *Firm specific.* These are factors unique to the firm like an unexpected labor strike or an unexpected technological advance. Variation in rates of return due to firm-specific factors is known as unsystematic risk.

2. *Market-wide.* These are factors that affect variability in a stock's rate of return that affect most firms like growth in GNP or unanticipated inflation. Variations in rates of return due to market-wide factors is known as systematic risk.

To summarize:

**Total Risk = Systematic Risk + Unsystematic Risk**

One would expect that the risk premium on a share of common stock would depend on systematic risk plus unsystematic risk. However, the CAPM tells us that since unsystematic risk can be diversified away, it won't be rewarded (i.e., priced) in financial markets. Moreover, it specifies the relationship between risk and return. This relationship is shown in Figure 8-1. We see that there is a linear relationship between risk and return, and Beta (discussed below) is the appropriate measure of risk. The equation for

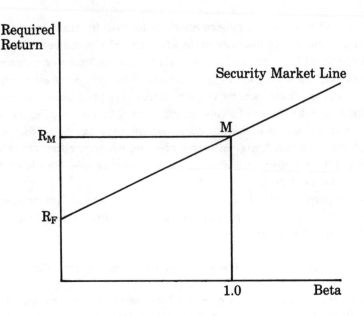

**Figure 8-1　Pictorial Representation of a Capital Asset Pricing Model (CAPM).**

this line, which is known as the Security Market Line (SML), is the following:

$$R_J = R_F + B_J (R_m - R_F)$$

Where:

$R_J$ = Required rate of return on investment J
$R_F$ = Risk-free rate
$B_J$ = Beta of investment J
$R_m$ = Required rate of return on the market

This equation says that the required rate of return equals the risk-free rate plus an appropriate risk premium. The appropriate risk premium is the risk premium on the market as a whole ($R_m - R_F$), adjusted for the investment's Beta which is a measure of the investment's systematic risk.

　Beta is a measure of systematic risk and indicates how the rate of return on the security is expected to vary with the rate of return on the market. For instance, if a common stock has a Beta of 1.5, this says that if there is an increase in the market rate of return of 10%, we expect the rate of return on this security to increase by 15%. A 10% decrease in the market would produce a 15% decrease for the stock. In other words, securities with a Beta greater than 1.0 are more variable than the market, and vice versa. Finally, by definition the market rate of return has a Beta of 1.0 and this is depicted as Point M in Figure 8-1.

All the variables in the equation are expected values and analysts generally rely on past data to estimate these variables. For instance, the rate of a specific Treasury security is often used for $R_F$, and past returns on a market index like the Standard and Poor's 500 are analyzed to predict $R_m$. Beta is usually estimated by relating historical rates or return on the security with historical rates on the market.

Given these estimates, we can estimate $R_J$ which is the required rate of return on Firm J, or in the language of this chapter it is the required risk-adjusted discount rate for an investment in the common stock of this firm. In other words, $R_J$ is the explicit cost of equity for Firm J.

Suppose the stock of Firm A has an estimated Beta of 1.4 and the estimates for the risk-free rate and the required rate on the market are 6% and 15%, respectively. Given these estimates, we can derive an estimate of Firm A's explicit cost of equity as follows:

$$
\begin{aligned}
R_A &= R_F + B_A \, (R_m - R_F) \\
&= 6\% + 1.4 \, (15\% - 6\%) \\
&= 18.6\%
\end{aligned}
$$

We need to examine one further issue pertaining to the CAPM. We will do so by investigating one more of its implications. Take the 18.6% rate just computed for Firm A's common stock. This is known as an equilibrium rate of return, meaning that it is the only stable rate. Say an analysis of the prospects of Firm A indicates an expected rate of return of 20%. If we plot this rate in Figure 8-1, we would see that the expected rate for Firm A lies above the Security Market Line. But this is not possible in a well-functioning market. Investors would see there is a "free lunch," in the sense that they can earn a rate greater than risk justifies. Hence, they would buy the stock causing the price to increase. This action would stop when the price increased to a point where the expected rate is 18.6%.

What if the market is not so well functioning? Then this buying activity might or might not occur. Well-functioning markets is one of many assumptions upon which the CAPM is based. Now, the realism of assumptions is not the critical issue when evaluating a theory like this. The crucial issue is: Does it work? In this case, we want to know whether or not the CAPM provides good predictions of required rates of return. Numerous empirical studies have focused on this point. It is beyond our scope to delve into these studies but we should point out that views vary regarding the CAPM'S ability to give good predictions. Our view is that the CAPM often will provide a decent estimate of a firm's cost of equity. However, we must recognize that it will not always give a good estimate and when it does not, another approach should be used. In any event, we should not lose sight of the fact that the CAPM provides a useful way of thinking about risk and return.

## Approach 3. Historical Rates of Return

Earlier we showed that the annual rate of return on a common stock can be computed as follows:

$$\text{Annual Rate of Return} = \frac{D_T + (P_{T+1} - P_T)}{P_T}$$

Where:

$$D_T = \text{Annual dividend}$$
$$P_T \text{ and } P_{T+1} = \text{Per share prices at the beginning and end of the year, respectively.}$$

What some analysts do is compute the annual rate of return for, say, the past five or ten years. They then rely on the average, adjusted perhaps for any apparent trends, and/or new information, as an estimate of the firm's explicit cost of equity capital.

We think this approach should be relied upon only when it is not possible to obtain a decent estimate with the dividend valuation model and/or the CAPM.

## Approach 4. Add Four to Six Percentage Points to YTM on a Firm's Long-Term Debt

Some analysts simply take the yield to maturity on a firm's debt and add four to six percentage points and use this total as an estimate of the firm's cost of equity. For instance, if the YTM on a firm's bonds is 13%, we would use 17% to 19% as the estimate of the firm's explicit cost of equity. The exact rate selected would depend on our assessment of how much risk is involved. The logic of this approach is that stockholders take more risk than bondholders and so the required rate is higher. The four to six percentage points over the required rate for debt (i.e., YTM) comes from the notion that for the typical firm this range provides a reasonable estimate of the appropriate risk premium.

This method, which can be considered as being related to the CAPM approach, is perhaps most appropriate when a firm's common stock is not publicly traded. However, we have seen it used productively for "quick and dirty analyses" for public companies. And, of course, it can be helpful when it is difficult to obtain a decent estimate by relying on one of the three approaches described above.

### Other Approaches

A number of other methods are used to estimate the cost of equity. We will mention two of them that we believe are still common despite their well-known shortcomings.

The first is the rate of return on net worth, which is simply the ratio of net income to owners' equity (excluding preferred stock). This is not a reliable approach because among other flaws, it is based on book values instead of market value. As owners, we want managers to increase the market value of the stock not its book value, and there is no guarantee that an increase in book value will also produce an increase in market value.

The second is to use the reciprocal of a firm's price earnings ratio. Recall that the price earnings ratio is defined as follows:

$$\text{Price Earnings Ratio} = \frac{\text{Market Price per Share}}{\text{Earnings per Share}}$$

Analysts take the reciprocal of this number. Say a firm has a price earnings ratio of ten. The reciprocal is 1/10 or 10% and some analysts would use this as the cost of equity. The trouble is that this number tells us how much must be earned on equity to increase earnings per share, and there is no assurance that this would produce an increase in market price.

Before concluding our discussion of the cost of equity, we must consider one more point. Equity flows from two sources: issuing common stock and retained earnings. Issuing common stock involves flotation costs so the estimates derived from the above approaches should be adjusted for these costs. To see how, it may help if we view an estimate derived from one of the above methods as the explicit cost of retained earnings. Given this, the explicit cost of new common stock can be derived as follows:

$$\frac{\text{Explicit Cost of}}{\text{New Common Stock}} = \frac{\text{Explicit Cost of Retained Earnings}}{1 - F}$$

**Where:**

**F** = Flotation costs stated as a percent of the total dollar amount of the issue

Say a firm has a $10 million stock issue and flotation costs are $500,000. F is 5%.

## USE OF COST OF CAPITAL FOR CAPITAL INVESTMENT ANALYSIS

Earlier in the chapter, we illustrated how to value an investment for a firm we called the Ablco Company. Think of Ablco as a company formed to undertake only one investment and think of the cash flows in that example as the returns from this single investment. What rate should be used to compute the value of the investment? The answer is Ablco's cost of capital. In other words, Ablco's weighted average cost of capital should be used as the appropriate risk-adjusted discount rate. Why? There is no difference between the risk of the firm and the risk of this investment. Hence, the firm's weighted average cost of capital is the same as the cost of capital for this investment (and the latter is known as the marginal cost of capital[14] for the investment, or, simply, the required rate for the investment).

As we have seen, it is the risk of the investment that determines the required rate of return for that investment. Hence, when a firm has a number of investment opportunities, its overall weighted average cost of capital can be used to evaluate these investments only when the following two conditions are met.

1. The investment possesses a degree of risk equal to the average of the firm as a whole.

2. The investment does not alter the firm's optimal capital structure. (Optimal capital structure is defined as the debt to total capital ratio that maximizes the value of the firm.)[15]

We will now turn our attention to what firms do to select risk-adjusted discount rates for analyzing capital investments when these conditions do

---

[14] The word "marginal" makes it clear that investments are undertaken with new capital, or marginal capital, and it is the cost of this additional capital that is relevant.

[15] We include this condition to be complete. Optimal capital structure is addressed briefly in the last chapter of the book. For our present purposes, while we should not ignore this condition, it is generally safe to say that if the first condition is met, the second one is met as well.

not prevail. In practice, these rates are frequently referred to as cutoff rates, screening rates, or simply, required rates. We prefer the last because we think it best signifies that it is the risk of the investment that determines its required rate of return.


## REQUIRED RATES FOR CAPITAL INVESTMENTS

From a theoretical point of view, if a firm is evaluating 50 capital investments, each possessing a different degree of risk, a separate rate should be used to evaluate each one. Specifically, each investment should be viewed as a separate firm, and a cost of capital should be estimated for each of these quasi-firms. Now as you can imagine, practitioners don't actually do this. We will turn to actual practices in a moment but before doing this let's point out one other message of the concepts discussed earlier.

Say a firm is considering an investment that costs $100,000, to be financed by debt. Despite the fact that it will be financed totally by debt, we would *not* use the cost of debt to evaluate this investment. In most practical cases, it just is not reasonable to think that an investment has 100% debt capacity. Hence, what we would do is estimate a realistic debt capacity for the investment, that is, how much debt financing could be used if this investment were viewed as a separate firm, and from there estimate the marginal cost of capital for this project. (Incidentally, we believe that most managers agree with this view.)

In practice, some firms use either the firm's weighted average cost of capital or some other predetermined cutoff rate to evaluate all capital investments, and subjectively account for differences in risk. Others establish risk classes, classify capital investments by class and use a separate risk-adjusted discount rate to evaluate investments in each class. For instance, the following categories might be used: high risk, average risk and low risk. The firm's weighted average cost of capital might be employed for those investments classified in the average risk category. Higher and lower rates would be used for the other two categories and these other rates likely would have been subjectively derived.

Some firms try to adhere to the theory more closely. However, they find that it just is not feasible to compute a separate rate for each investment, except perhaps for a very large investment. So what they do is compute a separate rate for each major line of business or a separate rate for each division. We will illustrate this latter approach, frequently referred to as the selection of divisional screening rates.

Suppose we form a holding company and purchase an airline and a retail supermarket chain. Figure 8-2 shows the two separate parts of our business which we call divisions. Now the required rates of return on our firm's common stock and debt reflect a weighted average of the risks of the two divisions. But these rates do not reflect the risk of investments in either, so we should not use the firm's cost of capital to evaluate capital investments. What we could do is compute the cost of capital for each division as if it were a separate firm. Specifically, we could analyze firms in each of these businesses to obtain estimates for our divisions. We will demonstrate this for the airline division.

Suppose we find that an airline just like ours has a Beta of 1.7. (Actually, we likely would use an average of Betas for several firms or the average for the entire industry.) One of the factors that determines this other firm's Beta is how much debt the firm employs. If we do not intend to use this level of debt, we must adjust the Beta. We do this by unlevering and then relevering the Beta. To do this we can rely on the following model.[16]

$$B_u = \frac{B_L}{[1 + (1 - TR) \frac{D}{E}]}$$

Where:

$B_u$ = Beta of a firm financed only with equity
$B_L$ = Beta of a firm with debt
$TR$ = Firm's tax rate
$D$ = Market value of debt
$E$ = Market value of equity

Suppose the market value of the debt and equity of this other firm is $300 million and $100 million, respectively, and its tax rate is 30%.

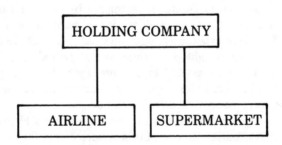

**Figure 8-2   Hypothetical Holding Company**

[16] Professor Robert Hamada performed much of the theoretical work for this model. See Hamada, "Portfolio Analysis, Market Equilibrium and Corporate Finance" *Journal of Finance* (March 1969).

$$B_u = \frac{1.7}{1 + (1 - .3)\dfrac{300}{100}} = .55$$

We are estimating that this firm would have a Beta of .55 if it had no debt.

Given our assessment that this firm is like ours, we are in effect, assuming that basic business risk is the same. Hence, our unlevered Beta is .55 for this division. Next we relever the Beta using our own division debt to equity ratio. Say it is two to one, based on market value, and that our firm's tax rate is 30%. We can derive an estimate of the levered Beta for this division by using the above model.

$$\begin{aligned} B_L &= B_u[1 + (1 - TR)\frac{D}{E}] \\ &= .55[1 + (1 - .3)\frac{2}{1}] \\ &= 1.3 \end{aligned}$$

This number, 1.3, is the estimate for Beta for the airline division.

The final step is to use the equation of the security market line to compute the explicit cost of equity for this division. Let's assume $R_F$ and $R_M$ are 6% and 15%, respectively.

$$\begin{aligned} R_i &= 6\% + (15\% - 6\%)\,1.3 \\ &= 17.7\% \end{aligned}$$

This rate, 17.7%, is an estimate of the explicit cost of common equity. We would then proceed to estimate the cost of capital for this division.

There are other ways of computing discount rates for divisions. Instead of relying on the CAPM and market value data for similar firms to help us derive an estimate, we could have relied on the DVM and the data for another firm or used a simpler approach. In any event, the point is this: The risk of an investment determines what its required rate of return should be. This should be the guiding principle in selecting discount rates for capital investment analysis or for evaluating any investment.

## PRICE VERSUS VALUE

Before closing, we should discuss a bit further the relationship between price and value. We will do so in the context of common stock prices because these securities are the most controversial when it comes to the question of whether prices equal values.

Many people, including the author, believe that financial markets in the United States are reasonably efficient. Among other things, this means that market prices reflect available information and also provide a good estimate of value. Furthermore, when some unexpected information arises that materially affects the prospects of a firm, like an unexpected discovery of oil, the market price of its stock will react rapidly and correctly to the new information. There are many implications of efficient markets. The one that has created all the fuss is the following: Performing analyses to identify undervalued or overvalued securities will not produce above average returns, at least not on a consistent enough basis to make the activity profitable.

As you can imagine, many people believe that markets are not nearly as efficient as the preceding paragraph would suggest. They argue that market prices can differ from value for prolonged periods of time. Thus, one can locate undervalued or overvalued securities and this activity can be quite profitable.

Our primary intent in raising the controversy over efficient markets is to make it clear that the basic principles of valuation that we have focused on in this chapter apply in any case. The value of an investment, which is the present value of the cash flows from the investment discounted at an appropriate risk-adjusted discount rate, is the maximum price that one should be willing to pay for that investment. The extent to which markets are efficient does not alter this basic point.

# Problems and Discussion Questions

## A. Solved Problems

### Problem 8-1A

One year ago a $1,000 par value, 8% coupon bond was selling for $814. Since then, the yield to maturity of the bond increased by one percentage point. If the bond pays interest annually and now has ten years to maturity, what is its current market price?

### Solution 8-1A

This problem required that we figure out what the yield to maturity was one year ago and then compute the price today.

One year ago, the bond had the following cash flow stream.

| End of Year | Cash Flow |
|:-----------:|:---------:|
| 1–11 | $ 80 |
| 11 | 1000 |

The price of the bond one year ago was $814. So we must find the rate that makes the bond's cash flows equal $814. We will rely on the trial and error procedure. Let's start with 10%.

#### Trial 1. 10%

| End of Year | Cash Flow | | (PVA$1, PV$1, 10%, n) | | Present Value |
|:-----------:|:---------:|:---:|:---------------------:|:---:|:-------------:|
| 1–11 | $ 80 | × | 6.4951 | = | $520 |
| 11 | 1,000 | × | .3505 | = | 350 |
| | | | | | $870 |

The result, $870, is too high. So we must try a rate that will produce a lower present value, which means trying a higher rate. Let's try 11%.

#### Trial 2. 11%

| End of Year | Cash Flow | | (PVA$1, PV$1, 11%, n) | | Present Value |
|:-----------:|:---------:|:---:|:---------------------:|:---:|:-------------:|
| 1–11 | $ 80 | × | 6.2065 | = | $497 |
| 11 | 1,000 | × | .3173 | = | 317 |
| | | | | | $814 |

The present value of the bond's cash flows discounted at 11% exactly equals (except for rounding) its market price one year ago. Thus, 11% was the bond's yield to maturity one year ago.

The bond's YTM has increased by one percentage point, so it is now 12%. The bond's current price can be found by computing the present value of the expected future cash flows discounted at this rate.

| End of Year | Cash Flow | | (PVA$1, PV$1, 12%, n) | | Present Value |
|:---:|:---:|:---:|:---:|:---:|:---:|
| 1–10 | $   80 | × | 5.6502 | = | $452 |
| 10 | 1,000 | × | .3220 | = | 322 |
| | | | | | $774 |

The current price of the bond is now $774.

### Problem 8-2A

You are asked to estimate the per share value for the common stock of the Acme Company. The firm pays a dividend once each year and today paid $2 per share. This amount is expected to grow by 10% per year for the next six years and 8% per year thereafter (i.e., end of years 7 to infinity). Although an appropriate risk-adjusted discount rate, $K_e$, at which to evaluate future dividends, is not readily available, you are advised that the Capital Asset Pricing Model may be employed to estimate that rate. Further, you are given the following estimates:

| | | |
|:---|:---:|:---:|
| Beta of Acme Company | = | .75 |
| Expected risk-free rate | = | 7.0% |
| Expected return on market | = | 15.0% |

Estimate the value of Acme's stock.

### Solution 8-2A

As noted we can rely on the CAPM to estimate the required rate on the stock.

$$R_{Acme} = R_F + B_{Acme} (R_m - R_F)$$
$$= .07 + .75 (.15 - .07)$$
$$= .13$$

Our estimate of $K_e$ is 13%. We now will use this rate to estimate the value of the stock.

Dividends will grow at 10% per year for the next six years and then 8% thereafter. We will first estimate dividends for each of the next six years.

| End of Year | Dividend Per Share |
|---|---|
| 1 | $2(1.10)^1 = \$2.20$ |
| 2 | $2(1.10)^2 = 2.42$ |
| 3 | $2(1.10)^3 = 2.66$ |
| 4 | $2(1.10)^4 = 2.93$ |
| 5 | $2(1.10)^5 = 3.21$ |
| 6 | $2(1.10)^6 = 3.54$ |

Given that there will be growth of 8% per year thereafter we can compute the value of the stock at the end of Year 6 as follows:

$$P_6 = \frac{D_7}{K_e - g} = \frac{(D_6)(1.08)}{K_e - g} = \frac{(\$3.54)(1.08)}{13\% - 8\%} = \$76.46$$

Finally, we compute the present value of the total stream at 13%.

| End of Year | Cash Flow | | (PV\$1, 13%, n) | | Present Value |
|---|---|---|---|---|---|
| 1 | $2.20 | × | .8850 | = | $ 1.95 |
| 2 | 2.42 | × | .7831 | = | 1.90 |
| 3 | 2.66 | × | .6931 | = | 1.84 |
| 4 | 2.93 | × | .6133 | = | 1.80 |
| 5 | 3.22 | × | .5428 | = | 1.75 |
| 6 | 3.54 + 76.46 = 80.00 | × | .4803 | = | 38.42 |
| | | | | | $47.66 |

This amount, $47.66 is the estimate of Acme's common stock price.

Because the initial growth rate (10%) does not exceed $K_3$ (13%), we can use the Dividend Valuation Model for the first six flows as well. We illustrate the procedure below which while somewhat involved, can be a handy shortcut. It is especially useful when the initial dividend flows are numerous, so that calculating their present values (as above) becomes tedious. Here's the procedure:

Step 1. *Compute the present value of dividend flows to infinity at a growth rate of 10%.*

$$P_o = \frac{D_1}{K - g} = \frac{\$2.20}{13\% - 10\%} = \$73.33$$

Step 2. *Compute the present value of dividend flows from the end of Year 7 to infinity at a growth rate of 10%.*

$$P_6 = \frac{D_7}{K - g} = \frac{\$2(1+.10)^7}{13\% - 10\%} = \frac{P_6}{\$129.91} \times \frac{(PV\$1,\ 13\%,\ 6)}{.4803} = \frac{P_o}{\$62.40}$$

Step 3. *Compute the present value of dividend flows from the end of Years 1 to 6 at a growth rate of 10%.*

| $P_o$ | PV of Dividend Years 1–∞ | | PV of Dividends Years 1–6 |
|---|---|---|---|
| $10.93 = | $73.33 | – | $62.40 |

Step 4. *Compute the present value of dividends flows from the end of Years 7 to infinity at a growth rate of 8%.*
This step was illustrated above. We derive price at the end of Year 6 of $76.46 and then find the present value of that amount which is $36.72 ($76.46 × .4803).

Step 5. *Compute the present value of all the stock's future dividend flows.*
*We simply add the amounts from steps 3 and 4.*

| $P_o$ | PV of Dividends Years 1–6 | | PV Dividends Years 7–∞ |
|---|---|---|---|
| $47.65 = | 10.93 | + | 36.72 |

## Problem 8-3A

The Britex Company has the following capital structure (book values):

| | |
|---|---|
| Secured bonds, $1,000 face value, 10% coupon | $250,000 |
| Debentures, $1,000 face value, 11% coupon | 500,000 |
| Common stock plus paid-in capital | 500,000 |
| (Par Value is 10¢ per share, 500,000 shares outstanding) | |
| Retained earnings | 750,000 |
| Total | $2,000,000 |

The following additional information is available:
Britex's tax rate:        40%
Secured bonds:        • Market price $1,000 per bond.
                    • Years to maturity is ten years.
                    • Interest paid annually.
Debentures:          • Market price $938 per bond.
                    • Years to maturity is 12 years from today.
                    • Interest paid annually, next payment in
                      one year.
Common stock:        • Market price $4 per share.
                    • Dividend just paid $.50 per share.
                    • Dividend growth rate expected 6% per
                      year, forever.

1. Compute the explicit after-tax cost of debt for Britex.

2. Compute the explicit cost of owners' equity for Britex using the Dividend Valuation Model.

3. Compute the weighted average cost of capital for Britex.

*Solution 8-3A*
1. Since Britex has two classes of bonds outstanding, the explicit cost of each must be computed, then a weighted average is calculated (using market weights).

*Secured Bonds:* Since the bond's market price equals its par value, its YTM equals the coupon rate of 10%. Furthermore, the bond's book value equals its market value.
*Debenture:* The cash flows of this unsecured bond are:

| End of Year | Cash Flow |
|---|---|
| 1–12 | $ 110 |
| 12 | 1,000 |

We must find the rate that makes the present value of the cash flows equal to its price of $938. Since the price is below the bond's face value, we know the YTM is above its coupon rate of 11%, so let's try 12%.

| End of Year | Cash Flow | (PVA$1,PV$1,12%, n) | Present Value |
|---|---|---|---|
| 1–12 | $ 110 × | 6.1944 | = $681.38 |
| 12 | 1,000 × | .2567 | = 256.70 |
| | | | $938.08 |

12% is the bond's YTM.

We know from the book value figures that there are 500 debentures outstanding, so the market value is 500 × \$938 = \$469,000. Hence, the weighted average before tax cost of debt can be computed as follows:

|  | Proportion | | YTM | | |
|---|---|---|---|---|---|
| Secured | $\dfrac{250,000}{719,000}$ | = .35 | × | .10 | = .035 |
| Debenture | $\dfrac{469,000}{719,000}$ | = .65 | × | .12 | = .078 |
|  |  |  |  |  | .113 |

The after-tax cost is:

$$\text{After-Tax Cost} = \text{Before-Tax Cost } (1-T)$$
$$6.78\% = 11.3\%(1-40\%)$$

2. When dividend growth is constant, the DVM reduces to:

$$P_o = \frac{D_1}{K_e - g}$$

Solving for $K_e$ and inserting data given, we have:

$$K_e = \frac{D_1}{P_o} + g$$
$$= \frac{D_o\,(1+g)}{P_o} + g$$
$$= \frac{(\$.50)\,(1+.06)}{\$4.00} + 6\%$$
$$= 19.25\%$$

This is the after-tax explicit cost of equity.

3. We multiply the explicit costs derived by the weight of each source in the firm's capital structure. The market value of debt is \$719,000 and the market value of stock is \$2 million (500,000 shares × \$4 price per share).

| Source | Weight | | After-Tax Cost | |
|---|---|---|---|---|
| Debt | $\dfrac{719,000}{2,719,000}$ = .264 | × | .0678 | = .0179 |
| Equity | $\dfrac{2,000,000}{2,719,000}$ = .736 | × | .1925 | = .1417 |
|  |  |  |  | .1596 |

The weighted average cost of capital is 15.96% for Britex.

## B. Discussion Questions

### Problem 8-1B
In the chapter we discussed a bond's coupon rate, current yield, and yield to maturity. Which of the three is most useful to an analyst? Why?

### Problem 8-2B
Explain why bond prices decrease when interest rates increase.

### Problem 8-3B
Is the fact that many firms do not pay any dividends proof that the Dividend Valuation Model is wrong? Explain.

### Problem 8-4B
A manager the author knows, who is skeptical of theory, once made the following remark regarding the valuation principles. "They are fine in theory but in the real world price is what someone is willing to pay." How would you defend the valuation principles in responding to this manager?

### Problem 8-5B
What is the difference between unsystematic and systematic risk? Are both types of risk equally important? Why?

### Problem 8-6B
Suppose two Government bonds that pay interest annually will mature one year from now. One, Bond X, will pay interest of $1,000 plus principal of $10,000 one year from today. The other, Bond Y, will pay interest of $1,050 plus principal of $10,000 one year from today. Can Bond X's price be higher than the price of Bond Y on the open market? Why or why not?

### Problem 8-7B
Can a firm's weighted average cost of capital be used to evaluate all its capital investment opportunities? Why?

## C. Study Problems

### Problem 8-1C
The Link Company has $1,000 face value, 10% coupon rate bonds outstanding. Interest is paid semi-annually and the bonds will mature six years from today. The next interest payment is due six months from now. What is the market price per bond if the yield to maturity is 12%? 8%?

### Problem 8-2C

A type of British Government bond, called a consol, has no maturity date, that is, it promises to pay interest to perpetuity. Assume that such a bond has a face value of $1,000, a coupon rate of 6% and a market price of $650. Interest is paid annually and the next payment is due one year from now. (Note that the bond would be denominated in British pounds instead of dollars.)

1. What is the bond's current yield?

2. What is the bond's yield to maturity?

### Problem 8-3C

Zero coupon bonds are debt instruments which offer no periodic interest payments. They only promise the investor a lump-sum payment equal to the bond's face value at maturity. Presume that a $1,000, ten year, zero coupon is priced to have a yield to maturity of 12% per year compounded semi-annually. What would the market price be?

### Problem 8-4C

A recently issued bond has a face value of $1,000, a coupon rate of 10%, matures ten years from today, and pays interest annually.

1. Compute the price of this bond assuming a yield to maturity of 10%, 6% and 16%.

2. Repeat the calculations in part (1) assuming the bond will mature in 40 years instead of ten years.

3. Comment on the relationship among coupon rate, market interest rates and maturity.

### Problem 8-5C

You are trying to estimate the value of a firm's common stock. You are confident that the per share dividend one year from now will be $1.61 and that this amount will grow at a constant annual rate in each subsequent year to infinity. However, there is considerable uncertainty regarding what the growth rate will be and what risk-adjusted discount rate should be employed to compute value. Hence, you decide to test the impact of growth rates of 4%, 6% and 8% and required rates ($K_e$) of 20%, 16% and 12%.

1. Use the Dividend Valuation Model to compute the possible values for the common stock.

2. Comment on the usefulness of the Dividend Valuation Model in this instance.

## Problem 8-6C

This problem is an extension of Problem 8-2A. Instead of assuming dividends will be paid to infinity, assume that they will be paid through the end of Year 30 and that the value of the stock will be zero after the last dividend payment. All the other facts are the same. Compute the value of Acme's stock based on this adjustment. Compare it with the value derived in Problem 8-2A and be prepared to comment on the use of infinite annuities in practical situations.

## Problem 8-7C

Mr. Arbucke just purchased a large block of common stock at a price of $80 per share. The stock is expected to pay a $5 per share dividend one year from today, and that annual dividend is expected to grow at a rate of 6.75% per year forever. As a gift to his college-bound son, Mr. Arbucke has promised him all dividend distributions from the stock for the next four years; hence the first dividend payment Mr. Arbucke will receive will be five years from today. Relying on the Dividend Valuation Model, compute the amount of the current value of $80 that Mr. Arbucke has given to his son. In other words, what is the per share value of this stock to Mr. Arbucke today?

## Problem 8-8C

The preferred stock of the MNP Corporation currently sells for $27 per share and just paid a dividend of $3 per share which is the fixed contractual annual amount. There is no call feature attached to this stock. The after-tax earnings of MNP Corporation are expected to grow at a rate of 8% per year, indefinitely. Finally, the firm's tax rate is 40%.

1. What is the after-tax explicit cost of preferred stock?

2. If the stock does have a call feature and is expected to be retired at a price of $35 per share seven years from now, what is its after-tax explicit cost? (Note that the dividend due also will be paid seven years from now.)

## Problem 8-9C

The common stock of the Albee Company has a Beta of 1.2 and a required return of 16%. The prevailing risk-free rate is 9%.

1. What is the prevailing required rate of return on the market? On Albee's common stock?

2. Draw the Security Market Line.

3. Compute the required rate of return for the common stock of the Jamke Company that has a Beta of .9.

4. Recompute your answers for parts (2) and (3) and compute Albee's new required rate of return assuming the risk-free rate increases by one percentage point and the risk premium on the market decreases by one-quarter of a percentage point.

### Problem 8-10C

The common stock of Oldtyme Corporation just paid a dividend of $7 per share and this is expected to *decline* at a rate of 5% per year, indefinitely. If the stock currently sells for $39 per share, what can you say about the required rate of return for this stock?

### Problem 8-11C

A firm's common stock is expected to pay a $1 per share dividend one year from now. This dividend will grow at a rate of 16% per year for two years and at an unknown constant rate thereafter. If the market's required rate of return for a stock of this risk class is 10% and the stock currently sells for $20 per share, what is the constant dividend growth expected after the 16% for two years?

### Problem 8-12C

The Dooning Corporation is considering acquiring a firm that has a debt to equity ratio of 33⅓% (market weights) and a Beta of 1.3. If the firm is acquired its debt to equity ratio will be changed to 50% (market weights). The interest rate on this debt will be 15% and the marginal tax rate will be 40%. The risk-free rate is 7% and the market risk premium is 8%. What discount rate should be used to evaluate this acquisition?

### Problem 8-13C

The following information is known about the Quepee Corporation.

| | |
|---|---|
| Common stockholders' required rate of return | 17% |
| Coupon rate on outstanding bond issue | 10% |
| Yield to maturity on outstanding bond issue | 12% |
| Explicit cost on non-callable preferred stock | 14% |

Tax rate: 46%
Capital structure:
Book value: 40% bonds
        20% preferred stock
        40% common equity
Market value: 30% bonds
        10% preferred stock
        60% common equity

1. What is the explicit after-tax cost of debt? Of preferred stock? Of common equity?

2. What is Quepee's weighted average cost of capital? (You may ignore flotation costs on newly-issued common stock.)

## Problem 8-14C

The following is known about the Inkman Company and capital market conditions:

*Capital Structure (book values)*

| | |
|---|---|
| Bonds | $ 85,000 |
| Preferred stock (15,000 shares) | 15,000 |
| Common stock (100,000 shares) | 200,000 |
| Retained earnings | 700,000 |

*Bonds*

| | |
|---|---|
| Coupon rate | 10% |
| Yield to maturity | 10% |
| Time to maturity | 12 years |

*Preferred Stock (non-callable)*

| | |
|---|---|
| Current market price | $5 per share |
| Current dividend | $.70 per share |

*Common Stock*

| | |
|---|---|
| Current market price | $15 per share |
| Dividend most recently paid | $.60 per share |
| Estimated Beta | 1.40 |

*Capital Market*

| | |
|---|---|
| Risk-free rate | 8% |
| Required return on market | 15% |

Finally, the firm's income tax rate is 40%.

1. What is the explicit after-tax cost of long-term debt? Of preferred stock? Of common equity?

2. What is Inkman's weighted average cost of capital? (You may ignore flotation costs on newly-issued common stock.)

# 9
# Capital Budgeting I

This chapter and the next explain the techniques and issues involved in capital investment decisions. The conceptual foundation laid in the previous chapter is an essential ingredient for this one.

We begin with a description of capital investments and a classification scheme for various types. Then we briefly review the conceptual foundation laid in the last chapter. After that we explain several capital budgeting techniques and briefly evaluate them. The final part of the chapter shows how to derive the relevant cash flows for capital investment analysis. The next chapter discusses a number of technical matters relating to the application of the techniques and also considers various methods of incorporating risk into capital budgeting analyses.

A primary message of this chapter and the next is that a primary motive for undertaking capital investment projects is to increase the value of the firm for its owners. This means selecting investments that promise a positive net present value *and* managing them well.

Many capital investment decisions are made by the top management of a firm. The firm's chief executive officer is frequently a key player in the decision, especially for large investments, and it also is not uncommon for the board of directors to take part. Why do these decisions receive so much attention? A fundamental reason is that a firm's very existence and its ability to create value for its owners depend critically on selecting good capital investments and managing them well.

# Capital Investment Decisions

Capital investment decisions are those involving the acquisition or divestiture of fixed assets such as land, buildings, and/or equipment. The process of selecting capital investments is known as capital budgeting and the procedures used to evaluate them are called capital budgeting techniques. Many capital investments also include the commitment of working capital. For instance, suppose a firm is contemplating a new product line. Not only would the acquisition of fixed assets normally be required but the higher sales would create the need for increased levels of current assets such as inventory and accounts receivable.

We will find it helpful to rely on a classification scheme for capital investments. Many taxonomies are employed in practice and none is perfect. However, the following will suit our needs: (1) strategic, (2) expansion, (3) replacement and (4) other.

1. *Strategic capital investments* usually are large projects or ventures. Typically included are major changes in direction such as introducing a new product line, entering a different business altogether and investing in a foreign country for the first time. Capital commitments to increase or maintain market share may also be included.

2. *Expansion* refers to acquiring new facilities to expand existing businesses. These investments include normal growth of existing products and the introduction of related products, and perhaps the decision to compete in a new geographic region of the same country. Classification schemes vary considerably. Hence, some of the investments we called strategic would be included in the expansion category in some firms and vice versa. In any case, both types generally receive considerable attention from top management.

3. *Replacements* represent the purchase of new fixed assets to replace existing ones and often these investments are divided into the following two subcategories: Routine (or normal) replacement and cost savings investments.

   *Routine replacement* refers to replacing worn out furniture and equipment. An example would be an analyst purchasing a new desk to replace an old one. Frequently, capital budgeting techniques are not used to evaluate these investments. However, typically a firm will have a budget for routine replacements which means there is a limit on how much will be spent on these fixed assets during a given period.

*Cost-saving replacements* are capital investments designed to produce reductions in operating costs. An example is the purchase of a machine that requires less labor to operate than existing equipment. Any new equipment designed to lower costs likely would be included in this category even if it was not replacing an existing fixed asset.

4. *The "other" category* refers to those capital investments that do not belong in one of the above categories. Examples are a new cafeteria for employees and the purchase of safety equipment necessitated by government regulation. Very often, no formal capital budgeting analysis is performed for this type of investment.

# *Conceptual Foundation*

In the last chapter we focused on two basic concepts in finance. These are:

1. The value of an investment is the present value of the cash flows that the investment will generate discounted at an appropriate risk-adjusted discount rate. This value represents the maximum price that one should be willing to pay for the investment.

2. The risk of an investment determines the required rate (i.e., appropriate risk-adjusted discount rate) that should be used to evaluate the investment.

These concepts apply to any investment and our objective in this chapter is to apply them to capital investments. More specifically, our primary goal is to show how to evaluate the impact of capital investments on a firm's value. To see this, let's look at a very simple example: Suppose you start a business and invest $5,000 in your firm's common stock. Your firm will only undertake riskless investments. Let us assume riskless investments are providing a return of 10%. This would be the rate you would use to evaluate capital investments. Now, assume you uncover an investment that requires an outlay of $5,000 today and promises a single definite return of $5,750 one year from now, the present value of this cash inflow at 10% is $5,227. Thus, you would accept this investment because the present value of its return is greater than its costs. Looking at it another way, this investment is a good one because if accepted it will increase the value of your firm from the $5,000 invested to $5,227.

As we will see below, the difference of $227 between the present value of the investment's cash inflow of $5,227 and its $5,000 cost is called Net Present Value (NPV). A more formal definition is provided later but note here that net present value is a measure of the change in a firm's value caused by the investment. We should add that here we know for sure how much value will change because it is a riskless investment, but generally we can only estimate an investment's NPV. We should also mention that we would not expect riskless investments to have a positive NPV; instead, we would expect a zero NPV which means the investment provides exactly its required rate of return.[1]

# Capital Budgeting Techniques

In this section, we will explain five techniques used to evaluate capital investments. They are:

1.  Average Rate of Return (ARR)

2.  Payback Period

3.  Net Present Value (NPV)

4.  Profitability Index (PI)

5.  Internal Rate of Return (IRR)

We will see that the first two are inconsistent with the valuation principles. The remaining three are consistent with valuation but we will argue here and in the next chapter that NPV is the best of the three. We should note that other capital budgeting procedures are used in practice. However, many of these other techniques are derived from the five discussed in this chapter, and more importantly, by relying on the concept of valuation, one can assess the validity of any technique.

To illustrate the application of the technique we rely on a simple example. Assume a firm is considering the purchase of a new machine to help perform a task that is currently being performed manually.[2] An immediate

---

[1] The reason is that riskless investments are generally traded in well-functioning markets and as explained in the previous chapter we would not expect to find a difference between price and value in a well-functioning market.
[2] We focus on replacement-type investments because it is easier to explain the application of the techniques for this kind of investment. However, you should not infer that replacements are the essence of capital budgeting.

cash outlay of $40,000, including installation costs, will be required. The labor savings over its five-year life will produce the following annual increments in after-tax net income and after-tax cash flows.

| End of Year | Net Income After Taxes | Cash Flow After Taxes[3] |
|---|---|---|
| 1 | $3,000 | $13,000 |
| 2 | 3,000 | 13,000 |
| 3 | 3,000 | 13,000 |
| 4 | 3,000 | 13,000 |

The difference between net income and cash flow was explained in an earlier chapter and we will review it later. Hence, do not try to reconcile the two amounts in this example (especially since it can't be done with the information provided). Deriving the relevant cash flow figures is a key part of capital budgeting but we think it will be easier for you if we defer discussion of this topic until the techniques are explained. Note here, however, that the cash flows and the discount rate we will discuss in a moment are after taxes. Enhancement of value is based on net returns, that is, after all costs including taxes. Now a capital budgeting system can be devised on a pretax basis and some firms do this, but, in our opinion, this approach needlessly complicates the analysis.

The last chapter discussed the processes used to select discount rates for capital budgeting. We will not repeat that discussion other than to note that the risk of the investment determines the appropriate rate. This rate is known by a variety of names including cutoff rate, screening rate, required rate, and the investment's marginal cost of capital. Generally we will refer to it as the required rate to focus attention on the idea that it is the risk of the investment that determines what discount rate should be used to evaluate the investment. Finally, for the above example, we will assume that 9% is the after-tax required rate.

## AVERAGE RATE OF RETURN (ARR)

The Average Rate of Return (ARR) is defined as:

$$\text{Average Rate of Return} = \frac{\text{Average Net Income After Taxes}}{\text{Average Book Value}}$$

[3] Throughout the chapter, we will assume that cash flows occur once each year, at the end of each year. This assumption simplifies the calculations. Also, to distinguish between cash inflows and cash outflows, the latter will be listed in parentheses.

The numerator refers to the average annual net income produced by the investment. Hence, we simply sum the annual figures and divide by the number of years.

$$\text{Average Net Income} = \frac{\$3{,}000 + \$3{,}000 + \$3{,}000 + \$3{,}000}{4 \text{ Years}}$$
$$= \$3{,}000$$

Recall that the book value of a fixed asset is defined as original cost less accumulated depreciation. To compute the average book value, we calculate the average book value for each year, sum the annual averages and divide by the number of years. To show the calculations, let's assume the average book value for each year for the above investment is:

| Year | Average Book Value |
|------|--------------------|
| 1 | $35,000 |
| 2 | 25,000 |
| 3 | 15,000 |
| 4 | 5,000 |
| | $80,000 |

$$\text{Average} = \frac{\$80{,}000}{4 \text{ years}} = \$20{,}000$$

Incidentally, here we assumed the fixed asset is being depreciated on a straight-line basis to a zero salvage value and when this is the case, average book value can be derived by dividing the original cost by 2.

We can now compute the average rate of return as follows:

$$\text{ARR} = \frac{\text{Average Net Income After Taxes}}{\text{Average Book Value}}$$
$$= \frac{\$3{,}000}{20{,}000}$$
$$= 15\%$$

This rate, 15%, is then compared to the required rate of 9%. It is greater, indicating it is an attractive investment.

This measure can be, and often is, misleading. The reason is simple: The ARR is inconsistent with the valuation principle in the sense that we can't tell from the ARR whether value is expected to increase or decrease. The fact that in our example the rate is substantially larger than the required rate is no assurance that value will increase if returns come in as expected. In fact, value might decrease; we just don't know. To see why, let's assume for a moment that the machine will produce no income or cash flow for the first three years. In the fourth year it produces a net income of $12,000 and cash flow of $52,000, the totals of the four annual amounts. The ARR would still be 15%, but in this instance, the investment clearly would be less attractive. Also, it is possible for the cash flows to be substantially less and still produce an ARR of 15%. Of course, the investment would be less attractive but the ARR would not show this.

We can see from the above the two fundamental weaknesses of the ARR. First, it relies on net income, not cash flows. Second, the measure ignores the time value of money. Because of these fatal flaws, the ARR is not a reliable method and should not be used to evaluate investments.

Why did we bother to explain the ARR? There are two reasons. First, although it is not nearly as common as it used to be, it still is employed and you may encounter the ARR or similar procedures in practice. Second, the critique of the ARR tells us that for a method to be useful, it must use cash flows and incorporate the time value of money. Any method that does not have these features will not give us information concerning the impact of the investment on the value of the firm.

## PAYBACK PERIOD

A widely-used measure is the payback period, which is defined as the number of years required for the cash inflows from an investment to recoup the cash outflows. In other words, this measure tells us how long it takes to get our money back. What we do is compute a cumulative sum of the cash flows to identify the payback year and compare this payback period to a predetermined required payback. We will illustrate with our example:

| End of Year | Cash Flow | Cumulative Amount |
|:-----------:|:---------:|:-----------------:|
| 1 | $13,000 | $13,000 |
| 2 | 13,000 | 26,000 |
| 3 | 13,000 | 39,000 |
| 4 | 13,000 | 52,000 |

The cumulative sum covers the initial cost in the fourth year so this is the payback period. Actually, it is almost covered by the end of the third year, and recognizing that in practice cash flows occur during the year, we would say that the payback period is a little more than three years. In any event, this number is then compared to a required payback period. For instance, a firm may have a policy of accepting cost-saving investments that have a payback period of no more than five years.

The payback period, like the ARR, is inconsistent with the valuation principle in the sense that we can't tell from payback whether value is expected to increase or decrease. This method does consider cash flow, but it does not consider all the cash flows from the investment. Furthermore, it does not properly account for the time value of money. For instance, say there were no cash flows in our example at the end of the first two years. Instead there was a lump sum of $39,000 at the end of Year 3 plus the $13,000 at the end of Year 4. We would still obtain the same payback but obviously the investment would be less attractive.

At one time, the ARR and the payback period were the primary methods used in practice to evaluate capital investments. Once the basic flaws were clearly understood, new methods were introduced. Many managers and academicians urged that practitioners stop relying on ARR and payback and adopt one of the other techniques. As it turned out, newer methods were adopted and many firms discarded the ARR. However, they continue to use the payback period along with one or more of the newer techniques, claiming that the payback method is easier to compute and that it can be used in a way that is consistent with other methods. We don't see how computational ease can be considered a relevant factor given that most managers use calculators and computers, and we believe that the payback period can be an unreliable proxy for one of the other methods. Frankly, we are not sure why the payback method has not been discarded, but in any event, it seems clear that many analysts find the information contained in the payback figure useful for evaluating capital investments.

## NET PRESENT VALUE

The Net Present Value (NPV) method[4] is a very useful tool for evaluating capital investments. We believe it is the best method because it gives clear information on the size of the impact of an investment on firm value and it is also the easiest to use. In fact we will see in the next chapter that the NPV is the standard used to judge other techniques. Specifically, we will show that if another method does not give the same message as the NPV method, then it is flawed.

Table 9-1 outlines the procedure. We will illustrate with our example. Recall that the required rate is 9%. Given this the next step is to compute the present value of the cash inflows as follows:

---

[4] As noted earlier, NPV is a measure. The entire process of computing and interpreting the NPV for an investment is called the NPV method or procedure. This designation is true for other methods as well.

| *End of Year* | *Cash Flow* | | *(PVA$1, 9%, 4)* | | *Present Value* |
|---|---|---|---|---|---|
| 1–4 | 13,000 | × | 3.2397 | = | $42,116 |

Next we compute the present value of the cash outflows at 9%. All the cash outflows occur at time zero, thus, the present value is $40,000. The NPV is $2,116 as shown below:

$$NPV = PVI - PVO$$
$$= \$42,116 - \$40,000$$
$$= \$2,116$$

The NPV is a positive $2,116 indicating that this is a good investment.

**Table 9-1**  *Net Present Value Method*

---

• Select an appropriate risk-adjusted discount rate.
• Compute the present value of the investment's cash inflows.
• Compute the present value of the investment's cash outflows.
• Compute the net present value by subtracting the present value of the cash outflows from the present value of the cash inflows. That is:

Net Present Value = Present Value of − Present Value of
                              Cash Inflows        Cash Outflows

*Interpretation Guides*
  *Guide 1*
  The NPV is a measure of the change in firm value produced by the investment. Hence, if the NPV is positive, we expect the firm's value to increase, so it is an acceptable investment.[5] If the NPV is negative, we expect a decrease in value and the investment should be rejected. If the NPV is zero we are indifferent because we expect no change in value.
  *Guide 2*
  If the NPV is positive this means the investment is expected to earn a rate greater than the risk-adjusted rate used to discount cash flows. If the NPV is negative, we expect a lower rate. If the NPV is zero, we expect exactly that rate.

---

[5] Generally, a firm should accept all investments with a positive NPV. However, in certain circumstances a firm cannot accept them all and this is why we say acceptable. For convenience we will simply say accept until this issue is discussed further in the next chapter.

As we've already noted, a positive NPV indicates the investment will increase value. But there's more to it than that. The NPV of $2,116 is an estimate of how much the firm's value will increase if this investment is accepted. Furthermore, we can conclude that as long as the firm pays less than $42,116 for this investment its value will increase. In the jargon of the last chapter, the value of this investment is the present value of the cash flows it will generate discounted at an appropriate risk-adjusted rate. This value represents the maximum price one should be willing to pay for the investment.

As you know, managers balance risk versus returns in making investments. Because of this they are accustomed to thinking in terms of rates of return rather than dollars of NPV. Hence, many rely on the second interpretation guide in Table 9-1 which tells us that the positive NPV indicates that the investment promises a rate of return greater than 9%. More specifically, it promises an internal rate of return of more than 9%.[6] To see this more clearly, assume you place $40,000 in a bank that pays interest of 9% per year compounded annually. You could withdraw $12,347 at the end of each year for four years and you would be left with a zero balance after the fourth withdrawal. Since this capital investment promises a return of more than $12,347 at the end of each year for four years, the rate of return is more than 9%. Suppose the cash inflows from the investment had been less than $12,347 each year. The net present value would have been negative, indicating a rate of return of less than 9%. Had the cash flows been equal to $12,347 each year, the net present value would have been zero, indicating a rate of 9%.

In summary, the NPV method is a reliable guide. It is telling us that the investment makes economic sense. We must keep in mind, however, that all the figures are estimates and so we cannot precisely measure the impact on value. Furthermore, sometimes noneconomic factors dominate a capital investment decision.

## PROFITABILITY INDEX

Many analysts rely on a measure called the Profitability Index (PI) which is derived from the NPV. It is defined as follows:

$$\text{Profitability Index (PI)} = \frac{\text{Present Value of Cash Inflows}}{\text{Present Value of Cash Outflows}}$$

---

[6] The internal rate of return was discussed in the previous two chapters and we will review it later.

For our example it is 1.05 as shown below.

$$PI = \frac{\$42,116}{\$40,000} = 1.05$$

As noted, the PI is derived from the NPV. Hence, we can summarize the interpretation guide as follows:

| When NPV is | | Pi will be |
|---|---|---|
| greater than zero | $\longrightarrow$ | greater than one |
| less than zero | | less than one |
| equal to zero | | equal to one |

All the earlier comments about NPV being positive or negative apply to the PI being greater or less than one. For example, a PI greater than one means we can expect a rate of return greater than the required rate.

The PI will always give the same accept/reject signal as the NPV. Hence, if this is all we want to know, it does not matter whether we use the NPV or the PI. However, sometimes we want to know more than this and in some of these instances, the PI is not as reliable a guide as the NPV. For example, sometimes we are comparing two investments each with a positive PI and can only take one. As it turns out, it is possible for the one with the higher PI to increase value less than the other. The NPV would not give this false signal.

## INTERNAL RATE OF RETURN

The Internal Rate of Return (IRR), also known by yield to maturity, discounted cash flow, yield, and the marginal efficiency of capital, is defined as the rate that makes the present value of the cash inflows from an investment equal to the present value of its cash outflows. We will first review how to compute it and then discuss the interpretation. Let's begin by restating the cash flows for our example.

| End of Year | Cash Flow |
|---|---|
| 0 | ($40,000) |
| 1 | 13,000 |
| 2 | 13,000 |
| 3 | 13,000 |
| 4 | 13,000 |

We want to find the rate that makes the present value of the cash inflows equal to $40,000, which is the present value of the cash outflows in this example. We can rely on a trial and error procedure. Let's begin by trying 15%:

| End of Year | Cash Flow | | (PVA$1, 15%, 4) | | Present Value |
|---|---|---|---|---|---|
| 0 | $(40,000) | × | 1.0000 | = | $(40,000) |
| 1–4 | 13,000 | × | 2.8550 | = | 37,115 |

The IRR is not 15% because at this rate the present value of the inflows is less than the present value of the outflows. We must try a lower rate. Let's pick 13%:

| End of Year | Cash Flow | | (PVA$1, 13%, 4) | | Present Value |
|---|---|---|---|---|---|
| 0 | $(40,000) | × | 1.0000 | = | $(40,000) |
| 1–4 | 13,000 | × | 2.9745 | = | 38,699 |

Still too high, let's try 11%:

| End of Year | Cash Flow | | (PVA$1, 13%, 4) | | Present Value |
|---|---|---|---|---|---|
| 0 | $(40,000) | × | 1.0000 | = | $(40,000) |
| 1–4 | 13,000 | × | 3.1024 | = | 40,331 |

Now the rate is too low; let's try 12%:

| End of Year | Cash Flow | | (PVA$1, 12%, 4) | | Present Value |
|---|---|---|---|---|---|
| 0 | $(40,000) | × | 1.0000 | = | $(40,000) |
| 1–4 | 13,000 | × | 3.0373 | = | 39,485 |

The internal rate of return on this investment is between 11% and 12%.

In Chapter 7 we explained a shortcut for computing the IRR that can be used when an investment has only one outlay at time zero and the inflows are an annuity. Recall that it was derived from the procedure for computing an annuity which is:

$$\text{Present Value} = \text{Annuity} \times (PVA\$1, i, n)$$

Here's how to apply it as a shortcut.

1. Divide the cash outflow by the annual inflow.

2. Go to Appendix P-2 to locate the factor for the appropriate n and that gives the IRR.

$$\begin{array}{lll} Present\ Value & Annuity & (PVA\$1,\ i,\ n) \\ \$40,000 & = \$13,000 & \times\ (PVA\$1,\ i,\ 4) \\ (PVA\$1,\ i,\ 4) & = \dfrac{\$40,000}{\$13,000} & = 3.0769 \end{array}$$

We then go to Appendix P-2 and look across the $n = 4$ row. The factor for 11% is 3.1024 and the factor for 12% is 3.0373. Since 3.0769 is between 11% and 12%, we know that the IRR for this investment is between 11% and 12%.

Another way of defining the IRR is as follows: The internal rate of return is the rate that makes the investment's net present value equal to zero. Hence, we can derive the following interpretation guide:

| When NPV is $\longrightarrow$ | IRR will be |
|---|---|
| Greater than zero | Greater than required rate |
| Less than zero | Less than required rate |
| Equal to zero | Equal to required rate |

All the earlier comments about the NPV being positive or negative apply to the IRR being greater than or less than the required rate.

As we can see the IRR can be used to judge whether or not an investment is expected to increase value.[7] Hence, if this is all we want to know, it does not matter whether we use the NPV or the IRR. However, sometimes we want to know more than this and in some of these instances, the IRR will not be as reliable a guide as the NPV.

We have completed our discussion of how to compute ARR, Payback Period, NPV, PI and IRR. We have been advocating the use of the NPV. The next chapter will provide an opportunity to illustrate more clearly why the NPV is best and easiest to use. We are devoting so much emphasis on this point because the IRR is used widely in practice, more commonly than the NPV. In our opinion, this is because managers are accustomed to working with rates of return and, hence, it is easier for them to work with an investment's (internal) rate of return than the dollars of NPV it will generate.

In illustrating the computations, the cash flows were given. Now we must turn our attention to explaining an investment's relevant cash flows and how to compute them.

---

[7] There is a qualification. For nonconventional investment this conclusion may not be warranted. Nonconventional investments are discussed in the next chapter. These investments involve net cash outflows in the later years of a project—a year subsequent to one in which the net cash flow is positive.

# Deriving Relevant Cash Flows

The relevant cash flows for computing an investment's NPV, PI and IRR are the *incremental operating after-tax cash flows* caused by the investment. We will review cash flow from operations after explaining what we mean by "incremental" and "operating."

Incremental means the change in cash flows caused by the investment. Basically, we can think of it as computing the difference between what the cash flows of the firm would be with and without the investment. Take our earlier example where a firm was considering a new piece of equipment that would require an initial outlay of $40,000. At time zero, the firm's cash would be $40,000 less than it would be without the investment. Thus, the incremental amount is a negative $40,000. We will discuss this more shortly but notice here that it doesn't matter whether the firm had the $40,000 in the bank or raised it by borrowing or issuing stock. In other words, the $40,000 outlay would be the incremental cash outflow regardless of the source of financing.

The word "operating" means we do not deduct interest or payments of principal or any debt used to finance the investment. In other words, we ignore interest expense and principal payments in making the computations. The reason is that the discount rate used for the NPV, PI, etc., incorporates the effect of interest, including the tax shield that interest expense creates. Thus, to deduct interest (or principal) in deriving cash flows for capital budgeting is counting interest twice. On this issue, many people ask whether the attractiveness of the investment is affected by favorable financing such as a government loan at an interest rate of 2%. It certainly is. But we would take this attractive financing into account another way. For instance, we would compute a marginal cost of capital for this project (as discussed in the last chapter), which includes the subsidized interest rate. In other words, the discount rate used to compute NPV, etc., would be lower because of the subsidized interest rate.[8]

Table 9-2 repeats a table from Chapter 3 which summarizes procedures for computing net working capital from operations. The procedure for de-

---

[8] Another way is to leave the discount rate as is and add to the cash flows the present value of the savings from the lower loan payments. We should add that a capital budgeting system can be devised that involves deducting interest and principal on debt. However, in our opinion the analysis would be much more complex and needlessly so. It is also possible to devise a system where we first value capital investments as if they were financed entirely by equity and then add the valuation impact of debt financing.

riving incremental operating cash flows for capital budgeting differs from the one shown in Table 9-2 in the following ways:

1. In capital budgeting we estimate future flows. We are not concerned with past flows.

2. When we compute the change in net income because of an investment, we will ignore interest on debt used to finance the investment.

3. Since we will deal only with the effect of investment decisions on actual tax liabilities, there will be no timing difference so deferred taxes don't enter the picture at all.

4. Incremental cash flow for capital budgeting includes changes in fixed assets caused by the investment and changes in other long-term assets as well. It also includes a change in the cash balance caused by the investment.

We will rely on this adjusted definition of cash flow from operations. However, we should point out that many analysts compute net working capital

**Table 9-2**  *Procedures for Estimating Net Working Capital and Cash Flow from Operations*

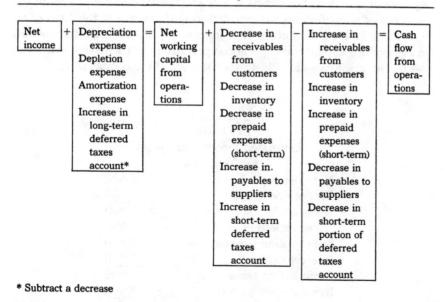

| Net income | + | Depreciation expense Depletion expense Amortization expense Increase in long-term deferred taxes account* | = | Net working capital from opera-tions | + | Decrease in receivables from customers Decrease in inventory Decrease in prepaid expenses (short-term) Increase in. payables to suppliers Increase in short-term deferred taxes account | − | Increase in receivables from customers Increase in inventory Increase in prepaid expenses (short-term) Decrease in payables to suppliers Decrease in short-term portion of deferred taxes account | = | Cash flow from opera-tions |

\* Subtract a decrease

from operations and call it cash flow. They then treat changes in net working capital as a capital flow, just as they would treat additional investments in or divestitures of fixed assets. This latter approach is quite common but we will not follow it because of the confusion it could create concerning cash flow.

The example below will illustrate a systematic approach for deriving the incremental cash flows from an investment. After that we will explain two shortcut procedures. Then we will raise a number of refinements. The example follows:

Table 9-3 has an estimated income statement for Aire, Inc. for the next year. This estimated statement assumes that Aire will not undertake the investment we will now describe: The firm is considering a new machine that will cost $10,000 and will save labor of $5,000 per year for its five-year life. Depreciation will be on a straight-line basis to a zero salvage value, so depreciation will be $2,000 per year. This investment will not affect the level of net working capital needed to support operations, that is, there will be no changes in current assets or current liabilities because of this investment. To finance the investment Aire will borrow $10,000 at 14%. Finally, the firm's income tax rate is 40%.

The cost of the machine is $10,000. We will assume that this is the net cash outflow at that time. Often the net outflow will be the net effect of items such as the cost of the new machine, proceeds from the sale of existing equipment including tax effects if any and the investment tax credit (for purposes of simplification, we are deferring discussion of this kind of refinement). To compute annual cash inflows, we first compute the increase in net working capital from operations produced by this investment. Table 9-4 has an analysis which illustrates the logic of the computations.

### TABLE 9-3
### AIRE, INC.
Estimated Income Statement
for Next Year

| | |
|---|---|
| Net sales | $100,000 |
| Cost of goods sold | 40,000 |
| Gross profit | $ 60,000 |
| Labor expense | 30,000 |
| Depreciation expense | 8,000 |
| Interest expense | 2,000 |
| Profit before taxes | $ 20,000 |
| Income taxes @ 40% | 8,000 |
| Net income | $ 12,000 |

## TABLE 9-4
## AIRE, INC.
### Adjusted Estimated Income Statement*
### for Next Year

| | Without Machine | With Machine | Incremental |
|---|---|---|---|
| Net sales | $100,000 | $100,000 | (no change) |
| Cost of goods sold | 40,000 | 40,000 | (no change) |
| Gross profit | $ 60,000 | $ 60,000 | (no change) |
| Labor expense | 30,000 | 25,000 | ($5,000 savings) |
| Depreciation expense | 8,000 | 10,000 | ($2,000 increase) |
| Earnings before interest & taxes | $ 22,000 | $ 25,000 | ($3,000 increase) |
| Income taxes | 8,800 | $ 10,000 | ($1,200 increase) |
| Net income | $ 13,200 | $ 15,000 | ($1,800 increase) |
| + Depreciation expense | 8,000 | 10,000 | ($2,000 increase) |
| Net working capital from operations (excluding interest) | $ 21,200 | $ 25,000 | ($3,800 increase) |

*Interest expense has been removed to ease the focus on operating flows.

The first column of Table 9-4 has a revised estimate of Aire, Inc.'s net working capital from operations next year assuming the investment is not taken. The difference from the estimated statement in Table 9-3 is that interest is omitted here. The reason is we want to focus on the operation cash flows. The second column has what net working capital from operations (excluding interest) would be if the investment is accepted. The difference between the flow "with" and "without" the investment is the incremental amount and is shown in the final column. As shown, the net effect is $3,800.

The next step is to compute cash inflows from operations because this is what we need. We adjust the net working capital figure of $3,800 for changes in those current assets and current liabilities caused by this investment.[9] But we are told that this investment will not affect the level of net working capital needed to support operations. Thus, in this instance net working capital from operations equals cash flow from operations. In other words, the cash inflow from operations for the first year is $3,800.

[9] Note the similarity and difference in computing cash flow from operations in flow of funds and capital budgeting analyses. Both include changes in spontaneous liabilities such as accounts payable and accrued expenses, but do not include any changes in short-term borrowing. On the other hand, in capital budgeting we include changes in all current assets, including cash, caused by the investment, whereas, in flow of funds analyses normally changes in cash are excluded in deriving cash flow from operations.

Notice from Table 9-4 that no matter what the estimated income statement is for the next year and the four years after that, the difference each year because of this investment would be $3,800. Hence, the incremental operating cash flows from this investment are the following:

| End of Year | Cash Flow |
|:-:|:-:|
| 0 | ($10,000) |
| 1 | 3,800 |
| 2 | 3,800 |
| 3 | 3,800 |
| 4 | 3,800 |
| 5 | 3,800 |

These are the figures we would use to compute the NPV, IRR, etc. We will illustrate the complete analysis, that is, derivation of cash flows and computation of NPV later.

It is important to stress that interest on the debt does not affect the above computations. We were told that the $10,000 would be borrowed at 14% but we ignored this in computing incremental operating cash flows. As explained earlier, an investment's debt capacity and the interest on this debt is captured in the discount rate selected.[10]

We could rely on the approach illustrated in Table 9-4 to derive net working capital from operations for any investment. However, usually it is convenient to employ a shortcut procedure which is derived from that analysis. We will show two such procedures that are quite common. They will give the same result as the analysis shown in Table 9-4.

### Shortcut Procedure 1

This approach computes the investment's impact on net working capital from operations directly, and although it can be used for any investment, it is especially convenient when the investment involves additional revenues. Below is an outline of the procedure:

Change in earnings before interest and taxes (EBIT)
± Change in income taxes
= Change in net income after taxes (excluding interest)
+ Expenses that do not decrease net working capital (often just depreciation expense)
= Change in net working capital from operations

---

[10] The fact that the entire $10,000 cost of the investment is being borrowed does not imply that the after-tax interest rate is the discount rate. In computing a marginal cost of capital, we should estimate the amount of debt (i.e. debt capacity) an investment can support and rely on this, not the specific amount of debt the firm employs. See the previous chapter for an elaboration of this point.

In our example, labor savings of $5,000 and added depreciation expense of $2,000 combine to increase the firm's EBIT by $3,000. From here we can derive the net impact as shown:

| | |
|---|---|
| Δ  EBIT | $3,000 |
| −Δ  Taxes | 1,200 |
| =Δ  NI | $1,800 |
| +Δ  Depreciation | 2,000 |
| =Δ  NWC from operations | $3,800 |

Notice that this method involves directly computing the figures in the final column of Table 9-4.

### Shortcut Procedure 2

This approach, which is most common for cost-saving investments like the one in our example, takes each income statement item impacted by the investment and computes its effect on net working capital from operations. For instance, labor savings of $5,000 will increase taxable income by $5,000 which in turn will increase taxes by $2,000 given the tax rate of 40%. Hence the net effect on net working capital from operations is $3,000. Let's state this impact in equation form.

Labor Savings − (Labor Savings) (Tax Rate) = After-Tax Labor Savings

This can be restated as follows:

Labor Savings (1 − Tax Rate) = After-Tax Labor Savings

The after-tax impact of any savings in operating costs can be computed in this way. In fact, the equation can be used to compute the impact on net working capital from operations of any income statement item that increases both taxable income and net working capital from operations, such as increased gross profit produced by an investment.

Depreciation is a non-cash expense so its only impact on net working capital from operations is through its effect on income taxes. Specifically, depreciation reduces the amount of income taxes that a firm must pay. The reduction is the tax shield and that is computed as follows:

Depreciation Expense × Tax Rate = Effect on NWC from Operations

Let's summarize the procedure for our example.

| Item | Amount × Tax Adjustment | | Effect on NWC from Operations |
|------|------------------------|---|------------------------------|
| Labor savings | 5,000 × (1 − .4) | = | $3,000 |
| Depreciation expense | 2,000 × (.40) | = | 800 |
| | | | $3,800 |

In our simple example, NWC from operations was equal to cash flow from operations. This often will not be the case; furthermore, an analysis will frequently involve the acquisition and/or sale of fixed assets in later years. When this is the case, it usually is a good idea to rely on a worksheet and to include on it the computation of the NPV, IRR or other technique employed. To illustrate, assume we want to compute the investment's NPV at a required rate of 15%. Table 9-5 summarizes the analysis.

## REFINEMENTS IN DERIVING INCREMENTAL OPERATING CASH FLOWS

Our example avoided a number of complexities and refinements. We will now show how to deal with some of them.

### Changes in Net Working Capital

Assume that the above investment will require Aire, Inc., to increase its raw materials inventory by $2,000 immediately and another $1,000 one year from now. This would result in an immediate increase in accounts payable of $500 and another increase of $250 one year from now. The extra inventory would not be needed when the farm disposes of this equipment, so the extra inventory would be freed up at that time. Accounts payable also would decrease. Below is a revision of part of the worksheet in Table 9-5 incorporating this new information.

**Table 9-5**   *Worksheet for Capital Budgeting Analysis*

| End of Year | Fixed Assets | | NWC From Operations | Changes in NWC | Cash Flow | | (PVA$1,15%,5) | | Present Value |
|---|---|---|---|---|---|---|---|---|---|
| 0 | ($10,000) | + | | + | = ($10,000) | × | 1.0000 | = | ($10,000) |
| 1 | | + | $3,800 | + | = | 3,800 | | | |
| 2 | | + | 3,800 | + | = | 3,800 | | | |
| 3 | | + | 3,800 | + | = | 3,800 | × | 3.3522 | = | 12,738 |
| 4 | | + | 3,800 | + | = | 3,800 | | | |
| 5 | | + | 3,800 | + | = | 3,800 | | | |
| | | | | | | | NPV @ 15% = | | $2,738 |

| End of Year | Fixed Assets | NWC From Operations | | Changes in NWC | | Cash Flow |
|---|---|---|---|---|---|---|
| 0 | ($10,000) | | + | ($1,500) | = | ($11,500) |
| 1 | | 3,800 | + | (750) | = | 3,050 |
| 2 | | 3,800 | + | | = | 3,800 |
| 3 | | 3,800 | + | | = | 3,800 |
| 4 | | 3,800 | + | | = | 3,800 |
| 5 | | 3,800 | + | 2,250 | = | 6,050 |

The $2,000 increase in inventory at time zero is offset partially by a simultaneous increase of $500 in accounts payable. The $1,000 increase one year from now is partially offset by the $250 increase in payables. Five years from now the $3,000 of inventory will be freed up but the firm would also lose the $750 source from accounts payable at that time.

All increases in current assets (including cash) caused by the investment have the effect of reducing cash flow. Decreases have the opposite effect. Increases in spontaneous liabilities such as accounts payable and accrued expenses have the effect of increasing cash flow. Decreases have the opposite effect.

### Replacing an Existing Machine

Our example assumed that Aire was not replacing an existing machine. Using the same example for a replacement, we will assume that labor savings and depreciation expenses will remain at $5,000 per year and $2,000 per year respectively. Suppose the machine to be replaced has a book value of $5,000, depreciation expense on it if retained would be $1,000 per year for the next five years, and the salvage value in five years is estimated at zero. Finally, we will assume the machine could be sold now for $3,000, and we will once again assume that this investment will not affect the level of current assets and current liabilities needed for operations.

Given the above revision, the net cash outflow at time zero and the annual inflows will be different from the amounts shown in Table 9-5. At time zero, there still will be an outlay of $10,000 for the new machine but there is an offsetting inflow of $3,000 from the sale of the old machine. Here's the complication: When we sell a fixed asset at a price different from its book value there may be a gain or a loss. The gain or loss is derived by subtracting the book value from the selling price as shown below.

|   | Selling price | $3,000 |
|---|---|---|
| − | Book value | 5,000 |
|   | Gain (loss) | ($2,000) |

This loss creates a tax shield as follows:

$$\text{Tax Shield} = \text{Loss} \times \text{Tax Rate}$$
$$\$800 \qquad = \$2,000 \times 40\%$$

If we assume this tax shield is received at time zero the incremental cash outflow at time zero is $6,200 as shown below:

|                            | *Initial Outlay* |
| -------------------------- | ---------------- |
| Purchase of machine        | ($10,000)        |
| Less sale of old machine   | 3,000            |
| Less tax shield on sale    | 800              |
| Net cash outflow           | ($ 6,200)        |

So in Table 9-5 a negative $6,200 would be shown instead of the negative $10,000.

If the selling price was greater than book value, a taxable gain would result, along with a cash outlay for taxes. Suppose the selling price was $6,000. The gain would be $1,000 and there would be an increase in taxes of $400.[11]Thus, the net outlay would be $4,400 as shown below:

|                            | *Initial Outlay* |
| -------------------------- | ---------------- |
| Purchase of machine        | ($10,000)        |
| Less sale of old machine   | 6,000            |
| Plus taxes on sale         | (400)            |
| Net cash outflows          | ($ 4,400)        |

If the old machine were not replaced, it would be depreciated at a rate of $1,000 per year. Hence, the incremental depreciation created by the investment would be $1,000, that is, depreciation increases by $2,000 because of the new equipment but the firm loses $1,000 per year, thus the change is $1,000 per year. Below is the impact of this revision on net working capital from operations derived by using the second shortcut procedure:

| *Item*           | *Amount*  |   | *Tax Adjustment* |   | *NWC from Operations* |
| ---------------- | --------- | - | ---------------- | - | --------------------- |
| Labor savings    | $5,000    | × | (1 − TR)         | = | $3,000                |
| New depreciation | 2,000     | × | (TR)             | = | 800                   |
| Old depreciation | (1,000)   | × | (TR)             | = | (400)                 |
|                  |           |   |                  |   | $3,400                |

---

[11] We are assuming $6,000 is less than the original cost of the old machine. When a machine is sold for more than its original cost, the difference between the selling price and original cost is taxed at a preferential rate. The remainder of the gain is taxed at ordinary rates.

Hence in Table 9-5, the new working capital from operation figures would be $3,400 instead of the $3,800 shown.

### Salvage Value

In the previous version of the example, we assumed a zero salvage value on both the new and old equipment. Suppose we still expected this for the old equipment but estimated a salvage value of $1,000 for the new equipment. We would show this amount as a cash inflow at the end of Year 5 in the fixed asset column in Table 9-5. Furthermore, there would be a change in annual depreciation on the new equipment. Recall that straight-line depreciation is computed as follows:

### Straight-Line Depreciation

$$\text{Annual Depreciation} = \frac{\text{Original Cost-Estimated Salvage Value}}{\text{Number of Years}}$$

$$= \frac{\$10,000 - \$1,000}{5}$$

$$= \$1,800$$

Of course, this change in depreciation would produce a change in the figures shown for net working capital from operations.

If the salvage value for the old equipment was positive, we would show the amount as a cash outflow at the end of Year 5 in the fixed assets column in Table 9-5. The reason is that by replacing the machine we would lose this inflow five years from now. This in effect is an incremental cash outflow produced by the new machine. (Note that, if the existing machine's estimated salvage value was above zero, then the annual depreciation lost and hence the tax shields lost, would be less than the amounts shown above.)

We should point out that some accelerated methods produce a book value at the end of the asset's life that is different from its salvage value. The result of this often will be a taxable gain at that time. For instance, suppose the estimated salvage value of the new equipment was $500 and that the depreciation method employed produced a book value of zero. There would be a taxable gain of $500 and given a tax rate of 40%, there would be an increase in taxes of $200 at that time. Consequently, the net cash inflow from the salvage would be $300, the $500 salvage value less the incremental taxes of $200.

### ITC/Accelerated Depreciation

The Investment Tax Credit (ITC) is a reduction of taxes earned by purchasing eligible property. Currently, it is generally available for all fixed asset purchases with a life of three years or more except for land and buildings. The current rate is 6% for qualifying assets with a life of 3–4 years and 10% for a life of five years or more. Note that the ITC is a direct reduction in taxes and not a tax shield.

Relying on the original version of our example (i.e., no existing equipment), the ITC would be $1,000 which is derived by multiplying 10% times the asset's $10,000 cost. Assuming the credit is received at time zero,[12] the net cash outflow shown in the fixed asset column in Table 9-5 would be $9,000 instead of $10,000.

We assumed the version of the example that did not involve existing equipment to avoid a complexity. Under current law, when an asset on which the ITC was taken is sold before the end of its useful life part or all of the ITC may be recaptured. Recapture means paying part of it back. It is beyond our scope to delve into the details of this.

The ITC may or may not affect the computation of depreciation. It depends on the depreciation method chosen. For instance, for straight-line depreciation which we have been using, the ITC does not affect the amount of depreciation. In other words, depreciation expense on the new equipment still would be $2,000 per year even though there is a tax credit of $1,000. For certain accelerated methods, the ITC will affect the amount of the asset's cost that can be depreciated.

With respect to accelerated methods, it is beyond our scope to delve into the available methods. However, we will illustrate one, called the Accelerated Cost Recovery System (ACRS) for the new equipment in our example. According to this method, we subtract one-half the ITC of $1,000 from the cost of $10,000. We then multiply the adjusted figure, $9,500, which is called the basis, by the following percents to compute the annual amounts.[13]

| Year | Basis | | Percentage | | Depreciation |
|------|-------|---|-----------|---|--------------|
| 1 | $9,500 | × | 15% | = | $1,425 |
| 2 | 9,500 | × | 22% | = | 2,090 |
| 3 | 9,500 | × | 21% | = | 1,995 |
| 4 | 9,500 | × | 21% | = | 1,995 |
| 5 | 9,500 | × | 21% | = | 1,995 |
| | | | Total | = | $9,500 |

---

[12] The impact of ITC would normally be taken on the next tax payment date. Since we are relying on annual intervals, we will usually assume for convenience that the cash inflow is received at time zero.

[13] Please keep in mind that tax laws are frequently revised. Hence, it is possible that the above illustrations regarding the applications of the ITC and ACRS no longer apply when you are reading this chapter

### Time Horizon

Many capital investments are expected to produce cash flows for a long but indefinite period. For instance, certain kinds of new products are expected to have a new life. Now, generally it is not feasible to estimate a precise life such as 43 years for a product. Furthermore, as we will see in the next chapter problems arise in comparing a project with say a 13-year life to one with a 16-year life. What many firms do is rely on a fixed horizon for analyzing certain kinds of investments. For instance, a firm may use 10 years as the limit for evaluating all investments classified as strategic or expansion. What this means is that a terminal value must be estimated which is an estimate of the market value of the fixed assets at that time and an estimate of working capital freed up. We then include these as cash inflows at the terminal date.

### Sunk Costs

In deriving incremental operating cash flows the analyst must be careful to exclude "sunk costs," expenditures already made but unable to be recouped. Suppose in January of Year 2 a firm is considering investing in a new product. During Year 1 the firm spent a considerable sum on market research for the product. In evaluating the capital investment in Year 2, we would not include the cost of the market research. The amount has been spent so it is a sunk cost. Looking at it another way, the amount is not incremental to the decision at hand in January of Year 2 because future cash flows of the firm would be the same whether the new product is accepted or rejected.

### Post-Audit

Value creation comes from selecting good investments and managing them well. Effective management includes many elements. For our purposes, it includes following-up to see that the investment is actually producing the promised cash flows. This is part of an audit or control function and it includes taking appropriate action when necessary. For instance, if an investment is not delivering the promised cash flows, it may make sense to abandon it. Many firms do not give this essential control function in capital budgeting the attention it deserves. This lack of attention is probably due to the stringent data requirements called for by this kind of audit and the fact that such data are not readily available. At any rate, it's not a "theory versus practice" issue. This control phase can and should be part of the capital budgeting process.

Often it is very difficult to develop reasonable estimates of cash flows.

This difficulty is especially severe for strategic and expansion type investments. Consider a business you would like to start and try to figure out how much profit you would earn from it five years from now and ten years from now. How confident are you in the estimates? This is precisely the problem we face when we do capital budgeting analyses for many investments. A similar difficulty is trying to isolate the impact of the investment. For instance, when computer firms analyzed entering the personal computer market, they encountered this difficulty (as well as a host of others) in trying to compute NPV, IRR, etc. They not only had to estimate the cash flows from the new line but they also had to figure out how much cash flow from existing products would have been lost had they not entered the personal computer market. We doubt that this was an easy task.

The above and other real world complexities make it difficult to apply the techniques described earlier in the chapter. The upshot is we cannot measure the value of a capital investment as precisely as we would like. This does not mean that capital budgeting techniques are not useful because they are very helpful. However, we must be aware of the practical difficulties that frequently arise and recognize the limitations.

# Problems and Discussion Questions

## A. Solved Problems

### Problem 9–1A

The Alfine Company is contemplating a capital investment that will require an immediate cash outlay of $75,000 and has the following expected annual cash inflows:

| End of Year | Cash Flow |
|:-----------:|:---------:|
| 1 | $25,000 |
| 2 | 27,000 |
| 3 | 26,000 |
| 4 | 22,000 |

For an investment in this risk class management has determined that 14% is an appropriate required return.

1. Evaluate the project using the NPV method.

2. Evaluate the project using the IRR method.

### Solution 9–1A

1. NPV method. Following the procedure in the chapter, the first step is to compute an appropriate risk-adjusted discount rate. We are told that this has been set at 14%. (Keep in mind that it is an after-tax rate and that the cash flows are after taxes.) The next step is to compute the present value of the cash inflows at this rate.

| End of Year | Cash Flow | | (PV$1, 14% n) | | Present Value |
|:-----------:|:---------:|:-:|:------------:|:-:|:------------:|
| 1 | $25,000 | × | .8772 | = | $21,930 |
| 2 | 27,000 | × | .7695 | = | 20,777 |
| 3 | 26,000 | × | .6750 | = | 17,550 |
| 4 | 22,000 | × | .5921 | = | 13,026 |
| | | | | Total = | $73,283 |

The third step is to compute the present value of the cash outflows, using the 14% required rate. Since the only outflow is the $75,000 at time zero this is the present value of the outflows. Note, however, that if outflows were spread over several years we would compute their present value just as we did for the inflows.

The next step is to compute the NPV which is a negative $1,717 as shown below:

$$NPV = PVI - PVO$$
$$= \$73,283 - \$75,000$$
$$= (\$1,717)$$

Finally, the interpretation of this result is that the project is expected to decrease the value of the firm, so it should be rejected. (The figure tells us that value is expected to decrease by $1,717.) Another way of looking at it is that the investment's rate of return is expected to be less than 14%.

2. *Internal Rate of Return Method.* The internal rate of return is the rate that makes the present value of an investment's cash inflows equal to its outflows, which is the same as saying that the net present value equals zero. We will use a trial and error procedure to compute the rate. Since the NPV was negative at 14%, we know it must be less than 14%. Let's try 12%.

### 12% Trial

| End of Year | Cash Flow | | (PV$1, 12%, n) | | Present Value |
|:-:|--:|:-:|:-:|:-:|--:|
| 1 | $25,000 | × | .8929 | = | $22,323 |
| 2 | 27,000 | × | .7972 | = | 21,524 |
| 3 | 26,000 | × | .7118 | = | 18,507 |
| 4 | 22,000 | × | .6355 | = | 13,981 |
| | | | | Total | $76,335 |

At 12% the present value of the cash inflows exceeds the present of the cash outflows, indicating that the IRR is more than 12%. Let's try 13%.

### 13% Trial

| End of Year | Cash Flow | | (PV$1, 13%, n) | | Present Value |
|:-:|--:|:-:|:-:|:-:|--:|
| 1 | $25,000 | × | .8850 | = | $22,125 |
| 2 | 27,000 | × | .7831 | = | 21,144 |
| 3 | 26,000 | × | .6931 | = | 18,021 |
| 4 | 22,000 | × | .6133 | = | 13,493 |
| | | | | Total | $74,783 |

This is very close, but still less than $75,000, indicating that the IRR is slightly less than 13%. (The actual IRR is 12.86% but that degree of precision is unnecessary and may even be misleading.) The IRR is less than the required rate of 14% so the project should be rejected; it is expected to decrease the value of the firm.

## Problem 9–2A

The Mateel Company is considering the replacement of an old machine with a technologically superior model that is expected to save cash operating costs. The existing machine was purchased three years ago at a cost of $33,000 and is being depreciated on a straight-line basis over an eight-year life to a $1,000 salvage value. The firm could sell this machine for $25,000 today. The replacement costs $100,000, including installation costs, and would be depreciated on a straight-line basis over its five-year life to a zero salvage value. The machine is expected to reduce cash operating costs by $30,000 per year for the next five years. The level of NWC needed to support operations would not change because of the replacement. Mateel's marginal tax rate is 46% and its required rate of return for investments like this one is 15%. (You may ignore the ITC.)

Utilizing the NPV method of analysis, recommend whether the existing machine should be replaced with the newer model.

## Solution 9–2A

The first step is to derive the cash flows for each period. At time zero two sets of flows are involved; the outlay of $100,000 for the new machine and the net (after-tax) inflow due to the sale of the old machine. Before the latter value can be determined, the current book value of the old machine must be computed.

| | |
|---|---|
| Initial cost | $33,000 |
| Less: accumulated depreciation | (12,000)[1] |
| Current book value | $21,000 |

If the machine is sold for $25,000, there will be a gain of $4,000 as shown below:

| | |
|---|---|
| Selling price | $25,000 |
| Less: Book value | 21,000 |
| Gain | $4,000 |

This amount is taxed at the ordinary tax rate.[2]

[1] Computed as follows: ($33,000 − $1,000) ÷ 8 years × 3.

[2] If the selling price is greater than the original cost of the asset, then part of the gain is taxed at a special rate. Specifically, the difference between selling price and original cost is taxed at a lower rate and the remainder of the gain, often referred to as depreciation recapture, is taxed at the regular tax rate.

| *Gain* | | *Tax Rate* | | *Tax Due* |
|---|---|---|---|---|
| $4,000 | × | 46% | = | $1,840 |

Putting this altogether, the net outlay at time zero is $76,840, assuming taxes on the sale are paid at time zero ($100,000 less $25,000 plus taxes of $1,840).

The annual incremental net working capital from operations can be derived as follows:

| *Item* | *Amount* | | *Tax Adjustment* | | *Effect on NWC from Operations* |
|---|---|---|---|---|---|
| Cash savings | $30,000 | × | (1 − .46) | = | $16,200 |
| New deprecia-tion | 20,000 | × | (.46) | = | 9,200 |
| Old depreciation | (4,000) | × | (.46) | = | (1,840) |
| | | | | | $23,560 |

The only other relevant cash flow is the loss of the $1,000 salvage value on the existing equipment. This is an incremental cash outflow because the firm would lose an inflow of $1,000 five years from now if the existing machine is sold today.

Table 9-6 has a worksheet summarizing the cash flow and the NPV computation. The NPV is positive, indicating that the replacement should be made. Given the expected costs and savings, the investment would cause the value of the firm to increase.

Some of you may need additional practice in computing the internal rate of return. If so, try it for the above investment.

Answer: The internal rate of return is 15.9%.

**Table 9-6**  *Worksheet for Capital Budgeting: Analysis of Mateel's Replacement*

| End of Year | Fixed Assets | NWC From Operations | NWC | Cash Flow | (PVA$1,PV$1,15%,n) | Present Value |
|---|---|---|---|---|---|---|
| 0 | ($76,840) + | | | = ($76,840) × | 1.0000 | = ($76,840) |
| 1 | | + $23,560 | | = 23,560 | | |
| 2 | | + 23,560 | | = 23,560 × | 2.8550 | = |
| 3 | | + 23,560 | | = 23,560 | | |
| 4 | | + 23,560 | | = 23,560 | | |
| 5 | (1,000) + | 23,560 | | = 22,560 × | .4972 | = 11,217 |
| | | | | | NPV @ 15% = | $ 1,641 |

# B. Discussion Questions

### Problem 9–1B

Explain why an investment's net present value is an estimate of how much the value of the firm will increase because of the investment.

### Problem 9–2B

Is it fair to say that the internal rate of return is the average rate of return adjusted for the time value of money?

### Problem 9–3B

Why should interest expense be excluded in computing an investment's relevant cash flows?

### Problem 9–4B

In the second shortcut procedure for computing incremental operating cash flows, why do we multiply certain items like labor savings by one minus the tax rate and multiply other items such as depreciation by the tax rate?

### Problem 9–5B

In the first shortcut procedure for computing incremental operating cash flows, we add depreciation expense in deriving NWC from operations but in the second we add depreciation times the tax rate. Why is there this difference in the two procedures?

### Problem 9–6B

Should straight line or an accelerated method of depreciation give a higher NPV, all other things being equal? Explain.

# C. Study Problems

### Problem 9–1C

The following cash flows are expected from a new investment:

| End of Year | Cash Flow |
|:-----------:|:---------:|
| 0 | ($150,000) |
| 1–10 | $ 35,778 |

1. Compute the IRR on the investment.

2. Compute this investment's NPV and PI using a discount rate of 18%.

3. Calculate the payback period of this investment.

### Problem 9–2C

A new project is under consideration which would require a cash outlay of $250,000 at time zero. The following cash inflows are expected over the project's three-year life.

| End of Year | Cash Flow |
|:-----------:|:---------:|
| 1 | $150,000 |
| 2 | 100,000 |
| 3 | 90,000 |

For investments in this risk class, a required rate of 18% is required.

1. Compute this project's NPV, PI and IRR.

2. What decision is implied by each of these methods?

3. Would your decision change if the required rate return is changed to 20%? Why or why not?

### Problem 9–3C

You are given the following cash flows for an investment:

| End of Year | Cash Flow |
|:-----------:|:---------:|
| 0 | ($80,000) |
| 1 | 40,000 |
| 2 | 40,000 |
| 3 | (10,000) |
| 4 | 40,000 |

The required rate of return for investments of this type is 14%.

1. Compute the NPV and PI of this investment.

2. If this firm has a payback rule to accept only projects with a payback period of three years or less, should this project be accepted or rejected? Why?

### Problem 9–4C

The following cash flows are expected from an investment:

| End of Year | Cash Flow |
|:-----------:|:---------:|
| 0 | ($18,000) |
| 1 | (5,000) |
| 2 | 10,000 |
| 3 | 10,000 |
| 4 | 10,000 |

The required rate of return is 8%.

1. Compute the NPV.

2. Compute the IRR.

3. Should the project be accepted?

### Problem 9–5C

An investment with one initial cash outflow at time zero promises the following cash inflows:

| End of Year | Cash Flow |
|:-----------:|:---------:|
| 1 | $37,000 |
| 2 | 42,000 |
| 3 | 48,000 |
| 4 | 35,000 |

The internal rate of return on this investment has been computed to be 16% and the firm's required rate of return on the investment is 12%.

1. What is the initial cash outflow associated with this investment?

2. Compute the NPV of this investment.

3. Compute the payback period of this investment.

### Problem 9–6C

The Dansel Company is considering a new machine which costs $80,000, including installation costs. It would be depreciated on a straight-line basis over a four-year life to a $20,000 salvage value. This investment will not cause Dansel's NWC to change. It is expected to increase the firm's net income after taxes by the following amounts, which include depreciation expense but not interest expense. (You may ignore the ITC.)

| Year | Net Income After Taxes |
|------|------------------------|
| 1    | $15,000                |
| 2    | 10,000                 |
| 3    | 10,000                 |
| 4    | 5,000                  |

1. Compute the Average Rate of Return for this investment.

2. Derive the incremental operating cash flows for this investment.

3. Compute the investment's IRR.

4. The required rate of return for this investment is 19%. Should it be accepted?

### Problem 9–7C

Lavalle Publishers wants to replace its old printer with a newer model. The new printer would cost $300,000, including installation costs, and would be depreciated on a straight-line basis over its ten-year life to a zero salvage value. The new printer would save cash operating costs of $60,000 per year for ten years. The old printer was purchased ten years ago and is being depreciated on a straight-line basis over a 20-year life to a zero salvage value. It could be sold now for $100,000, which is $50,000 less than its book value. The replacement would not affect the level of NWC needed to support operations. The firm's marginal tax rate is 46% and its required rate of return for investments like this one is 16%. (You may ignore the ITC.)

1. Compute the NPV, IRR, PI and payback period for this replacement.

2. What would you recommend to Lavalle?

### Problem 9–8C

The Filtrex Company must purchase a new water filtration system. Its old system has a book value of zero but could be sold for $5,000. Two alternatives are being considered. The first costs $180,000, including installation costs, and is expected to have cash operating costs of $40,000 per year. The second costs $270,000 but is expected to have cash operating costs of only $20,000 per year. Both machines have a six-year life and would be depreciated on a straight-line basis to a zero salvage value. Each system would require the same level of NWC to operate as the existing system. Filtrex's marginal tax rate is 45% and the required rate for this type of investment is 12%. (You may ignore the ITC.)

1. Relying on the NPV method, recommend which alternative should be selected.

### Problem 9–9C

Because of previously unexpected high demand for its natural peanut butter, Captain Carrot's Health Foods is considering replacing its old manually-operated peanut butter maker with a new automated model. The old machine was purchased five years ago for $20,000 and has been depreciated on a straight-line basis over a ten-year life to a zero salvage value. This machine could be sold today for $8,000. The new machine costs $50,000, including installation, and it would be depreciated on a straight-line basis over a five-year life to a zero salvage value. This machine would reduce labor costs by $18,000 per year and would not affect the level of NWC needed to support operations. Captain Carrot's marginal tax rate is 40% and its required rate of return for this replacement proposal is 15%. (You may ignore the ITC.)

1. Evaluate this replacement decision using the NPV method and prepare a recommendation to Captain Carrot.

### Problem 9–10C

The HKB Company could increase its sales of widgits if it had the capacity to increase production volume. It has identified one machine which is creating a bottleneck. If that machine is replaced with a larger model, total production of widgits could increase. The existing machine was purchased four years ago at a cost of $200,000 and is being depreciated on a straight-line basis over a ten-year life to a $20,000 salvage value. It could be sold today for $100,000. The model being considered as a replacement costs $350,000, including installation, and would be depreciated on a straight-line basis over a six-year life to a $50,000 salvage value.

If the new model is purchased, HKB would borrow $250,000, at 14% per year compounded annually, with interest payments due annually at the end of each for six years and the total principal repaid six years from the date of the loan. The new model would increase sales volume and this would cause inventory, accounts receivable and accounts payable to increase. Specifically, there would be an immediate increase in inventory of $25,000, and increases of $5,000 in receivables and $10,000 in payables one year from now. There would be no further changes in these accounts until the end of the project's life when they would each decrease by the same amount at which they increased at times zero and the end of Year 1.

It is estimated that earnings before depreciation and taxes (that is, sales minus all expenses including interest on the loan described above except for depreciation and taxes) would be $80,000 higher each year for each of the next six years. HKB's marginal tax rate is 46% and its required rate for this project is 16%. (You may ignore the ITC.)

1. Compute the NPV and IRR for this investment proposal.

2. What would you recommend based on your analysis?

### Problem 9–11C

The management of Archer, Inc. is contemplating investing in a new product. Initial cash outlays at time zero are: $1.98 million for plant and equipment, $100,000 for land, and $400,000 for NWC. The life of the project is 15 years and there would be no further outlays for fixed assets and no further changes in NWC until the termination date, even though, as explained below, there are two separate phases for the project. Plant and equipment will be depreciated on a straight-line basis over a 15-year life to a zero salvage value, the land has an estimated market value of $100,000 at the end of 15 years, and all NWC will be freed up at the end of the project's life.

Archer projects two phases in the product's life: Phase I will last for five years and Phase II will last for ten years. Forecasted income statements for each phase are as follows:

| | Forecasted Income Statement ($000) | |
| --- | --- | --- |
| | *Phase I* Years 1–5 | *Phase II* Years 6–15 |
| Net sales | $1,200 | $2,000 |
| Cost of goods sold | 800 | 1,300 |
| Gross profit | $ 400 | $ 700 |
| Operating expenses | 175 | 300 |
| Earnings before interest & taxes | $ 225 | $ 400 |
| Interest | 0 | 0 |
| Earnings before taxes | $ 225 | $ 400 |
| Income taxes @ 40% | 90 | 160 |
| Net income | $ 135 | $ 240 |

Depreciation expense on the new plant and equipment is included in the above expenses.

Archer's required rate of return on this investment is 12%. (You may ignore the ITC.)

1. Compute the NPV for this investment.

2. Based on NPV should the project be accepted?

### Problem 9–12C

Cyberton, Inc. has idle plant, equipment, and property as a result of a closed division. The land has a market value of $50,000, which is equal to its original cost. The plant and equipment are all fully depreciated, but could be sold today for $200,000.

The management of Cyberton is faced with two alternatives: (1) sell the surplus property or (2) re-equip the plant to begin production of a new product. Re-equipment costs would be $360,000, which would be depreciated on an ACRS basis. This means that one-half of the ITC would be deducted from the initial cost with the remainder being depreciated over five years according to the following schedule:

| Year | ACRS Percents |
|:----:|:-------------:|
| 1 | 15% |
| 2 | 22% |
| 3 | 21% |
| 4 | 21% |
| 5 | 21% |

The new product is expected to generate earnings before interest, depreciation and taxes of $325,000 per year for ten years. Net working capital needs will increase by $400,000 at time zero in order to support this project, but this entire amount will be freed up at the end of ten years. In addition, it is expected that the land could be sold for $50,000 at the end of ten years.

Cyberton's marginal tax rate is 46% and its required rate of return for this re-equipment proposal is 18%.

1. Use the NPV method to evaluate this proposal.

2. Based on your analysis what recommendation would you make to Cyberton regarding the sale of the surplus property versus re-equipment for the new product?

### Problem 9–13C

Management of Sallspace, Inc., is trying to decide whether to replace one of its existing machines and if so, which of two competing models, A or B, should be selected? The existing machine has been depreciated down to its (originally estimated) salvage value of $10,000, but it could be sold today for only $5,000. Although the machine has been depreciated to its salvage value, it would last five more years. Because it is now estimated that it could be sold for $2,000 five years from now, annual depreciation on this machine would be $1,600.

Model A costs $100,000, including installation costs, and would be depreciated on a straight-line basis over its five year life to a $10,000 salvage value. This model would reduce cash operating costs (relative to the existing machine) by $60,000 per year for each year except Year 3 when the reduction would be $55,000. Inventory needs are expected to increase by $4,000 immediately due to this new model, but accounts payable will rise by $2,500 at the same time. These are the only changes in NWC expected because of Model A until the end of its life when inventory and accounts payable will decrease by $4,000 and $2,500, respectively.

Model B costs $230,000, including installation costs, and would be depreciated on a straight-line basis over its five-year life to a $10,000 salvage value. Cash operating costs are expected to decline (relative to the existing machine) by $90,000 per year for all five years. If the model is accepted, the firm's NWC would decrease by $10,000 at time zero and there would be no further changes until the end of the model's life when NWC needed to support operations would increase by $10,000.

The firm's marginal tax rate is 40% and its required rate of return for this type of replacement is 15%. (You may ignore the ITC.)

1. Use the NPV method to determine if replacement is desireable.

2. If replacement is desirable, which model should be selected?

### Problem 9–14C

The Sultan Company is considering two alternatives for replacing an existing machine and is also considering introducing a new product. This problem requires that you evaluate each of these investment decisions. The firm's marginal income tax rate is 54% and you may ignore the ITC.

*Replacement.* The firm is using a machine that has cash operations costs of $150,000 per year. It was purchased five years ago for $100,000 and is being depreciated on a straight-line basis over a ten-year life to a zero salvage value. The machine requires a major overhaul that is so costly management has decided to replace the machine. Because of the major work required, it has a zero sale value; in fact, management estimates it will cost $1,000 to get rid of it.

Two replacement options are being considered. The first costs $200,000, including installation, and will require cash operating costs of $150,000 per year. The second costs $250,000, including installation, and will require cash operating costs of $135,000 per year. Both machines will be depreciated on a straight-line basis over a five-year life to a zero salvage value. Finally, NWC needed to support operations will not be affected by this decision and the required rate for this type of investment is 12%.

*New Product.* The new product will have a five-year life and sales, and EBIT (earnings before interest and taxes) generated by the new product are expected to be the following:

| End of Year | Net Sales | EBIT |
|---|---|---|
| 1 | $1.0 million | $ 70,000 |
| 2 | 1.5 million | 150,000 |
| 3 | 2.0 million | 200,000 |
| 4 | 2.0 million | 200,000 |
| 5 | .5 million | 100,000 |

Below are estimates of net working capital for the firm with and without the investment. (The firm's only current liabilities are accounts payable and accrued expenses.)

| End of Year | Total NWC of Firm Without Product | Total NWC of Firm With Product |
|---|---|---|
| 0 | $10.0 million | $10.1  million |
| 1 | 10.5 million | 10.65 million |
| 2 | 11.0 million | 11.2  million |
| 3 | 13.0 million | 13.2  million |
| 4 | 13.5 million | 13.55 million |
| 5 | 14.5 million | 14.5  million |

Equipment costing $400,000 would be purchased at time zero to produce the product. Depreciation on this equipment would be:

| End of Year | Depreciation Expense |
|:---:|:---:|
| 1 | $ 60,000 |
| 2 | 88,000 |
| 3 | 84,000 |
| 4 | 84,000 |
| 5 | 84,000 |
| Total | $400,000 |

Although the full $400,000 could be depreciated for tax purposes, management estimates the equipment could be sold for $20,000 five years from now. Finally, as you know, depreciation expense is deducted from revenue in computing EBIT. In other words, these depreciation amounts were deducted from the sales estimates in deriving the EBIT estimates shown above.

The firm estimates that 16% is an appropriate required rate of return to evaluate this investment.

Use the NPV method to make a recommendation on the replacement and new product.

# 10
# Capital Budgeting II

This chapter continues our treatment of capital budgeting by discussing a number of issues that were only mentioned or not discussed at all in the previous chapter. In the first part of the chapter a number of technical matters are addressed. These include multiple internal rates of return, contradictory rankings, capital rationing, unequal lives, replacement cycles, inflation and abandonment. The purpose of this discussion is to enhance your understanding of the topics covered in the last chapter and to help you deal with complexities that can and do arise in applying capital budgeting techniques in practice. The second part of the chapter discusses various methods of incorporating risk in capital budgeting analysis.

## MULTIPLE INTERNAL RATES OF RETURN

Let's assume you have the opportunity to deposit or withdraw money from a savings account at any time during the next two years and that the account pays interest of 10% per year compounded annually. Assume further that you have $5,000 which you are contemplating putting into that savings account for two years. If you do, it would grow to $6,050 in two years. Now suppose you are offered the following riskless investment.

| End of Year | Cash Flow |
|:---:|:---:|
| 0 | ($5,000) |
| 1 | 14,773 |
| 2 | (10,000) |

Which of the two alternatives is a better investment for you?

One's initial reaction might be to forget about the second alternative because it involves more cash outflows than inflows. If this was your reaction, you made the error of ignoring the time value of money. As it turns out, the second alternative is better than the first. Looking more closely at the second alternative, one year from now it will give you $14,773 which can be invested at 10%. Hence, this amount would grow to $16,250 by the end of Year 2. After the cash outflow of $10,000 at the end of the second year, you would be left with $6,250. If, instead of accepting this alternative, you put the $5,000 in the savings account at time zero, you would have $6,050 in two years which is $200 less than this investment provides. Looking at this point in a conceptual context, both investments have the same risk (i. e., they are riskless) and the second promises a greater return; hence, the second alternative dominates the first.

If we wanted to evaluate the second alternative using the Internal Rate of Return (IRR) method, we would get 5% for the IRR. This is less than the required rate indicating rejection, but we just saw that it is better than a 10% investment. As it turns out, this investment has two internal rates of return: 5% and 90%. That is, at a rate of 5% the present value of the inflows equals the present value of the outflows. This is also true for 90%. Nonconventional investments (defined below) like this one can have two or more internal rates of return. The number of internal rates of return is not important for our purposes. What is important is that we must interpret the internal rate of return in a fundamentally different way when there is more than one IRR.

A nonconventional investment is one where there is more than one switch from net cash outflows to net cash inflows or vice versa. Think of a net cash outflow as a negative number and a net cash inflow as a positive number. In practice, we frequently encounter the following types of cash flow patterns.

| Time | Cash Flow |
|:----:|:---------:|
| 0 | − − |
| 1 | + − |
| 2 | + + |
| 3 | + + |
| 4 | + + |

That is, there is one or more net outflows followed only by net cash inflows, which means there is only one change in sign from negative to positive. This is called a conventional investment and for this type there can be only one IRR. Sometimes, we encounter the following kind of cash flow streams.

| Time | Cash Flow |
|------|-----------|
| 0 | − − − |
| 1 | + − + |
| 2 | + + + |
| 3 | + + − |
| 4 | − − + |

Here we have net outflows followed by net inflows and then more net outflows. That is, there is more than one change in sign. This type is called a nonconventional investment, and nonconventional investments can have more than one IRR.

The NPV Discount Rate Graph in Figure 10-1 will help us explain the interpretation of multiple internal rates of return. The curve was drawn by plotting a series of points with each point being an NPV computed at a specific rate. In other words, we selected a range of rates from 0% to 100% and computed an NPV for each rate. We then plotted the NPV numbers. For instance, at 5%, the NPV is zero which means that point is on the horizontal axis as shown. The graph shows that the curve cuts the horizontal axis at two places, 5% and 90%. Notice that at any point between 5% and 90%, the NPV is positive, meaning a good investment. At any other rate NPV is negative. Hence, we interpret the dual rates in this example as follows: For any required rate of return between 5% and 90%, this investment should be accepted because it would increase value, otherwise it should be rejected.

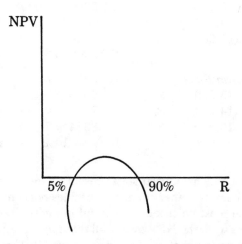

**Figure 10-1  NPV Discount Rate Graph**

There is nothing fundamentally wrong with multiple rates of return as long as one is careful in interpreting them. Keep in mind that the interpretation depends on the shape of the curve on an NPV Discount Rate Graph. For instance, say the cash flows in our investment were as follows:

| End of Year | Cash Flow |
|---|---|
| 0 | $ 5,000 |
| 1 | (14,773) |
| 2 | 10,000 |

This investment has the same two IRRs (5% and 90%) only now we interpret them as follows: At any required rate between 5% and 90% this investment should be rejected because it would decrease value; at required rates less than 5% or more than 90% it should be accepted because it would increase value. (If you were to plot the second investment, you would see that the curve is the flip side of the one shown.)

When there are more than two internal rates of return for a nonconventional investment it gets even more complex. We can still rely on the IRR method but we think it's much simpler to use the NPV. Below is the NPV at 10% for the two versions of the nonconventional investment in our example.

| End of Year | Cash Flow | | (PV$1, 10%, n) | | Present Value |
|---|---|---|---|---|---|
| 0 | ($5,000) | × | 1.0000 | = | ($5,000) |
| 1 | 14,773 | × | .9091 | = | 13,430 |
| 2 | (10,000) | × | .8264 | = | (8,264) |
| | | | NPV @ 10% | = | $166 |

| End of Year | Cash Flow | | (PV$1, 10%, n) | | Present Value |
|---|---|---|---|---|---|
| 0 | $5,000 | × | 1.0000 | = | $5,000 |
| 1 | (14,773) | × | .9091 | = | (13,430) |
| 2 | 10,000 | × | .8264 | = | 8,264 |
| | | | NPV @ 10% | = | ($166) |

Note that nonconventional investments present no special problems for the NPV method. There are other situations, besides nonconventional investments, where one must be especially careful in interpreting the IRR, and for these others as well, the NPV avoids all these interpretation difficulties. Hence, it is not merely a matter of saying that the NPV method is superior theoretically to the IRR; it is also much easier to use in practice. Now we realize that the IRR is used widely in practice and that its popularity likely will continue. We suggest that if you work in an environment where it is not feasible to discard the IRR, that you also compute the NPV when analyzing capital investments.


## CONTRADICTORY RANKINGS

In the previous chapter we saw that the NPV, PI and IRR all give the same information regarding whether or not an investment increases or decreases value. Thus, if this is all we want to know, it does not matter which technique we use. However, sometimes we need more than a simple accept/reject signal for an investment. When we do, the choice of a technique can matter. In this section, we look at one such situation: contradictory ranking that can arise when evaluating mutually exclusive investment alternatives. We begin by defining mutually exclusive alternatives and contradictory rankings.

*Mutually exclusive investment alternatives* are those where accepting one precludes the possibility of accepting others. Suppose you own a vacant piece of land and are considering the following three options: (1) construct an office building, (2) build an apartment complex and (3) construct a manufacturing facility. Obviously, you cannot select all three and you must choose one. Hence, they are mutually exclusive investment alternatives. Now, say you evaluate them using the NPV and IRR. The IRR may say that the apartment complex is best and the NPV may say that the office building is best. This is what we mean by *contradictory rankings*.

We will rely on an example to illustrate the problem more clearly and to show how to deal with it. The example will involve the NPV and IRR, but keep in mind that we can also obtain contradictory rankings between PI and NPV and between PI and IRR. Also keep in mind that contradictory rankings will not always arise when choosing among mutually exclusive alternatives.

Suppose we are evaluating the following two mutually exclusive alternatives and the required rate for each is 8%.

| End of Year | Investment A | Investment B |
|:---:|:---:|:---:|
| 0 | ($29,645) | ($90,000) |
| 1 | 17,772 | 52,555 |
| 2 | 17,772 | 52,555 |
| NPV @ 8% | 2,048 | 3,721 |
| IRR | 13% | 11% |

The IRR is indicating that Investment A is better than Investment B, and the NPV is saying that B is better than A. Note that both investments increase value, so if we could accept both we would. However, we can only take one and so we must select the better alternative.

We should first explain why we are getting contradictory rankings. This result is possible when investments have differing cash flow patterns. This means two (or more) investments are of different size as is the case in our example, or they require the same initial outlay but differ with respect to the amount and timing of subsequent cash flows. Figure 10-2 has an NPV Discount Rate Graph for the two investments in our example. Each curve was derived by plotting several points. For example, Investment B has an NPV of $15,110 at a rate of zero percent and an NPV of zero at 11%. By computing several more NPV values for B, we were able to draw the curve shown in the figure for Investment B. We repeated this process for In-

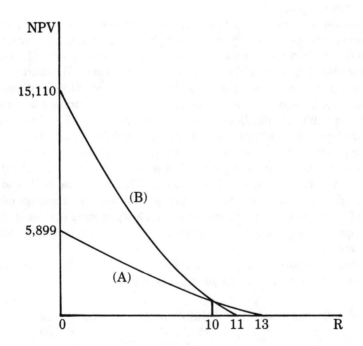

**Figure 10-2   NPV Discount Rate Graph Illustrating Contradictory Rankings for Mutually Exclusive Alternatives**

vestment A. Because of the differing cash flow patterns the two curves cross and because they cross above the horizontal axis, we are obtaining contradictory rankings.[1]

How do we resolve contradictory rankings? It depends on the circumstances. Specifically, it depends on whether or not a firm is in a position to accept all investments that are expected to increase value. If the firm can accept all value enhancing investments, then we do not have to be concerned about the contradictory rankings at all and we simply select the mutually exclusive alternative with the higher (or highest) NPV. When a firm cannot accept all projects that are expected to increase value, then further analysis is necessary. The difference between these two circumstances will become more clear as we proceed.

Some analysts use a procedure to resolve contradictory rankings that is based on the IRR method. We will explain this procedure and begin by providing an intuitive sense of its underlying logic. An example will be the vehicle for explaining this logic.[2]

Suppose you have $90,000 and decide to use this amount to provide income for your family for the next two years. You plan to put the $90,000 in one or more savings accounts at a bank and make two equal annual withdrawals starting one year from now. Most of the banks you investigate offer an interest rate of 10.5% or less depending on the nature of the account, but two, Banks A and B, are willing to offer a higher rate. Bank A is willing to accept a deposit of $29,645 and will allow you to withdraw $17,772 at the end of each of the next two years at which time there would be a zero balance in the account. Bank A is offering an interest rate of 13% per year compounded annually on this account. Now Bank A is happy to accept additional deposits as well but the interest rate on them would be much lower. Bank B is willing to give you 11% per year compounded annually, provided you deposit the entire $90,000 in the account. If you do, you will be able to withdraw $52,555 at the end of each of the next two years.

Note that the cash flows for the two bank options are the same as the cash flows for the two investment alternatives presented earlier. We can see the essence of the conflict. Bank A and Bank B are both offering attractive rates, and while Bank A is offering a higher rate, it is on a smaller amount. Which alternative should you choose? That depends on what you could earn on other alternatives. Specifically, it depends on how much you

---

[1] The curves will not always cross jabove the horizontal axis when there are differing cash flow patterns between two investments. In such a case, we would not get contradictory rankings.

[2] It should be noted that analysts who rely on this procedure to resolve contradictory rankings do so whenever they arise and not only when a firm cannot accept all value enhancing investments. We will see the implications of this later.

could earn on the remaining $60,355 should you deposit $29,645 with Bank A. To figure out what the interest rate must be on other alternatives to make Bank A better than Bank B we can rely on the following procedure: Compute the difference in the cash flows between the two alternatives and calculate the IRR on the differential. This is shown below:

| End of Year | Difference (Bank B - Bank A) |
|:-----------:|:----------------------------:|
| 0 | ($60,355) |
| 1 | 34,783 |
| 2 | 34,783 |
| IRR | 10% |

Notice this difference plus Bank A's cash flows equals Bank B's cash flows.

| End of Year | Difference | | Bank A | | Bank B |
|:-----------:|:----------:|:---:|:----------:|:---:|:----------:|
| 0 | ($60,355) | + | ($29,645) | = | ($90,000) |
| 1 | 34,783 | + | 17,772 | = | 52,555 |
| 2 | 34,783 | + | 17,772 | = | 52,555 |

If you select Bank A and can earn more than $34,783 per year on the remaining $60,355, this would be better than Bank B's offer. On the other hand, if you earn less than $34,783 per year on the difference of $60,355, you would be better off with Bank B's offer. And you would be indifferent if you could earn just $34,783 per year on the remaining $60,355.

Say another bank offers you $34,783 for two years on a deposit of $60,355. This is an interest rate of 10%, the rate that makes you indifferent between Bank A's and Bank B's offer. If you could earn an interest rate higher than 10% you would be better off accepting Bank A's offer and Bank B's offer would be better at a lower interest rate.

Some analysts resolve contradictory rankings by the procedure we just described. The two investments in the example presented earlier in this section have the same cash flows as Bank A and Bank B offer. Therefore, an analyst comparing those two mutually exclusive investments would conclude that Investment A should be chosen if more than 10% could be earned on other opportunities and Investment B should be recommended if less than 10% could be earned. To compute this indifference IRR, analysts would compute the IRR on the differential just like we did or they would construct an NPV Discount Rate Graph. The place where the two curves cross is the indifference rate. Figure 10-2 shows that the intersection point is 10% for the two mutually exclusive options in our example. Notice in Figure 10-2, that Investment B has a higher NPV than Investment A at required rates less than 10% and a lower NPV at higher rates.[3]

Assume the firm in our example uncovers an investment opportunity, Investment C, which requires an initial outlay of $60,355, has a required rate of 8%, and promises the following cash flows:

| End of Year | Investment C |
|:---:|:---:|
| 0 | ($60,355) |
| 1 | 35,711 |
| 2 | 35,711 |

Finally, assume that this is the only other investment opportunity available. The IRR on this investment is 12%. Hence, according to the IRR procedure, the firm should choose Investment A rather than Investment B because it can earn more than 10% on the remaining funds. This conclusion is incorrect unless the firm cannot raise more than $90,000. If capital is not limited, the firm should choose Investment B and Investment C.

In the example where you were choosing between two banks, we made an important but subtle assumption to justify the analysis we performed. Specifically, we assumed you had only $90,000 to invest.[4] Many firms do not face such capital constraints and if we assume the firm in our example does not, then Investment B should be chosen along with this other option. To see why, let's summarize the NPV for each of the investments and the total NPV for the two combinations available.

| Investment | NPV |
|:---:|:---:|
| A | $2,048 |
| B | 3,721 |
| C | 3,327 |

| Possible Combinations | Total NPV |
|:---:|:---:|
| A and C | $5,375 |
| B and C | 7,048 |

The second combination is better because it has a higher NPV. Recall that NPV is a measure of how much the value of the firm will increase and the

---

[3] When contradictory rankings arise due to cash flow patterns that are the result of differences in size like our example, it does not matter how you compute the breakeven rate. For other differing cash flow patterns—say, two investments requiring the same initial outlay but differing with respect to the amount and time of inflows—it usually will be easier to work with an NPV Discount Rate Graph.

[4] We also assumed that all alternatives had the same risk (i. e., riskless) which is another crucial assumption to justify the analysis.

firm in our example would increase the value of the firm more by selecting Investments B and C. Of course, this means investing more money but it should be done because it's profitable.

Now many firms often have a limit on the size of their capital budgets. Say the firm in our example only had $90,000 to invest just like you did. Then it should choose Investment A and Investment C, the answer obtained from the IRR procedure described above. However, the reason we got the correct answer is because the NPV of A plus C is $5,375, and this is higher than the $3,721 NPV of Investment B. In other words, if the firm had only $90,000 to invest it would be facing the following combinations:

| Possible Combinations | Total NPV |
|---|---|
| A + C | $5,375 |
| B | 3,721 |

It should select the first combination because that one would increase the value of the firm more.

The point is that the IRR procedure described earlier will be reliable only when capital is limited and the required rate of return is the same for all capital investment alternatives. To see this, let's retain the assumption that the required rate of Investments A and B is still 8%, but Investment C is riskier and has a required rate of 11%. Investment C still would have an IRR of 12%, which is above the breakeven rate on the differential cash flows between Investments B and A. However, its NPV would be $801. Hence, if the firm had only $90,000 to invest, it would choose between the following combinations.

| Possible Combinations | Total NPV |
|---|---|
| A + C | $2,849 |
| B | 3,721 |

The better choice is Investment B because it has a higher NPV and thus would increase value more.

The upshot of the above discussion is that the popular IRR procedure is reliable only when the required rate is the same for all capital investments and capital is limited. Here is a simpler procedure, that will work whether or not the required rate is the same for all investment. It involves two guidelines.

1. When the size of the capital budget is not limited pick the mutually exclusive alternative that has the higher (or highest) NPV.

2. When the capital budget is limited, select that combination of investments that has the highest NPV. (Limitations on the size of the capital budget is frequently known as capital rationing. We will discuss this topic in the next section.)

One final point before we conclude this section. Earlier we mentioned that some analysts use the IRR procedure to resolve all contradictory rankings even when capital is not limited. Given that the required rate is the same for all investments, this procedure can be used as a reliable guide for choosing among mutually exclusive alternatives even when capital is not limited. However, it will always give the same answer as one obtains by simply picking the mutually exclusive alternative with the higher (or highest) NPV. In other words, to apply this procedure in such circumstances is to perform an unnecessary analysis.

## CAPITAL RATIONING

Here we show how to select investments when the size of a firm's capital *budget is* limited. Say a firm has five independent[5] investments available and each has a positive NPV. It should take all five. The reason is that since NPV is a measure of how much the value of the firm is expected to increase because of an investment, accepting all five would increase the value of the firm most. In practice we frequently encounter situations where firms are unable to accept all investments with a positive NPV. There are two basic reasons for this: First, the firm faces capital rationing, which means it simply cannot raise money. Second, top management sets a limit on how much will be expended on capital investments in a particular year. (In the context of capital budgeting both of these reasons are referred to as capital rationing but strictly speaking, capital rationing refers only to the inability to raise money.)

Whether artificial limits[6] should be set by top management, and the size of these artificial limits, are interesting and important issues. Some argue that executives are reducing value creation opportunities by not accepting all positive NPV investments. Others argue that it is the positive NPVs that are artifical, so limiting the size of the capital budget is top management's way of forcing middle managers not to be too optimistic in predicting

---

[5] Independent means the firm can take all of them. In the last section we described mutually exclusive investments. Mutually exclusive investment alternatives are those where selecting one alternative precludes the possibility of choosing the others.

[6] Artificial means the limit is not market driven, that is, the firm could raise the capital if it chose to do so.

cash flows and motivating them to set priorities. Another important and interesting issue is the extent to which firms are unable to raise capital to fund capital investments with a positive NPV. One would not expect this to be a serious problem, given well-functioning financial markets. It is beyond our scope to delve into these issues. For our purposes, it is sufficient to note that the size of capital budgets are limited in practice so we need to discuss the implications of this for applying capital budgeting techniques.

When the size of the capital budget is limited, the firm should select the combination of capital investments that gives the highest NPV. Let's assume a firm has the following independent investment opportunities:

| Project | | Investment Amount | NPV |
|---------|---|-------------------|-----|
| A | | $100,000 | $25,000 |
| B | | 60,000 | 40,000 |
| C | | 130,000 | 60,000 |
| D | | 200,000 | 110,000 |
| | Total | $490,000 | $235,000 |

Assume further that only $300,000 is available. What we do is examine each combination that meets the constraint and pick the one that has the highest NPV. Each individual project should be treated as a combination because the alternative is available to select only one. We will not list these because a glance at the opportunities indicates that some combination of two will dominate the option of taking one.

| Combinations | Projects | Investment Amount | Total NPV |
|--------------|----------|-------------------|-----------|
| 1 | A, B | $160,000 | $ 65,000 |
| 2 | A, C | 230,000 | 85,000 |
| 3 | A, D | 300,000 | 135,000 |
| 4 | A, B, C | 290,000 | 125,000 |
| 5 | B, C | 190,000 | 100,000 |
| 6 | B, D | 260,000 | 150,000 |

The firm should select the sixth combination because this one has the highest NPV and hence would increase the value of the firm the most.

Notice that the ideal combination involves investing $260,000 instead of the full $300,000 available. The extra $40,000, and in fact the remaining amounts for each combination except the third, should be viewed as having an NPV of zero. The reason is that it is reasonable to assume management would take action with the unused portion that would be equivalent to investing it at an NPV of zero.

As you know, large firms normally invest more than $300,000 annually and evaluate more than four investments each year. Further, there is the added complexity of considering future opportunities and constraints. Thus, usually there will be many more than six combinations to consider as was the case in the above example. Complex quantitative models are available that can help one choose the combination with the highest NPV. An example is linear programming.

Other procedures besides the one described above are used in practice to select the ideal combination when capital is limited. We will not delve into these procedures and will merely note that these other methods will be reliable only if they give the same answer as the NPV procedure we have discussed.

## UNEQUAL LIVES

Earlier in the chapter we explained how to choose among mutually exclusive investment alternatives. (Mutually exclusive means that by accepting one alternative we preclude the others.) We showed that in the absence of capital limits, we simply pick the alternative with the higher (or highest) NPV. An additional complexity arises when these alternatives have unequal lives, which means that further analysis is required. Here we show how to deal with the "unequal lives" problem.

To see how we avoided the issue thus far think back to the last chapter where we relied on several examples involving the possible replacement of existing equipment with new equipment. Every example involved the purchase of a new machine that had a useful life equal to the remaining useful life of the existing equipment. Frequently there are several replacement alternatives available and if these and the existing equipment all do not have the same life, then a more detailed analysis is needed than what was explained in the last chapter. We will rely on an example to show the additional analysis that is required.

A firm which accepts all investments with a positive NPV[7] is considering replacing a piece of equipment with a more efficient model. Two options are available, which we will call Model X and Model Y, that have the same required rate of 10% and promise a positive NPV at this rate as shown below:

---

[7] We assume this only to avoid the complexity that may arise when capital is limited.

| End of Year | Model X | End of Year | Model Y |
|:---:|:---:|:---:|:---:|
| 0 | ($50,000) | 0 | ($90,000) |
| 1–4 | 17,500 | 1–8 | 18,500 |
| NPV @ 10% | 5,473 | NPV @ 10% | 8,696 |

Because they are mutually exclusive alternatives with unequal lives we cannot simply pick the one with the higher NPV. (Note that the fact that they are mutually exclusive is the reason why we need more analysis. In other words, if these were independent investments we would take both of them and not worry about unequal lives.) The reason we can't pick the higher NPV is that Model X, if selected, would have to be replaced four years from now and its replacement might also have a positive NPV compared to the existing machine. Thus, a proper evaluation between Models X and Y involves an analysis of cash flows over the same time period.

Various methods are used in practice to deal with this complexity. One is to assume that the alternative with the longer life is sold at the end of the life of the one with the shorter life. In this example, assuming that Model Y would be sold four years from now, we estimate the terminal value, which includes an estimate of the market value of the equipment at that time net of any taxes plus the free up of any working capital, and calculate the NPV for Model Y over a four-year life. We then compare this revised NPV to Model X's NPV and pick the alternative with the higher NPV. This method is perhaps most appropriate when each of the mutually exclusive alternatives has a relatively long life, say, ten years or more.

When one of the alternatives has a relatively short life, like Model X in this example, it probably is better to estimate cash flows, assuming one or more replacements until a common time horizon is reached. For example, we could assume Model X is replaced once, which allows us to compare cash flows for each over eight years. As you know, a firm often does not know what kind of replacement would be sought in four years. For the purpose of this kind of analysis frequently it makes most sense to assume that Model X would be replaced with a similar machine four years from now. To illustrate, let's assume that Model X could be replaced for $50,000 four years from now and that it would continue to generate annual inflows of $17,500. The cash flows for Model X over an eight-year period would be:

| End of Year | Model X |
|:---:|:---:|
| 0 | ($50,000) |
| 1–3 | 17,500 |
| 4 | (32,500) [50,000 − 17,500] |
| 5–8 | 17,500 |
| NPV @ 10% | 9,211 |

Over a common horizon of eight years Model X has an NPV of $9,211, which is higher than Model Y's NPV of $8,696. Thus, Model X is the better choice and should be selected.

One replacement of Model X gave a common time period. Suppose Model X had a life of five years. The lowest number that is divisible by both five and eight is 40. So, theoretically, we would have to examine eight replacements of X and five replacements in Y. In this instance, most analysts would sacrifice theoretical purity in the interest of practicality and would probably assume three replacements of X and two for Y. This means we are comparing cash flows over 15 years for one alternative and 16 years for the other but usually this would not make a difference.

We mentioned theoretical purity for the benefit of those practitioners who wrestle with real world complexities on a day-to-day basis. Most people realize that theory cannot provide an exact prescription. Adjustments are needed to translate theory into practice. Learning how to do this effectively takes experience and a good deal of common sense.

## REPLACEMENT CYCLES

Sometimes we have to figure out how often an asset should be replaced. Here we illustrate how capital budgeting techniques can be used to help deal with this issue. Suppose a firm needs a van to make deliveries and that management is trying to decide whether to replace it every two or every three years. The cash outflows for the cost of the asset and cash operating costs net of taxes (including depreciation tax shields) for each replacement cycle alternative is:

| End of Year | Two-Year Cycle | Three-Year Cycle |
|:-:|:-:|:-:|
| 0 | ($12,500) | ($12,500) |
| 1 | (4,000) | (4,200) |
| 2 | (5,000) | (5,400) |
| 3 | | (6,000) |

The initial cash outlay of $12,500 is the same for each alternative. Subsequent outlays are higher for the three-year cycle because we assume more would be spent to keep the van on the road for the extra year.

Notice that both alternatives involve only cash outflows. Hence we are trying to figure out which is cheaper. Specifically, we want to select the alternative that has the lower present value of cash outflows, computed at an appropriate required rate, because this decision would lead to higher firm value. One method of doing this is to select a common time horizon for the analysis such as twelve years, estimate cash outflows for each and select an appropriate risk-adjusted rate. We then would compute the present value of each alternative and select the alternative that has the lower present value. Since we illustrated this kind of analysis in the last section, we will not show it again. However, we should note that the common-horizon approach is often most appropriate for this kind of analysis. Furthermore, we should mention that although a six-year period would be common in this example, it likely makes sense to analyze cash flows for at least twelve years.

Sometimes analysts assume for simplicity that cash outflows for each alternative will be the same for each replacement cycle. This simplifying assumption, which perhaps permits only "quick and dirty" analysis, enables one to apply a variety of simple techniques, including computing the present value for an infinite time horizon. Here we will illustrate an approach that is frequently referred to as the Equivalent Annuity Method. What this procedure involves is the conversion of the cash outlays for each cycle to an equivalent annuity and the comparison of the equivalent annuity for each replacement cycle alternative. It sounds a bit ominous but actually it is fairly simple. We will illustrate it for the above example, assuming that 12% is the appropriate risk-adjusted rate.

First we compute the present value of the outflows for one cycle for each alternative. The present value of the outflows for the two-year cycle is $20,058 as shown below.

| End of Year | Cash Flow | | (PV$1, 12%, n) | | Present Value |
|---|---|---|---|---|---|
| 0 | ($12,500) | × | 1.0000 | = | ($12,500) |
| 1 | (4,000) | × | .8929 | = | (3,572) |
| 2 | (5,000) | × | .7972 | = | (3,986) |
| | | | Total | = | ($20,058) |

For the three-year cycle the present value of the outflows for the three-year cycle is $24,826, as shown next:

| End of Year | Cash Flows | | (PV$1, 12%, n) | | Present Value |
|---|---|---|---|---|---|
| 0 | ($12,500) | × | 1.0000 | = | ($12,500) |
| 1 | (4,200) | × | .8929 | = | (3,750) |
| 2 | (5,400) | × | .7972 | = | (4,305) |
| 3 | (6,000) | × | .7118 | = | (4,271) |
| | | | Total | = | ($24,826) |

Next, we convert each of these sums to an equivalent annuity. For instance, for the two-year cycle we want to find a two-year annuity that is the same

(i. e., equivalent) in present value terms to $20,058. We do this by relying on the format for computing the present value of an annuity (just as we did to compute loan amounts and the IRR in previous chapters). Here's how we do it:

| Present Value of Annuity | | Annuity | | (PVA$1, i, n) |
|---|---|---|---|---|
| $20,058 | = | Annuity | × | (PVA$1, 12%, 2) |
| $20,058 | = | Annuity | × | 1.6901 |
| $\dfrac{\$20,058}{1.6901}$ | = | Annuity | = | $11,868 |

This two-year annuity of $11,868 is the same as the present value of $20,058 computed earlier. Putting it another way, at 12%, paying out $12,500 today, $4,000 one year from now and $5,000 two years from now, is the same as paying out $11,868 at the end of Years 1 and 2.

Using the same procedure we compute the equivalent annuity for the three-year cycle and the amount is $10,336 as shown below:

| Present Value of Annuity | | Annuity | | (PVA$1, i, n) |
|---|---|---|---|---|
| $24,826 | = | Annuity | × | (PVA$1, 12%, 3) |
| $24,826 | = | Annuity | × | 2.4018 |
| $\dfrac{\$24,826}{2.4018}$ | = | Annuity | = | $10,336 |

The next step is to compare the two equivalent annuities and select the lower one, the three-year cycle in this example. This has the lower cost and hence would lead to higher firm value. To show that this conclusion is warranted despite the fact that we analyzed only one cycle, we will extend the analysis a bit. Let's compute the present value of the two-year alternative for two cycles:

| End of Year | Cycle 1 | Cycle 2 | | Total Cash Flow | | (PV$1, 12%, n) | | Present Value |
|---|---|---|---|---|---|---|---|---|
| 0 | ($12,500) | | = | $12,500 | × | 1.0000 | = | ($12,500) |
| 1 | (4,000) | | = | 4,000 | × | .8929 | = | (3,572) |
| 2 | (5,000) + | ($12,500) | = | 17,500 | × | .7972 | = | (13,951) |
| 3 | | (4,000) | = | 4,000 | × | .7118 | = | (2,847) |
| 4 | | (5,000) | = | 5,000 | × | .6355 | = | (3,178) |
| | | | | | | | Total = | ($36,048) |

Let's convert the total present value over four years to an equivalent annuity.

| Present Value of Annuity | | Annuity | | (PVA$1, i, n) |
|---|---|---|---|---|
| $36,048 | = | Annuity | × | (PVA$1,12%,4) |
| $36,048 | = | Annuity | × | 3.0373 |
| $\dfrac{\$36,048}{3.0373}$ | = | Annuity | = | $11,868 |

The present value of outlays over four years for the two-year cycle is $36,048 and at 12% this is the same as paying out $11,868 at the end of Years 1 to 4. But this equal annual amount is what we got for examining the first cycle. We would get this amount, $11,868, regardless of how many cycles we tried, including replacement to infinity. For the three-year cycle, we would get $10,336 regardless of the number of cycles analyzed. We can conclude that the three-year cycle is the better alternative.

In capital budgeting, this equivalent annuity method is likely useful only for "quick and dirty" analyses. It certainly is a handy tool because as we showed, we only have to compute the present value for one cycle to figure out which option is cheaper. This is due to the fact that we would get the same equal annual amount no matter how many cycles we try. However, this result is due in turn to the assumption that the cash outlays will be the same for each cycle. As you know, costs likely will increase in later cycles because of inflation (discussed in the next section), so for a thorough analysis you normally would have to rely on the common-horizon approach described in the previous section. Of course, estimating cash outflows for subsequent cycles would not be an easy task in practice. Nevertheless, generally you would obtain more useful information.

## INFLATION

Inflation's impact on capital budgeting is incorporated in two ways: the risk-adjusted discount rate and cash flows. An earlier chapter discussed the selection of appropriate risk-adjusted discount rates for capital budgeting. Recall that we relied on market values to derive explicit costs of debt and equity. These market-determined rates incorporate expectations regarding inflation. For instance, you would not accept a rate of return of 8% on a bond maturing in one year if you expected inflation to be 10% for the next year. If you did you would suffer a loss of purchasing power which means a negative real return.[8]

Given that the discount rate we use to compute NPV, etc., incorporates inflation, we can easily obtain misleading signals if we do not account for inflation in estimating cash flows. That is, we could get a positive NPV when it is actually negative and vice versa. We will look at a simple example that shows how this can happen if one ignores inflation.

Suppose we use a machine that will last another five years and labor costs to operate this machine next year are $100,000. A newer model requiring an outlay at time zero of $200,000 is available. It has an estimated useful life of five years. We estimate that labor costs to operate this machine next year will be $50,000. To keep the example simple we will assume a zero tax-rate, which enables us to avoid computing after-tax labor savings and depreciation tax shields. In other words, the cash inflow from the investment next year will be $50,000, the reduction in labor savings. In this kind of situation, often it is very tempting to say for simplicity that labor savings would be $50,000 for each of the next five years. Let's assume this and also assume a required rate of 10%. Given these assumptions, the NPV for the replacement is a negative $10,461, indicating the existing machine should not be replaced. Now suppose we expect labor costs to increase by 6% per year. Let's compute the annual savings for the five years incorporating this estimate:

| End of Year | Existing Machine | | New Machine | | Savings |
|---|---|---|---|---|---|
| 1 | $100,000 | − | $50,000 | = | $50,000 |
| 2 | 106,000 | − | 53,000 | = | 53,000 |
| 3 | 112,360 | − | 56,180 | = | 56,180 |
| 4 | 119,102 | − | 59,551 | = | 59,551 |
| 5 | 126,248 | − | 63,124 | = | 63,124 |

The NPV using the cash inflows incorporating inflation is a positive $11,329, indicating that this is a good investment. Had we ignored inflation, we would have rejected a good investment.

The above example showed how failing to incorporate inflation can lead one to reject a value-enhancing investment. The opposite case is also possible, that is, we accept bad investments. Consider new products which are often priced to produce a targeted net profit margin. Analysts assume some-

---

[8] Sometimes the actual inflation rate is greater than the anticipated rate so the rate of return actually realized may be negative. However, it is expectations regarding inflation that influence interest rates. In other words, a rational person would not invest to earn a negative return (unless a decrease in the price level was expected).

times that the targeted margin will be maintained for the life of the investment. This can be quite an assumption, particularly when inflation rates
are high and vary a great deal. The real complexity, in our view, is due to
the fact that inflation can impact the price of the product or service, the
cost of labor and other costs in a variety of ways. For instance, if all the
needed fixed assets are purchased at time zero, depreciation expense will
be the same regardless of inflation, but this will not be the case if subsequent
fixed asset expenditures are required. The point is that the impact of inflation on each item affecting an investment's cash flows must be separately
estimated. This certainly is no easy task, but it must be done.

Practicing analysts hesitate to make assumptions, particularly because
they are often asked to defend them. This may be the reason why inflation
is sometimes ignored. Predicting inflation is like predicting interest rates.
It's hard enough to predict next month's interest rates, never mind rates
five or ten years from now. Hence, in estimating future cash flows that
incorporate inflation, we have to make assumptions. When you ignore inflation in estimating cash flows, you are in effect assuming an inflation rate
of zero. It may be tough to make reasonable assumptions regarding inflation
but assuming a zero rate is certainly not reasonable.

## ABANDONMENT

In the previous chapter, we explained that as part of the control function
analysts should check the progress of capital investments to see if the actual
cash flows are as expected. One of the reasons for doing this is to judge
whether a project should be liquidated (i. e., abandoned) before the end of
its life. To make this assessment, we must estimate the investment's liquidating value and compare this to the present value of the remaining cash
flows. In doing this, we make adjustments to the original cash flow estimates,
if appropriate, and perhaps revise the required rate as well. If the present
value of the remaining cash flows is less than the liquidated value today
then the project should be abandoned. In other words, we perform an
analysis all over again using the liquidating value as the outlay at time
zero. We will illustrate with a simple example:

Suppose a firm accepted an investment with a four-year life because
it had a positive NPV at a required rate of 12%. One year later management decides to review the project. The analyst would review the original
cash flow projections and make appropriate modifications. Let's assume re-
visions are necessary as shown below along with the original cash flow
estimates:

| End of Year | Original Cash Flows | Revised Cash Flows |
|:---:|:---:|:---:|
| 1 | $75,000 | $65,000 |
| 2 | 70,000 | 60,000 |
| 3 | 60,000 | 50,000 |

Suppose the analyst estimates that the same required rate of 12% is appropriate and that the investment could be liquidated today for $170,000. The analyst would compute the NPV to assess whether liquidation is in order.

| End of Year | Cash Flow | | (PV$1, 12%, n) | | Present Value |
|:---:|:---:|:---:|:---:|:---:|:---:|
| 0 | (170,000) | × | 1.0000 | = | ($170,000) |
| 1 | 65,000 | × | .8929 | = | 58,039 |
| 2 | 60,000 | × | .7972 | = | 47,832 |
| 3 | 50,000 | × | .7118 | = | 35,590 |
| | | | NPV@ 12% | = | ($28,539) |

The project should be abandoned because at 12%, $170,000 today is worth more than the cash flows that the investment promises to return.

The fact that the remaining cash was revised downward is not the sole factor in deriving a signal regarding abandonment. It is a function of the remaining cash flows, the liquidating value and the discount rate. In the above example, even if the original cash flow estimates were expected, the liquidating value would produce a negative NPV of $4,525 at 12%.

It is important to keep in mind that we review the progress of projects for other reasons besides possible abandonment. For instance, this kind of analysis is useful for judging the people who submit proposals. Executives are often concerned that middle managers may be too optimistic in estimating cash flows. As you can imagine, middle managers develop more reasonable estimates when they realize they will be reviewed. Of course, a healthy control system must take into account the difficulty often encountered in developing reasonable estimates.


## ESTIMATING CASH FLOWS/COMPETITIVE ANALYSIS

Throughout this chapter and the previous one we frequently referred to the difficulty involved in deriving reasonable cash flow estimates in practice. The difficulty is due not only to the uncertainty of future events but also to the near impossibility of isolating the impact of certain investments. Shortly, we will turn our attention to methods of incorporating uncertainty in capital budgeting analyses. Basically, the message will be this: We cannot measure the impact of an investment on value as precisely as we would like. Hence, it is crucial to keep in mind that when we apply the techniques *we get information not decisions.* This is generally true for most techniques of financial analysis.

Many capital budgeting analyses must include an assessment of the competitive environment. Who are our competitors? How will they respond, if at all, to our investment? Considering how competitors may react is especially critical if the investment is intended to take away someone else's market share, more so if we are aiming directly to capture some of their existing business. We must estimate their ability to respond and their likely intentions. "Ability" means an evaluation of their financial and other resources; and "intentions" refers to assessing their strategies and analyzing the temperament and personalities of their executives.

# *Incorporating Risk in Capital Budgeting Analysis*

Chapter 7 explained that the risk of an investment determines what required rate should be employed to evaluate an investment. Hence, the process of estimating an appropriate risk-adjusted discount rate is a way of incorporating risk in capital budgeting. Many analysts adjust the discount rate to account for differences in risk among projects; however, they often do more than this and here we briefly discuss some of the methods they use.

## *DISCOUNTED PAYBACK PERIOD*

Traditionally, the payback period, as described in the previous chapter, has been viewed by managers as a useful way of assessing risk. It is still used for this purpose but some analysts now rely on a different version. This newer version is frequently referred to as discounted payback and is defined as the number of years it takes for the present value of an investment's cash inflows to recoup the present value of the outflows, all discounted at an appropriate risk-adjusted discount rate. This measure, in effect, tells us how long it will take the capital investment to attain an NPV of zero. (This is the same as saying that the measure tells us how long it will take the IRR to equal the required rate.)

Discounted payback is certainly an improvement over the undiscounted version of payback. Still, it is only partially consistent with the valuation principle because it does not account for cash flows after the discounted payback period. We should point out, however, that capital budgeting analysts have told us they consider discounted payback a useful measure. These people recognize the limitations with respect to theory. Nevertheless, they have found that it provides useful information for decision-making purposes.

## SENSITIVITY ANALYSIS

Many analysts rely on sensitivity analysis which means that NPV, IRR, etc. calculations are made for more than one set of cash flow estimates. For instance, the analyst might derive three sets of cash flow estimates—most likely, optimistic, pessimistic—and compute the NPV for each set. Alternatively, the analyst might begin with the most likely estimate and then redo the computations for a series of what-if questions. The advantage of this is it enables one to focus on key areas of interest. For example, suppose we expect a market share of 10% for a product we are considering introducing and compute the NPV assuming this market share is obtained. We might redo the analysis assuming a lower market share like 8%.

We have used sensitivity analysis often in practice and have found it very useful. Many practitioners rely on it a great deal and now that the assistance of computers is readily available this kind of analysis is not a burdensome task. We should point out, however, that pushing too many numbers can create an information overload and hence, can substantially diminish the utility of this kind of analysis.

## SIMULATION[9]

Simulation is another way of obtaining useful information about the variability of returns. The analysis involves estimating a series of values for each item, like working capital levels or selling price per unit, affecting

---

[9] A classic article on this topic is: David Hertz, "Risk Analysis in Capital Budgeting," *Harvard Business Review* (January-February 1964). Our discussion is based on this excellent article.

cash flows, and assigning a probability to each value. We will illustrate this with a simple example:

Let's assume we are considering a machine that will cost $10,000 and be depreciated at a rate of $2,000 per year for five years. The machine will produce savings in labor and raw materials. To simplify the application, we will assume that the level of raw materials savings is independent of the level of labor savings and that annual savings in each item are independent over time.[10] Finally, the investment will not affect the level of net working capital, this machine does not replace an existing machine, and the firm's tax rate is 40%.

We must estimate a range of values for each item and assign a probability to each. Given we know for sure that the machine will cost $10,000, we don't have to estimate a range of values and we simply assign a probability of 100% to this estimate. Assuming we are equally confident of our salvage value and tax rate estimates (which we normally would not be), we would assign a probability of 100% to the $800 tax shield created by depreciation. For labor and raw materials, let's assume we develop the values and probabilities shown below:

| Labor Savings | | Raw Materials Savings | |
|---|---|---|---|
| *Amount* | *Probability* | *Amount* | *Probability* |
| 1,000 | .10 | 500 | .10 |
| 1,500 | .40 | 800 | .70 |
| 2,000 | .40 | 1,000 | .20 |
| 2,500 | .10 | | |

We have estimated that there is a 10% chance that the after-tax cash inflow produced by labor savings will be $1,000, a 40% chance it will be $1,500, and so on.

Given these estimates the next step is to make several hundred NPV or IRR calculations. Specifically, relying on a computer we select at random one value from each cash flow distribution and compute the NPV or IRR using the four cash flows selected and repeat the process many times.

Consider each cash flow distribution as a hat containing 100 pieces of paper. Each piece of paper has a cash flow value on it, and the number of pieces with the same cash flow depends on the probability distribution. For example, all the pieces of paper in the investment outlay hat would have a cash outflow of $10,000 written on it. In the labor savings hat, 10 pieces

---

[10] Simulation could still be used if they were not independent, but the model would be more complex. Incidentally, if the probability distributions were independent as described here, we probably would not use simulation because there is an easier way to assess risk in such circumstances.

would have an inflow of $1,000 written on it, 40 pieces would have $1,500, 40 pieces would have $2,000 and ten would have $2,500. To illustrate the simulation procedure, we will rely on the IRR method.

We select a piece of paper from each of the four hats. We compute the IRR based on these four cash flows, write it down and then put the pieces of paper back in their respective hats. This process is repeated many times. By summarizing the results, we are able to see what percentage of the total number of trials the IRR was above or below a certain level. For example, we might generate the following summary:

| Internal Rate of Return | Cumulative Probability |
|:---:|:---:|
| −5% | 4% |
| 0% | 6% |
| +5% | 10% |
| +10% | 20% |
| +12% | 40% |
| +15% | 80% |
| +18% | 90% |
| +20% | 100% |

The IRR was a negative 5% or less in 4% of the trials. It was zero or less for 6% of total calculations, a positive 5% or less for 10% of total calculations, and so on.

This chapter was designed to help you learn how to apply capital budgeting in practice. In closing we will merely remind you that effective capital budgeting analysis requires an understanding of concepts and tools along with judgment and common sense. Lastly, it is important to keep in mind that value creation comes from selecting capital investments that promise a positive NPV *and* from managing them well.

# Problems and Discussion Questions

## A. Solved Problems

### Problem 10-1A

Management of Visal, Inc., has been presented with two investment opportunities. Each has a required rate of 10%, and information on their cash flows, NPV and IRR is presented below:

| End of Year | Investment X | Investment Y |
|---|---|---|
| 0 | ($20,000) | ($45,000) |
| 1–10 | 4,770 | 9,310 |
| NPV @ 10% | $ 9,310 | $12,206 |
| IRR | 20% | 16% |

1. If these are mutually exclusive investments and there are no capital limits, which one would you select? Why?

2. Construct an NPV Discount Rate Graph for these investments and clearly identify the intersection point between their curves. What is the interpretation of this point?

3. Suppose Visal is approached with a third opportunity, which also has a required rate of 10%, and the following characteristics:

| End of Year | Investment Z |
|---|---|
| 0 | ($25,000) |
| 1–10 | 4,640 |
| NPV @ 10% | $3,511 |
| IRR | 13.2% |

If Investments X, Y and Z are not mutually exclusive (that is, any one or more can be selected) and Visal has no capital constraints, which investment(s) should be selected? Would your answer change if capital rationing limits Visal's total capital budget to $45,000? (In answering this, continue to assume that Investments X, Y and Z are independent.)

### Solution 10-1A

1. Mutually exclusive means that only one can be selected. In this case, the NPV and IRR are giving contradictory rankings; the NPV for Y is higher than the NPV for X, but the IRR for X is

greater than the IRR for Y. In the chapter, we explained that in the absence of capital limits, we simply select the alternative with the higher NPV, which means Investment Y is a better choice because this would increase firm value more. Now, given that the required rate for each alternative is the same, we could rely on the IRR procedure discussed in the chapter. However, when capital is not limited, that procedure would always select the one with the higher NPV.

2. In order to construct a NPV Discount Rate Graph, the curves of both investments must be plotted. To do this, we first compute a number of points for each investment.

| Investment X | | Investment Y | |
|---|---|---|---|
| *NPV* | *Discount Rate* | *NPV* | *Discount Rate* |
| $27,700 | 0% | $48,100 | 0% |
| 16,833 | 5% | 26,889 | 5% |
| 12,007 | 8% | 17,471 | 8% |
| 6,951 | 12% | 7,603 | 12% |
| 3,054 | 16% | 0 | 16% |
| 1,437 | 18% | (3,160) | 18% |
| 0 | 20% | (5,968) | 20% |
| (1,286) | 22% | (8,475) | 22% |

The actual curves are shown in Figure 10-3; the rate at the intersection point, Point L, is the rate at which the NPV for both investments are equal. The IRR and NPV values at that point can be read off the graph or can be derived by computing the IRR on the difference between the cash flows of the two investments as shown below:

| End of Year | Investment Y − Investment X |
|---|---|
| 0 | ($25,000) |
| 1–10 | 4,540 |
| IRR | 12.6%[1] |

At this rate the NPV for each is about $6,260.

This tells us that at any required rate below 12.6%, Y is preferred to X, and X is better at higher rates. Since the required rate is 10%, Investment Y should be selected. This is the answer we got in Part 1.

---

[1] Such precision in capital budgeting is usually unnecessary, and can, in fact, be misleading; it is mentioned only for the benefit of those who may have computed an exact rate in solving the problem.

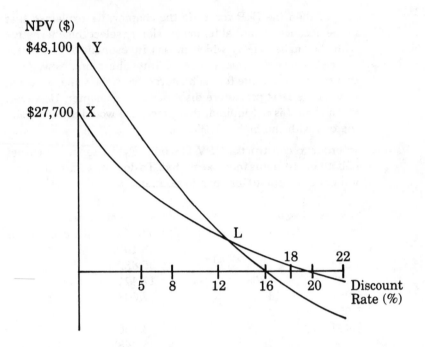

**Figure 10-3    NPV Discount Rate Graph Displaying
Investments X and Y**

3. If Visal has no capital limits, it should accept all projects with
   a positive NPV because this would increase the value of the
   firm most. Hence, Investments X, Y and Z should all be selected
   because they all have NPVs above zero.

   With a capital limit of $45,000 we must look at each com-
   bination, including treating each alternative as a combination,
   and pick the one with the highest NPV.

| Combination | Amount Invested | Total NPV |
|---|---|---|
| Investment X | $20,000 | $ 9,310 |
| Investment Y | 45,000 | 12,206 |
| Investment Z | 25,000 | 3,511 |
| Investments X & Z | 45,000 | 12,821 |

The firm should select Investments X and Z.

Notice that if we go back to Part 1 and consider X and Y mutually exclusive and Z as the third opportunity, the IRR procedure would tell us to pick X and Z which is the conclusion we reached in Parts 1 and 2. However, this is due to the fact that the required rate is the same for all three choices and so in this case the IRR procedure leads to the same choice as selecting the combination with the highest NPV. This will not always be the case. For instance, if the required rate for Investment Z was 11%, its NPV would be $2,326. Hence, the NPV for Investments X and Z would be $11,635. This is less than the NPV for Investment Y, so Y should be selected. The IRR procedure would still tell us to select X + Z.

### Problem 10-2A

The Dresden Company is considering replacing a machine with a model that will reduce spoilage, and two mutually exclusive alternatives have been identified. Each model has the following cash flows:

| Model A | | Model B | |
|---|---|---|---|
| End of Year | Cash Flow | End of Year | Cash Flow |
| 0 | ($50,000) | 0 | ($70,000) |
| 1–3 | 27,500 | 1–4 | 29,000 |

Both investments are of the same risk class and management has determined 16% to be an appropriate required rate of return.

When the time comes to replace either model, it is expected that annual operating cash savings will remain the same, but that the cost of replacement will increase by 3% per year.

Adjust the cash flows of both alternatives so that they have a common time horizon and advise Dresden which model it should select based on an NPV analysis.

### Solution 10-2A

The first step is to compute the NPV for each model before considering replacements. Model A has an NPV of $11,762 and Model B has an NPV of $11,148. The reason this step is necessary first is because each mutually exclusive alternative with unequal lives (or with contradictory rankings) must be acceptable to begin with to warrant further attention. Suppose Model A had a positive NPV but Model B's NPV was negative. No further analysis would be necessary and we simply would select Model A.

The two alternatives have unequal lives and so their NPV's cannot be compared directly; a common time period must be selected and cash flows must be estimated for the entire period. Here we will use 12 years.

### Model B

| End of Year | Cash Flow | | (PV$1, PVA$1, 16%, n) | | Present Value |
|---|---|---|---|---|---|
| 0 | ($70.000) | × | 1.0000 | = | ($ 70,000) |
| 4 | (78,786) | × | .5523 | = | (43,514) |
| 8 | (88,674) | × | .3050 | = | (27,046) |
| 1–12 | 29,000 | × | 5.1971 | = | 150,716 |
| | | | | NPV = | $ 10,156 |

### Model A

| End of Year | Cash Flow | | (PV$1, PVA$1, 16%, n) | | Present Value |
|---|---|---|---|---|---|
| 0 | ($50,000) | × | 1.0000 | = | ($ 50,000) |
| 3 | (54,636) | × | .6407 | = | (35,005) |
| 6 | (59,703) | × | .4104 | = | (24,502) |
| 9 | (65,239) | × | .2630 | = | (17,158) |
| 1–12 | 27,500 | × | 5.1971 | = | 142,920 |
| | | | | NPV = | $ 16,255 |

Based on the above analysis, Model A should be selected because it has the higher NPV.

## B. Discussion Questions

### Problem 10-1B

Explain the following terms: capital rationing, sensitivity analysis, mutually exclusive alternatives, independent investments and contradictory rankings.

### Problem 10-2B

If a project has two internal rates of return, how can an accept/reject rule based on the IRR be stated?

### Problem 10-3B

Should abandonment analysis be done only when a project appears to be failing?

### Problem 10-4B

Explain why an NPV procedure is preferred to an IRR procedure for selecting mutually exclusive alternatives when contradictory rankings arise.

### Problem 10-5B

When two mutually exclusive alternatives have unequal lives, we cannot simply pick the one with the higher NPV because further analysis is needed. Explain why further analysis is necessary.

## C. Study Problems

### Problem 10-1C

Two mutually exclusive investments are available to a firm. Both are in the same risk class for which the firm's required rate of return is 10%.

| End of Year | Option A | Option B |
|---|---|---|
| 0 | ($150,000) | ($100,000) |
| 1–6 | 42,000 | 30,000 |

1. Compute the NPV and IRR for each alternative. Assuming no capital limits, which alternative should be chosen?

2. Compute the indifference IRR for these two alternatives both graphically and arithmetically. For what range of required rates would A be preferred to B and for which range of required rates would B be preferred to A?

### Problem 10-2C

The same firm as in 10-1C has two other investment opportunities in addition to A and B (which are still mutually exclusive). These are not mutually exclusive with each other or with A or B.

| | Option X | Option Y |
|---|---|---|
| Capital Outlay | $50,000 | $130,000 |
| NPV | $ 8,200 | $ 40,000 |

1. If the firm has no capital rationing, which option(s) should it select? Why?

2. If the firm has only $150,000 to invest, which option(s) should it select? Why?

### Problem 10-3C

The Mallon Company needs advice on whether to replace one of its machines every three or every four years. Replacement every three years involves a major capital outlay more frequently, but a replacement every four years involves higher annual maintenance costs. Relevant cash flows are as follows:

| End of Year | Three-Year Cycle | Four-Year Cycle |
|:---:|:---:|:---:|
| 0 | ($50,000) | ($50,000) |
| 1 | (18,000) | (19,000) |
| 2 | (20,000) | (21,000) |
| 3 | (22,000) | (23,000) |
|  |  | (26,000) |

Management estimates that these cash flows will remain the same in the future and that the appropriate required rate for each cycle is 12%. Use the Equivalent Annuity Method as discussed in the chapter to select the better replacement cycle for Mallon.

### Problem 10-4C

Le Bon Pain has an oven which currently has a book value of $80,000 and could be sold for $80,000. It is being depreciated on a straight-line basis to a zero salvage value with eight years of life remaining. Newer convection ovens are available which would save operating costs, and management is considering two alternatives.

Oven A costs $120,000, including installation, and would be depreciated on a straight-line basis over an eight-year life to a zero salvage value. It would save $30,000 per year in cash operating costs.

Oven B costs $100,000, including installation, and would be depreciated on a straight-line basis over four years to a zero salvage value. It would have to be replaced at the end of four years with another similar oven, and the estimated capital outlay at that time is $110,000. This type of oven would save $27,000 per year in cash operating costs over the next eight years.

NWC needs will not change due to the change in ovens. Le Bon Pain's marginal tax rate is 40% and its required rate of return for this type of investment is 14%. (You may ignore the ITC.)

1. Use the NPV method of analysis to determine if the old oven should be replaced.

2. If replacement is desirable, which new oven should be selected?

### Problem 10-5C

You have just been approached with a rather bizarre proposal: its cash flows are as follows:

| End of Year | Cash Flow |
|:---:|:---:|
| 0 | ($2,500) |
| 1 | 6,250 |
| 2 | (3,850) |

1. Should you even bother to analyze this opportunity since its total cash outflows obviously exceed its inflows? Could it possibly increase the value of your firm?

2. Compute the internal rates of return for this proposal. How should such multiple rates be interpreted?

3. What should you do with this opportunity if your required rate of return is 8%? 10%? 20%? 45%?

## Problem 10-6C

Your firm has a limit on capital spending of $800,000 for the coming year. The following projects have been identified and they all have positive NPVs:

| Project | Capital Outlay | NPV |
|:---:|:---:|:---:|
| A | $200,000 | $ 63,000 |
| B | 400,000 | 100,000 |
| C | 350,000 | 90,000 |
| D | 250,000 | 75,000 |
| E | 100,000 | 20,000 |

Determine which projects should be selected.

## Problem 10-7C

Greenwood, Inc., has developed a new product which it proposes to introduce as part of its garden supply line. It is expected that the product will have a six-year life and annual unit sales are expected to be as follows:

| Year | Unit Sales |
|:---:|:---:|
| 1 | 10,000 |
| 2 | 14,000 |
| 3 | 20,000 |
| 4 | 18,000 |
| 5 | 12,000 |
| 6 | 12,000 |

Initial cash outlays include $250,000 for plant and equipment and $300,000 for increased net working capital. The plant and equipment will be depreciated on a straight-line basis over six years to a $10,000 salvage value. All NWC will be recovered at the end of the project's life.

The product will be priced at $18 per unit in Year 1 and the price will increase by 5% per year thereafter. Cash operating costs will be $7 per unit in Year 1 and this per unit amount is expected to increase by 8% per year thereafter.

Greenwood's marginal tax rate is 40% and its required rate of return for this investment is 16%. (You may ignore the ITC.)

1. Use the NPV method of analysis to evaluate this proposal. Should it be accepted?

2. Would your decision change if the effect of inflation had been ignored and a constant price per unit and operating cost per unit were maintained throughout the life of the project?

3. Explain the importance of incorporating an estimated inflation impact in capital budgeting decisions of this type.

### Problem 10-8C

This problem requires the use of the CAPM which was covered in an earlier chapter. The Barlow Company is considering a project that has the following expected cash flows:

| End of Year | Cash Flows |
| --- | --- |
| 0 | ($475,000) |
| 1–12 | 100,000 |

To select a discount rate for this project, an analyst has analyzed several firms in the industry engaged exclusively in this type of project and the Betas of these firms are all very close to 1.40. These firms do not employ any debt financing and Barlow agrees that only equity financing is appropriate for a project of this type. The prevailing risk-free rate is 9% and the required rate of return on the market is estimated at 17.5%.

1. Compute the risk-adjusted discount rate for this project.

2. Utilize the NPV method to determine whether Barlow should accept this project.

### Problem 10-9C

The Blue Cliffs Laboratories has developed a new chemical preservative which it hopes to introduce as a new product. Management has estimated a four-year life for the product and unit sales have been forecast under three different economic scenarios.

| Year | Optimistic | Most Likely | Pessimistic |
|------|-----------|-------------|-------------|
| 1 | 5,000 | 4,000 | 2,000 |
| 2 | 8,000 | 7,000 | 4,000 |
| 3 | 10,000 | 8,000 | 5,000 |
| 4 | 5,000 | 4,000 | 2,000 |

The project would cost $500,000 in new plant and equipment, including installation, which would be depreciated on a straight-line basis to a zero salvage value over four years. In addition, the following estimates have been made under the three possible scenarios.

|  | Optimistic | Most Likely | Pessimistic |
|--|-----------|-------------|-------------|
| NWC needed (Year 0) | ($300,000) | ($200,000) | ($100,000) |
| Price per Unit | $80 | $80 | $80 |
| Operating Costs (Cash) per unit | $30 | $40 | $50 |

Net working capital would be recovered at the end of four years, the firm's marginal income tax rate is 40% and its required rate of return for this investment is 16%. (You may ignore the ITC.)

1. Compute the NPV for the project for each economic scenario.

2. If you believed there was a 10% chance that the pessimistic scenario would prevail, a 30% chance that the optimistic scenario would prevail and a 60% chance that the most likely scenario would prevail, what would you recommend?

### Problem 10-10C

A firm wants to purchase a new piece of equipment which costs $132,000, including installation, and is expected to last four years. It will be depreciated on a straight-line basis to a zero salvage value over the four years. While the initial cost and salvage value of the equipment is known with certainty, the annual cash savings expected from the investment are described in the following probability distribution.

| Savings in Operating Costs Per Year | Probability |
|---|---|
| $35,000 | .10 |
| 45,000 | .20 |
| 55,000 | .50 |
| 65,000 | .20 |

In addition, there is a 50% chance that the firm's marginal tax rate will be 45% for each of the next four years and a 50% chance that it will be 40% for each of the next four years. There are no expected changes in NWC needs due to the acquisition of this piece of equipment.

Following the simulation procedure described in the chapter, compute 15 internal rates of return for this project and summarize your findings. You may assume that all probability distributions are independent of each other and independent over time.

# 11
# Analysis of Financing Decisions

This chapter discusses the analysis of the choice among debt, preferred stock and common stock, and explains methods for evaluating the decision to lease versus borrowing to buy. A thorough treatment of these complex topics are beyond the scope of this book. The chapter provides an overview of the analysis of financing decisions. References at the end of the book will enable you to pursue various issues in more depth.

To provide a conceptual framework for the discussion, we begin with a brief description of capital structure theory. Then we explain an organized method for analyzing a financing choice. The final part of the chapter discusses leasing.

## *Capital Structure Theory*

Capital structure theory is concerned with guiding managers in deciding on a financing mix, that is, the proportions of debt, preferred stock and common equity that should be used to finance the firm. To crystalize the topic, let's divide a firm's financing decisions into three basic categories: investment, financing and dividend decisions. (Up to now we have generally treated dividends as part of the firm's financing decision.) In previous chapters, we explained how valuation provides the framework for investment decisions. That is, the firm should choose investments and pursue an overall investment strategy that increases the value of the firm the most.

The same principle applies to the area of financing. Specifically, the firm should make financing decisions and establish financing policies that increase the value of the firm the most. Unlike the investments' arena, however, there is considerable disagreement over whether and how the firm's financing choices affect its value. Thus, capital structure theory tries to answer the following questions: Given a firm's investment and dividend decisions (that is, holding them constant), can the way a firm chooses to finance itself impact its value? If so, how? Putting it another way, does the use of debt financing affect a firm's value?

Figure 11-1 has a graphical view of a position frequently called the traditional view. It depicts the hypothesized relationship between the proportion of debt employed and a firm's cost of capital. The cost of debt, $K_i$, remains level and then increases, depicting the widely-held view that a firm can borrow up to a certain amount at the same interest rate but that

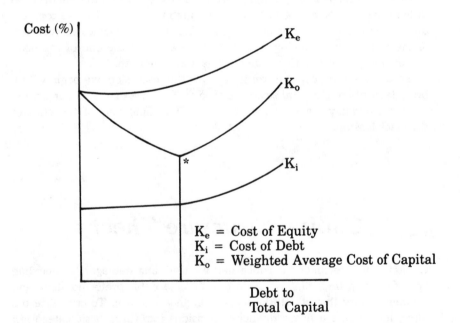

$K_e$ = Cost of Equity
$K_i$ = Cost of Debt
$K_o$ = Weighted Average Cost of Capital

**Figure 11-1   Traditional View of Impact of Financing on Value**

borrowing more forces interest rates to increase. The cost of equity, $K_e$, increases as debt increases because of greater risk.[1] The weighted average cost of capital, $K_o$, is a (weighted) average of the two curves. Note that $K_o$ decreases, levels off and then increases. The supposed logic of each of these phases is the following:

1. The $K_o$ curve decreases up to a point because of the advantage of low-cost debt. The cost of equity increases during this phase but not enough to offset the advantage of low-cost debt.

2. The $K_o$ curve levels off beyond some point because here the increase in the cost of equity offsets the advantage of low-cost debt. We show an asterisk (*) at the lowest point in Figure 11-1. (Some proponents of the traditional view say it's better to think of a minimum range instead of a single point, that is, the $K_o$ curve may have a horizontal stretch.)

3. Beyond some level of debt, the $K_o$ curve increases. The cost of equity rises rapidly because considerable risk is involved with the heavy use of debt. The higher rate of increase in $K_e$ more than offsets the advantage of low-cost debt.

The implication is that a firm should choose a capital structure that minimizes its cost of capital (i. e., the low point or range of the $K_o$ curve in Figure 11-1). The capital structure that minimizes the firm's cost of capital is the one that maximizes its value. This is called the firm's optimal capital structure. In other words, when we say a firm's cost of capital increases or decreases that is the same as saying its value decreases or increases.[2]

In the late 1950s this traditional view was challenged by the seminal contribution of Professors F. Modigliani and M. Miller. They showed that in a world of perfect markets (among other things no income taxes), a firm's cost of capital is unaffected by its financing mix.[3] Their position created controversy which continues to this day. There have been many extensions

---

[1] It might be helpful to think of the impact of increased debt on risk and hence required return in the context of the Capital Asset Pricing Model (CAPM) discussed in Chapter 8. Recall that the higher the Beta, the measure of systematic risk, on a firm's stock, the higher the required rate of return on the stock, which is the same as saying the higher the cost of equity. Now as a firm's debt usage increases, the Beta on its stock increases, which in turn increases its cost of equity, assuming no change in the risk-free rate and the required rate of return on the market.

[2] It may help to think of the value function as the mirror image (inverted) of the $K_o$ curve. For this to be exactly the case, however, we must assume that the capital structure choice does not affect operating profits.

[3] F. Modigliani and M. Miller, "The Cost of Capital, Corporate Finance and the Theory of Investment," *American Economic Review*, June 1958.

and refinements including additional contributions by Professors Modigliani and Miller.

Many authors have argued that when you relax some of the assumptions of MM's model, you end up with a $K_o$ curve that has a U shape similar to the one in Figure 11-1. When income taxes on corporate income are introduced into the model, the $K_o$ curve decreases and this decline is due to the tax shield created by interest expense. When the costs of financial distress (e. g., bankruptcy and reorganization costs) are introduced, this eventually causes $K_o$ to increase because the costs of financial distress increase with higher proportions of debt and beyond some point they offset the interest tax shields.

Incorporating other factors into these models complicates matters further. Examples of these factors are the difference between the personal tax rate on interest income and capital gains; the costs involved in sheltering income such as transaction costs and fees paid to purchase ownership in a limited partnership leasing equipment; and the costs of formulating and enforcing loan provisions such as bond covenants. The upshot of all this work seems at this writing to be that most people agree debt financing can have a positive effect on firm value and the $K_o$ curve has a shape similar to the one shown in Figure 11-1. However, it is not clear just how much of an impact on value debt financing can have, particularly for firms with low marginal income tax rates.

Before proceeding, we should say something about the many empirical studies that have been conducted to test the impact of the firm's financing mix on value. The results have been inconclusive since it is very difficult to isolate the effect of a firm's financing mix and hence difficult to analyze the impact of financing on value. Recall that we are studying the effect on value of the firm's financing choice, holding other decision areas constant. These other decisions obviously are not constant in practice and this is the laboratory in which empirical tests are conducted. Finally, it is important to keep in mind that a firm's investment, financing and dividend decisions are related in a fundamental way. The importance of this basic relationship will be seen more clearly in the ensuing discussion.

# Choosing Among Debt, Preferred and Common Stock

To finance long term or permanent capital requirements, firms rely on both internal (profits retained) and external sources. This discussion is concerned with deciding which external source to employ. There are three basic external sources: long-term debt, preferred stock and common stock. Sometimes a feature is added to make the financial instrument more attractive. For instance, a bond may be convertible, which means that it can be changed for another security, typically, a stated number of shares of common stock.[4]

Valuation is the guide for making the choice. That is, given that a firm's financing mix can affect its value, it should choose the financing alternative that produces the highest firm value.[5] Instead of relying on a complete analytical model like net present value, analysts make a decision based on an analysis of the following factors: analysis of supply, control, flexibility, income and risk. We will now discuss each of them.

### *Analysis of Supply*

Individuals, financial institutions, and other organizations purchase a firm's securities. As explained in Chapter 8, purchasers of securities should be willing to pay a price equal to the security's value. But translating theory into practice means designing the financial instrument so that it is attractive to the potential purchaser. Hence, it is imperative that the firm analyze the needs and conditions of the segments of the financial markets it is trying to attract. Let's look at two examples.

1. Suppose we plan to issue common stock. Our analysis reveals that the stock of our firm would probably be attractive to individual investors instead of financial institutions. We certainly should not divide up our equity into a number of outstanding shares that would produce a per share price of $1,000.

2. Suppose our firm wanted to issue long-term debt. We would not design a debt instrument appealing primarily to life insurance companies if at that time life insurance companies were already heavily invested in firms in our industry and had no plans to add to their investments.

In performing this task, many firms rely on the expertise of investment

---

[4] When a firm issues a convertible bond it is in effect issuing a package containing two instruments: a bond and an option to purchase a firm's common stock. One would expect that the issue price (i. e., price investors would pay for the convertible) would equal the value of the bond plus the value of the option. Our reason for explaining this is to point out that when special features are added to securities, we should expect them to be valued according to the principles explained in Chapter 8.

[5] Generally, we have been assuming, at least implicitly, that increasing the value of the firm is the same as increasing the value of the firm's common stock. This is not necessarily the case. However, for our purposes, it has not been necessary to delve into the possible distinctions.

bankers. (An investment banker is an intermediary who for a fee assists a firm in designing and issuing securities.) In addition, many firms have investor relations departments that monitor the supply side of the market and respond to the needs of individuals and institutions investing in the firm.

### Control

By control we refer to the effect of the firm's financing choice on management's discretion to make decisions. In our opinion, a firm gives up a certain amount of control with every dollar it raises, so what we are discussing here is the degree of control lost.

The board of directors of a firm is elected by the common share holders, with each common share typically having one vote. When a firm issues new shares, there are additional votes and hence a greater chance that a party hostile to existing management can gain a slot on the board or even gain control (i. e., a majority of the seats on the board). The board is responsible for broad policy decisions and hiring and firing managers.

Preferred stockholders typically are promised a fixed dividend. While no legal obligation exists to meet the payment each year, often the agreement includes a cumulative feature, which means that dividends omitted in any year must be made up before common stockholders are entitled to any dividends. Moreover, often there is a clause stating that if dividends are not paid for a certain period, then preferred stockholders can elect a certain portion of the board of directors.

A debt instrument has provisions or covenants outlining the nature of the agreement. In addition to specifying the amount of interest and principal to be paid and when the payment is to be made, these provisions might include restrictions on the payment of dividends, on salary increases, on fixed asset expenditures and on the freedom of the firm to raise additional debt. Typically, an acceleration clause is part of the agreement. This means that if the covenant is broken and not amended within a certain period, say 30 days, the entire loan becomes due. Often a firm would not be in a position to make full payment on such short notice so the lender can legally enforce his or her claim in court, leading perhaps to bankruptcy and liquidation. Generally, lenders do not want to do this when a covenant is broken. Instead they want to work something out with management.

Management's objective with respect to the "control" factor is to maintain the freedom to act in the firm's best interests. There is no general rule regarding which type of financial instrument (e. g., stock versus bond) is best from a control point of view because it depends on the particular circumstances. We should point out, however, that when investors want to exercise strong control over management, they typically opt for a debt instrument. For instance, suppose you wanted to exert substantial control in a small firm while owning less than 50% of the equity. You would probably prefer a debt instrument convertible into stock or with warrants attached.[6] The reason is that many investors believe that covenants on a debt instrument are an effective means of exerting control.

### Flexibility

Flexibility refers here to the effect of the financing alternative selected on future financing decisions. In this regard, managers ask the following questions: If we raise debt now, will we have to raise equity the next time? If so, what if the equity market is not receptive? Even if we have more debt-raising ability, will we have to pay a very high price for it?

In our view, firms must be certain they have ready access to capital. If capital-raising ability is not strong, then greater emphasis should be placed on internal sources such as maintaining a liquid reserve invested in marketable securities. At any rate, the more external and internal sources a firm has, the more financial flexibility it enjoys. While financial flexibility is important for all firms, it is especially crucial for firms requiring substantial amounts of capital. Hence, one would expect firms having large capital needs to choose to operate under a debt to equity ratio that permits the firm to add additional debt if it needs it. This is precisely what we observe in practice.

Generally, choosing equity financing is best for preserving and enhancing financial flexibility. Very often enlarging the equity base creates the opportunity for more debt financing, thus increasing the financing alternatives available to the firm.

### Income

This factor is concerned with the effect of the financing choice on the level and movement of Earning Per Share (EPS). We will show that because debt and preferred stock involve a fixed dollar dilution versus a fixed percentage dilution for common stock, they can provide an opportunity for a higher level of EPS and greater growth in EPS. However, they also create financial risk, that is, they make EPS more variable.

Let's look at an example. Table 11-1 has a projected income statement

---

[6] The owner of warrants has the option to buy a specified number of shares at a specified price.

**TABLE 11-1**
**AN-MA COMPANY**
Projected Income Statement
for Next Year
(000 omitted)

| | |
|---|---:|
| Net sales | $20,000 |
| Cost of goods sold | 14,000 |
| Gross profit | $ 6,000 |
| Selling, general and administrative expenses | 4,500 |
| Operating profit (earnings before interest and taxes) | $ 1,500 |
| Interest expense | 200 |
| Earnings before taxes | $ 1,300 |
| Income taxes @ 50% | 650 |
| Net income | $    650 |
| Less preferred dividends | 50 |
| Earnings available to common stock | $    600 |
| Number of common shares outstanding | 450 |
| Earnings per share (not in $ thousands) | $    1.33 |

for next year for the An-Ma Company. Management is considering an investment which will increase Earnings Before Interest and Taxes (EBIT) by $500,000. (That is, next year EBIT will be $2 million instead of the $1.5 million shown in Table 11-1 if the investment is taken.) The firm needs $1 million of external capital and is considering the following three possibilities.

1. Long-term debt with an interest rate of 13%. Principal payments of $100,000 per year would be required commencing one year from now.

2. Preferred stock with a dividend rate of 11%. The firm expects to call the preferred in about six years.

3. Issue 100,000 shares of common stock to net the firm $10 after transaction costs.

If EBIT is $2 million, EPS will be $1.74, $1.64 or $1.55, depending on the alternative selected. Table 11-2 shows the calculations. (These computations and others discussed below are known as EBIT-EPS analysis.) EBIT is the same for all three alternatives. Existing interest and preferred dividends refer to the amounts that will be due on instruments already outstanding. New interest for debt is $130,000 (13% times $1 million) and

**TABLE 11-2**
**AN-MA COMPANY**
EBIT - EPS Analysis
for Next Year
(000 omitted)

| | Debt | Preferred | Common |
|---|---|---|---|
| Earnings before interest and taxes (EBIT) | $2,000 | $2,000 | $2,000 |
| Existing interest | 200 | 200 | 200 |
| New interest | 130 | 0 | 0 |
| Earnings before taxes | $1,670 | $1,800 | $1,800 |
| Income taxes @ 50% | 835 | 900 | 900 |
| Net income | $ 835 | $ 900 | $ 900 |
| Existing preferred dividends | 50 | 50 | 50 |
| New preferred dividends | 0 | 110 | 0 |
| Earnings available to common | $ 785 | $ 740 | $ 850 |
| Number of common shares | 450 | 450 | 550 |
| Earnings per share (EPS) | 1.74 | 1.64 | 1.55 |

new preferred dividends are $110,000 (11% times $1 million). If the firm issues stock, there will be 100,000 new shares outstanding, so the total would be 550,000 if this alternative is chosen. Finally, principal payments are not involved because they are not expenses and hence do not affect EPS.

We can readily see that common stock has the lowest level of EPS because of the larger number of shares. But this will not always be the case. In fact, had EBIT been below a certain level (discussed later), common stock would have produced the highest level of EPS. To understand why, we must appreciate the difference in the nature of the cost of each alternative for existing stockholders.

Debt and preferred stock involve a fixed dollar cost, which means the same amount is due regardless of the level of EBIT. For debt, the after-tax dollar cost is $65,000 ($130,000 times one minus the tax rate). It is $110,000 for preferred because preferred does not create a tax shield. Since the after-tax cost of debt is lower, it will give a higher level of EPS than preferred no matter what the level of EBIT (assuming EBIT will be high enough to permit the tax shield on interest.)

Common stock involves a fixed percentage dilution. There will be 100,000 new shares, making for a new total of 550,000. So, the percentage dilution is 18.2% as shown below:

$$\text{Dilution} = \frac{\text{Number of New Shares}}{\text{Number of New Shares} + \text{Existing Shares Outstanding}}$$
$$= \frac{100,000}{100,000 + 450,000}$$
$$= 18.2\%$$

This figure means that the new owners are entitled to 18.2% of the earnings regardless of the level. Say earnings are $1. Well, they own 18.2 cents. Say they are $100 million; they own $18.2 million. It is these converted dollar figures that are comparable to the dollar costs of debt and preferred. The alternative with the lowest dollar cost has the highest EPS and vice versa.

Figure 11-2 is a pictorial representation of the relationship between EBIT and EPS for each alternative. It is known as an EBIT-EPS Chart. To draw each line two points were plotted for each alternative. The first was the level of EPS at an EBIT level of $2 million. The second was the

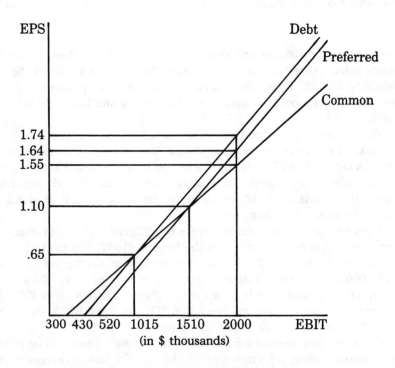

**Figure 11-2   EBIT-EPS Chart**

EBIT level that produces a zero level of EPS. For debt it is $430,000, for preferred it is $520,000 and for common it is $300,000. You can easily verify that these levels of EBIT would produce a zero level of EPS for each option by performing the analysis shown in Table 11-2.

Notice that the debt and preferred stock lines are parallel indicating both are fixed dollar cost instruments. The debt line is above the preferred stock line at all levels of EBIT. This is because the after-tax cost of debt is less than the after-tax cost of preferred. Hence, EPS will always be higher than the debt alternative, as long as EBIT is large enough to permit the firm to use the tax shield on interest. This is often the case in practice and one reason that many firms do not rely heavily on preferred stock. However, EBIT-EPS analysis focuses on the impact of the choice on EPS. We must consider all factors—analysis of supply, control, flexibility, income and risk—when making a decision between debt and preferred.

The common stock line intersects the other two displaying the difference between securities that involve a fixed dollar cost and one that involves a fixed percentage dilution. Take the intersection point between debt and common. At any EBIT level to the left of that point, EPS will be higher with common; to the right, EPS will be higher with debt; and the intersection point is the level of EBIT at which EPS will be the same for each option. The same interpretation applies to the intersection between common stock and preferred. It is useful to know what that point is and one way of computing it is to rely on the graph. Alternatively, we can rely on simple algebra and we will now explain how to do that.

Let's begin by restating the EPS computation in equation format.

$$EPS = \frac{(EBIT - I)(1 - TR) - P}{n}$$

Where:

- EBIT = Earnings before interest and taxes
- I = Total dollars of interest (existing plus new interest)
- TR = Tax rate
- P = Total dollars of preferred dividends (existing plus new preferred dividends)
- n = Number of common shares outstanding
- EPS = Earnings per share

Setting the right hand side of the equation for the common stock alternative equal to the right hand side of the equation for one of the fixed dollar cost alternatives and solving for EBIT gives the intersection point between the two. We will illustrate for each pair.

$$\frac{\text{(EBIT} - 330,000)\,(1-50\%)-50,000}{450,000} = \frac{\text{(EBIT} - 200,000)(1-50\%)-50,000}{550,000}$$

Debt | | | Common

$$\text{EBIT} = \$1,015,000$$
$$\text{EPS} = \$.65$$

| | Debt* | Common* |
|---|---|---|
| Earnings before interest and taxes (EBIT) | $1,015 | $1,015 |
| Interest | 330 | 200 |
| Earnings before taxes (EBT) | $ 685 | $ 815 |
| Taxes | 342.5 | 407.5 |
| Net income | $ 342.5 | $ 407.5 |
| Preferred dividends | 50 | 50 |
| Earnings available to common stock (EATCS) | $ 292.5 | $ 357.5 |
| Number of shares | 450 | 550 |
| Earnings per share (EPS) | $ .65 | $ .65 |

* All figures except EPS are 000 omitted

At any level of EBIT above $1,015,000 EPS will be higher with debt, and at any level below $1,015,000 EPS will be higher with common stock.

$$\frac{\text{(EBIT} - 200,000)\,(1-50\%)-160,000}{450,000} = \frac{\text{(EBIT} - 200,000)\,(1-50\%)-50,000}{550,000}$$

Preferred | | | Common

$$\text{EBIT} = \$1,510,000$$
$$\text{EPS} = \$1.10$$

| | Preferred* | Common* |
|---|---|---|
| Earnings before interest and taxes (EBIT) | $1,510 | $1,510 |
| Interest | 200 | 200 |
| Earnings before taxes (EBT) | $1,310 | $1,310 |
| Taxes | 655 | 655 |
| Net income | $ 655 | $ 655 |
| Preferred dividends | 160 | 50 |
| Earnings available to common stock (EATCS) | $ 495 | $ 605 |
| Number of shares | 450 | 550 |
| Earnings per share (EPS) | $ 1.10 | $ 1.10 |

* All figures except EPS are 000 omitted

Before continuing we should mention a practical issue that may seem confusing. Often in practice the interest rate on debt is not fixed for the life of the loan and "floats." In these cases, the rate is linked to and changes with a benchmark rate. The above analysis still can be used. However, instead of an exact dollar figure for the interest, we would have to rely on an estimate or several estimates.

We have just seen that debt (and preferred stock) can give a higher level of EPS than stock. This is why we discuss debt in terms of financial leverage; it acts as a lever to EPS. In addition, as Figure 11-2 indicates, the debt line has a steeper slope than common stock line. This tells us that if EBIT grows, EPS will grow at a faster rate with debt than with stock. Hence, debt not only can permit higher EPS but it also can produce a greater growth rate.

But the difference in slopes also tells us that if EBIT decreases, EPS will decrease at a greater rate with debt than with common stock. Also, debt (and preferred) makes EPS more variable assuming EBIT changes. That is, there is more risk.

### Risk

We will focus here on the risk involved in debt financing, but much of what we say applies to preferred stock. From a conceptual point of view, we are evaluating the impact of the financing alternative selected on the required rates for the firm's securities. For our present purposes, we will translate this into analyzing the following two issues:

1. Ability to service debt, that is, ability to meet interest and principal payments on a timely basis.

2. Impact on variability of EPS.

We discuss each separately but the two are related in a fundamental way.

Analysts evaluate ability to service debt, also known as debt capacity, in many ways. A popular approach is to rely on selected ratios. For instance, a ratio that is commonly employed to help assess debt capacity is the earnings coverage ratio which you may recall is defined as follows:

$$\text{Earnings Coverage} = \frac{\text{EBIT}}{\text{I} + \dfrac{\text{SF}}{(1 - \text{TR})}}$$

Where:

$$\begin{aligned}
\text{EBIT} &= \text{Earnings before interest and taxes} \\
\text{I} &= \text{Dollars of interest} \\
\text{SF} &= \text{Sinking fund payments} \\
\text{TR} &= \text{Tax rate}
\end{aligned}$$

Sinking fund payment is a frequently used name for a required principal payment on debt. It is divided by one minus the tax rate because a sinking fund payment is not an expense and hence not tax deductible. Thus, dividing by one minus the tax rate converts it to an equivalent pretax amount.

Other ratios are used together with the earnings coverage ratio to evaluate debt-servicing ability. The chapter on ratio analysis explained that while ratios can provide insight into debt capacity, there are basic limitations and so, generally, ratios alone are not sufficient for a thorough appraisal of debt capacity. We will not repeat that chapter's discussion of this issue here; instead we will only mention a couple of key points. Earnings coverage and other ratios have two basic weaknesses when it comes to assessing debt capacity: (1) earnings and cash flow are not the same thing and debt payments are made with cash and (2) computing ratios based on past financial statements is backward-looking and a proper assessment of debt capacity must be forward-looking in nature. Hence, what the analyst must do is estimate future cash flows under a variety of assumed conditions to appraise the ability of a firm to meet its debt payments in a timely manner.

With respect to the variability issue, we need to review the notion of operating leverage, which was discussed in the chapter on cost/volume/profit analysis and relate this to financial leverage. Recall that operating leverage is concerned with the impact of fixed operating expenses on the level and variability of operating profits. Financial leverage is concerned with the impact of fixed cost financing on the level and variability of EPS. The following income statement format will help to illustrate the relationship between the two types of leverage:

Operating leverage
- Sales
- − Cost of goods sold
- = Gross profit
- − Operating expense

Financial leverage
- = Operating profit, earnings before interest and taxes (EBIT)
- − Interest expense
- = Earnings before taxes
- − Income taxes
- = Net income
- − Preferred dividends
- = Earnings available to common stock
- ÷ Common shares outstanding
- = Earnings per share (EPS)

In the chapter on cost/volume/profit analysis, we explained the degree of operating leverage, which is a measure of the sensitivity of operating profits to a change in sales. There is a similar measure for financial leverage called the degree of financial leverage (DOF). This measure provides insight into how variable EPS will be for a given change in EBIT at a given level EBIT. It is computed as follows:

$$DOF = \frac{EBIT}{EBIT - I - \dfrac{P}{1 - TR}}$$

Where:
  DOF = Degree of financial leverage
    I = Dollars of interest
    P = Preferred dividends
   TR = Tax rate

Preferred dividends are divided by one minus the tax rate because they are not tax deductible and we want to convert them to an equivalent pretax amount.

We will rely on the debt and common stock alternatives for the An-Ma company discussed earlier to illustrate the computations. These are shown below for the $2 million EBIT level that the firm expects:

*Debt Alternative*

$$DOF = \frac{2,000,000}{2,000,000 - 330,000 - 100,000}$$
$$= 1.27$$

*Common Stock Alternative*

$$DOF = \frac{2,000,000}{2,000,000 - 200,000 - 100,000}$$
$$= 1.18$$

The 1.27 figure for debt tells us that for any percentage change in EBIT from the $2 million level EPS will change by 1.27 times that percentage. For instance, if EBIT increases by 10%, EPS will increase by 12.7% if we choose debt. If we choose common stock, EPS will increase by 11.8% if EBIT increases by 10%. This magnification of the rate of change applies to percentage decreases as well.

If a firm does not rely on debt or preferred stock financing, its DOF will be 1.0 at any level of EBIT, that is, EPS will change at the same rate that EBIT changes at any EBIT level. The DOF will be greater than 1.0 at any level of EBIT if debt and/or preferred stock are employed. This is what we mean when we say debt/and/or preferred stock lever a firm's earnings. Note that while debt or preferred stock will cause the firm's DOF to be greater than 1.0, the actual DOF depends on the level of EBIT and will be different at different EBIT levels. Finally, it is important to keep in mind that the variability of EPS is affected by both operating and financial leverage.[7]

It may be useful, before closing, to think of the variability issue in the context of the Capital Asset Pricing Model (CAPM) which was discussed in Chapter 8. You may recall that the equation for the security market line is:

$$R_i = R_F + B_i(R_m - R_F)$$

Where:

$R_i$ = Required rate of return
$R_F$ = Risk-free rate
$B_i$ = Security's Beta which is a measure of systematic risk
$R_m$ = Required return on the market

In the context of common stock, $R_i$ is the required rate of return demanded by stockholders. It is also the rate used to compute the present value of future dividends.

We can see from the above equation that the higher a stock's Beta, the higher the required rate (also known as the cost of equity) and hence the lower the present value of future dividends. Now, we saw in Chapter 8 that as a firm increases its use of debt, its Beta increases because of the increased risk. To see this more clearly, recall the following relationship between a stock's levered and unlevered Beta.

$$B_L = B_u[1 + (1 - TR)\frac{D}{E}]$$

Where:

$B_L$ = Beta for a given level of financial leverage
$B_u$ = Beta if the firm had no financial leverage
$TR$ = Tax rate
$D$ = Market value of debt
$E$ = Market value of equity

---

[7] Sometimes it is useful to compute a degree of combined leverage which is a measure of the sensitivity of EPS to changes in sales. It is computed by multiplying the equation for the DOF presented above by the equation for the degree of operating leverage (DOL) explained in Chapter 4. Finally, keep in mind that it is sales variability that drives the changes in EPS. For instance, a firm can have a high DOL and a high DOF, but EPS will be stable if sales are stable.

This shows that if a firm had no debt its Beta would be $B_u$. With debt, its Beta becomes $B_L$. The essential point for our purpose is that a firm's Beta increases as the amount of financial leverage employed increases.

When we discussed the income factor, we saw that debt can produce a higher EPS, which could produce higher cash flows accruing to common stock. Here we see that debt also means that these cash flows are discounted at a higher rate. Whether the net result is an increase or decrease in value depends on the magnitudes of the two effects. In sum, we make a tradeoff between risk and return. We should add that a consideration of the first three factors—analysis of supply, control and flexibility, also provides insight on risk and return. In other words, we consider the five factors described above, using both quantitative and qualitative factors, to assess the impact on the firm's value.

# Leasing

When one party, the lessee, pays another party, the lessor, for the use of an asset, the transaction is known as a lease. We will focus on one kind of lease in particular. This type, which is similar to a loan, is known by a variety of names including financial lease, capital lease, full payout lease and finance lease.

Why do people choose a lease arrangement instead of owning the asset? There are many reasons and we will discuss the following four: (1) necessity, (2) convenience, (3) risk shifting and (4) tax benefit shifting. By "necessity" we are referring to situations where an option to own does not exist. For instance, suppose a firm wants to open a retail outlet in a particular shopping center. It might prefer to buy the space but, as is often the case, the owner is not willing to sell and will only lease. Convenience refers to those situations where it may not be feasible to own. For example, suppose your car breaks down on a Friday. You need a car badly for the weekend but you are unable to borrow one. You could conceivably buy a car Friday and sell it Monday. But this would be too costly and too inconvenient so you would most likely lease a car for the weekend.

An important reason for leasing is to shift the risk of ownership to someone who is in a better position to bear it or to one who is willing to assume the risk (in the hope of a reasonable return). For example, some firms in the 1960s and 1970s were reluctant to purchase large computers because they were concerned about technological obsolescence. So, many of these firms arranged for a short-term renewable lease with a computer manufacturer or a finance company. Some of these leases extended for only one year, although both the lessor and lessee expected that the lease would be renewed for several years. Nevertheless, the firm was incurring a legal commitment to make lease payments only for one year. This kind of short-term commitment is known as an operating lease. The key criterion for our purposes is that the lessee is incurring an obligation for only a short period. This would include leases that extend for a short time[8] or leases that can be cancelled on short notice, say, 30 days, with little or no penalty.

The shifting of tax benefits is a major reason for the existence of leasing, particularly, the existence of financial leases. Users of assets who have low marginal tax rates find it beneficial to trade the tax benefit of ownership to an individual or institution who can make better use of them. Specifically, these low marginal tax rate individuals and firms become lessees instead of owners and they get part of the tax benefit back in the form of lower lease payments.

For example, suppose you have a marginal income tax rate of 50% and the author's firm has a marginal income tax rate of 10%. Assume further that his firm recently bought a piece of electrical manufacturing equipment that will be depreciated at a rate of $10,000 per year over its ten-year life. This depreciation deduction will create a tax shield of $1,000 per year given the 10% tax rate. Now you and the author could benefit at the expense of the U.S. Treasury if we could get the depreciation deduction on your tax return. If we could, there would be tax shield of $5,000, each year, given your 50% tax bracket, and we would find an equitable way of splitting the difference of $4,000 (i. e., the $5,000 tax shield versus the $1,000 tax shield if the author deducted the depreciation). One method of accomplishing this transfer is to arrange a lease transaction. For instance, the author could sell you the asset and then lease it back from you. This sounds great but we should address several concerns that you and the author would have. We will start with yours.

Suppose the lease payment does not arrive when it is supposed to and the author tells you, "The check is in the mail." In other words, you are incurring credit risk for which you would want an adequate return if you were willing to accept it at all.[9] Another concern you would have is the duration of the agreement. Suppose the author does not want to use the equipment in a couple of years. What would you do with a piece of electrical

---

[8] There is no universal agreement on exactly how short the period must be for the lease to be classified as operating. For instance, we suspect that some analysts would not agree with our classifying a one-year commitment as an operating lease.

[9] Many of these arrangements are structured in such a way that the credit risk is low. However, usually there are some credit risk and other risks as well. For instance, to meet tax regulations often the lease period cannot extend over the entire useful life of the asset.

manufacturing equipment? You could have him commit himself to a long period payment plan.[10] This would make it a financial lease. Of course, the author would prefer as much flexibility as possible and the more he is constrained the more he must be offered with respect to the share of the tax benefits.

A final concern you likely would have is machine maintenance. It is unlikely that you would want to service the machine on a regular basis, nor would you cherish the thought of insuring it. One way around this is to structure the deal so that the author's firm would be responsible for maintenance, insurance, etc. This generally is not a major issue because he would have to do this anyhow if he owned the asset. This kind of arrangement is known as a net financial lease, or simply, a net lease, implying that the lessor is focusing on advancing capital. Putting it another way, the lessor is an investor, not an asset manager.

Turning to the author's concerns, we should first observe that he would not be the owner of the asset. However, unless there is some pride of ownership issue involved, he would probably be primarily concerned with the use of the asset for the intended time period. This would be accomplished by structuring the arrangement to include lease renewal options and/or a purchase option. On the other hand, the cash inflow from the salvage value of the asset would flow to you instead of the author; he would expect the lease payments to reflect this.[11]

The author's firm is incurring a legal obligation to make lease payments for a given period. He is practically borrowing to buy the asset. Look at it this way: If he did not want to utilize debt financing for his firm, for whatever reason, it is unlikely that he would enter into a financial lease arrangement. Given that debt is acceptable for his firm and the nature of the arrangement discussed above, the issue for his firm boils down to this: Should the firm lease or borrow to buy?[12]

To answer that question one must figure out which financing alternative has the lower financing cost. We will now show how to analyze these costs.

We will explain two methods for evaluating the cost of a financial lease. Before doing that, however, we should point out that many techniques are used in practice and it is likely that you will encounter some of these as

---

[10] Here is where we see considerable variety. Sometimes financial leases include a cancellation option, one requiring payment of a substantial penalty, especially if exercised several years prior to the expected terminal date. Furthermore, very often there must be some useful life remaining after the terminal date. When this is the case, there typically is a provision to release or sell the asset.

[11] For some equipment, the expected salvage value is a very small amount. In such cases, salvage value obviously would not be an important consideration in structuring the arrangement.

[12] In the example, the author already owns the asset so the issue is to lease or to find another way to rely on the asset's debt capacity. However, in practice, we more often see firms contemplating financial leases prior to purchasing the asset.

part of the financing proposals prepared by firms and individuals that arrange leases for a fee. We mention this because in our opinion, many of these techniques are flawed. Here are the three most common errors we have encountered:

1. *Improper comparison.* Often these analyses compare a financial lease alternative to a financing alternative that includes some equity financing. Frequently, these analyses are biased in favor of the lease alternative.
2. *Cost of capital.* Very often the cost of capital is used as the discount rate in these analyses. Recall that it is the risk of the cash flows that determines what the appropriate required rate should be. The cost of capital reflects the average risk of the firm as a whole and it is unlikely that this is appropriate for a lease analysis. The firm's interest rate on new borrowing generally is more suitable.
3. *Interest cost of lease.* Many of these analyses quote an equivalent interest rate for the lease. Often, the cited rate will not be meaningful because it likely will not be the same as an effective after-tax interest rate, the rate needed to make a proper assessment.

We will now explain two methods of analysis which we will call the value method and the internal rate of return method. These methods assume that a financial lease is the same as a debt or, to be more precise, the amount of financing provided by the lease alternative utilizes this amount of debt capacity.[13] Very often this assumption will be reasonable enough to make a proper appraisal of the cost of a financial lease alternative. To illustrate the methods we will rely on the following example:

The Sentinel Company has decided to acquire a piece of equipment and is deciding whether to finance it with a financial lease arrangement or to borrow the funds from its commercial bank. The cost of the equipment is $100,000. It would be depreciated on a straight-line basis over a five-year life to a $20,000 salvage value. This equipment would be entitled to an Investment Tax Credit (ITC) of $10,000 and we will assume that the credit would be received at time zero.[14] If the purchase alternative is selected,

---

[13] For an excellent treatment of the conceptual issues involved see: Richard Brealey and Stewart Myers, *Principles of Corporate Finance* (McGraw-Hill) and, James Van Horne, *Financial Management and Policy* (Prentice-Hall).
[14] The ITC does not affect the computation of depreciation when the straight-line method is used. In this example, depreciation expense would be $16,000 per year, which is derived as follows:

$$\text{Straight-Line Depreciation} = \frac{\text{Original Cost} - \text{Salvage Value}}{\text{Number of Years}}$$

$$\$16,000 = \frac{\$100,000 - \$20,000}{5}$$

Sentinel would borrow $90,000 from its bank at an interest rate of 15%. The loan would be repaid in five equal amounts starting one year from now. Sentinel could lease the machine from the manufacturer. The firm would have to make annual lease payments of $21,500, starting one year from now, for five years. There would be no cancellation option, nor would there be an option to renew the lease or purchase the equipment five years from now. Further, Sentinel would have to pay for all maintenance costs, insurance, etc., just as if it owned the machine (i. e., a net lease). Finally, the firm's marginal income tax rate is 40%.

By leasing the machine, the lessor is in effect providing the firm with $90,000 of financing, the cost less the ITC.[15] Looking at it another way, there is an incremental cash outflow of $90,000 foregone by leasing instead of buying. The firm has to make lease payments and these create a tax shield. However, the firm loses the tax shield on depreciation, the tax shield on interest and the salvage value of the equipment. Both of the methods we will explain incorporate the lost tax shields and the salvage value. The salvage value and depreciation tax shield are incorporated in deriving the relevant cash flows and the interest tax shield is incorporated in the discount rate as we will see in a moment.

The value method computes the present value of the cash outflows created by the lease and compares this to the amount of financing provided. If the financing provided is greater than the present value then the lease alternative is cheaper and vice versa. Table 11-3 has the analysis.

Column one has the amount of financing provided by the financial lease alternative. Column two has the lease payments. The next column has the tax shields that the lease payments would create given a 40% rate. The fourth column has the depreciation tax shields lost. They are outflows because the firm foregoes receiving these shields by leasing because it would

**Table 11-3**  *Value Method*

|  | (1) | (2) | (3) Lease | (4) Depreciation | (5) | (6) | | (7) | | (8) |
|---|---|---|---|---|---|---|---|---|---|---|
| End of Year | Financing Provided | Lease Payments | Tax Shields | Tax Shield Foregone | Residual Value | Net Cash Flow | | (PV$1,9%,n) | | Present Value |
| 0 | $90,000 | | | | | $90,000 | × | 1.0000 | = | $90,000 |
| 1 | | ($21,500) | $8,600 | ($6,400) | | (19,300) | × | .9174 | = | (17,706) |
| 2 | | (21,500) | 8,600 | (6,400) | | (19,300) | × | .8417 | = | (16,245) |
| 3 | | (21,500) | 8,600 | (6,400) | | (19,300) | × | .7722 | = | (14,903) |
| 4 | | (21,500) | 8,600 | (6,400) | | (19,300) | × | .7084 | = | (13,672) |
| 5 | | (21,500) | 8,600 | (6,400) | (20,000) | (39,300) | × | .6499 | = | (25,541) |
| | | | | | | | | Value | = | $1,933 |

[15] In some lease arrangements the ITC is "passed through" which means the firm would be entitled to claim it on its tax return.

not be able to deduct depreciation.[16] Interest tax shields are also lost but incorporate this in the rate as we will see. Column five has the salvage value that would be lost by leasing.[17] The sixth column has the sum of the nrst four and notice that except for the fifth year, the amounts are computed s follows:

Lease payment
− Lease tax shield
+ Depreciation tax shield foregone
= Net cash flow

In the last year we add the lost salvage value.

The net cash flow figures in column six are the relevant cash flows for the analysis. We compute the present value of these cash flows at the after-tax interest rate on the debt alternative which is 9% as shown below.[18]

$$\text{Discount Rate} = \text{Interest Rate} \times (1 - \text{Tax Rate})$$
$$9\% \quad = \quad 15\% \quad \times (1 - 40\%)$$

Column eight has the present value of these cash flows and as shown, the sum of these is a positive $1,933. We call this the value of the lease and we interpret it in the following way: If the value is positive, the lease alternative has a lower financing cost than the debt alternative. If the value is negative, the debt alternative is cheaper. Here we have a positive value of $1,933 indicating that lease financing is cheaper than the debt alternative. Hence, if there are no other factors to offset this cost advantage, then Sentinel should select the lease alternative.

The internal rate of return method uses the same relevant cash flows as the value method. What we are trying to do is to compute an after-tax interest rate for the lease. We do this by computing the internal rate of return for the cash flows shown in column six of Table 11-3. Specifically, we find the rate that makes the present value of the cash outflows in column six equal to the $90,000 which is the outlay saved at time zero. The IRR of this stream is 8.25%. We then compare this rate to the after-tax interest

[16] Keep in mind that we are talking about the tax treatment. For financial accounting purposes, this lease might have to be capitalized and if so depreciation expense would be recorded on the books.
[17] It is called residual value instead of salvage value because the end of the lease period may not coincide with the end of the asset's useful life. Also, we should point out that the salvage value estimate is typically less certain than the other cash flow estimates. When this is the case, many analysts alter the analysis. Specifically, they either test the impact of various salvage value estimates on the lease's value or IRR or employ a higher rate to compute the present value of the salvage value in calculating the value of the lease.
[18] If a specific debt alternative was not being considered, we would rely on an estimate of the interest rate on similar debt, that is, the rate on debt with the same maturity and payment flow as the lease alternative.

rate which is 9%. The IRR is lower indicating that the lease alternative is cheaper.

Before closing, we should mention another caveat about techniques used in practice. Earlier we noted that often interest rates for the lease are cited in these analyses. What many do is compute the rate that makes the before-tax lease payments equal to the cost of the asset. For instance, for Sentinel these analysts would find the discount rate that makes the lease payments of $21,500 shown in column two of Table 11-3 equal to the $100,000 cost of the asset. This is about 2.5% which obviously seems very attractive. The trouble is it is not comparable to a pretax or after-tax interest rate on debt financing or anything else for that matter.

# Problems and Discussion Questions

## A. Solved Problems

### Problem 11-1A

The Martex Company has decided to undertake a new project which is expected to increase operating income (i. e., EBIT) above the projected $2 million level. The project will require $1.2 million of new external capital and the following three alternatives are being considered.

- Raise all $1.2 million through the issue of new common stock at a price of $12 per share, net of transaction costs.

- Raise half the capital through the issue of new common stock at the same price, and the other half through long-term debt at a rate of 14%.

- Raise half the capital through the issue of long-term debt at 14% and the other half through the issue of new preferred stock at a dividend rate of 10%.

Interest next year on existing long-term debt will be $198,000, preferred dividends on existing preferred will be $40,000, and there are currently 800,000 shares of common stock outstanding. Finally, the firm's income tax rate is 50%.

1. What will EPS be for each financing alternative if the project increases EBIT by $1 million?

2. Identify the EBIT-EPS indifference levels between the first and second, first and third, and the second and third alternatives utilizing the equation format explained in the chapter.

3. Does the EBIT-EPS indifference point indicate the level of EBIT at which one is indifferent between two financing alternatives? Explain.

### Solution 11-1A

1. We will begin by stating a pro forma analysis assuming the project is not accepted ($000 omitted).

| EBIT | $2,000 |
|---|---|
| Interest | 198 |
| EBT | $1,802 |
| Income tax @ 50% | 901 |
| EAT | $ 901 |
| Preferred dividends | 40 |
| EATCS | $ 861 |
| Number of common shares | 800 |
| EPS | $1.076 |

Let's now evaluate each of the three alternatives before computing EPS for each.

- *Raise $1.2 million by issuing common stock at $12 per share.*
  This involves increasing the number of common shares outstanding by 100,000 shares, to a new total of 900,000 shares. There would be no change in interest or preferred dividend obligations.

- *Raise $1.2 million by issuing $600,000 of common stock at $12 per share and $600,000 of long-term debt at 14%.*
  This involves increasing the number of common shares outstanding by 50,000 shares, to a new total of 850,000 shares. Interest expense would increase by $84,000 per year, to a new total of $282,000. There would be no change in preferred stock dividends.

- *Raise $1.2 million by issuing $600,000 of long-term debt at 14% and $600,000 of 10% preferred stock.*
  This involves increasing interest expense by $84,000 per year, to a new total of $282,000. Preferred stock dividends would increase by $60,000 per year, to a new total of $100,000. There would be no change in the number of shares of common stock outstanding.

### EBIT-EPS Analysis
#### (000 omitted)

| | Common | ½ Common and ½ Debt | ½ Debt and ½ Preferred |
|---|---|---|---|
| EBIT | $3,000 | $3,000 | $3,000 |
| Existing interest | 198 | 198 | 198 |
| New interest | 0 | 84 | 84 |
| EBT | $2,802 | $2,718 | $2,718 |
| Income taxes @ 50% | 1,401 | 1,359 | 1,359 |
| EAT | $1,401 | $1,359 | $1,359 |

*EBIT-EPS Analysis (Cont.)*
*(000 omitted)*

|  | Common | ½ Common and ½ Debt | ½ Debt and ½ Preferred |
|---|---|---|---|
| Existing preferred | 40 | 40 | 40 |
| New preferred | 0 | 0 | 60 |
| EATCS | $1,361 | $1,319 | $1,259 |
| Number of common shares | 900 | 850 | 800 |
| EPS | $1.512 | $1.552 | $1.574 |
| EBIT | $2,200 | $2,200 | $2,200 |
| EPS | $1.068 | 1.081 | 1.074 |

At an EBIT of $3 million EPS is highest with the third alternative, and the second alternative gives the highest EPS at an EBIT of $2.2 million. This shows the difference between a fixed dollar cost security and a security that involves a fixed percentage dilution. The higher EBIT is, the greater the impact of the new common shares (i. e., fixed percentage dilution) and vice versa.

2. The indifference EBIT level between alternatives 1 and 2 is $1.79 million as shown below:

*All Common*　　　　　　　　　　　　*½ Common and ½ Debt*

$$\frac{(EBIT - \$198,000)(1-.5) - \$40,000}{900,000} = \frac{(EBIT - \$282,000)(1-50\%) - \$40,000}{850,000}$$

$$EBIT = \$1,790,000$$
$$EPS = \$.84$$

At any level of EBIT above $1.79 million, the ½ common and ½ debt alternative will give a higher EPS than the all common alternative and vice versa. (Incidentally, as explained in the chapter, you should check your answer. That is, you should compute EPS for each alternative at an EBIT $1.79 million to check that EPS for each is $ .84.)

The intersection point for the first and third alternatives is $2.114 million as shown below:

*All Common*　　　　　　　　　　　　*½ Debt + ½ Preferred*

$$\frac{(EBIT - \$198,000)(1-.5) - \$40,000}{900,000} = \frac{(EBIT - \$282,000)(1-.5) - \$100,000}{800,000}$$

$$EBIT = \$2,114,000$$
$$EPS = \$1.02$$

Finally, the intersection point for the second and third alternatives is $2.402 million as shown below:

$$\underset{850,000}{\underbrace{\frac{(EBIT-\$282,000)(1-.5)-\$40,000}{}}_{\frac{1}{2}\ Common+\frac{1}{2}\ Debt}} = \underset{800,000}{\underbrace{\frac{(EBIT-\$282,000)(1-.5)-\$100,000}{}}_{\frac{1}{2}\ Debt+\frac{1}{2}\ Preferred}}$$

$$EBIT = \$2,402,000$$
$$EPS = \$1.20$$

3. The answer is "no." An analysis of EPS is an assessment of the income factor only and one must also consider supply, flexibility, control, and risk.

## Problem 11-2A

For the Martex Company (Problem 11-1A) compute the Degree of Financial Leverage (DOF) at an EBIT level of $2.2 million for each alternative. What is the interpretation of each of these numbers? Relate your findings to those of Problem 11-1A.

## Solution 11-2A

The DOF measures the percentage change in EPS that will result from a given percentage change in EBIT at a given EBIT level. It can be computed as follows:

$$DOF = \frac{EBIT}{EBIT - Interest - \dfrac{Preferred\ Dividends}{1 - Tax\ Rate}}$$

We will now compute the DOF for each.

*Alternative 1. All Common Stock*
$$DOF = \frac{\$2,200}{\$2,200 - \$198 - \$80} = 1.145$$

*Alternative 2. ½ Common Stock, ½ Debt*
$$DOF = \frac{\$2,200}{\$2,200 - \$282 - \$80} = 1.197$$

*Alternative 3. ½ Debt, ½ Preferred Stock*
$$DOF = \frac{\$2,200}{\$2,200 - \$282 - \$200} = 1.281$$

Each computed value of DOF indicates the multiplier effect of financial leverage (the extent to which there are fixed charges—interest and preferred stock dividends—in financing) on EPS. Recall from Problem 11-1A that an EBIT level of $3 million is expected. This potential change of EBIT from $2.2 million to $3 million represents a percentage change of 36.4%. The resulting percentage and dollar changes in EPS can be summariz·d as follows:

| | % Change EBIT | × | DOF | = | % Change EPS | EPS at $2.2 Million EBIT Level + Increase | = | EPS at $3 million EBIT Level |
|---|---|---|---|---|---|---|---|---|
| All common | 36.4% | × | 1.145 | = | 41.68% | $1.068 + $1.068(.4168) | = | $1.513 |
| ½ Common | | | | | | | | |
| ½ Preferred | 36.4% | × | 1.197 | = | 43.57% | $1.081 + $1.081(.4357) | = | $1.552 |
| ½ Debt | | | | | | | | |
| ½ Preferred | 36.4% | × | 1.281 | = | 46.63% | $1.074 + $1.074(.4663) | = | $1.575 |

Comparing these results with those of Problem 11-1A we see that the EPS figures are identical except for rounding. We are, of course, measuring the same thing in both cases: the expected EPS given a certain increase (or decrease) in EBIT from a given EBIT level for each financial alternative. Note that the DOF is highest for Alternative 3 and lowest for Alternative 1. This illustrates that financial leverage makes a firm's EPS more variable (i. e., riskier).

## Problem 11-3A

The Buffington Company needs to raise $70,000 in cash and is considering either borrowing the necessary funds or entering into a sale-and-leaseback arrangement with its data processing equipment. The equipment involved currently has a book value of $100,000 and is being depreciated on a straight-line basis to a $10,000 salvage value with three years of life remaining. Buffington fully intends to replace the equipment at the end of three years and is not interested in continued ownership or leasing beyond three years. The following two financing alternatives are being considered:

*Three-year bank loan.* A loan for $70,000 can be obtained at a rate of 16% from a commercial bank. The loan would be paid in three equal annual installments starting one year from now. The equipment would serve as collateral for the loan.

*Sale-and-leaseback arrangement.* A leasing company has offered to purchase the equipment for $70,000 today,[1] then lease back the equipment to Buffington for the next three years. Annual lease payments of $28,000 would be required starting one year from now. Buffington would not have the option to cancel during the

---

[1] Ignore the potential to impact on the sale of the equipment.

three years, nor would there be an option to purchase the equipment or release it in three years. Finally, Buffington would have to pay to maintain the equipment (i. e., it is a net financial lease) and its marginal income tax rate is 30%.

1. Derive the relevant cash flows for the lease versus borrow and buy analysis.

2. Relying on the Value and IRR methods, determine whether it is cheaper to lease or borrow. In computing a discount rate, round to the nearest full percent.

*Solution 11-3A*

1. The analysis is in Table 11-4. The first column shows the financing provided by the lease, the next has the lease payments, and after that there are the lease tax shields which were derived by multiplying 30% times the lease payments. Depreciation is $30,000 per year, given the $100,000 book value and $10,000 salvage value, and at 30% the tax shield lost will be $9,000 per year. The last two columns have the salvage value that would be foregone and the net cash flows which are derived by summing the previous columns. These net cash flow figures are used for both the Value and IRR methods.

2. The lease's value is the present value of the cash inflows at the after-tax interest rate, which is 11.2% in this case (16% times one minus 30%). This rate was rounded to 11% and as shown in Table 11-4, the value at this rate is a negative $7,202. The negative value indicates that it would be cheaper for the firm to borrow. The IRR is the rate that makes the present value of the outflows equal to $70,000. It is between 16%–17% as shown in Table 11-4. The IRR is greater than the after-tax interest rate of 11% indicating it would be cheaper to borrow.

**Table 11-4**   *Analysis for Lease versus Borrow Decision for Buffington*

| End of Year | Financing Provided | Lease Payments | Lease Tax Shield | Depreciation Tax Shield Foregone | Residual Value | Net Cash Flows |
|---|---|---|---|---|---|---|
| 0 | $70,000 | | | | | $70,000 |
| 1 | | ($28,000) | $8,400 | ($9,000) | | (28,600) |
| 2 | | (28,000) | 8,400 | (9,000) | | (28,600) |
| 3 | | (28,000) | 8,400 | (9,000) | ($10,000) | (38,600) |
| | | | | | PV@11% = | ($7,202) |
| | | | | | IRR = | 16% to 17% |

## B. Discussion Questions

### Problem 11-1B

Suppose a firm can raise preferred with a dividend rate of 10% and the same quantity of debt at an interest rate of 12%. Since the dividend rate is less than the interest rate, does it follow that the preferred stock alternative would produce a higher level of EPS than debt? Explain.

### Problem 11-2B

Explain why, according to the traditional view, a firm's cost of capital tends first to decrease and then to increase as the firm increases its debt to equity ratio.

### Problem 11-3B

The EBIT-EPS Chart shown in the text is similar to actual situations in the sense that generally the lines for the debt and common stock alternatives will intersect. Why do they intersect?

### Problem 11-4B

Say an evaluation of debt and preferred stock alternatives for a given firm shows that EPS would be higher with debt at all levels of EBIT. Should the firm even consider preferred stock?

### Problem 11-5B

Is it true for all firms that the DOF for a given firm will vary with EBIT? Explain.

### Problem 11-6B

Why are sinking fund payments *not* deducted from EBIT in computing EPS? Does this imply sinking fund payments are unimportant?

## C. Study Problems

### Problem 11-1C

The Arnone Company is considering the following three alternatives for raising $5 million of capital.

- Issue long-term debt with an interest rate of 12%. The debt would require annual sinking fund payments of $1 million starting one year from now.

• Issue 500,000 shares of common stock to net the firm $10 per share. There are currently four million common shares outstanding.

• Raise $5 million of preferred stock with a dividend rate of 11%. Dividends on existing preferred will be $100,000 next year and interest on existing debt outstanding will be $400,000 next year.

    This $5 million of capital will fund a project that is expected to increase operating profit (EBIT) from $18 million to $20 million. Finally the firm's marginal income tax rate is 40%.

1. Compute EPS for each financing alternative at the projected level of EBIT.

2. Compute the EBIT-EPS indifference levels relying on the equation format illustrated in the text. Interpret what these indifference levels mean.

3. What other factors should the Arnone Company consider in making this financing decision?

## Problem 11-2C

Prepare an EBIT-EPS Chart for the Arnone Company (Problem 11-1C) depicting the debt and common stock alternatives only. Answer the following:

1. Do the lines for each alternative have the same slope? What are the implications of this?

2. At what level of EBIT does each line cross the horizontal axis? How would you interpret these EBIT levels?

3. If the firm could issue shares at a net price of more than $10 per share, what would happen to the intersection point between the debt and common stock lines? What are the implications of this, if any, for the relative attractiveness of debt and common stock financing?

## Problem 11-3C

The following questions pertain to the Arnone Company (Problem 11-1C).

1. Compute the DOF for each financing alternative at the $20 million projected EBIT level. Explain what these numbers mean.

2. Compute the DOF for each financing alternative at EBIT levels of $15 million and $25 million. Comment on your answer.

### Problem 11-4C

The Flint Company needs to raise $200,000 to finance a new project that is expected to increase the firm's EBIT to $600,000 next year. The following financing alternatives are being considered:

- Issue 10,000 shares of common stock to net the firm $20 per share. The firm currently has 60,000 shares of common stock outstanding.

- Borrow $200,000 at an interest rate of 14%. The loan would require five equal annual payments starting one year from now.

- Issue 5,000 common shares at a net price of $20 per share and borrow $100,000 at an interest rate of 12%. The loan would be repaid in equal annual installments over the next five years.

The firm currently has no debt or preferred stock and its tax rate is 50%.

1. Calculate EPS for each of the three financing alternatives at the $600,000 projected EBIT level.

2. Compute the EBIT-EPS indifference level between the first and second, the first and third, and the second and third alternatives.

3. Comment on your answer.

### Problem 11-5C

Harold Smith is about to form a new firm and needs $10 million of capital. He has been advised that he can issue stock at a net price of $25 per share provided that the long-term debt to capital ratio is 20% or less and a net price of $20 per share if the debt to capital ratio is between 21% and 50%. Debt financing above the 50% is believed to be unfeasible. With respect to the cost of debt, Harold has been advised that the interest rate will average 14% if the debt to capital ratio is 20% or less and the rate will average 16% for all debt at debt levels between 21% to 50%. Finally, the new firm will have a tax rate of 50%.

1. Assuming an EBIT level of $5 million the first year, compute EPS for the following two financing alternatives.

- • $2 million of long-term debt and $8 million of common stock.

- • $5 million of long-term debt and $5 million of common stock.

2. Calculate the EBIT indifference level for the financing alternatives noted in 1.

3. Compute the DOF for each alternative noted in 1 at the $5 million projected EBIT level.

## Problem 11-6C

The Ralston Company needs to raise $5 million and is considering the following two alternatives:

- • Issue bonds with a coupon rate of 14%.

- • Issue common stock at a net price of $20 per share.

Interest on existing long-term debt will be $200,000 next year, dividends on preferred stock will be $50,000, the firm currently has 750,000 shares of common stock outstanding and its income tax rate is 40%. Management estimates that if the debt alternative is chosen EPS will be $2 next year.

1. What is the projected EBIT level for next year?

2. Compute EPS for the common stock alternative at the projected EBIT level.

3. Compute the EBIT indifference level for the two financing alternatives.

## Problem 11-7C

The Dresden Company has decided to acquire a piece of equipment that will cost $1 million, including installation costs, and will be depreciated on a straight-line basis over its five-year useful life to an estimated salvage value of $100,000. The firm has considered numerous financing alternatives and has narrowed the choice to the following two:

- • Borrow $1 million from a commercial bank at 15%. The loan would require five equal annual installments starting one year from now.
- • Lease the equipment from the manufacturer. The arrangement would be noncancellable, would require five equal annual payments of $250,000 starting one year from now, and there would

be no option to release or purchase. Finally, the firm would have to pay for all maintenance, insurance, and other operating costs just as if it owned the asset.

The firm's marginal income tax rate is 40%. Finally, you may ignore the Investment Tax Credit (ITC).

Relying on the Value and IRR methods determine which finan _ng alternative is cheaper.

## Problem 11-8C

The Carter Company needs to raise $10 million to purchase a piece of equipment that would be depreciated at a rate of $2 million per year over its five year life. The equipment is not entitled to an ITC and management of Carter fully intends to purchase a newer model five years from now. Further, management is confident that the equipment will have a zero salvage value five years from now. The following two financing alternatives are being considered:

• Borrow $10 million from a commercial bank. The loan would be secured by the equipment and would require five equal annual installments of $2,912,835 starting one year from now.

• Lease the equipment from the manufacturer. It would be a net lease requiring five equal annual payments of $3 million starting one year from now. The lease could not be cancelled, however, there would be the option to purchase the equipment for $100,000 five years from now.

The firm's marginal income tax rate is 50%.

1. Determine whether it would be cheaper for Carter to lease or to borrow and buy.

## Problem 11-9C

The Jones Company needs to buy a piece of equipment for $2 million. There would be no ITC on the equipment and annual depreciation charges over its five-year life would be the following:

| Year | Depreciation Expenses |
|---|---|
| 1 | $300,000 |
| 2 | 440,000 |
| 3 | 420,000 |
| 4 | 420,000 |
| 5 | 420,000 |
| Total | $2,000,000 |

Although the machine could be fully depreciated for tax purposes, it is estimated that it would have a salvage value of $200,000 five years from now.

Management can borrow $2 million at 15% for five years to finance the equipment. Alternatively, it could lease the equipment from the manufacturer. It would be a net lease that could not be cancelled and there would be no option to release or purchase five years from now. The lease would require five equal annual payments of $640,000 with the first payment due one year from now. Finally, the firm's marginal income tax rate would be 40%.

1. Determine whether it is cheaper to lease or borrow using the value method of analysis.

2. Explain how an option to release or to purchase would affect the analysis.

# References

Below are the references for each major section of the book. For textbooks, we generally will not cite specific editions (unless the topic is likely edition-specific) because they probably will be in newer editions by the time you are seeking them out. For articles, we generally will cite those published from 1980 onward. These articles will include references to earlier publications.

## Part I
### (Chapters 1, 2, and 3)

Anthony and Welsch, *Fundamentals of Financial Accounting* (Irwin)

Bernstein, *Financial Statement Analysis: Theory, Application and Interpretation* (Irwin)

Chen and Shimerda, "An Empirical Analysis of Useful Financial Ratios," *Financial Management* Spring 1981.

Davidson, Schindler, Stickney, and Weil, *Accounting, the Language of Business* (Horton Company)

Ford, *A Framework for Financial Analysis* (Prentice-Hall)

Foster, *Financial Statement Analysis* (Prentice-Hall)

Harrington and Wilson, *Corporate Financial Analysis* (Business Publications)

Helfert, *Techniques of Financial Analysis* (Irwin)

Higgins, *Analysis for Financial Management* (Irwin)

Meigs, Mosick, and Johnson, *Intermediate Accounting* (McGraw-Hill)

Minard, Lawrence, and Wilson, editors, *Forbes Numbers Game* (Prentice-Hall, 1980)

Ohlson, "Financial Ratios and Probablistic Prediction of Bankruptcy," *Journal of Accounting Research*, Spring 1980

Viscione, *Analyzing Ratios: A Perceptive Approach* (National Association of Credit Management)

Viscione, *Flow of Funds and Other Financial Concepts* (National Association of Credit Management)

Welsch, Zlatkovich, and White, *Intermediate Accounting* (Irwin)

## Part II
## (Chapters 4, 5, and 6)

Ford, *A Framework for Financial Analysis* (Prentice-Hall)

Harrington and Wilson, *Corporate Financial Analysis* (Business Publications)

Higgins, *Analysis for Financial Management* (Irwin)

Horngren, *Cost Accounting: A Managerial Approach* (Prentice-Hall)

Van Horne, *Financial Management and Policy* (Prentice-Hall)

Viscione, *How to Construct Pro Forma Statements* (National Association of Credit Management)

Weston and Brigham, *Managerial Finance* (Harper & Row)

## Part III
## (Chapters 7, 8, 9, 10 and 11)

Ang and Lewellen, "Risk Adjustment in Capital Investment Project Evaluations," *Financial Management* Summer 1982

Barnea, Haugen, and Senbet, "An Equilibrium Analysis of Debt Financing Under Costly Tax Arbitrage and Agency Problems," *Journal of Finance* June 1981

Bierman and Smidt, *The Capital Expenditure Decision* (Macmillan)

Brealey and Myers, *Principles of Corporate Finance* (McGraw-Hill)

Clark, Hindelang, and Prichard, *Capital Budgeting: Planning and Control of Capital Expenditures* (Prentice-Hall)

Crawford, Harpert, and McConnell, "Further Evidence on the Terms of Financial Leases," *Financial Management* Autumn 1981

DeAngelo and Masulis, "Leverage and Dividend Irrelevancy Under Corporate and Personal Taxation," *Journal of Finance* May 1980

Dorfman, "The Meanings of Internal Rates of Return," *Journal of Finance* December 1981

Emery, "Some Guidelines fjor Evaluating Capital Investment Alternatives with Unequal Lives," *Financial Management* Spring 1982

Fuller and Kerr, "Estimating the Divisional Cost of Capital: An Analysis of the Pure-Play Technique," *Journal of Finance* December 1981

Gitman and Mercurio, "Cost of Capital Techniques Used by Major U.S. Firms: Survey and Analysis of Fortune's 1000," *Financial Management* Winter 1982

Kim, "Miller's Equilibrium, Shareholder Leverage Clienteles and Optimum Capital Structure," *Journal of Finance* May 1982

Marsh, "The Choice Between Equity and Debt, An Empirical Study," *Journal of Finance* March 1982

Masulis, "The Impact of Capital Structure Change on Firm Value: Some Estimates," *Journal of Finance* March 1983

McCarthy and McDaniel, "A Note on Expensing Versus Depreciating Under the Accelerated Cost Recovery System: Comment," *Financial Management* Summer 1983

McConnell and Schallheim, "Valuation of Asset Leasing Contracts," *Journal of Financial Economics* August 1983

Modigliani, "Debt, Dividend Policy, Taxes, Inflation and Market Valuation" *Journal of Finance* May 1982

O'Brien and Nunnally, "A 1982 Survey of Corporate Leasing Analysis," *Financial Management* Summer 1983

Osteryoung, *Capital Budgeting: Long-Term Asset Selection* (Grid)

Schall and Haley, *Introduction to Financial Management* (McGraw-Hill)

Schneller, "Taxes and the Optimal Capital Structure of the Firm," *Journal of Finance* March 1980

Scott and Johnson, "Financing Policies and Practices in Large Corporations," *Financial Management* Summer 1982

Taggart, "Taxes and Corporate Capital Structure in an Incomplete Market," *Journal of Finance* June 1980

Van Horne, *Financial Management and Policy* (Prentice-Hall)

Weston and Brigham, *Managerial Finance* (Harper & Row)

Weston, "Developments in Finance Theory," *Financial Management,* Tenth Anniversary Issue 1981

# Appendixes

# Appendix F-1

## TABLE OF FUTURE VALUE FACTORS OF $1 FOR VARIOUS INTEREST RATES AND PERIODS

| RATE PERIOD | 1% | 2% | 3% | 4% | 5% | 6% | 7% | 8% | 9% | 10% | 11% | 12% | 13% | 14% | 15% |
|---|---|---|---|---|---|---|---|---|---|---|---|---|---|---|---|
| 1 | 1.0100 | 1.0200 | 1.0300 | 1.0400 | 1.0500 | 1.0600 | 1.0700 | 1.0800 | 1.0900 | 1.1000 | 1.1100 | 1.1200 | 1.1300 | 1.1400 | 1.1500 |
| 2 | 1.0201 | 1.0404 | 1.0609 | 1.0816 | 1.1025 | 1.1236 | 1.1449 | 1.1664 | 1.1881 | 1.2100 | 1.2321 | 1.2544 | 1.2769 | 1.2996 | 1.3225 |
| 3 | 1.0303 | 1.0612 | 1.0927 | 1.1249 | 1.1576 | 1.1910 | 1.2250 | 1.2597 | 1.2950 | 1.3310 | 1.3676 | 1.4049 | 1.4429 | 1.4815 | 1.5209 |
| 4 | 1.0406 | 1.0824 | 1.1255 | 1.1699 | 1.2155 | 1.2625 | 1.3108 | 1.3605 | 1.4116 | 1.4641 | 1.5181 | 1.5735 | 1.6305 | 1.6890 | 1.7490 |
| 5 | 1.0510 | 1.1041 | 1.1593 | 1.2167 | 1.2763 | 1.3382 | 1.4026 | 1.4693 | 1.5386 | 1.6105 | 1.6851 | 1.7623 | 1.8424 | 1.9254 | 2.0114 |
| 6 | 1.0615 | 1.1262 | 1.1941 | 1.2653 | 1.3401 | 1.4185 | 1.5007 | 1.5869 | 1.6771 | 1.7716 | 1.8704 | 1.9738 | 2.0820 | 2.1950 | 2.3131 |
| 7 | 1.0721 | 1.1487 | 1.2299 | 1.3159 | 1.4071 | 1.5036 | 1.6058 | 1.7138 | 1.8280 | 1.9487 | 2.0762 | 2.2107 | 2.3526 | 2.5023 | 2.6600 |
| 8 | 1.0829 | 1.1717 | 1.2668 | 1.3686 | 1.4775 | 1.5938 | 1.7182 | 1.8509 | 1.9926 | 2.1436 | 2.3045 | 2.4760 | 2.6584 | 2.8526 | 3.0590 |
| 9 | 1.0937 | 1.1951 | 1.3048 | 1.4233 | 1.5513 | 1.6895 | 1.8385 | 1.9990 | 2.1719 | 2.3579 | 2.5580 | 2.7731 | 3.0040 | 3.2519 | 3.5179 |
| 10 | 1.1046 | 1.2190 | 1.3439 | 1.4802 | 1.6289 | 1.7908 | 1.9672 | 2.1589 | 2.3674 | 2.5937 | 2.8394 | 3.1058 | 3.3946 | 3.7072 | 4.0456 |
| 11 | 1.1157 | 1.2434 | 1.3842 | 1.5395 | 1.7103 | 1.8983 | 2.1049 | 2.3316 | 2.5804 | 2.8531 | 3.1518 | 3.4785 | 3.8359 | 4.2262 | 4.6524 |
| 12 | 1.1268 | 1.2682 | 1.4258 | 1.6010 | 1.7959 | 2.0122 | 2.2522 | 2.5182 | 2.8127 | 3.1384 | 3.4985 | 3.8960 | 4.3345 | 4.8179 | 5.3503 |
| 13 | 1.1381 | 1.2936 | 1.4685 | 1.6651 | 1.8856 | 2.1329 | 2.4098 | 2.7196 | 3.0658 | 3.4523 | 3.8833 | 4.3635 | 4.8980 | 5.4924 | 6.1528 |
| 14 | 1.1495 | 1.3195 | 1.5126 | 1.7317 | 1.9799 | 2.2609 | 2.5785 | 2.9372 | 3.3417 | 3.7975 | 4.3104 | 4.8871 | 5.5348 | 6.2613 | 7.0757 |
| 15 | 1.1610 | 1.3459 | 1.5580 | 1.8009 | 2.0789 | 2.3966 | 2.7590 | 3.1722 | 3.6425 | 4.1772 | 4.7846 | 5.4736 | 6.2543 | 7.1379 | 8.1371 |
| 16 | 1.1726 | 1.3728 | 1.6047 | 1.8730 | 2.1829 | 2.5404 | 2.9522 | 3.4259 | 3.9703 | 4.5950 | 5.3109 | 6.1304 | 7.0673 | 8.1372 | 9.3576 |
| 17 | 1.1843 | 1.4002 | 1.6528 | 1.9479 | 2.2920 | 2.6928 | 3.1588 | 3.7000 | 4.3276 | 5.0545 | 5.8951 | 6.8660 | 7.9861 | 9.2765 | 10.761 |
| 18 | 1.1961 | 1.4282 | 1.7024 | 2.0258 | 2.4066 | 2.8543 | 3.3799 | 3.9960 | 4.7171 | 5.5599 | 6.5436 | 7.6900 | 9.0243 | 10.575 | 12.375 |
| 19 | 1.2081 | 1.4568 | 1.7535 | 2.1068 | 2.5270 | 3.0256 | 3.6165 | 4.3157 | 5.1417 | 6.1159 | 7.2633 | 8.6128 | 10.197 | 12.056 | 14.232 |
| 20 | 1.2202 | 1.4859 | 1.8061 | 2.1911 | 2.6533 | 3.2071 | 3.8697 | 4.6610 | 5.6044 | 6.7275 | 8.0623 | 9.6463 | 11.523 | 13.743 | 16.367 |
| 21 | 1.2324 | 1.5157 | 1.8603 | 2.2788 | 2.7860 | 3.3996 | 4.1406 | 5.0338 | 6.1088 | 7.4002 | 8.9492 | 10.804 | 13.021 | 15.668 | 18.822 |
| 22 | 1.2447 | 1.5460 | 1.9161 | 2.3699 | 2.9253 | 3.6035 | 4.4304 | 5.4365 | 6.6586 | 8.1403 | 9.9336 | 12.100 | 14.714 | 17.861 | 21.645 |
| 23 | 1.2572 | 1.5769 | 1.9736 | 2.4647 | 3.0715 | 3.8197 | 4.7405 | 5.8715 | 7.2579 | 8.9543 | 11.026 | 13.552 | 16.627 | 20.362 | 24.891 |
| 24 | 1.2697 | 1.6084 | 2.0328 | 2.5633 | 3.2251 | 4.0489 | 5.0724 | 6.3412 | 7.9111 | 9.8497 | 12.239 | 15.179 | 18.788 | 23.212 | 28.625 |
| 25 | 1.2824 | 1.6406 | 2.0938 | 2.6658 | 3.3864 | 4.2919 | 5.4274 | 6.8485 | 8.6231 | 10.835 | 13.585 | 17.000 | 21.231 | 26.462 | 32.919 |
| 26 | 1.2953 | 1.6734 | 2.1566 | 2.7725 | 3.5557 | 4.5494 | 5.8074 | 7.3964 | 9.3992 | 11.918 | 15.080 | 19.040 | 23.991 | 30.167 | 37.857 |
| 27 | 1.3082 | 1.7069 | 2.2213 | 2.8834 | 3.7335 | 4.8223 | 6.2139 | 7.9881 | 10.245 | 13.110 | 16.739 | 21.325 | 27.109 | 34.390 | 43.535 |
| 28 | 1.3213 | 1.7410 | 2.2879 | 2.9987 | 3.9201 | 5.1117 | 6.6488 | 8.6271 | 11.167 | 14.421 | 18.580 | 23.884 | 30.633 | 39.204 | 50.066 |
| 29 | 1.3345 | 1.7758 | 2.3566 | 3.1187 | 4.1161 | 5.4184 | 7.1143 | 9.3173 | 12.172 | 15.863 | 20.624 | 26.750 | 34.616 | 44.693 | 57.575 |
| 30 | 1.3478 | 1.8114 | 2.4273 | 3.2434 | 4.3219 | 5.7435 | 7.6123 | 10.063 | 13.268 | 17.449 | 22.892 | 29.960 | 39.116 | 50.950 | 66.212 |
| 35 | 1.4166 | 1.9999 | 2.8139 | 3.9461 | 5.5160 | 7.6861 | 10.677 | 14.785 | 20.414 | 28.102 | 38.575 | 52.800 | 72.069 | 98.100 | 133.18 |
| 40 | 1.4889 | 2.2080 | 3.2620 | 4.8010 | 7.0400 | 10.286 | 14.974 | 21.725 | 31.409 | 45.259 | 65.001 | 93.051 | 132.78 | 188.88 | 267.86 |
| 45 | 1.5648 | 2.4379 | 3.7816 | 5.8412 | 8.9850 | 13.765 | 21.002 | 31.920 | 48.327 | 72.890 | 109.53 | 163.99 | 244.64 | 363.68 | 538.77 |
| 50 | 1.6446 | 2.6916 | 4.3839 | 7.1067 | 11.467 | 18.420 | 29.457 | 46.902 | 74.358 | 117.39 | 184.56 | 289.00 | 450.74 | 700.23 | 1083.7 |
| 75 | 2.1091 | 4.4158 | 9.1789 | 18.945 | 38.833 | 79.057 | 159.88 | 321.20 | 641.19 | 1271.9 | 2507.4 | 4913.1 | 9569.4 | 18530. | 35673. |
| 100 | 2.7048 | 7.2446 | 19.219 | 50.505 | 131.50 | 339.30 | 867.72 | 2199.8 | 5529.0 | 13781. | 34064. | 83522. | ****** | ****** | ****** |

| RATE PERIOD | 16% | 17% | 18% | 19% | 20% | 21% | 22% | 23% | 24% | 25% | 30% | 35% | 40% | 45% | 50% |
|---|---|---|---|---|---|---|---|---|---|---|---|---|---|---|---|
| 1 | 1.1600 | 1.1700 | 1.1800 | 1.1900 | 1.2000 | 1.2100 | 1.2200 | 1.2300 | 1.2400 | 1.2500 | 1.3000 | 1.3500 | 1.4000 | 1.4500 | 1.5000 |
| 2 | 1.3456 | 1.3689 | 1.3924 | 1.4161 | 1.4400 | 1.4641 | 1.4884 | 1.5129 | 1.5376 | 1.5625 | 1.6900 | 1.8225 | 1.9600 | 2.1025 | 2.2500 |
| 3 | 1.5609 | 1.6016 | 1.6430 | 1.6852 | 1.7280 | 1.7716 | 1.8158 | 1.8609 | 1.9066 | 1.9531 | 2.1970 | 2.4604 | 2.7440 | 3.0486 | 3.3750 |
| 4 | 1.8106 | 1.8739 | 1.9388 | 2.0053 | 2.0736 | 2.1436 | 2.2153 | 2.2889 | 2.3642 | 2.4414 | 2.8561 | 3.3215 | 3.8416 | 4.4205 | 5.0625 |
| 5 | 2.1003 | 2.1924 | 2.2878 | 2.3864 | 2.4883 | 2.5937 | 2.7027 | 2.8153 | 2.9316 | 3.0518 | 3.7129 | 4.4840 | 5.3782 | 6.4097 | 7.5938 |
| 6 | 2.4364 | 2.5652 | 2.6996 | 2.8398 | 2.9860 | 3.1384 | 3.2973 | 3.4628 | 3.6352 | 3.8147 | 4.8268 | 6.0534 | 7.5295 | 9.2941 | 11.391 |
| 7 | 2.8262 | 3.0012 | 3.1855 | 3.3793 | 3.5832 | 3.7975 | 4.0227 | 4.2593 | 4.5077 | 4.7684 | 6.2749 | 8.1722 | 10.541 | 13.476 | 17.086 |
| 8 | 3.2784 | 3.5115 | 3.7589 | 4.0214 | 4.2998 | 4.5950 | 4.9077 | 5.2389 | 5.5895 | 5.9605 | 8.1573 | 11.032 | 14.758 | 19.541 | 25.629 |
| 9 | 3.8030 | 4.1084 | 4.4355 | 4.7854 | 5.1598 | 5.5599 | 5.9874 | 6.4439 | 6.9310 | 7.4506 | 10.604 | 14.894 | 20.661 | 28.334 | 38.443 |
| 10 | 4.4114 | 4.8068 | 5.2338 | 5.6947 | 6.1917 | 6.7275 | 7.3046 | 7.9259 | 8.5944 | 9.3132 | 13.786 | 20.107 | 28.925 | 41.085 | 57.665 |
| 11 | 5.1173 | 5.6240 | 6.1759 | 6.7767 | 7.4301 | 8.1403 | 8.9117 | 9.7489 | 10.657 | 11.642 | 17.922 | 27.144 | 40.496 | 59.573 | 86.498 |
| 12 | 5.9360 | 6.5801 | 7.2876 | 8.0642 | 8.9161 | 9.8497 | 10.872 | 11.991 | 13.215 | 14.552 | 23.298 | 36.644 | 56.694 | 86.381 | 129.75 |
| 13 | 6.8858 | 7.6987 | 8.5994 | 9.5964 | 10.699 | 11.918 | 13.264 | 14.749 | 16.386 | 18.190 | 30.288 | 49.470 | 79.371 | 125.25 | 194.62 |
| 14 | 7.9875 | 9.0075 | 10.147 | 11.420 | 12.839 | 14.421 | 16.182 | 18.141 | 20.319 | 22.737 | 39.374 | 66.784 | 111.12 | 181.62 | 291.93 |
| 15 | 9.2655 | 10.539 | 11.974 | 13.590 | 15.407 | 17.449 | 19.742 | 22.314 | 25.196 | 28.422 | 51.186 | 90.158 | 155.57 | 263.34 | 437.89 |
| 16 | 10.748 | 12.330 | 14.129 | 16.172 | 18.488 | 21.114 | 24.086 | 27.446 | 31.243 | 35.527 | 66.542 | 121.71 | 217.80 | 381.85 | 656.84 |
| 17 | 12.468 | 14.426 | 16.672 | 19.244 | 22.186 | 25.548 | 29.384 | 33.759 | 38.741 | 44.409 | 86.504 | 164.31 | 304.91 | 553.68 | 985.26 |
| 18 | 14.463 | 16.879 | 19.673 | 22.901 | 26.623 | 30.913 | 35.849 | 41.523 | 48.039 | 55.511 | 112.46 | 221.82 | 426.88 | 802.83 | 1477.9 |
| 19 | 16.777 | 19.748 | 23.214 | 27.252 | 31.948 | 37.404 | 43.736 | 51.074 | 59.568 | 69.389 | 146.19 | 299.46 | 597.63 | 1164.1 | 2216.8 |
| 20 | 19.461 | 23.106 | 27.393 | 32.429 | 38.338 | 45.259 | 53.358 | 62.821 | 73.864 | 86.736 | 190.05 | 404.27 | 836.68 | 1688.0 | 3325.3 |
| 21 | 22.574 | 27.034 | 32.324 | 38.591 | 46.005 | 54.764 | 65.096 | 77.269 | 91.592 | 108.42 | 247.06 | 545.77 | 1171.4 | 2447.5 | 4987.9 |
| 22 | 26.186 | 31.629 | 38.142 | 45.923 | 55.206 | 66.264 | 79.418 | 95.041 | 113.57 | 135.53 | 321.18 | 736.79 | 1639.9 | 3548.9 | 7481.8 |
| 23 | 30.376 | 37.006 | 45.008 | 54.649 | 66.247 | 80.180 | 96.889 | 116.90 | 140.83 | 169.41 | 417.54 | 994.66 | 2295.9 | 5145.9 | 11223. |
| 24 | 35.236 | 43.297 | 53.109 | 65.032 | 79.497 | 97.017 | 118.21 | 143.79 | 174.63 | 211.76 | 542.80 | 1342.8 | 3214.2 | 7461.6 | 16834. |
| 25 | 40.874 | 50.658 | 62.669 | 77.388 | 95.396 | 117.39 | 144.21 | 176.86 | 216.54 | 264.70 | 705.64 | 1812.8 | 4499.9 | 10819. | 25251. |
| 26 | 47.414 | 59.270 | 73.949 | 92.092 | 114.48 | 142.04 | 175.94 | 217.54 | 268.51 | 330.87 | 917.33 | 2447.2 | 6299.8 | 15688. | 37877. |
| 27 | 55.000 | 69.345 | 87.260 | 109.59 | 137.37 | 171.87 | 214.64 | 267.57 | 332.95 | 413.59 | 1192.5 | 3303.8 | 8819.8 | 22748. | 56815. |
| 28 | 63.800 | 81.134 | 102.97 | 130.41 | 164.84 | 207.97 | 261.86 | 329.11 | 412.86 | 516.99 | 1550.3 | 4460.1 | 12348. | 32984. | 85223. |
| 29 | 74.009 | 94.927 | 121.50 | 155.19 | 197.81 | 251.64 | 319.47 | 404.81 | 511.95 | 646.23 | 2015.4 | 6021.1 | 17287. | 47827. | ****** |
| 30 | 85.850 | 111.06 | 143.37 | 184.68 | 237.38 | 304.48 | 389.76 | 497.91 | 634.82 | 807.79 | 2620.0 | 8128.5 | 24201. | 69349. | ****** |
| 35 | 180.31 | 243.50 | 328.00 | 440.70 | 590.67 | 789.75 | 1053.4 | 1401.8 | 1861.1 | 2465.2 | 9727.9 | 36449. | ****** | ****** | ****** |
| 40 | 378.72 | 533.87 | 750.38 | 1051.7 | 1469.8 | 2048.4 | 2847.0 | 3946.4 | 5455.9 | 7523.2 | 36119. | ****** | ****** | ****** | ****** |
| 45 | 795.44 | 1170.5 | 1716.7 | 2509.7 | 3657.3 | 5313.0 | 7694.7 | 11110. | 15995. | 22959. | ****** | ****** | ****** | ****** | ****** |
| 50 | 1670.7 | 2566.2 | 3927.4 | 5988.9 | 9100.4 | 13781. | 20797. | 31279. | 46890. | 70065. | ****** | ****** | ****** | ****** | ****** |
| 75 | 68289. | ****** | ****** | ****** | ****** | ****** | ****** | ****** | ****** | ****** | ****** | ****** | ****** | ****** | ****** |
| 100 | ****** | ****** | ****** | ****** | ****** | ****** | ****** | ****** | ****** | ****** | ****** | ****** | ****** | ****** | ****** |

# Appendix F-2

## TABLE OF FUTURE VALUE FACTORS FOR ANNUITIES FOR VARIOUS INTEREST RATES AND PERIODS

| RATE PERIOD | 1% | 2% | 3% | 4% | 5% | 6% | 7% | 8% | 9% | 10% | 11% | 12% | 13% | 14% | 15% |
|---|---|---|---|---|---|---|---|---|---|---|---|---|---|---|---|
| 1 | 1.0000 | 1.0000 | 1.0000 | 1.0000 | 1.0000 | 1.0000 | 1.0000 | 1.0000 | 1.0000 | 1.0000 | 1.0000 | 1.0000 | 1.0000 | 1.0000 | 1.0000 |
| 2 | 2.0100 | 2.0200 | 2.0300 | 2.0400 | 2.0500 | 2.0600 | 2.0700 | 2.0800 | 2.0900 | 2.1000 | 2.1100 | 2.1200 | 2.1300 | 2.1400 | 2.1500 |
| 3 | 3.0301 | 3.0604 | 3.0909 | 3.1216 | 3.1525 | 3.1836 | 3.2149 | 3.2464 | 3.2781 | 3.3100 | 3.3421 | 3.3744 | 3.4069 | 3.4396 | 3.4725 |
| 4 | 4.0604 | 4.1216 | 4.1836 | 4.2465 | 4.3101 | 4.3746 | 4.4399 | 4.5061 | 4.5731 | 4.6410 | 4.7097 | 4.7793 | 4.8498 | 4.9211 | 4.9934 |
| 5 | 5.1010 | 5.2040 | 5.3091 | 5.4163 | 5.5256 | 5.6371 | 5.7507 | 5.8666 | 5.9847 | 6.1051 | 6.2278 | 6.3528 | 6.4803 | 6.6101 | 6.7424 |
| 6 | 6.1520 | 6.3081 | 6.4684 | 6.6330 | 6.8019 | 6.9753 | 7.1533 | 7.3359 | 7.5233 | 7.7156 | 7.9129 | 8.1152 | 8.3227 | 8.5355 | 8.7537 |
| 7 | 7.2135 | 7.4343 | 7.6625 | 7.8983 | 8.1420 | 8.3938 | 8.6540 | 8.9228 | 9.2004 | 9.4872 | 9.7833 | 10.089 | 10.405 | 10.730 | 11.067 |
| 8 | 8.2857 | 8.5830 | 8.8923 | 9.2142 | 9.5491 | 9.8975 | 10.260 | 10.637 | 11.028 | 11.436 | 11.859 | 12.300 | 12.757 | 13.233 | 13.727 |
| 9 | 9.3685 | 9.7546 | 10.159 | 10.583 | 11.027 | 11.491 | 11.978 | 12.488 | 13.021 | 13.579 | 14.164 | 14.776 | 15.416 | 16.085 | 16.786 |
| 10 | 10.462 | 10.950 | 11.464 | 12.006 | 12.578 | 13.181 | 13.816 | 14.487 | 15.193 | 15.937 | 16.722 | 17.549 | 18.420 | 19.337 | 20.304 |
| 11 | 11.567 | 12.169 | 12.808 | 13.486 | 14.207 | 14.972 | 15.784 | 16.645 | 17.560 | 18.531 | 19.561 | 20.655 | 21.814 | 23.045 | 24.349 |
| 12 | 12.683 | 13.412 | 14.192 | 15.026 | 15.917 | 16.870 | 17.888 | 18.977 | 20.141 | 21.384 | 22.713 | 24.133 | 25.650 | 27.271 | 29.002 |
| 13 | 13.809 | 14.680 | 15.618 | 16.627 | 17.713 | 18.882 | 20.141 | 21.495 | 22.953 | 24.523 | 26.212 | 28.029 | 29.985 | 32.089 | 34.352 |
| 14 | 14.947 | 15.974 | 17.086 | 18.292 | 19.599 | 21.015 | 22.550 | 24.215 | 26.019 | 27.975 | 30.095 | 32.393 | 34.883 | 37.581 | 40.505 |
| 15 | 16.097 | 17.293 | 18.599 | 20.024 | 21.579 | 23.276 | 25.129 | 27.152 | 29.361 | 31.772 | 34.405 | 37.280 | 40.417 | 43.842 | 47.580 |
| 16 | 17.258 | 18.639 | 20.157 | 21.825 | 23.657 | 25.673 | 27.888 | 30.324 | 33.003 | 35.950 | 39.190 | 42.753 | 46.672 | 50.980 | 55.717 |
| 17 | 18.430 | 20.012 | 21.762 | 23.698 | 25.840 | 28.213 | 30.840 | 33.750 | 36.974 | 40.545 | 44.501 | 48.884 | 53.739 | 59.118 | 65.075 |
| 18 | 19.615 | 21.412 | 23.414 | 25.645 | 28.132 | 30.906 | 33.999 | 37.450 | 41.301 | 45.599 | 50.396 | 55.750 | 61.725 | 68.394 | 75.836 |
| 19 | 20.811 | 22.841 | 25.117 | 27.671 | 30.539 | 33.760 | 37.379 | 41.446 | 46.018 | 51.159 | 56.939 | 63.440 | 70.749 | 78.969 | 88.212 |
| 20 | 22.019 | 24.297 | 26.870 | 29.778 | 33.066 | 36.786 | 40.995 | 45.762 | 51.160 | 57.275 | 64.203 | 72.052 | 80.947 | 91.025 | 102.44 |
| 21 | 23.239 | 25.783 | 28.676 | 31.969 | 35.719 | 39.993 | 44.865 | 50.423 | 56.765 | 64.002 | 72.265 | 81.699 | 92.470 | 104.77 | 118.81 |
| 22 | 24.472 | 27.299 | 30.537 | 34.248 | 38.505 | 43.392 | 49.006 | 55.457 | 62.873 | 71.403 | 81.214 | 92.503 | 105.49 | 120.44 | 137.63 |
| 23 | 25.716 | 28.845 | 32.453 | 36.618 | 41.430 | 46.996 | 53.436 | 60.893 | 69.532 | 79.543 | 91.148 | 104.60 | 120.20 | 138.30 | 159.28 |
| 24 | 26.973 | 30.422 | 34.426 | 39.083 | 44.502 | 50.816 | 58.177 | 66.765 | 76.790 | 88.497 | 102.17 | 118.16 | 136.83 | 158.66 | 184.17 |
| 25 | 28.243 | 32.030 | 36.459 | 41.646 | 47.727 | 54.865 | 63.249 | 73.106 | 84.701 | 98.347 | 114.41 | 133.33 | 155.62 | 181.87 | 212.79 |
| 26 | 29.526 | 33.671 | 38.553 | 44.312 | 51.113 | 59.156 | 68.676 | 79.954 | 93.324 | 109.18 | 128.00 | 150.33 | 176.85 | 208.33 | 245.71 |
| 27 | 30.821 | 35.344 | 40.710 | 47.084 | 54.669 | 63.706 | 74.484 | 87.351 | 102.72 | 121.10 | 143.08 | 169.37 | 200.84 | 238.50 | 283.57 |
| 28 | 32.129 | 37.051 | 42.931 | 49.968 | 58.403 | 68.528 | 80.698 | 95.339 | 112.97 | 134.21 | 159.82 | 190.70 | 227.95 | 272.89 | 327.10 |
| 29 | 33.450 | 38.792 | 45.219 | 52.966 | 62.323 | 73.640 | 87.347 | 103.97 | 124.14 | 148.63 | 178.40 | 214.58 | 258.58 | 312.09 | 377.17 |
| 30 | 34.785 | 40.568 | 47.575 | 56.085 | 66.439 | 79.058 | 94.461 | 113.28 | 136.31 | 164.49 | 199.02 | 241.33 | 293.20 | 356.79 | 434.75 |
| 35 | 41.660 | 49.994 | 60.462 | 73.652 | 90.320 | 111.43 | 138.24 | 172.32 | 215.71 | 271.02 | 341.59 | 431.66 | 546.68 | 693.57 | 881.17 |
| 40 | 48.886 | 60.402 | 75.401 | 95.026 | 120.80 | 154.76 | 199.64 | 259.06 | 337.88 | 442.59 | 581.83 | 767.09 | 1013.7 | 1342.0 | 1779.1 |
| 45 | 56.481 | 71.893 | 92.720 | 121.03 | 159.70 | 212.74 | 285.75 | 386.51 | 525.86 | 718.90 | 986.64 | 1358.2 | 1874.2 | 2590.6 | 3585.1 |
| 50 | 64.463 | 84.579 | 112.80 | 152.67 | 209.35 | 290.34 | 406.53 | 573.77 | 815.08 | 1163.9 | 1668.8 | 2400.0 | 3459.5 | 4994.5 | 7217.7 |
| 75 | 110.91 | 170.79 | 272.63 | 448.63 | 756.65 | 1300.9 | 2269.7 | 4002.6 | 7113.2 | 12709. | 22785. | 40934. | 73603. | ****** | ****** |
| 100 | 170.48 | 312.23 | 607.29 | 1237.6 | 2610.0 | 5638.4 | 12382. | 27485. | 61423. | ****** | ****** | ****** | ****** | ****** | ****** |

| RATE PERIOD | 16% | 17% | 18% | 19% | 20% | 21% | 22% | 23% | 24% | 25% | 30% | 35% | 40% | 45% | 50% |
|---|---|---|---|---|---|---|---|---|---|---|---|---|---|---|---|
| 1 | 1.0000 | 1.0000 | 1.0000 | 1.0000 | 1.0000 | 1.0000 | 1.0000 | 1.0000 | 1.0000 | 1.0000 | 1.0000 | 1.0000 | 1.0000 | 1.0000 | 1.0000 |
| 2 | 2.1600 | 2.1700 | 2.1800 | 2.1900 | 2.2000 | 2.2100 | 2.2200 | 2.2300 | 2.2400 | 2.2500 | 2.3000 | 2.3500 | 2.4000 | 2.4500 | 2.5000 |
| 3 | 3.5056 | 3.5389 | 3.5724 | 3.6061 | 3.6400 | 3.6741 | 3.7084 | 3.7429 | 3.7776 | 3.8125 | 3.9900 | 4.1725 | 4.3600 | 4.5525 | 4.7500 |
| 4 | 5.0665 | 5.1405 | 5.2154 | 5.2913 | 5.3680 | 5.4457 | 5.5242 | 5.6038 | 5.6842 | 5.7656 | 6.1870 | 6.6329 | 7.1040 | 7.6011 | 8.1250 |
| 5 | 6.8771 | 7.0144 | 7.1542 | 7.2966 | 7.4416 | 7.5892 | 7.7396 | 7.8926 | 8.0484 | 8.2070 | 9.0431 | 9.9544 | 10.946 | 12.022 | 13.188 |
| 6 | 8.9775 | 9.2068 | 9.4420 | 9.6830 | 9.9299 | 10.183 | 10.442 | 10.708 | 10.980 | 11.259 | 12.756 | 14.438 | 16.324 | 18.431 | 20.781 |
| 7 | 11.414 | 11.772 | 12.142 | 12.523 | 12.916 | 13.321 | 13.740 | 14.171 | 14.615 | 15.073 | 17.583 | 20.492 | 23.853 | 27.725 | 32.172 |
| 8 | 14.240 | 14.773 | 15.327 | 15.902 | 16.499 | 17.119 | 17.762 | 18.430 | 19.123 | 19.842 | 23.858 | 28.664 | 34.395 | 41.202 | 49.258 |
| 9 | 17.519 | 18.285 | 19.086 | 19.923 | 20.799 | 21.714 | 22.670 | 23.669 | 24.712 | 25.802 | 32.015 | 39.696 | 49.153 | 60.743 | 74.887 |
| 10 | 21.321 | 22.393 | 23.521 | 24.709 | 25.959 | 27.274 | 28.657 | 30.113 | 31.643 | 33.253 | 42.619 | 54.590 | 69.814 | 89.077 | 113.33 |
| 11 | 25.733 | 27.200 | 28.755 | 30.404 | 32.150 | 34.001 | 35.962 | 38.039 | 40.238 | 42.566 | 56.405 | 74.697 | 98.739 | 130.16 | 171.00 |
| 12 | 30.850 | 32.824 | 34.931 | 37.180 | 39.581 | 42.142 | 44.874 | 47.788 | 50.895 | 54.208 | 74.327 | 101.84 | 139.23 | 189.73 | 257.49 |
| 13 | 36.786 | 39.404 | 42.219 | 45.244 | 48.497 | 51.991 | 55.746 | 59.779 | 64.110 | 68.760 | 97.625 | 138.48 | 195.93 | 276.12 | 387.24 |
| 14 | 43.672 | 47.103 | 50.818 | 54.841 | 59.196 | 63.909 | 69.010 | 74.528 | 80.496 | 86.949 | 127.91 | 187.95 | 275.30 | 401.37 | 581.86 |
| 15 | 51.660 | 56.110 | 60.965 | 66.261 | 72.035 | 78.330 | 85.192 | 92.669 | 100.82 | 109.69 | 167.29 | 254.74 | 386.42 | 582.98 | 873.79 |
| 16 | 60.925 | 66.649 | 72.939 | 79.850 | 87.442 | 95.780 | 104.93 | 114.98 | 126.01 | 138.11 | 218.47 | 344.90 | 541.99 | 846.32 | 1311.7 |
| 17 | 71.673 | 78.979 | 87.068 | 96.022 | 105.93 | 116.89 | 129.02 | 142.43 | 157.25 | 173.64 | 285.01 | 466.61 | 759.78 | 1228.2 | 1968.5 |
| 18 | 84.141 | 93.406 | 103.74 | 115.27 | 128.12 | 142.44 | 158.40 | 176.19 | 195.99 | 218.04 | 371.52 | 630.92 | 1064.7 | 1781.8 | 2953.8 |
| 19 | 98.603 | 110.28 | 123.41 | 138.17 | 154.74 | 173.35 | 194.25 | 217.71 | 244.03 | 273.56 | 483.97 | 852.75 | 1491.6 | 2584.7 | 4431.7 |
| 20 | 115.38 | 130.03 | 146.63 | 165.42 | 186.69 | 210.76 | 237.99 | 268.79 | 303.60 | 342.94 | 630.17 | 1152.2 | 2089.2 | 3748.8 | 6648.5 |
| 21 | 134.84 | 153.14 | 174.02 | 197.85 | 225.03 | 256.02 | 291.35 | 331.61 | 377.46 | 429.68 | 820.22 | 1556.5 | 2925.9 | 5436.7 | 9973.8 |
| 22 | 157.41 | 180.17 | 206.34 | 236.44 | 271.03 | 310.78 | 356.44 | 408.88 | 469.06 | 538.10 | 1067.3 | 2102.3 | 4097.2 | 7884.3 | 14962. |
| 23 | 183.60 | 211.80 | 244.49 | 282.36 | 326.24 | 377.05 | 435.86 | 503.92 | 582.63 | 673.63 | 1388.5 | 2839.0 | 5737.1 | 11433. | 22443. |
| 24 | 213.98 | 248.81 | 289.49 | 337.01 | 392.48 | 457.22 | 532.75 | 620.82 | 723.46 | 843.03 | 1806.0 | 3833.7 | 8033.0 | 16579. | 33666. |
| 25 | 249.21 | 292.10 | 342.60 | 402.04 | 471.98 | 554.24 | 650.96 | 764.61 | 898.09 | 1054.8 | 2348.8 | 5176.5 | 11247. | 24041. | 50500. |
| 26 | 290.09 | 342.76 | 405.27 | 479.43 | 567.38 | 671.63 | 795.17 | 941.46 | 1114.6 | 1319.5 | 3054.4 | 6989.3 | 15747. | 34860. | 75752. |
| 27 | 337.50 | 402.03 | 479.22 | 571.52 | 681.85 | 813.68 | 971.10 | 1159.0 | 1383.1 | 1650.4 | 3971.8 | 9436.5 | 22047. | 50548. | ****** |
| 28 | 392.50 | 471.38 | 566.48 | 681.11 | 819.22 | 985.55 | 1185.7 | 1426.6 | 1716.1 | 2064.0 | 5164.3 | 12740. | 30867. | 73296. | ****** |
| 29 | 456.30 | 552.51 | 669.45 | 811.52 | 984.07 | 1193.5 | 1447.6 | 1755.7 | 2129.0 | 2580.9 | 6714.6 | 17200. | 43214. | ****** | ****** |
| 30 | 530.31 | 647.44 | 790.95 | 966.71 | 1181.9 | 1445.2 | 1767.1 | 2160.5 | 2640.9 | 3227.2 | 8730.0 | 23222. | 60501. | ****** | ****** |
| 35 | 1120.7 | 1426.5 | 1816.7 | 2314.2 | 2948.3 | 3755.9 | 4783.6 | 6090.3 | 7750.2 | 9856.8 | 32423. | ****** | ****** | ****** | ****** |
| 40 | 2360.8 | 3134.5 | 4163.2 | 5529.8 | 7343.9 | 9749.5 | 12937. | 17154. | 22729. | 30089. | ****** | ****** | ****** | ****** | ****** |
| 45 | 4965.3 | 6879.3 | 9531.6 | 13203. | 18281. | 25295. | 34971. | 48302. | 66640. | 91831. | ****** | ****** | ****** | ****** | ****** |
| 50 | 10436. | 15090. | 21813. | 31515. | 45497. | 65617. | 94525. | ****** | ****** | ****** | ****** | ****** | ****** | ****** | ***** |
| 75 | ****** | ****** | ****** | ****** | ****** | ****** | ****** | ****** | ****** | ****** | ****** | ****** | ****** | ****** | ****** |
| 100 | ****** | ****** | ****** | ****** | ****** | ****** | ****** | ****** | ****** | ****** | ****** | ****** | ****** | ****** | ****** |

# Appendix P-1

## TABLE OF PRESENT VALUE FACTORS OF $1
## FOR VARIOUS INTEREST RATES AND PERIODS

| RATE PERIOD | 1% | 2% | 3% | 4% | 5% | 6% | 7% | 8% | 9% | 10% | 11% | 12% | 13% | 14% | 15% |
|---|---|---|---|---|---|---|---|---|---|---|---|---|---|---|---|
| 1 | .9901 | .9804 | .9709 | .9615 | .9524 | .9434 | .9346 | .9259 | .9174 | .9091 | .9009 | .8929 | .8850 | .8772 | .8696 |
| 2 | .9803 | .9612 | .9426 | .9246 | .9070 | .8900 | .8734 | .8573 | .8417 | .8264 | .8116 | .7972 | .7831 | .7695 | .7561 |
| 3 | .9706 | .9423 | .9151 | .8890 | .8638 | .8396 | .8163 | .7938 | .7722 | .7513 | .7312 | .7118 | .6931 | .6750 | .6575 |
| 4 | .9610 | .9238 | .8885 | .8548 | .8227 | .7921 | .7629 | .7350 | .7084 | .6830 | .6587 | .6355 | .6133 | .5921 | .5718 |
| 5 | .9515 | .9057 | .8626 | .8219 | .7835 | .7473 | .7130 | .6806 | .6499 | .6209 | .5935 | .5674 | .5428 | .5194 | .4972 |
| 6 | .9420 | .8880 | .8375 | .7903 | .7462 | .7050 | .6663 | .6302 | .5963 | .5645 | .5346 | .5066 | .4803 | .4556 | .4323 |
| 7 | .9327 | .8706 | .8131 | .7599 | .7107 | .6651 | .6227 | .5835 | .5470 | .5132 | .4817 | .4523 | .4251 | .3996 | .3759 |
| 8 | .9235 | .8535 | .7894 | .7307 | .6768 | .6274 | .5820 | .5403 | .5019 | .4665 | .4339 | .4039 | .3762 | .3506 | .3269 |
| 9 | .9143 | .8368 | .7664 | .7026 | .6446 | .5919 | .5439 | .5002 | .4604 | .4241 | .3909 | .3606 | .3329 | .3075 | .2843 |
| 10 | .9053 | .8203 | .7441 | .6756 | .6139 | .5584 | .5083 | .4632 | .4224 | .3855 | .3522 | .3220 | .2946 | .2697 | .2472 |
| 11 | .8963 | .8043 | .7224 | .6496 | .5847 | .5268 | .4751 | .4289 | .3875 | .3505 | .3173 | .2875 | .2607 | .2366 | .2149 |
| 12 | .8874 | .7885 | .7014 | .6246 | .5568 | .4970 | .4440 | .3971 | .3555 | .3186 | .2858 | .2567 | .2307 | .2076 | .1869 |
| 13 | .8787 | .7730 | .6810 | .6006 | .5303 | .4688 | .4150 | .3677 | .3262 | .2897 | .2575 | .2292 | .2042 | .1821 | .1625 |
| 14 | .8700 | .7579 | .6611 | .5775 | .5051 | .4423 | .3878 | .3405 | .2992 | .2633 | .2320 | .2046 | .1807 | .1597 | .1413 |
| 15 | .8613 | .7430 | .6419 | .5553 | .4810 | .4173 | .3624 | .3152 | .2745 | .2394 | .2090 | .1827 | .1599 | .1401 | .1229 |
| 16 | .8528 | .7284 | .6232 | .5339 | .4581 | .3936 | .3387 | .2919 | .2519 | .2176 | .1883 | .1631 | .1415 | .1229 | .1069 |
| 17 | .8444 | .7142 | .6050 | .5134 | .4363 | .3714 | .3166 | .2703 | .2311 | .1978 | .1696 | .1456 | .1252 | .1078 | .0929 |
| 18 | .8360 | .7002 | .5874 | .4936 | .4155 | .3503 | .2959 | .2502 | .2120 | .1799 | .1528 | .1300 | .1108 | .0946 | .0808 |
| 19 | .8277 | .6864 | .5703 | .4746 | .3957 | .3305 | .2765 | .2317 | .1945 | .1635 | .1377 | .1161 | .0981 | .0829 | .0703 |
| 20 | .8195 | .6730 | .5537 | .4564 | .3769 | .3118 | .2584 | .2145 | .1784 | .1486 | .1240 | .1037 | .0868 | .0728 | .0611 |
| 21 | .8114 | .6598 | .5375 | .4388 | .3589 | .2942 | .2415 | .1987 | .1637 | .1351 | .1117 | .0926 | .0768 | .0638 | .0531 |
| 22 | .8034 | .6468 | .5219 | .4220 | .3418 | .2775 | .2257 | .1839 | .1502 | .1228 | .1007 | .0826 | .0680 | .0560 | .0462 |
| 23 | .7954 | .6342 | .5067 | .4057 | .3256 | .2618 | .2109 | .1703 | .1378 | .1117 | .0907 | .0738 | .0601 | .0491 | .0402 |
| 24 | .7876 | .6217 | .4919 | .3901 | .3101 | .2470 | .1971 | .1577 | .1264 | .1015 | .0817 | .0659 | .0532 | .0431 | .0349 |
| 25 | .7798 | .6095 | .4776 | .3751 | .2953 | .2330 | .1842 | .1460 | .1160 | .0923 | .0736 | .0588 | .0471 | .0378 | .0304 |
| 26 | .7720 | .5976 | .4637 | .3607 | .2812 | .2198 | .1722 | .1352 | .1064 | .0839 | .0663 | .0525 | .0417 | .0331 | .0264 |
| 27 | .7644 | .5859 | .4502 | .3468 | .2678 | .2074 | .1609 | .1252 | .0976 | .0763 | .0597 | .0469 | .0369 | .0291 | .0230 |
| 28 | .7568 | .5744 | .4371 | .3335 | .2551 | .1956 | .1504 | .1159 | .0895 | .0693 | .0538 | .0419 | .0326 | .0255 | .0200 |
| 29 | .7493 | .5631 | .4243 | .3207 | .2429 | .1846 | .1406 | .1073 | .0822 | .0630 | .0485 | .0374 | .0289 | .0224 | .0174 |
| 30 | .7419 | .5521 | .4120 | .3083 | .2314 | .1741 | .1314 | .0994 | .0754 | .0573 | .0437 | .0334 | .0256 | .0196 | .0151 |
| 35 | .7059 | .5000 | .3554 | .2534 | .1813 | .1301 | .0937 | .0676 | .0490 | .0356 | .0259 | .0189 | .0139 | .0102 | .0075 |
| 40 | .6717 | .4529 | .3066 | .2083 | .1420 | .0972 | .0668 | .0460 | .0318 | .0221 | .0154 | .0107 | .0075 | .0053 | .0037 |
| 45 | .6391 | .4102 | .2644 | .1712 | .1113 | .0727 | .0476 | .0313 | .0207 | .0137 | .0091 | .0061 | .0041 | .0027 | .0019 |
| 50 | .6080 | .3715 | .2281 | .1407 | .0872 | .0543 | .0339 | .0213 | .0134 | .0085 | .0054 | .0035 | .0022 | .0014 | .0009 |
| 75 | .4741 | .2265 | .1089 | .0528 | .0258 | .0126 | .0063 | .0031 | .0016 | .0008 | .0004 | .0002 | .0001 | .0001 | .0000 |
| 100 | .3697 | .1380 | .0520 | .0198 | .0076 | .0029 | .0012 | .0005 | .0002 | .0001 | .0000 | .0000 | .0000 | .0000 | .0000 |

| RATE PERIOD | 16% | 17% | 18% | 19% | 20% | 21% | 22% | 23% | 24% | 25% | 30% | 35% | 40% | 45% | 50% |
|---|---|---|---|---|---|---|---|---|---|---|---|---|---|---|---|
| 1 | .8621 | .8547 | .8475 | .8403 | .8333 | .8264 | .8197 | .8130 | .8065 | .8000 | .7692 | .7407 | .7143 | .6897 | .6667 |
| 2 | .7432 | .7305 | .7182 | .7062 | .6944 | .6830 | .6719 | .6610 | .6504 | .6400 | .5917 | .5487 | .5102 | .4756 | .4444 |
| 3 | .6407 | .6244 | .6086 | .5934 | .5787 | .5645 | .5507 | .5374 | .5245 | .5120 | .4552 | .4064 | .3644 | .3280 | .2963 |
| 4 | .5523 | .5337 | .5158 | .4987 | .4823 | .4665 | .4514 | .4369 | .4230 | .4096 | .3501 | .3011 | .2603 | .2262 | .1975 |
| 5 | .4761 | .4561 | .4371 | .4190 | .4019 | .3855 | .3700 | .3552 | .3411 | .3277 | .2693 | .2230 | .1859 | .1560 | .1317 |
| 6 | .4104 | .3898 | .3704 | .3521 | .3349 | .3186 | .3033 | .2888 | .2751 | .2621 | .2072 | .1652 | .1328 | .1076 | .0878 |
| 7 | .3538 | .3332 | .3139 | .2959 | .2791 | .2633 | .2486 | .2348 | .2218 | .2097 | .1594 | .1224 | .0949 | .0742 | .0585 |
| 8 | .3050 | .2848 | .2660 | .2487 | .2326 | .2176 | .2038 | .1909 | .1789 | .1678 | .1226 | .0906 | .0678 | .0512 | .0390 |
| 9 | .2630 | .2434 | .2255 | .2090 | .1938 | .1799 | .1670 | .1552 | .1443 | .1342 | .0943 | .0671 | .0484 | .0353 | .0260 |
| 10 | .2267 | .2080 | .1911 | .1756 | .1615 | .1486 | .1369 | .1262 | .1164 | .1074 | .0725 | .0497 | .0346 | .0243 | .0173 |
| 11 | .1954 | .1778 | .1619 | .1476 | .1346 | .1228 | .1122 | .1026 | .0938 | .0859 | .0558 | .0368 | .0247 | .0168 | .0116 |
| 12 | .1685 | .1520 | .1372 | .1240 | .1122 | .1015 | .0920 | .0834 | .0757 | .0687 | .0429 | .0273 | .0176 | .0116 | .0077 |
| 13 | .1452 | .1299 | .1163 | .1042 | .0935 | .0839 | .0754 | .0678 | .0610 | .0550 | .0330 | .0202 | .0126 | .0080 | .0051 |
| 14 | .1252 | .1110 | .0985 | .0876 | .0779 | .0693 | .0618 | .0551 | .0492 | .0440 | .0254 | .0150 | .0090 | .0055 | .0034 |
| 15 | .1079 | .0949 | .0835 | .0736 | .0649 | .0573 | .0507 | .0448 | .0397 | .0352 | .0195 | .0111 | .0064 | .0038 | .0023 |
| 16 | .0930 | .0811 | .0708 | .0618 | .0541 | .0474 | .0415 | .0364 | .0320 | .0281 | .0150 | .0082 | .0046 | .0026 | .0015 |
| 17 | .0802 | .0693 | .0600 | .0520 | .0451 | .0391 | .0340 | .0296 | .0258 | .0225 | .0116 | .0061 | .0033 | .0018 | .0010 |
| 18 | .0691 | .0592 | .0508 | .0437 | .0376 | .0323 | .0279 | .0241 | .0208 | .0180 | .0089 | .0045 | .0023 | .0012 | .0007 |
| 19 | .0596 | .0506 | .0431 | .0367 | .0313 | .0267 | .0229 | .0196 | .0168 | .0144 | .0068 | .0033 | .0017 | .0009 | .0005 |
| 20 | .0514 | .0433 | .0365 | .0308 | .0261 | .0221 | .0187 | .0159 | .0135 | .0115 | .0053 | .0025 | .0012 | .0006 | .0003 |
| 21 | .0443 | .0370 | .0309 | .0259 | .0217 | .0183 | .0154 | .0129 | .0109 | .0092 | .0040 | .0018 | .0009 | .0004 | .0002 |
| 22 | .0382 | .0316 | .0262 | .0218 | .0181 | .0151 | .0126 | .0105 | .0088 | .0074 | .0031 | .0014 | .0006 | .0003 | .0001 |
| 23 | .0329 | .0270 | .0222 | .0183 | .0151 | .0125 | .0103 | .0086 | .0071 | .0059 | .0024 | .0010 | .0004 | .0002 | .0001 |
| 24 | .0284 | .0231 | .0188 | .0154 | .0126 | .0103 | .0085 | .0070 | .0057 | .0047 | .0018 | .0007 | .0003 | .0001 | .0001 |
| 25 | .0245 | .0197 | .0160 | .0129 | .0105 | .0085 | .0069 | .0057 | .0046 | .0038 | .0014 | .0006 | .0002 | .0001 | .0000 |
| 26 | .0211 | .0169 | .0135 | .0109 | .0087 | .0070 | .0057 | .0046 | .0037 | .0030 | .0011 | .0004 | .0002 | .0001 | .0000 |
| 27 | .0182 | .0144 | .0115 | .0091 | .0073 | .0058 | .0047 | .0037 | .0030 | .0024 | .0008 | .0003 | .0001 | .0000 | .0000 |
| 28 | .0157 | .0123 | .0097 | .0077 | .0061 | .0048 | .0038 | .0030 | .0024 | .0019 | .0006 | .0002 | .0001 | .0000 | .0000 |
| 29 | .0135 | .0105 | .0082 | .0064 | .0051 | .0040 | .0031 | .0025 | .0020 | .0015 | .0005 | .0002 | .0001 | .0000 | .0000 |
| 30 | .0116 | .0090 | .0070 | .0054 | .0042 | .0033 | .0026 | .0020 | .0016 | .0012 | .0004 | .0001 | .0000 | .0000 | .0000 |
| 35 | .0055 | .0041 | .0030 | .0023 | .0017 | .0013 | .0009 | .0007 | .0005 | .0004 | .0001 | .0000 | .0000 | .0000 | .0000 |
| 40 | .0026 | .0019 | .0013 | .0010 | .0007 | .0005 | .0004 | .0003 | .0002 | .0001 | .0000 | .0000 | .0000 | .0000 | .0000 |
| 45 | .0013 | .0009 | .0006 | .0004 | .0003 | .0002 | .0001 | .0001 | .0001 | .0000 | .0000 | .0000 | .0000 | .0000 | .0000 |
| 50 | .0006 | .0004 | .0003 | .0002 | .0001 | .0001 | .0000 | .0000 | .0000 | .0000 | .0000 | .0000 | .0000 | .0000 | .0000 |
| 75 | .0000 | .0000 | .0000 | .0000 | .0000 | .0000 | .0000 | .0000 | .0000 | .0000 | .0000 | .0000 | .0000 | .0000 | .0000 |
| 100 | .0000 | .0000 | .0000 | .0000 | .0000 | .0000 | .0000 | .0000 | .0000 | .0000 | .0000 | .0000 | .0000 | .0000 | .0000 |

# Appendix P-2

## TABLE OF PRESENT VALUE FACTORS FOR ANNUITIES FOR VARIOUS INTEREST RATES AND PERIODS

| RATE PERIOD | 1% | 2% | 3% | 4% | 5% | 6% | 7% | 8% | 9% | 10% | 11% | 12% | 13% | 14% | 15% |
|---|---|---|---|---|---|---|---|---|---|---|---|---|---|---|---|
| 1 | 0.9901 | 0.9804 | 0.9709 | 0.9615 | 0.9524 | 0.9434 | 0.9346 | 0.9259 | 0.9174 | 0.9091 | 0.9009 | 0.8929 | 0.8850 | 0.8772 | 0.8696 |
| 2 | 1.9704 | 1.9416 | 1.9135 | 1.8861 | 1.8594 | 1.8334 | 1.8080 | 1.7833 | 1.7591 | 1.7355 | 1.7125 | 1.6901 | 1.6681 | 1.6467 | 1.6257 |
| 3 | 2.9410 | 2.8839 | 2.8286 | 2.7751 | 2.7232 | 2.6730 | 2.6243 | 2.5771 | 2.5313 | 2.4869 | 2.4437 | 2.4018 | 2.3612 | 2.3216 | 2.2832 |
| 4 | 3.9020 | 3.8077 | 3.7171 | 3.6299 | 3.5460 | 3.4651 | 3.3872 | 3.3121 | 3.2397 | 3.1699 | 3.1024 | 3.0373 | 2.9745 | 2.9137 | 2.8550 |
| 5 | 4.8534 | 4.7135 | 4.5797 | 4.4518 | 4.3295 | 4.2124 | 4.1002 | 3.9927 | 3.8897 | 3.7908 | 3.6959 | 3.6048 | 3.5172 | 3.4331 | 3.3522 |
| 6 | 5.7955 | 5.6014 | 5.4172 | 5.2421 | 5.0757 | 4.9173 | 4.7665 | 4.6229 | 4.4859 | 4.3553 | 4.2305 | 4.1114 | 3.9975 | 3.8887 | 3.7845 |
| 7 | 6.7282 | 6.4720 | 6.2303 | 6.0021 | 5.7864 | 5.5824 | 5.3893 | 5.2064 | 5.0330 | 4.8684 | 4.7122 | 4.5638 | 4.4226 | 4.2883 | 4.1604 |
| 8 | 7.6517 | 7.3255 | 7.0197 | 6.7327 | 6.4632 | 6.2098 | 5.9713 | 5.7466 | 5.5348 | 5.3349 | 5.1461 | 4.9676 | 4.7988 | 4.6389 | 4.4873 |
| 9 | 8.5660 | 8.1622 | 7.7861 | 7.4353 | 7.1078 | 6.8017 | 6.5152 | 6.2469 | 5.9952 | 5.7590 | 5.5370 | 5.3282 | 5.1317 | 4.9464 | 4.7716 |
| 10 | 9.4713 | 8.9826 | 8.5302 | 8.1109 | 7.7217 | 7.3601 | 7.0236 | 6.7101 | 6.4177 | 6.1446 | 5.8892 | 5.6502 | 5.4262 | 5.2161 | 5.0188 |
| 11 | 10.368 | 9.7868 | 9.2526 | 8.7605 | 8.3064 | 7.8869 | 7.4987 | 7.1390 | 6.8052 | 6.4951 | 6.2065 | 5.9377 | 5.6869 | 5.4527 | 5.2337 |
| 12 | 11.255 | 10.575 | 9.9540 | 9.3851 | 8.8633 | 8.3838 | 7.9427 | 7.5361 | 7.1607 | 6.8137 | 6.4924 | 6.1944 | 5.9176 | 5.6603 | 5.4206 |
| 13 | 12.134 | 11.348 | 10.635 | 9.9856 | 9.3936 | 8.8527 | 8.3577 | 7.9038 | 7.4869 | 7.1034 | 6.7499 | 6.4235 | 6.1218 | 5.8424 | 5.5831 |
| 14 | 13.004 | 12.106 | 11.296 | 10.563 | 9.8986 | 9.2950 | 8.7455 | 8.2442 | 7.7862 | 7.3667 | 6.9819 | 6.6282 | 6.3025 | 6.0021 | 5.7245 |
| 15 | 13.865 | 12.849 | 11.938 | 11.118 | 10.380 | 9.7122 | 9.1079 | 8.5595 | 8.0607 | 7.6061 | 7.1909 | 6.8109 | 6.4624 | 6.1422 | 5.8474 |
| 16 | 14.718 | 13.578 | 12.561 | 11.652 | 10.838 | 10.106 | 9.4466 | 8.8514 | 8.3126 | 7.8237 | 7.3792 | 6.9740 | 6.6039 | 6.2651 | 5.9542 |
| 17 | 15.562 | 14.292 | 13.166 | 12.166 | 11.274 | 10.477 | 9.7632 | 9.1216 | 8.5436 | 8.0216 | 7.5488 | 7.1196 | 6.7291 | 6.3729 | 6.0472 |
| 18 | 16.398 | 14.992 | 13.754 | 12.659 | 11.690 | 10.828 | 10.059 | 9.3719 | 8.7556 | 8.2014 | 7.7016 | 7.2497 | 6.8399 | 6.4674 | 6.1280 |
| 19 | 17.226 | 15.678 | 14.324 | 13.134 | 12.085 | 11.158 | 10.336 | 9.6036 | 8.9501 | 8.3649 | 7.8393 | 7.3658 | 6.9380 | 6.5504 | 6.1982 |
| 20 | 18.046 | 16.351 | 14.877 | 13.590 | 12.462 | 11.470 | 10.594 | 9.8181 | 9.1285 | 8.5136 | 7.9633 | 7.4694 | 7.0248 | 6.6231 | 6.2593 |
| 21 | 18.857 | 17.011 | 15.415 | 14.029 | 12.821 | 11.764 | 10.836 | 10.017 | 9.2922 | 8.6487 | 8.0751 | 7.5620 | 7.1016 | 6.6870 | 6.3125 |
| 22 | 19.660 | 17.658 | 15.937 | 14.451 | 13.163 | 12.042 | 11.061 | 10.201 | 9.4424 | 8.7715 | 8.1757 | 7.6446 | 7.1695 | 6.7429 | 6.3587 |
| 23 | 20.456 | 18.292 | 16.444 | 14.857 | 13.489 | 12.303 | 11.272 | 10.371 | 9.5802 | 8.8832 | 8.2664 | 7.7184 | 7.2297 | 6.7921 | 6.3988 |
| 24 | 21.243 | 18.914 | 16.936 | 15.247 | 13.799 | 12.550 | 11.469 | 10.529 | 9.7066 | 8.9847 | 8.3481 | 7.7843 | 7.2829 | 6.8351 | 6.4338 |
| 25 | 22.023 | 19.523 | 17.413 | 15.622 | 14.094 | 12.783 | 11.654 | 10.675 | 9.8226 | 9.0770 | 8.4217 | 7.8431 | 7.3300 | 6.8729 | 6.4641 |
| 26 | 22.795 | 20.121 | 17.877 | 15.983 | 14.375 | 13.003 | 11.826 | 10.810 | 9.9290 | 9.1609 | 8.4881 | 7.8957 | 7.3717 | 6.9061 | 6.4906 |
| 27 | 23.560 | 20.707 | 18.327 | 16.330 | 14.643 | 13.211 | 11.987 | 10.935 | 10.027 | 9.2372 | 8.5478 | 7.9426 | 7.4086 | 6.9352 | 6.5135 |
| 28 | 24.316 | 21.281 | 18.764 | 16.663 | 14.898 | 13.406 | 12.137 | 11.051 | 10.116 | 9.3066 | 8.6016 | 7.9844 | 7.4412 | 6.9607 | 6.5335 |
| 29 | 25.066 | 21.844 | 19.188 | 16.984 | 15.141 | 13.591 | 12.278 | 11.158 | 10.198 | 9.3696 | 8.6501 | 8.0218 | 7.4701 | 6.9830 | 6.5509 |
| 30 | 25.808 | 22.396 | 19.600 | 17.292 | 15.372 | 13.765 | 12.409 | 11.258 | 10.274 | 9.4269 | 8.6938 | 8.0552 | 7.4957 | 7.0027 | 6.5660 |
| 35 | 29.409 | 24.999 | 21.487 | 18.665 | 16.374 | 14.498 | 12.948 | 11.655 | 10.567 | 9.6442 | 8.8552 | 8.1755 | 7.5856 | 7.0700 | 6.6166 |
| 40 | 32.835 | 27.355 | 23.115 | 19.793 | 17.159 | 15.046 | 13.332 | 11.925 | 10.757 | 9.7791 | 8.9511 | 8.2438 | 7.6344 | 7.1050 | 6.6418 |
| 45 | 36.095 | 29.490 | 24.519 | 20.720 | 17.774 | 15.456 | 13.606 | 12.108 | 10.881 | 9.8628 | 9.0079 | 8.2825 | 7.6609 | 7.1232 | 6.6543 |
| 50 | 39.196 | 31.424 | 25.730 | 21.482 | 18.256 | 15.762 | 13.801 | 12.233 | 10.962 | 9.9148 | 9.0417 | 8.3045 | 7.6752 | 7.1327 | 6.6605 |
| 75 | 52.587 | 38.677 | 29.702 | 23.680 | 19.485 | 16.456 | 14.196 | 12.461 | 11.094 | 9.9921 | 9.0873 | 8.3316 | 7.6915 | 7.1425 | 6.6665 |
| 100 | 63.029 | 43.098 | 31.599 | 24.505 | 19.848 | 16.618 | 14.269 | 12.494 | 11.109 | 9.9993 | 9.0906 | 8.3332 | 7.6923 | 7.1428 | 6.6667 |

| RATE PERIOD | 16% | 17% | 18% | 19% | 20% | 21% | 22% | 23% | 24% | 25% | 30% | 35% | 40% | 45% | 50% |
|---|---|---|---|---|---|---|---|---|---|---|---|---|---|---|---|
| 1 | 0.8621 | 0.8547 | 0.8475 | 0.8403 | 0.8333 | 0.8264 | 0.8197 | 0.8130 | 0.8065 | 0.8000 | 0.7692 | 0.7407 | 0.7143 | 0.6897 | 0.6667 |
| 2 | 1.6052 | 1.5852 | 1.5656 | 1.5465 | 1.5278 | 1.5095 | 1.4915 | 1.4740 | 1.4568 | 1.4400 | 1.3609 | 1.2894 | 1.2245 | 1.1653 | 1.1111 |
| 3 | 2.2459 | 2.2096 | 2.1743 | 2.1399 | 2.1065 | 2.0739 | 2.0422 | 2.0114 | 1.9813 | 1.9520 | 1.8161 | 1.6959 | 1.5889 | 1.4933 | 1.4074 |
| 4 | 2.7982 | 2.7432 | 2.6901 | 2.6386 | 2.5887 | 2.5404 | 2.4936 | 2.4483 | 2.4043 | 2.3616 | 2.1662 | 1.9969 | 1.8492 | 1.7195 | 1.6049 |
| 5 | 3.2743 | 3.1993 | 3.1272 | 3.0576 | 2.9906 | 2.9260 | 2.8636 | 2.8035 | 2.7454 | 2.6893 | 2.4356 | 2.2200 | 2.0352 | 1.8755 | 1.7366 |
| 6 | 3.6847 | 3.5892 | 3.4976 | 3.4098 | 3.3255 | 3.2446 | 3.1669 | 3.0923 | 3.0205 | 2.9514 | 2.6427 | 2.3852 | 2.1680 | 1.9831 | 1.8244 |
| 7 | 4.0386 | 3.9224 | 3.8115 | 3.7057 | 3.6046 | 3.5079 | 3.4155 | 3.3270 | 3.2423 | 3.1611 | 2.8021 | 2.5075 | 2.2628 | 2.0573 | 1.8829 |
| 8 | 4.3436 | 4.2072 | 4.0776 | 3.9544 | 3.8372 | 3.7256 | 3.6193 | 3.5179 | 3.4212 | 3.3289 | 2.9247 | 2.5982 | 2.3306 | 2.1085 | 1.9220 |
| 9 | 4.6065 | 4.4506 | 4.3030 | 4.1633 | 4.0310 | 3.9045 | 3.7863 | 3.6731 | 3.5655 | 3.4631 | 3.0190 | 2.6653 | 2.3790 | 2.1438 | 1.9480 |
| 10 | 4.8332 | 4.6586 | 4.4941 | 4.3389 | 4.1925 | 4.0541 | 3.9232 | 3.7993 | 3.6819 | 3.5705 | 3.0915 | 2.7150 | 2.4136 | 2.1681 | 1.9653 |
| 11 | 5.0286 | 4.8364 | 4.6560 | 4.4865 | 4.3271 | 4.1769 | 4.0354 | 3.9018 | 3.7757 | 3.6564 | 3.1473 | 2.7519 | 2.4383 | 2.1849 | 1.9769 |
| 12 | 5.1971 | 4.9884 | 4.7932 | 4.6105 | 4.4392 | 4.2784 | 4.1274 | 3.9852 | 3.8514 | 3.7251 | 3.1903 | 2.7792 | 2.4559 | 2.1965 | 1.9846 |
| 13 | 5.3423 | 5.1183 | 4.9095 | 4.7147 | 4.5327 | 4.3624 | 4.2028 | 4.0530 | 3.9124 | 3.7801 | 3.2233 | 2.7994 | 2.4685 | 2.2045 | 1.9897 |
| 14 | 5.4675 | 5.2293 | 5.0081 | 4.8023 | 4.6106 | 4.4317 | 4.2646 | 4.1082 | 3.9616 | 3.8241 | 3.2487 | 2.8144 | 2.4775 | 2.2100 | 1.9931 |
| 15 | 5.5755 | 5.3242 | 5.0916 | 4.8759 | 4.6755 | 4.4890 | 4.3152 | 4.1530 | 4.0013 | 3.8593 | 3.2682 | 2.8255 | 2.4839 | 2.2138 | 1.9954 |
| 16 | 5.6685 | 5.4053 | 5.1624 | 4.9377 | 4.7296 | 4.5364 | 4.3567 | 4.1894 | 4.0333 | 3.8874 | 3.2832 | 2.8337 | 2.4885 | 2.2164 | 1.9970 |
| 17 | 5.7487 | 5.4746 | 5.2223 | 4.9897 | 4.7746 | 4.5755 | 4.3908 | 4.2190 | 4.0591 | 3.9099 | 3.2948 | 2.8398 | 2.4918 | 2.2182 | 1.9980 |
| 18 | 5.8178 | 5.5339 | 5.2732 | 5.0333 | 4.8122 | 4.6079 | 4.4187 | 4.2431 | 4.0799 | 3.9279 | 3.3037 | 2.8443 | 2.4941 | 2.2195 | 1.9986 |
| 19 | 5.8775 | 5.5845 | 5.3162 | 5.0700 | 4.8435 | 4.6346 | 4.4415 | 4.2627 | 4.0967 | 3.9424 | 3.3105 | 2.8476 | 2.4958 | 2.2203 | 1.9991 |
| 20 | 5.9288 | 5.6278 | 5.3527 | 5.1009 | 4.8696 | 4.6567 | 4.4603 | 4.2786 | 4.1103 | 3.9539 | 3.3158 | 2.8501 | 2.4970 | 2.2209 | 1.9994 |
| 21 | 5.9731 | 5.6648 | 5.3837 | 5.1268 | 4.8913 | 4.6750 | 4.4756 | 4.2916 | 4.1212 | 3.9631 | 3.3198 | 2.8519 | 2.4979 | 2.2213 | 1.9996 |
| 22 | 6.0113 | 5.6964 | 5.4099 | 5.1486 | 4.9094 | 4.6900 | 4.4882 | 4.3021 | 4.1300 | 3.9705 | 3.3230 | 2.8533 | 2.4985 | 2.2216 | 1.9997 |
| 23 | 6.0442 | 5.7234 | 5.4321 | 5.1668 | 4.9245 | 4.7025 | 4.4985 | 4.3106 | 4.1371 | 3.9764 | 3.3254 | 2.8543 | 2.4989 | 2.2218 | 1.9998 |
| 24 | 6.0726 | 5.7465 | 5.4509 | 5.1822 | 4.9371 | 4.7128 | 4.5070 | 4.3176 | 4.1428 | 3.9811 | 3.3272 | 2.8550 | 2.4992 | 2.2219 | 1.9999 |
| 25 | 6.0971 | 5.7662 | 5.4669 | 5.1951 | 4.9476 | 4.7213 | 4.5139 | 4.3232 | 4.1474 | 3.9849 | 3.3286 | 2.8556 | 2.4994 | 2.2220 | 1.9999 |
| 26 | 6.1182 | 5.7831 | 5.4804 | 5.2060 | 4.9563 | 4.7284 | 4.5196 | 4.3278 | 4.1511 | 3.9879 | 3.3297 | 2.8560 | 2.4996 | 2.2221 | 1.9999 |
| 27 | 6.1364 | 5.7975 | 5.4919 | 5.2151 | 4.9636 | 4.7342 | 4.5243 | 4.3316 | 4.1542 | 3.9903 | 3.3305 | 2.8563 | 2.4997 | 2.2221 | 2.0000 |
| 28 | 6.1520 | 5.8099 | 5.5016 | 5.2228 | 4.9697 | 4.7390 | 4.5281 | 4.3346 | 4.1566 | 3.9923 | 3.3312 | 2.8565 | 2.4998 | 2.2222 | 2.0000 |
| 29 | 6.1656 | 5.8204 | 5.5098 | 5.2292 | 4.9747 | 4.7430 | 4.5312 | 4.3371 | 4.1585 | 3.9938 | 3.3317 | 2.8567 | 2.4999 | 2.2222 | 2.0000 |
| 30 | 6.1772 | 5.8294 | 5.5168 | 5.2347 | 4.9789 | 4.7463 | 4.5338 | 4.3391 | 4.1601 | 3.9950 | 3.3321 | 2.8568 | 2.4999 | 2.2222 | 2.0000 |
| 35 | 6.2153 | 5.8582 | 5.5386 | 5.2512 | 4.9915 | 4.7559 | 4.5411 | 4.3447 | 4.1644 | 3.9984 | 3.3330 | 2.8571 | 2.5000 | 2.2222 | 2.0000 |
| 40 | 6.2335 | 5.8713 | 5.5482 | 5.2582 | 4.9966 | 4.7596 | 4.5439 | 4.3467 | 4.1659 | 3.9995 | 3.3332 | 2.8571 | 2.5000 | 2.2222 | 2.0000 |
| 45 | 6.2421 | 5.8773 | 5.5523 | 5.2611 | 4.9986 | 4.7610 | 4.5449 | 4.3474 | 4.1664 | 3.9998 | 3.3333 | 2.8571 | 2.5000 | 2.2222 | 2.0000 |
| 50 | 6.2463 | 5.8801 | 5.5541 | 5.2623 | 4.9995 | 4.7616 | 4.5452 | 4.3477 | 4.1666 | 3.9999 | 3.3333 | 2.8571 | 2.5000 | 2.2222 | 2.0000 |
| 75 | 6.2499 | 5.8823 | 5.5555 | 5.2631 | 5.0000 | 4.7619 | 4.5455 | 4.3478 | 4.1667 | 4.0000 | 3.3333 | 2.8571 | 2.5000 | 2.2222 | 2.0000 |
| 100 | 6.2500 | 5.8824 | 5.5556 | 5.2632 | 5.0000 | 4.7619 | 4.5455 | 4.3478 | 4.1667 | 4.0000 | 3.3333 | 2.8571 | 2.5000 | 2.2222 | 2.0000 |

# Index

# Financial Analysis:
## Tools and Concepts

Also by Jerry A. Viscione

*Analyzing Ratios: A Perceptive Approach*
*Cases in Financial Management*
*Financial Analysis: Principles and Procedures*
*Flow of Funds and Other Financial Concepts*
*How to Construct Pro Forma Statements*

# Financial Analysis:

## Tools
## and
## Concepts

## Jerry A. Viscione

Professor of Finance
Boston College

Publications Division
National Association of Credit Management
475 Park Avenue South, New York, N.Y. 10016

Library of Congress Cataloging in Publication Data

Viscione, Jerry A.
  Financial analysis.

  Bibliography: p.
  Includes index.
  1. Corporations—Finance.  2. Business enterprises—Finance.  I. Title.
  HG4026.V577  1984     658.1'51      84-16530
  ISBN 0-934914-56-7

Manufactured in the United States of America

First Printing

*To Albert, Keith, Kelly and Joe*

# Table of Contents

# PART II: FINANCIAL PLANNING
# AND CONTROL

# Tables